# 60 HIKES within 60 MILES
# NEW YORK CITY

## INCLUDING NORTHERN NEW JERSEY, WESTERN LONG ISLAND, AND SOUTHWESTERN CONNECTICUT

# 60 Hikes
## within 60 MILES

## NEW YORK CITY

### INCLUDING NORTHERN NEW JERSEY, WESTERN LONG ISLAND, AND SOUTHWESTERN CONNECTICUT

## Christopher and Catherine Brooks

MENASHA RIDGE PRESS
Birmingham, Alabama

Library of Congress Cataloging-in-Publication Data

Brooks, Christopher, 1959–
60 Hikes within 60 miles, New York/Christopher and Catherine Brooks.—1st ed.
p. cm.
ISBN 0-89732-546-X
1. Hiking—New York Region—Guidebooks. 2. New York Region—Guidebooks. I.
Title: Sixty hikes within 60 miles, New York City. II. title: Sixty hikes within sixty
miles, New York City. III. Brooks, Catherine. IV. Title

GV199.42.N64B76 2004
796.51'09747'1—dc22

2004049903
CIP

Cover design by Grant M. Tatum and Travis Bryant
Text design by Karen Ocker
Cover photo by Hardie Truesdale
All other photos by Christopher and Catherine Brooks
Maps and elevation profiles drawn by Christopher and Catherine Brooks

Menasha Ridge Press
P.O. Box 43673
Birmingham, AL 35243
www.menasharidge.com

To those people inspired with the vision
to set this precious space aside.
And those enlightened hikers, bikers, and riders
with the grace to tread the land lightly.

# TABLE OF CONTENTS

# TABLE OF CONTENTS

# ACKNOWLEDGMENTS

Like the many trees, shrubs, and ground cover that compose a forest, a number of people have been involved in the successful completion of this book. We would like to thank the following for helping to nurture this work along:

Catherine's parents, Jan and Liliane, taught her the importance of respecting nature. They loved to stroll through fields and forests, they planted many a tree and fed the birds that came to roost in them, and they made sure that their five daughters had a spacious back yard in which to play.

Likewise, Christopher's parents, Patricia and Lester, introduced him to the delights of the wide-open woods. Some of his earliest, fondest memories are of family outings to Ward Pound Ridge, where Chris, barely able to walk, roamed the forest floor, gathering fiddlehead ferns for the family meal.

Wilhelmina Peters has an inexhaustible knowledge of plants. The input of this dear friend and trail companion has aided us in identifying numerous species.

As soon as they heard of this undertaking, our friends Nancy and Allan Mitchell brought several splendid hikes to our attention. Their enthusiastic support gave us a great head start.

Without the selfless efforts of trail volunteers, venturing into the wilds would be a considerably different—and more taxing—experience. While they all deserve our gratitude, we would like to send a special thank you to the New York–New Jersey Trail Conference, which has been highly active in developing and maintaining a vast network of paths in this region.

We are grateful to the many people who took the time to answer our questions about their respective domains and who granted us permission to publish our photographs of those areas. The following, in alphabetical order, were particularly helpful: Tom McFadden of the Great Swamp National Wildlife Refuge; Luke Mason of the Morris County Parks; John Matthiessen of the Nature Conservancy, Connecticut Chapter; Amy Berridge of the Nature Conservancy, New Jersey Field Office; Marie Jones of the Nature Conservancy, Eastern New York Chapter; Michele Stelle of New Jersey State Parks; Ann Cassidy of New York State Office of Parks, Recreation, and Historic Preservation; Carole Nolan of the Palisades Interstate Park Commission; Dave Dendler of Somerset County Parks; Iris Stevens of the Westchester County Film Office; Paul Gallay and Paul Zofnass of the Westchester Land Trust; and Stephen A.Ricker of the Westmoreland Sanctuary.

# ACKNOWLEDGMENTS

Although New York has one of the best mass-transit systems in the world, we found a few hikes that were beyond the reach of the MTA. To get to those, we relied on a safe, reliable, fuel-efficient automobile, and we appreciate the manufacturing smarts of the Honda Motor Company that went into its design.

And finally, special recognition is due to Chris Mohney, our keen-eyed editor, and to the rest of the Menasha Ridge Press team for giving us the opportunity to write this book.

—*Christopher and Catherine Brooks*

# ABOUT THE AUTHORS

Christopher Brooks brings to *60 Hikes within 60 Miles: New York City* more than two decades of writing experience. In addition to a 5-year stint as contributing editor at *Market Watch* (a sister publication to *Wine Spectator*) and 14 years as contributing editor and columnist at Hearst's *Country Living,* his many credits include the *New York Times, Family Circle, Christian Science Monitor, Cigar Aficionado,* the *Chicago Tribune,* the *International Herald Tribune, USA Today*, and *Diversion.* Brooks also serves as articles editor of the occasionally published English edition of *Beer Passion* magazine, an interest that goes well with hiking, he claims.

Catherine Brooks, née Van der Maat, spent her childhood in Belgium, delving often into the forests around Brussels while raising rabbits and roosters as pets. Her enjoyment of nature falls under a large umbrella of passions, including photography, birding, zoology, mycology, and botany. With a university degree in languages, Catherine started her career as an interpreter-translator. Later, she went to work for a United States–based multinational corporation, with marketing responsibilities spread over six European countries.

Together, the Brookses wrote the California half of *The Unofficial Guide to Campgrounds in California and the West* and team up monthly to write restaurant reviews for *Westport* magazine. They have hiked the Appalachian Trail, the Pacific Crest Trail, the Inca Trail, and extensively explored the U.S., Mexico and South America, Europe, Asia, and northern Africa. As a unit, they are fluent in five languages, all of which facilitate the interpretation of occasionally cryptic trail maps and signposts. "That doesn't prevent us from periodically confusing our dexter from our sinister," one of the Brookses confesses.

# PREFACE

"You'll never come up with 60 hikes," we were warned before undertaking this book. "40, sure—maybe even 50. But *60?* No way, not with so many millions of people living within a 60-mile radius of Manhattan." This armchair advisor felt sure that we would have to include strolls in Central Park and the Brooklyn Botanical Gardens—Wave Hill, too, perhaps—just to reach our quota. He even suggested we visit the Meadowlands. "You could easily log a couple of miles wandering around its parking complex," he chortled.

No doubt shopping malls would have been his next proposal, but we had other ideas. First among them was the notion that only walks in natural settings would make the cut, thus excluding with one blow city parks, botanical gardens, and arboretums. No question, such open spaces serve a useful purpose within a metropolitan environment, but most are already quite well known and would simply be filler in a guide like this. Similarly, to our minds, the surface of a trail should be grounded in the natural world. Many excellent hikes briefly overlap macadam, but those that are paved from start to finish were dropped from consideration. Then there are the "rails to trails" paths, and other long, level, linear treks. We're all for greenways like the Old Croton Aqueduct, but too often they feel like bicycle freeways, and hiking loses its allure when you are jarred out of peaceful reveries by the need to dodge speeding objects hurtling down the track. So those, too, were eliminated.

What was left over, you wonder? Plenty. It is no secret that this is one of the richest cultural centers on the planet. What we were delighted to discover during our peregrinations was that the New York area is no less blessed with an increasing number of stellar hikes. Admittedly, in the end we did have trouble settling on 60. The difficulty arose from the limit; we might easily have given you a volume of 70, 80, or even 90 hikes, but that would have been a different book. Instead, we restricted ourselves to simply one hike profile per park, even though many, like Bear Mountain/Harriman, Wawayanda, Stokes, High Point, and Ward Pound Ridge (to name a mere handful), deserved to have several of their superb trails featured. No matter; once you go there and get your feet wet, you'll soon be venturing out on your own, discovering other exciting treks.

It is customary in a preface to include remarks relating to the history of the region. Rather than bore you, though, with too many words about stuff we all should know anyway, we decided to leave the history lesson up to you, in the form of fieldwork. Would you like to see where Indians lived long ago? Several of these hikes, including

# PREFACE

Devil's Den, High Mountain, and Ramapo-Ringwood, showcase Paleolithic rock shelters. Care to learn about some of the first settlers on Long Island? Caleb Smith Full Circuit and Connetquot State Parks are great starting points. Do you have an interest in the Revolutionary War period? There is a connection at Sourland Mountain and Sterling Forest, to name just two. And in Wawayanda and Westchester Wilderness you will find a link (albeit a tenuous one) to the Civil War. Curious about how the Big Apple roared back to life after the Great Fire of 1835? Look for the answers at Clay Pit Ponds and Croton Point. Then there is the question of how the city and its harbor were defended against the possibility of foreign attack during the cold war and before. Sandy Hook and Hartshorne Woods provide an insight into that. On the other hand, if your taste flows more toward social history than bellicose matters, the historic mines of the Black River Trail and Norvin Green, the Leatherman's Cave at Ward Pound Ridge, and the abandoned lunatic asylum at Sunken Meadow should all make your short list. And for that *fin-de-siècle* sense of a golden era coming to an end, the ruins at Muttontown and Hudson Highlands are among the most expressive and atmospheric we've seen. A small slice of history surrounded by the beauty of the backwoods is about as sweet a classroom as there is. Best of all, the only tests you are likely to face concern stamina, and how long a wait you will have to endure until the next outing.

At one time or another we have all heard it said that when it comes to hitting the wilderness, the west is best. Well, after spending months at a time on the trails in the west, from the Rocky Mountains on out to the coast, we have arrived at a simple conclusion: It's not true. Why sugarcoat what we should be yodeling from the crest of Storm King Mountain? The New York City region has some of the best hiking trails in the country, maybe even the world. True, there are no killer mountains out here, no death-defying climbs to nosebleed altitudes. But then, we don't have to schlep 10-plus miles just to see a different kind of cactus. Our woods and lowlands and granite-graced mountains are so rich in beauty and rife with diversity that it doesn't require a marathon trek to fill our souls with the sweet honey of nature. Sure, our eastern peaks are lower than those in the Sierra Nevada range and the Cascades, but for better views than what you will find atop Schunemunk Mountain or the spires of Black Rock Forest Peaks to Ponds Trail, you'll have to hire a blimp.

Oddly enough, as ever-more houses are shoehorned into the region, New York has become an even better place in which to hike. Not because of the influx of people, but rather as a reaction to it. Recognizing the imperative to preserve whatever remains of

# PREFACE

large blocks of open space, grassroots conservationists have waged determined and sustained drives, resulting in the creation of a number of great parks in recent years. We have included a handful of those in this volume—preserves so diverse, and of such head-turning beauty, that we feel certain you will want to visit them again and again. But don't take our word for it . . . go see for yourself with a hearty scramble along the towering limestone cliffs of Johnsonburg Swamp (established in 1990), and a quiet stroll by the pastoral pond at Weir Farm (1990, Connecticut's first—and only—national park). Have your binoculars handy for those far-reaching vistas from atop High Mountain (1993), and for the great birding along the water at Nissequogue River State Park (1999). You probably won't require an energy bar during the peaceful ramble by the streams, swamps, and granite bluffs of Westchester Wilderness (2001), but an extra apple or pack of trail mix will be a welcome restorative after the exhilarating climbs up Sterling Ridge (2000), and Turkey and Pyramid mountains (1987, with preservation efforts ongoing).

As conservation campaigns continue, additional parks will no doubt be established. Already, there is talk of a Meadowlands Preserve opening within a year or two. With several thousand acres tucked into its borders, it is predicted that this park will have about 35 miles of hiking trails, some of which will traverse scenic swamps and a rambling riverside. Then there is the new Highlands Trail, stretching west from the Hudson River all the way to the Delaware Water Gap. Volunteers have finished nearly 140 miles of this path, with the remaining 20 or so miles scheduled for completion by 2006. We have already gamboled along parts of this route and found that it incorporates some of the most wild and wonderful land between the Big Apple and Pennsylvania. This truly is a magnificent time to be a hiker.

Some of the trails included in this guide are all but impassable when snow covers the ground. Most, however, are still navigable and take on a lustrous appearance when in the icy grip of winter. Sight lines are clearer, hitherto hidden rock formations rise into high relief, streams magically become more beautiful than Waterford crystal, and animal tracks in the snow reinforce just how abundantly our woodlands teem with wildlife. You may not be able to see as much in summer, but the long days and warm, humid weather lend a pleasurable lassitudinousness to an excursion, transforming the outing from a brisk march to one that is more pensive, seemingly pregnant with possibilities. Most of our black bear sightings have occurred when it was so uncomfortably sticky that the beasts couldn't be bothered to duck into hiding. There are a number of dark, densely forested swamp and river hikes included in this book that you will find enticingly cool and welcoming when the streets and sidewalks are sizzling. Autumn means leaf-peeping, and we know of no better place to enjoy the annual fall foliage displays than deep in our New York area woods. There is an invigorating sharpness to the air, most biting bugs are gone, and animals tend to be more visible as they engage in a final, frantic foraging for wild nuts and seeds. Autumn is also hunting season, a sport that is permitted in many of the parks listed in these pages. We suggest you call ahead to confirm when and where such activities are taking place. Then there is spring, our favorite time to be out, to witness Nature renewing itself. With streams and rivers running high, the tiny spear-like tips of skunk cabbage are among the first greens to surface from the soft ground. Soon, though, the entire forest, great swaths of swampland, and sandy stretches of pine barrens all erupt in a kaleidoscope of colorful flowers. Simultaneously, migratory birds return, contributing a chatty insouciance to the realm as they build their nests and defend their territory.

Spring also marks the return of bugs, and two varieties, ticks and mosquitoes, merit special attention. Deer ticks, which are a little larger than a poppy seed, are known for transmitting Lyme disease, while mosquitoes are the vector for west Nile virus. Neither of these concerns should inhibit you from lacing up your boots and setting off on the trail. We have met more people who have caught Lyme by lolling about in their own backyard than from any backwoods adventure. Basically, if you wear light-colored clothing, check yourself regularly for ticks, and lather on a DEET-rich insect repellant (especially around the ankles, wrists, and neck), you'll be more likely to bump into Mayor Bloomberg out in the forest than come down with Lyme disease. Bug spray also wards off mosquitoes, giving you added insurance against west Nile virus. (And keeping your dog on a leash will help to minimize its exposure to parasites.)

If you plan to spend a fair amount of time out in the woods—and we hope that you do—consider investing in an Empire Passport or New Jersey State Park Pass. For a set fee, both programs permit unlimited day-use admission to nearly all New York and Garden State parks. Westchester County provides a discount on the admission fee through a similar plan for its residents. And in those parks where fishing is allowed, you will need to purchase a license unless otherwise noted in the text.

# PREFACE

Finally, while we have made every effort to be accurate in our trail maps and descriptions, conditions change over time. Trees fall, causing paths to be rerouted. Erosion from equestrians and bikers alters the appearance of intersections. Right-of-ways and easements are revoked, forcing the creation of new connector trails. We apologize in advance should you encounter any such circumstance. Remember, though, that these sorts of challenges are but a small part of the thrill and pleasure of a few hours or a day spent in the woods. And in the most densely populated area of the country, where else but in the woods can you find yourself both alone and at home?

# HIKING RECOMMENDATIONS

## ▶ 1 TO 3 MILES

Clay Pit Ponds Connector
Croton Point Discovery Trail
Great Kills Crooke's Point Labyrinth
Holmdel Big Loop
Jamaica Bay West Pond Trail
Johnsonburg Swamp Trail
Mercer Lake Trail
Pelham Bay Hunter Island Loop

Storm King Summit Trail
Tallman Mountain Hudson River Overlook
  Trail
Teatown Lake Loop (Hidden Valley Trail)
Turkey Swamp Sampler
Uplands Farm Loop
Weir Pond and Swamp Loops
Westchester Wilderness Walk (South Loop)

## ▶ 3 TO 6 MILES

Allaire Southern Loop
Babcock Circumference Trail
Blue Mountain Twin Summits Trail
Butler Outer Loop Trail
Caleb Smith Full Circuit
Cheesequake Natural Area Trail
David Weld Sanctuary Tour
Fishkill Ridge Trail
Great Swamp Wilderness Trail
Hartshorne Woods Grandest Tour
Jenny Jump Mountain Lake Trail
Mianus River Gorge Trail
Muttontown Mystery Trail
Shark River Circuit

Sourland Mountain Track (without spur trails)
Stillwell Woods Stroll
Sunken Meadow to Nissequogue River Trail
Swartswood Spring Lake Trail
Teatown Lake Loop
Thompson Park Red and Blue Combo
Turkey–Egypt Connection (either loop)
Walt Whitman Revisited
Ward Pound Ridge Main Loop
Wawayanda Way Way Yonder (Bearfort
  Mountain Natural Area loop)
Westchester Wilderness Walk (without either
  the North or East Loop)
Westmoreland Grand Tour

## ▶ 6 TO 9 MILES

Allamuchy Natural Area Amble
Bear Mountain Doodletown Circuit
Black River Trail
Caumsett Neck Loop
Connetquot Contour
Devil's Den Concourse
Fahnestock Hidden Lake Loop
Fitzgerald Falls to Little Dam Lake
  Appalachian Trail (with car shuttle)

High Mountain Summit Loop
Hudson Highlands Breakneck Ridge Loop
Rockefeller Medley
Shark River Circuit (with Pine Hills Trail
  extension)
Sourland Mountain Track
Watchung Sierra Sampler
Westchester Wilderness Walk

# HIKING RECOMMENDATIONS

## ▶ OVER 9 MILES

Black Rock Forest Peaks to Ponds Trail
Fitzgerald Falls to Little Dam Lake
  Appalachian Trail
Harriman Highlands Trail
High Point Duet
Norvin Green's Heart
Ramapo–Ringwood Rally

Sandy Hook Hiking Trail
Schunemunk Mountain Ridge Loop
Sterling Ridge Trail
Stokes Select
Turkey–Egypt Connection
Wawayanda Way Way Yonder

## ▶ GOOD FOR YOUNG CHILDREN

Babcock Circumference Trail
Butler Outer Loop Trail
Caleb Smith Full Circuit
Cheesequake Natural Area Trail
Clay Pit Ponds Connector
Croton Point Discovery Trail
David Weld Sanctuary Tour
Great Kills Crooke's Point Labyrinth
Great Swamp Wilderness Trail
Holmdel Big Loop
Jamaica Bay West Pond Trail
Johnsonburg Swamp Trail
Mercer Lake Trail
Mianus River Gorge Trail

Muttontown Mystery Trail
Pelham Bay Hunter Island Loop
Shark River Circuit
Stillwell Woods Stroll
Swartswood Spring Lake Trail
Tallman Mountain Hudson River Overlook
  Trail
Teatown Lake Loop
Thompson Park Red and Blue Combo
Turkey Swamp Sampler
Uplands Farm Loop
Ward Pound Ridge Main Loop
Weir Pond and Swamp Loops
Westchester Wilderness Walk (South Loop)

## ▶ ACCESSIBLE BY PUBLIC TRANSPORTATION (NO CABS REQUIRED)

Blue Mountain Twin Summits Trail (1.5-mile
  walk to trailhead)
Caleb Smith Full Circuit
Clay Pit Ponds Connector (0.3-mile walk)
Connetquot Contour (1.5-mile walk)
Croton Point Discovery Trail (0.5-mile walk)
Great Kills Crooke's Point Labyrinth (1.5-
  mile walk)
Hartshorne Woods Grandest Tour
Hudson Highlands Breakneck Ridge Loop
  (0.9-mile walk)

Jamaica Bay West Pond Loop (0.5-mile walk)
Pelham Bay Hunter Island Loop
Sandy Hook Hiking Trail (2-mile walk)
Sterling Ridge Trail
Stillwell Woods Stroll (2-mile walk)
Walt Whitman Revisited (1.5-mile walk)
Watchung Sierra Sampler (1.25-mile walk)
Weir Pond and Swamp Loops (1.8-mile
  walk)
Westchester Wilderness Walk (1.8-mile
  walk)

# HIKING RECOMMENDATIONS

## ▶ GOOD FOR DOGS

Allamuchy Natural Area Amble
Babcock Circumference Trail
Bear Mountain Doodletown Circuit
Black River Trail
Caumsett Neck Loop
Cheesequake Natural Area Trail
Fahnestock Hidden Lake Loop
Harriman Highlands Trail
High Point Duet

Holmdel Big Loop
Ramapo–Ringwood Rally
Sterling Ridge Trail
Stokes Select
Turkey Swamp Sampler
Ward Pound Ridge Main Loop
Wawayanda Way Way Yonder
Westchester Wilderness Walk

## ▶ FLAT HIKES

Caumsett Neck Loop
Clay Pit Ponds Connector
Connetquot Contour
Croton Point Discovery Trail
David Weld Sanctuary Tour
Great Kills Crooke's Point Labyrinth
Great Swamp Wilderness Trail
Jamaica Bay West Pond Trail

Mercer Lake Trail
Pelham Bay Hunter Island Loop
Sandy Hook Hiking Trail
Tallman Mountain Hudson River Overlook
   Trail
Thompson Park Red and Blue Combo
Turkey Swamp Sampler

## ▶ HIKES WITH STEEP SECTIONS

Bear Mountain Doodletown Circuit
Black Rock Forest Peaks to Ponds Trail
Fishkill Ridge Trail
Fitzgerald Falls to Little Dam Lake
   Appalachian Trail
Harriman Highlands Trail
High Mountain Summit Loop
Hudson Highlands Breakneck Ridge Loop
Jenny Jump Mountain Lake Trail

Norvin Green's Heart
Ramapo–Ringwood Rally
Schunemunk Mountain Ridge Loop
Sterling Ridge Trail
Stokes Select
Storm King Summit Trail
Turkey–Egypt Connection
Wawayanda Way Way Yonder

## ▶ SOLITUDINOUS HIKES

Black Rock Forest Peaks to Ponds Trail
Butler Outer Loop Trail
Devil's Den Concourse
Fishkill Ridge Trail
Fitzgerald Falls to Little Dam Lake
   Appalachian Trail

Harriman Highlands Trail
High Mountain Summit Loop
High Point Duet
Jenny Jump Mountain Lake Trail
Norvin Green's Heart
Ramapo–Ringwood Rally

# HIKING RECOMMENDATIONS

## ▶ SOLITUDINOUS HIKES (continued)

Schunemunk Mountain Ridge Loop
Sterling Ridge Trail
Stokes Select

Turkey–Egypt Connection
Wawayanda Way Way Yonder
Westmoreland Grand Tour

## ▶ RURAL HIKES

Caleb Smith Full Circuit
Caumsett Neck Loop
Connetquot Contour
David Weld Sanctuary Tour
Johnsonburg Swamp Trail

Rockefeller Medley
Stillwell Woods Stroll
Uplands Farm Loop
Weir Pond and Swamp Loops

## ▶ LEAF-PEEPING HIKES

Bear Mountain Doodletown Circuit
Black Rock Forest Peaks to Ponds Trail
Blue Mountain Twin Summits Trail
Devil's Den Concourse
Fishkill Ridge Trail
Fitzgerald Falls to Little Dam Lake
  Appalachian Trail
Harriman Highlands Trail
High Mountain Summit Loop
High Point Duet

Hudson Highlands Breakneck Ridge Loop
Norvin Green's Heart
Ramapo–Ringwood Rally
Schunemunk Mountain Ridge Loop
Sterling Ridge Trail
Stokes Select
Storm King Summit Trail
Turkey–Egypt Connection
Ward Pound Ridge Main Loop
Wawayanda Way Way Yonder

## ▶ HIKES ALONG WATER

Black River Trail
Black Rock Forest Peaks to Ponds Trail
Caumsett Neck Loop
Cheesequake Natural Area Trail
Connetquot Contour
Croton Point Discovery Trail
David Weld Sanctuary Tour
Fahnestock Hidden Lake Loop
Fitzgerald Falls to Little Dam Lake
  Appalachian Trail
Great Kills Crooke's Point Labyrinth
Great Swamp Wilderness Trail
Jamaica Bay West Pond Trail
Mercer Lake Trail
Mianus River Gorge Trail

Norvin Green's Heart
Pelham Bay Hunter Island Loop
Ramapo–Ringwood Rally
Rockefeller Medley
Sandy Hook Hiking Trail
Shark River Circuit
Sunken Meadow to Nissequogue
  River Trail
Swartswood Spring Lake Trail
Teatown Lake Loop
Turkey–Egypt Connection
Turkey Swamp Sampler
Watchung Sierra Sampler
Wawayanda Way Way Yonder
Weir Pond and Swamp Loops

# HIKING RECOMMENDATIONS

## ▶ HIKES FOR BIRDING

Allamuchy Natural Area Amble
Black River Trail
Black Rock Forest Peaks to Ponds Trail
Butler Outer Loop Trail
Caumsett Neck Loop
Cheesequake Natural Area Trail
Clay Pit Ponds Connector
Connetquot Contour
Croton Point Discovery Trail
David Weld Sanctuary Tour
Fahnestock Hidden Lake Loop
Great Kills Crooke's Point Labyrinth
Great Swamp Wilderness Trail
Jamaica Bay West Pond Trail
Jenny Jump Mountain Lake Trail
Johnsonburg Swamp Trail
Mercer Lake Trail
Mianus River Gorge Trail

Muttontown Mystery Trail
Pelham Bay Hunter Island Loop
Ramapo–Ringwood Rally
Rockefeller Medley
Sandy Hook Hiking Trail
Schunemunk Mountain Ridge Loop
Sourland Mountain Track
Stillwell Woods Stroll
Sunken Meadow to Nissequogue River Trail
Tallman Mountain Hudson River Overlook
    Trail
Teatown Lake Loop
Thompson Park Red & Blue Combo
Turkey–Egypt Connection
Uplands Farm Loop
Ward Pound Ridge Main Loop
Wawayanda Way Way Yonder
Westmoreland Grand Tour

## ▶ WILDLIFE VIEWING

Bear Mountain Doodletown Circuit
Black River Trail
Black Rock Forest Peaks to
    Ponds Trail
Butler Outer Loop Trail
Caumsett Neck Loop
Connetquot Contour
Croton Point Discovery Trail
David Weld Sanctuary Tour
Devil's Den Concourse
Fitzgerald Falls to Little Dam Lake
    Appalachian Trail

Harriman Highlands Trail
High Mountain Summit Loop
Johnsonburg Swamp Trail
Mianus River Gorge Trail
Muttontown Mystery Trail
Ramapo–Ringwood Rally
Schunemunk Mountain Ridge Loop
Turkey–Egypt Connection
Ward Pound Ridge Main Loop
Wawayanda Way Way Yonder
Westchester Wilderness Walk
Westmoreland Grand Tour

## ▶ SEASONAL WILDFLOWERS

Allamuchy Natural Area Amble
Black River Trail
Caumsett Neck Loop
Cheesequake Natural Area Trail
Connetquot Contour

David Weld Sanctuary Tour
Devil's Den Concourse
Fitzgerald Falls to Little Dam Lake
    Appalachian Trail
High Mountain Summit Loop

# HIKING RECOMMENDATIONS

## ▶ SEASONAL WILDFLOWERS (continued)

Jamaica Bay West Pond Trail
Johnsonburg Swamp Trail
Mianus River Gorge Trail
Norvin Green's Heart
Ramapo–Ringwood Rally
Schunemunk Mountain Ridge Loop
Stillwell Woods Stroll
Stokes Select

Swartswood Spring Lake Trail
Teatown Lake Loop
Turkey–Egypt Connection
Uplands Farm Loop
Ward Pound Ridge Main Loop
Wawayanda Way Way Yonder
Westchester Wilderness Walk

## ▶ SCENIC HIKES

Bear Mountain Doodletown Circuit
Black Rock Forest Peaks to Ponds Trail
Blue Mountain Twin Summits Trail
Caumsett Neck Loop
Devil's Den Concourse
Fishkill Ridge Trail
Fitzgerald Falls to Little Dam Lake
  Appalachian Trail
Harriman Highlands Trail
High Mountain Summit Loop
High Point Duet
Hudson Highlands Breakneck Ridge Loop
Norvin Green's Heart

Ramapo–Ringwood Rally
Sandy Hook Hiking Trail
Schunemunk Mountain Ridge Loop
Sterling Ridge Trail
Stokes Select
Storm King Summit Trail
Sunken Meadow to Nissequogue River Trail
Tallman Mountain Hudson River Overlook
  Trail
Turkey–Egypt Connection
Ward Pound Ridge Main Loop (with
  Leatherman's Cave side trip)
Wawayanda Way Way Yonder

## ▶ HIKES WITH GOOD WINTER SCENERY

Allamuchy Natural Area Amble
Bear Mountain Doodletown Circuit
Black Rock Forest Peaks to Ponds Trail
Caumsett Neck Loop
Devil's Den Concourse
Fishkill Ridge Trail
Fitzgerald Falls to Little Dam Lake
  Appalachian Trail
Harriman Highlands Trail
High Point Duet
Hudson Highlands Breakneck
  Ridge Loop

Norvin Green's Heart
Ramapo–Ringwood Rally
Sandy Hook Hiking Trail
Schunemunk Mountain Ridge Loop
Sterling Ridge Trail
Stokes Select
Storm King Summit Trail
Turkey–Egypt Connection
Ward Pound Ridge Main Loop
Westmoreland Loop

# HIKING RECOMMENDATIONS

## ▶ GOOD TRAILS FOR RUNNERS

Allaire Southern Loop
Black Rock Forest Peaks to Ponds Trail
Black River Trail
Cheesequake Natural Area Trail
Fahnestock Hidden Lake Loop
Hartshorne Woods Grandest Tour
Holmdel Big Loop

Rockefeller Medley
Shark River Circuit
Stillwell Woods Stroll
Sunken Meadow to Nissequogue River Trail
Thompson Park Red and Blue Combo
Ward Pound Ridge Main Loop
Watchung Sierra Sampler

## ▶ MULTI-USE TRAILS

Allaire Southern Loop
Allamuchy Natural Area Amble
Babcock Circumference Trail
Blue Mountain Twin Summits Trail
Caumsett Neck Loop
Cheesequake Natural Area Trail
Connetquot Contour
Hartshorne Woods Grandest Tour
High Point Duet
Jenny Jump Mountain Lake Trail
Mercer Lake Trail
Muttontown Mystery Trail
Ramapo–Ringwood Rally (bicycles prohibited
   in many areas)
Rockefeller Medley

Shark River Circuit
Sourland Mountain Track
Stillwell Woods Stroll
Stokes Select
Sunken Meadow to Nissequogue River
   Trail
Swartswood Spring Lake Trail
Tallman Mountain Hudson River Overlook
   Trail
Teatown Lake Loop
Turkey Swamp Sampler
Walt Whitman Revisited
Ward Pound Ridge Main Loop (bicycles
   prohibited)
Watchung Sierra Sampler

## ▶ HISTORIC TRAILS

Bear Mountain Doodletown Circuit
Black River Trail
Caumsett Neck Loop
Clay Pit Ponds Connector
Connetquot Contour
Croton Point Discovery Trail
Devil's Den Concourse
Harriman Highlands Trail
Hartshorne Woods Grandest Tour
Hudson Highlands Breakneck Ridge Loop
Muttontown Mystery Trail

Norvin Green's Heart
Ramapo–Ringwood Rally
Sandy Hook Hiking Trail
Sterling Ridge Trail
Sunken Meadow to Nissequogue River Trail
Turkey–Egypt Connection
Ward Pound Ridge Main Loop
Watchung Sierra Sampler
Weir Pond and Swamp Loops

# 60 Hikes within 60 MILES

## NEW YORK CITY

### INCLUDING NORTHERN NEW JERSEY, WESTERN LONG ISLAND, AND SOUTHWESTERN CONNECTICUT

# INTRODUCTION

Welcome to *60 Hikes within 60 Miles: New York City*. If you're new to hiking or even if you're a seasoned trail-smith, take a few minutes to read the following introduction. We explain how this book is organized and how to use it.

## ▶ HIKE DESCRIPTIONS

Each hike contains eight key items: a locator map, an "In Brief" description of the trail, a key at-a-glance information box, directions to the trail, a trail map, an elevation profile, a trail description, and nearby activities. Combined, the maps and information provide a clear method to assess each trail from the comfort of your favorite reading chair.

### LOCATOR MAP

After narrowing down the general area of the hike on the overview map (see inside front cover), the locator map, along with directions given in the narrative, enable you to find the trailhead. Once at the trailhead, park only in designated areas.

### IN BRIEF

A "taste of the trail." Think of this section as a snapshot focused on the historical landmarks, beautiful vistas, and other sights you may encounter on the trail.

### KEY AT-A-GLANCE INFORMATION

The information in the key at-a-glance boxes gives you a quick idea of the specifics of each hike. There are 13 basic elements covered.

**LENGTH** The length of the trail from start to finish. There may be options to shorten or extend the hikes, but the mileage corresponds to the described hike. Consult the hike description to help decide how to customize the hike for your ability or time constraints.

**CONFIGURATION** A description of what the trail might look like from overhead. Trails can be loops, out-and-backs (that is, along the same route), figure eights, or balloons.

**DIFFICULTY** The degree of effort an "average" hiker should expect on a given hike. For simplicity, difficulty is described as "easy," "moderate," or "difficult."

**SCENERY** Rates the overall environs of the hike and what to expect in terms of plant life, wildlife, streams, and historic buildings.

**EXPOSURE** A quick check of how much sun you can expect on your shoulders during the hike. Descriptors used are self-explanatory and include terms such as shady, exposed, and sunny.

**TRAFFIC** Indicates how busy the trail might be on an average day, and if you might be able to find solitude out there. Trail traffic, of course, varies from day to day and season to season.

# INTRODUCTION

**TRAIL SURFACE**  Indicates whether the trail is paved, rocky, smooth dirt, or a mixture of elements.

**HIKING TIME**  How long it takes to hike the trail. A slow but steady hiker will average 2 to 3 miles an hour depending on the terrain. Most of the estimates in this book reflect a speed of about 2 mph.

**SEASON**  Times of year when this trail is accessible. In most cases, the limiting factor is snow on the trail or the road to the trailhead, but in some cases trails are closed for reasons relating to wildlife habitat. In any case, if it's a transitional time for the trail you want to hike, call the information number to be sure you can hike it.

**ACCESS**  Notes fees or permits needed to access the trail (if any) and whether pets and other forms of trail use are permitted.

**MAPS**  Which maps are the best, or easiest, for this hike and where to get them.

**FACILITIES**  What to expect in terms of rest rooms, phones, water, and other amenities available at the trailhead or nearby.

**SPECIAL COMMENTS**  These comments cover little extra details that don't fit into any of the above categories. Here you'll find information on trail-hiking options and facts, or tips on how to get the most out of your hike.

## DIRECTIONS TO THE TRAIL
Used with the locator map, the directions will help you locate each trailhead.

## TRAIL DESCRIPTIONS
The trail description is the heart of each hike. Here, the authors provide a summary of the trail's essence as well as highlight any special traits the hike offers. Ultimately, the hike description will help you choose which hikes are best for you.

## NEARBY ACTIVITIES
Look here for information on nearby activities or points of interest

## ▶ WEATHER

In an average year, the New York region receives 49 inches of rainfall and 26 inches of snow. And yet every month is well suited to hiking. Spring opens with a burst of wildflowers, songbirds, and cacophonous cascades. Even at its wettest, the unfolding forest canopies act as an umbrella, partially shielding hikers from precipitation. In summer, the woods become luminescent green; no matter how hot the days, there are always shady spots where you can mop the sweat from your brow and bathe your feet in the cool flow of clear-running streams. Autumn is leaf-peeping time, when hitting the trail allows you to enjoy the fall colors far from the crowds. There are still fewer people out in winter, when a trip to a bald summit on a bright, crisp day can yield a

# INTRODUCTION

spectacular view of the Manhattan skyline. And while snow may turn a path into a treacherous toboggan run, its glistening white carpet transforms the landscape into a different sort of paradise.

## AVERAGE DAILY TEMPERATURES BY MONTH

|        | JAN | FEB | MAR | APR | MAY | JUN |
|--------|-----|-----|-----|-----|-----|-----|
| MIN.   | 28  | 27  | 34  | 43  | 53  | 63  |
| MAX.   | 40  | 40  | 48  | 59  | 71  | 80  |

|        | JUL | AUG | SEP | OCT | NOV | DEC |
|--------|-----|-----|-----|-----|-----|-----|
| MIN.   | 69  | 68  | 61  | 51  | 41  | 30  |
| MAX.   | 85  | 83  | 76  | 66  | 54  | 42  |

## ▶ ALLOCATING TIME

On flat or lightly undulating terrain, the authors average 3 mph when hiking. That speed drops in direct proportion to the steepness of a path, and it does not reflect the many pauses and forays off trail in pursuit of yet another bird sighting, wildflower, or photograph. Give yourself plenty of time. Few people enjoy rushing through a hike, and fewer still take pleasure in bumping into trees after dark. Remember, too, that your pace naturally slackens over the back half of a long trek.

## ▶ MAPS

The maps in this book have been produced with great care and, used with the hiking directions, will help you stay on course. But as any experienced hiker knows, things can get tricky off the beaten path.

When used with the route directions present in each chapter, the maps are sufficient to direct you to the trail and guide you on it. However, you will find superior detail and valuable information in the United States Geological Survey's 7.5-minute series topographic maps. Topo maps are available online in many locations. The easiest single Web resource is located at terraserver.microsoft.com. You can view and print topos of the entire United States there, and view aerial photographs of the same area. The downside to topos is that most of them are outdated, having been created 20 to 30 years ago. But they still provide excellent topographic detail.

If you're new to hiking, you might be wondering, "What's a topographic map?" In short, a topo indicates not only linear distance but elevation as well, using contour lines. Contour lines spread across the map like dozens of intricate spider webs. Each line represents a particular elevation, and at the base of each topo, a contour's interval designation is given. If the contour interval is 200 feet, then the distance between each contour line is 200 feet. Follow five contour lines up on a map, and the elevation has increased by 1,000 feet.

# INTRODUCTION

Let's assume that the 7.5-minute series topo reads "Contour Interval 40 feet," that the short trail we'll be hiking is two inches in length on the map, and that it crosses five contour lines from beginning to end. What do we know? Well, because the linear scale of this series is 2,000 feet to the inch (roughly two and three-quarters inches representing one mile), we know our trail is approximately four-fifths of a mile long (2 inches are 2,000 feet). But we also know we'll be climbing or descending 200 vertical feet (5 contour lines are 40 feet each) over that distance. And the elevation designations written on occasional contour lines will tell us if we're heading up or down.

In addition to outdoor shops and bike shops, you'll find topos at major universities and some public libraries, where you might try photocopying the ones you need to avoid the cost of buying them. But if you want your own and can't find them locally, visit the United States Geological Survey website at topomaps.usgs.gov. The authors also recommend topozone.com as a resource for topographic maps and software.

## ▶ TRAIL ETIQUETTE

Whether you're on a city, county, state, or national park trail, always remember that great care and resources (from Nature as well as from your tax dollars) have gone into creating these trails. Treat the trail, wildlife, and fellow hikers with respect.

1.  Hike on open trails only. Respect trail and road closures (ask if not sure), avoid possible trespassing on private land, and obtain all permits and authorization as required. Also, leave gates as you found them or as marked.

2.  Leave only footprints. Be sensitive to the ground beneath you. This also means staying on the existing trail and not blazing any new trails. Be sure to pack out what you pack in. No one likes to see the trash someone else has left behind.

3.  Never spook animals. An unannounced approach, a sudden movement, or a loud noise startles most animals. A surprised snake or skunk can be dangerous for you, for others, and to themselves. Give animals extra room and time to adjust to your presence.

4.  Plan ahead. Know your equipment, your ability, and the area in which you are hiking—and prepare accordingly. Be self-sufficient at all times; carry necessary supplies for changes in weather or other conditions. A well-executed trip is a satisfaction to you and to others.

5.  Be courteous to other hikers, bikers, or equestrians you meet on the trails.

# INTRODUCTION

## ▶ WATER

"How much is enough? One bottle? Two? Three?! But think of all that extra weight!" Well, one simple physiological fact should convince you to err on the side of excess when it comes to deciding how much water to pack: A hiker working hard in 90-degree heat needs approximately ten quarts of fluid every day. That's two and a half gallons—12 large water bottles or 16 small ones. In other words, pack along one or two bottles even for short hikes.

Serious backpackers hit the trail prepared to purify water found along the route. This method, while less dangerous than drinking it untreated, comes with risks. Purifiers with ceramic filters are the safest, but are also the most expensive. Many hikers pack along the slightly distasteful tetraglycine hydroperiodide tablets (sold under the names Potable Aqua, Coughlan's, and others).

Probably the most common waterborne "bug" that hikers face is *Giardia,* which may not hit until one to four weeks after ingestion. It will have you passing noxious rotten-egg gas, vomiting, shivering with chills, and living in the bathroom. But there are other parasites to worry about, including *E. coli* and *Cryptosporidium* (that are harder to kill than *Giardia*).

For most people, the pleasures of hiking make carrying water a relatively minor price to pay to remain healthy. If you're tempted to drink "found water," do so only if you understand the risks involved. Better yet, hydrate prior to your hike, carry (and drink) six ounces of water for every mile you plan to hike, and hydrate after the hike.

## ▶ FIRST-AID KIT

A typical kit may contain more items than you might think necessary. These are just the basics:

Ace bandages or Spenco joint wraps

Antibiotic ointment (Neosporin or the generic equivalent)

Aspirin or acetaminophen

Band-Aids

Benadryl or the generic equivalent— diphenhydramine (an antihistamine, in case of allergic reactions)

Butterfly-closure bandages

Epinephrine in a prefilled syringe (for those known to have severe allergic reactions to such things as bee stings)

Gauze (one roll)

Gauze compress pads (a half-dozen 4 in. x 4 in.)

Hydrogen peroxide or iodine

Matches or pocket lighter

Moleskin/Spenco "Second Skin"

Snakebite kit

Sunscreen

Water purification tablets or water filter (on longer hikes)

Whistle (more effective in signaling rescuers than your voice)

# INTRODUCTION

## ▶ HIKING WITH CHILDREN

No one is too young for a hike in the woods or through a city park. Be mindful, though. Flat, short trails are best with an infant. Toddlers who have not quite mastered walking can still tag along, riding on an adult's back in a child carrier. Use common sense to judge a child's capacity to hike a particular trail, and always rely on the possibility that the child will tire quickly and need to be carried. To determine which trails are suitable for children, a list of good hikes for children is provided in the "Hiking Recommendations" section earlier in this book.

## ▶ SNAKES

Snakes, like bears and bobcats, tend to appear when you least expect them. They like warm—but not hot—weather, and are active from mid-spring through mid-autumn. Most of the authors' encounters with such reptiles have involved benign garter snakes, rat snakes, ribbon snakes, and black racers. Venomous rattlesnakes and copperheads are also native to the New York area, but we have only rarely come across them. In general, their heads are more triangular than their nonvenomous cousins. You might spend a few minutes studying snakes before heading into the woods, but in any case, a good rule of thumb is to give whatever animal you encounter a wide berth and leave it alone.

## ▶ TICKS

Ticks tend to lurk in the brush, leaves, and grass that grow alongside trails. April through mid-July is the peak period for ticks in this area, but the authors have managed to pick up stray ticks in every month of the year. Scientifically, ticks are arachnids (of the spider family) and ectoparasites which live on the outside of a host for the majority of their life cycle in order to reproduce. Of the two varieties that may hitch a ride on you while hiking—wood ticks and deer ticks—extensive research suggests that both need several hours of actual bloodsucking attachment before they can transmit any disease. Deer ticks, the primary vector for Lyme disease, are very small (often as tiny as a poppy seed), and you may not be aware of their presence until you feel the itchiness of their bite. The best avoidance strategy is to wear light-colored clothing (so that you can spot the ticks more easily); tuck the bottom of your pant legs into your socks (sure it looks geeky, but it helps); lather your ankles, wrists, and neck with a DEET-rich insect repellant; and remain on the beaten path. At the end of the hike, check yourself thoroughly before getting in the car, bus, or train; and later, when you take a post-hike shower, do an even more thorough check of your entire body (this is more fun with a partner or spouse). Ticks that haven't bitten you are easily removed, but not easily killed, unless you burn or crush them. Tweezers work best for plucking off attached ticks.

# INTRODUCTION

## ▶ POISON IVY

Recognizing and avoiding contact with poison ivy is the most effective way to prevent the painful, itchy rashes associated with it. In the Northeast, poison ivy occurs as a vine or ground cover. Its leaves, which are notched on one edge, are clustered in groups of three (hence the expression, "leaves of three, leave it be"). This is a chameleon plant, with its leaves—sometimes shiny, sometimes matte—assuming the tint and overall size of neighboring vegetation. Urushiol, the oil in its sap, is responsible for the rash. Thus, you may contract a case of poison ivy either by direct contact with the plant, or by touching something—your clothing, boots, or pets—that has brushed against it. Within 12 to 24 hours of exposure, raised lines and/or blisters will appear, accompanied by a terrible itch. As with insect bites, scratching makes the situation worse, and bacteria under your fingernails may cause an infection. Wash and dry the rash thoroughly, applying a calamine lotion or another desiccant to help dry out the rash. If the itching or blistering is severe, seek medical attention.

## ▶ BEARS

Many of the denser forests referred to in this book feature black bears as their largest and most fearsome residents. On emerging from hibernation in April, they start foraging for food, relying on their exceptional sense of smell to sniff out edible plants, nuts, and fruit, and fattening up for eight months before returning to their winter dens. While some truant bears have learned that there are easy pickings in campgrounds and suburban garbage cans, these are, in general, shy animals. You are more likely to walk away a winner at three-card Monte than encounter one on the trail. Should you be fortunate enough to come across an *Ursus americanus* waddling through the woods, give it plenty of space (getting off the path, if necessary), avoid direct eye contact, and don't offer it any food.

# ALLAIRE SOUTHERN LOOP

## ▶ IN BRIEF

Look closely at this hilly terrain and you may see the dug-out remnants of old bog mines, now overgrown by pine barren thickets, dense oak forests, and clusters of mountain laurel, with the latter in dynamic bloom early in June. Deer and wild turkeys frequent these woods, along with mountain bikers and equestrians.

## ▶ DESCRIPTION

Gertrude Stein once commented about Oakland, California, that "There's no there, there." She could hardly say the same about Allaire State Park. There is, in fact, so much "there" to Allaire, including a well-preserved nineteenth-century iron mining town, a narrow-gauge steam-powered railroad, river canoeing, and camping, that you very well might overlook its several miles of hiking trails.

The focal point of this 3,068-acre park is its namesake village, where costumed volunteers demonstrate (in summer) various crafts and explain the history of the community. By all means, visit its historic brick row houses, chapel, general store, and carpentry and smithy shops. Take a ride, too, on its railroad—if you *must*. Just be sure to reserve sufficient time for a romp through Allaire's laurel forests and pine barrens, which reflect so well the natural diversity of New Jersey's Coastal Plain.

## ▶ DIRECTIONS

Follow I-95 across the George Washington Bridge into New Jersey and continue south, switching to the Garden State Parkway south at Exit 11. Take Exit 98 off the Garden State Parkway onto I-195 west. At Exit 35, proceed south on SR 34. At the traffic circle, head right onto CR 524 west. After passing under the Garden State Parkway, turn left onto Hospital Road. Proceed for 1 mile to the trailhead parking lot on the right.

## ① KEY AT-A-GLANCE INFORMATION

**LENGTH:** 4.6 miles

**CONFIGURATION:** Loop

**DIFFICULTY:** Easy

**SCENERY:** Sandy pine barrens alternate with thick hardwood forests and gnarly laurel patches

**EXPOSURE:** A few open stretches, but mostly shielded

**TRAFFIC:** Multi-use trails make this area popular year-round

**TRAIL SURFACE:** Dirt and sand, deeply rutted in places, some roots

**HIKING TIME:** 2.5 hours

**SEASON:** Year-round, 8 a.m.–dusk

**ACCESS:** No fee for trailhead parking; summer parking fee for Allaire Village; pets must be leashed

**MAPS:** USGS Farmingdale, available at Visitor Center and posted at trailhead kiosk

**FACILITIES:** Vault toilets at trailhead, no water; Visitor Center and Nature Interpretive Center in the northern part of park, off CR 524, with campground and picnic area nearby

**SPECIAL COMMENTS:** Be alert for seasonal bow hunters.

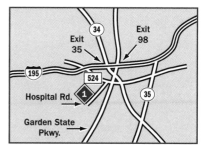

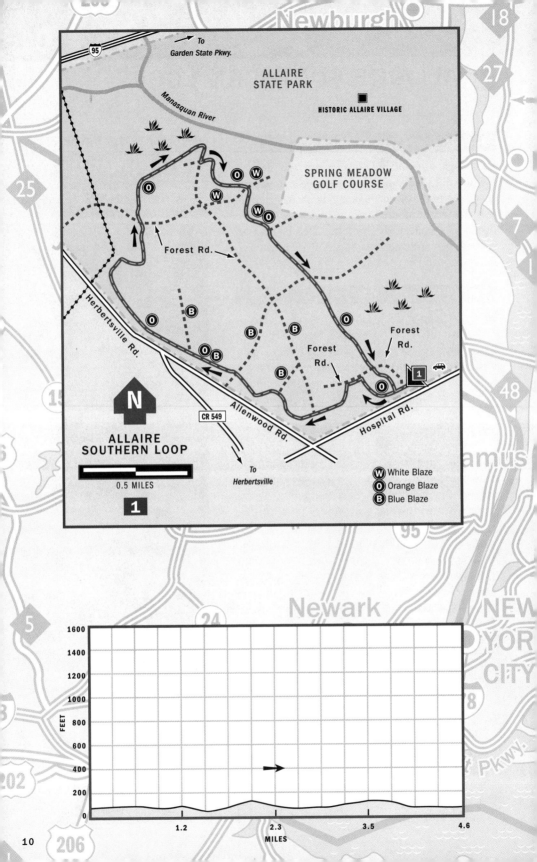

ALLAIRE STATE PARK

HISTORIC ALLAIRE VILLAGE

SPRING MEADOW
GOLF COURSE

To
Garden State Pkwy.

Manasquan River

Forest Rd.

Forest
Rd.

Forest
Rd.

Herbertsville Rd.

CR 549

Allenwood Rd.

Hospital Rd.

To
Herbertsville

**N**

**ALLAIRE
SOUTHERN LOOP**

0.5 MILES

**1**

W  White Blaze
O  Orange Blaze
B  Blue Blaze

FEET

1600
1400
1200
1000
800
600
400
200
0

1.2    2.3    3.5    4.6
MILES

Sandy pine barrens and thick clusters of mountain laurel are part of the allure of Allaire State Park.

This hike begins by the kiosk at the southwestern end of the Hospital Road parking area. It is an easy trek, with little sustained elevation change, but be advised that Allaire allows hunting in this section of the park, typically late in the fall. Strike out on the orange-blazed trail (OT) as it crosses a gravel forest road and, shortly after, forks right and left. Keep left, passing meanwhile among cedars, pines, scrub oaks, and black birch trees. Ignore the many side spurs that have been worn into the loamy soil by bikers, hunters, and deer, and in 15 minutes turn left onto the sandy forest road. Just as this track narrows to single-file, you'll step left at a fork. In roughly 100 feet the orange blazes veer sharply right, tending downhill among oaks and white birch trees, through an area of odd mounds. These latter, incidentally, are the slowly healing scars of the bog-mining industry that thrived here from the 1790s through 1848.

On emerging from this sandy depression, the path is joined by a blue-blazed trail (BT), and they flow concurrently for 250 yards through more oaks and pines, until the BT branches off to the right by a green metal shed. Stay straight with the OT and, in five minutes, it will roll to the right toward higher ground. Blue blazes reappear shortly, as you stroll through a four-way intersection. When the moss-sided track hits a dense cluster of pines, the OT swerves left, once again diverging from the BT.

On heading toward a string of high-tension wires, you may notice, as we did, a spent tire off to the side, the third such eyesore along this route. (The fourth may still be attached to an automobile, buried beneath the bog out here.) Moving along, the trail shifts from under the cover of trees and slices to the right, just shy of the power-line stanchion, and then returns to the shade of oaks and pines. This stretch is deeply grooved, having been well chewed by bikes and horses, which share the terrain. Cross the wide forest road, remaining with the OT, and be alert for the wild turkeys that frequent this mountain laurel covered hillside.

The meandering track gradually ascends one such laurel-wrapped ridge via a couple of switchbacks, with this refreshing change of scenery continuing as you swing left at a four-way crossing and enter into one of the more peaceful parts of the forest. Press on through the next junction, where the OT is joined by white blazes, and watch for the sharp left bend by a split-rail fence. From the following ridge, you face perhaps the steepest descent of the hike, though the elevation loss is a piddling 50 feet or so. A spur to the left shortly after leads to the Spring Meadows Golf Course, which you can see through the laurels and oaks.

The intrusion of road noises signals that you are nearing the trail's end. There are still some turns to navigate, though. Once the path tops another ridge, amid a jungle of laurel, head through a four-way intersection. Cross over the broken-up roadbed a few minutes later, plunging back among oaks, holly, and pines, with cat briar hugging the ground. The somewhat disheveled, upended look to the soil is further evidence of bog mining. On cutting toward the right, you'll come to a fork; stay left with the rectangular blazes, which will quickly deliver you to the start of the loop.

## ▶ NEARBY ACTIVITIES

Historic Allaire Village, a beautifully preserved bog-iron company town, dates to about 1830. Costumed interpreters demonstrate crafts on a seasonal basis using period tools. The nearby Nature Interpretive Center, housed in a handsome log cabin, includes exhibits on indigenous fauna and flora. You can also ride the narrow-gauge, steam-powered Pine Creek Railroad. For details, call (908) 938-2371.

History buffs should plan to check out Monmouth Battlefield State Park in Freehold. One of the longest battles in the American Revolution took place in this now-peaceful rural setting. Call (732) 462-9616 for information.

# ALLAMUCHY NATURAL AREA AMBLE

## ▶ IN BRIEF

Whether the quarry is birds, the backwoods, or beautiful bodies of water, Allamuchy has what it takes to make your outing a success. In fact, the combination of a wild, untended woodland with countless streams, several swamps, and a couple of lakes adds up to an environment that birds find irresistible. Most hikers do, too, what with the miles of trails that snake through an underpopulated backcountry.

## ▶ DESCRIPTION

Most people who are aware of Allamuchy Mountain State Park know of it only parenthetically as the setting for Waterloo Village. Within the loose structure of an early 1800s community, visitors there pass through time, from a recreated Lenape Indian settlement to a thriving port by the once-bustling Morris Canal. There are sawmills, gristmills, a blacksmith shop, and general store, along with a variety of historic homes. Everything, it seems, except the mountain to which the name of this park refers. For that—and a highly enchanting hike—you need to venture into the Allamuchy Natural Area, a 2,440-acre chunk of hilly hardwood forestland tucked into the western part of the park.

Allamuchy draws its name from Chief Allamuchahokkingen ("place within the hills") of the Lenape tribe. After the natives were displaced by European settlers, most of this locale was absorbed by the estates of the Rutherford and Stuyvesant families, descendants of New Amsterdam's final governor, Peter Stuyvesant. More recently, the

## ▶ DIRECTIONS

Follow I-95/I-80 west across the George Washington Bridge. Leave I-80 at Exit 19 and drive south on CR 517 for 2.1 miles to Deer Park Road. Turn left on Deer Park Road and proceed straight for 0.6 miles to the parking area.

## ⓘ KEY AT-A-GLANCE INFORMATION

**LENGTH:** 7.5 miles

**CONFIGURATION:** Loop

**DIFFICULTY:** Moderate

**SCENERY:** A succession of mixed hardwood forests, grassy fields, marshlands, and a lovely fishing pond in the center

**EXPOSURE:** Half exposed, half shady

**TRAFFIC:** Light on weekdays, popular summer spot

**TRAIL SURFACE:** Dirt with alternating grass, rocks, and roots

**HIKING TIME:** 4 hours

**SEASON:** Year-round, sunrise–sunset

**ACCESS:** Memorial Day–Labor Day, $5 weekdays, $10 on weekends; free rest of year; $50 parks pass provides access to all New Jersey state parks for one calendar year

**MAPS:** At trailhead kiosk

**FACILITIES:** Portable toilet

**SPECIAL COMMENTS:** In spring, a wild variety of feathered creatures can be spotted; a true birder's special.

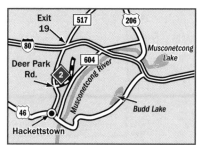

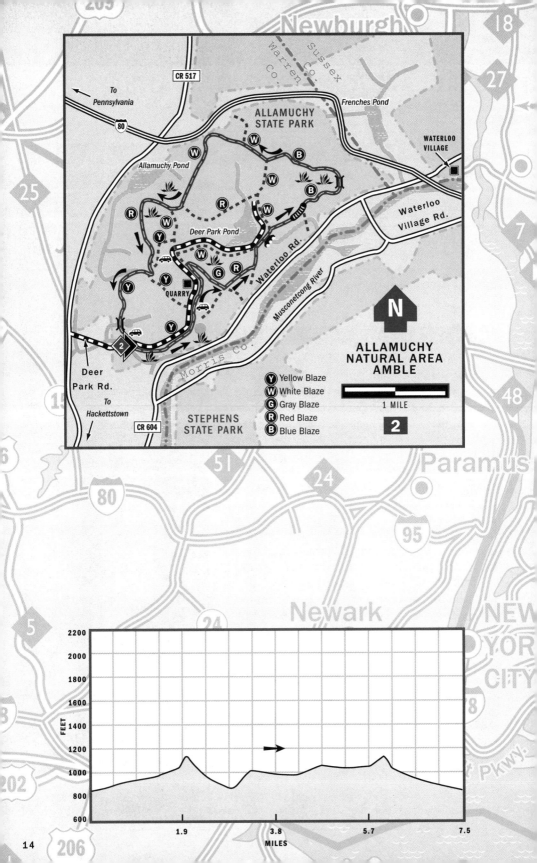

# ALLAMUCHY
# NATURAL AREA
# AMBLE

Y Yellow Blaze
W White Blaze
G Gray Blaze
R Red Blaze
B Blue Blaze

1 MILE

2

ALLAMUCHY
STATE PARK

Frenches Pond

WATERLOO
VILLAGE

Waterloo
Village Rd.

CR 517

To
Pennsylvania

80

Allamuchy Pond

Deer Park Pond

Waterloo Rd.

Musconetcong River

QUARRY

Morris Co.

Deer
Park Rd.

To
Hackettstown

CR 604

STEPHENS
STATE PARK

Warren Co.

Sussex Co.

Musconetcong River, south of the park, has become renowned as one of the best trout fishing spots in New Jersey. The Allamuchy Natural Area—as already noted—enjoys no such fame, which works to the advantage of anyone with an interest in great birding opportunities, unsullied beauty, and a secluded system of trails.

The first part of this hike follows yellow blazes along the dirt road by the kiosk. It is usually possible to drive a mile farther to a different parking lot, one that is closer to Deer Park Pond, but we suggest you walk this stretch. It is attractively overgrown by cedar, maple, flowering dogwood, oak, apple, and tulip trees, with a lowland swamp below the road's right shoulder. This combination makes for an amateur ornithologist's wonderland, one in which we've seen a rose-breasted grosbeak, a redstart, an oriole, and a flock of goldfinches, among many species. You should also see, if you're here in spring, lavender-colored wild geraniums, yellow asters, violets, and white anemones, to name just a few of the wildflowers that highlight the groundcover. The spur to the right, after 15 minutes

In springtime, lavender geraniums are among the many wildflowers that cover the forest floor in Allamuchy State Park.

of walking, dead-ends in a few paces at a picturesque pond, with sheep laurel and chokeberry encroaching and purple irises rising up out of the mud. We once observed half a dozen painted turtles slumbering on the rock to the left, their wet carapaces glistening in the morning sun.

Back on the main track, the dirt road skims by a ranger's residence and then swerves to the right, just as the yellow blazes veer left onto a side trail. Remain with the road as it proceeds past a parking area and slips around a pipe gate. In a couple hundred yards there is a spur to the left, with the shallow tunnel of an old mine a few feet away; swallows like to nest in its carved-out ceiling. Your turnoff is just beyond the quarry on the right side of the forest road. (If you reach parking area 2 you have gone too far.) Though it starts out as an overgrown trace, this gray-blazed route soon widens to comfortable single-file dimensions, snaking through a swamp made all the more colorful by a scattering of glacial erratics among the flowering azalea, mayapple, skunk cabbage, and ferns. You may even see tiger and spicebush swallowtail butterflies brightly fluttering through this zone. As the trail begins to descend, high water or muddy conditions often require that you hop from one moss-coated rock to the next to keep your boots dry. Swing left at the fork, by the low-hung power line, now heading uphill.

The blazes along this somewhat rocky stretch are supposed to be red, though some of the more weathered ones look to be salmon or orange. The forest is rather open here, with an appealing amount of glacial debris littering the slope up to the right. In ten minutes, the serpentine ascent ends as the path levels off, and then descends with Deer Park Pond straight ahead, partially screened by maples and oaks. Bear left at the fork, still treading downward, and hang a right when you reach the forest road. Stay with the road as it crosses the dam, and if you brought a lunch along, you might avail yourself of the hemlock-shaded spot by the pond, where a fair-size rock makes a comfortable seat.

Blue blazes mark the next leg of the hike, a right fork just as the wide dirt road enters tree cover. This path gains ground initially, then loses it, while meandering from rock-pocked forest to fern-flecked swamp, from glacial erratics to a muck-crusted boardwalk. Just after the latter, the track swerves left; 15 feet beyond, there is a spur to the right heading to Waterloo Road. Stay with the main trail as it commences to climb, passing by great, granite-struck leavings of the last glacier to scrape through New Jersey. More erratics follow as the path dips into another bog patch, fording the muck via a rickety bridge. In a little more than a mile, this enjoyable track ends at a fork. With white blazes going both left and right, you should steer right, in a westward direction.

At first, the wide rocky path resembles an old forest road until, having gently ascended for a few minutes, it narrows significantly to single-file. You may notice a boundary fence to the right as the path arcs toward the south, with a couple of traces leading that way a few steps later. Stay with the main trail as it again rises slightly, cresting in 60 seconds among rocky mounds—terrain that is strikingly similar to the undulating blue-blazed stretch. A notable difference, however, is that this region is a bit more open, with an increasing number of dogwood, white birch, and cedar trees entering the arboreal mix. In due time, you arrive at a junction with a red-blazed track merging from the left. Continue straight, with concurrent markings of red and white, as the pebbly path drops through another bog, where purple irises flower in spring. Just after a log puncheon crossing, the red route forks to the right, and you should, too.

From this swampy setting, the path gradually moves toward an attractive mound of fractured granite, with a seasonal bog stream serenely rippling by its base. The trail climbs from there, rapidly entering a boulder-blasted landscape before tapering downward again to another boggy patch. Bear to the right at the fork with a yellow-blazed track and then, in another few yards, right again as the red blazes end. Now walking with yellow markings, this is the home stretch of the hike. The fence to your right is so rusty it is hardly noticeable in an area choked with sarsaparilla and prickler bushes, where large-trunked black birches are the dominant tree. After drifting under a pair of power lines, the path bottoms out by a sweet little pond. Step around the reeds and ferns for a closer look at the shallow water, and you just might spy a few spirited trout and possibly some frogs. A couple of yards farther on is a mowed lawn. Scoot left there to return to your car.

## ▶ NEARBY ACTIVITIES

A bustling port in the nineteenth century, the handsomely restored Waterloo Village is now a living-history museum. It contains a working mill complex, several historic buildings, a recreated Lenape Indian village, and a preserved farm site, with costumed interpreters demonstrating traditional trades. It is also a great venue for summer music concerts. For details, call (973) 347-0900.

# BABCOCK CIRCUMFERENCE TRAIL

## ▶ IN BRIEF

Only ogres and elves are missing from this enchanting hike that threads by bogs, boulders, and fallen trees along several meandering trails. Stone walls and cat briar carpet the undulating forest floor, making this charming preserve seem far larger than it actually is.

## ▶ DESCRIPTION

The Babcock Preserve is a fairy-tale example of conservation overcoming Grimm development. Once upon a time, the 297-acre tract was owned by the local water company. After the always-busy Merritt Parkway was built a half mile away, this hobbit-size hollow was acquired by Charles and Mary Babcock. Their heirs later donated part and sold the rest of this land to the town of Greenwich, allowing for the creation of a wild, shady park that seems, magically, far larger and more remote than it really is.

Nearly 25 years ago, excavators found evidence of an American Indian presence dating back to 2,500 B.C. More recently, through the 1700s and much of the ensuing century, the trees were cleared and the land used for farming. Densely forested once more, all that remains of that latter era is a series of stone walls that run almost haphazardly among the vast stands of birch, beech, maple, and mixed oaks, over a rolling landscape spiced with boulders and bogs.

## ▶ DIRECTIONS

Drive north on the Hutchinson River Parkway and continue as it changes to the Merritt Parkway. Take Exit 31 and, at the end of the ramp, turn right on North Street and proceed for a half mile to the preserve entrance on the left. The trailhead is a quarter mile ahead, with parking available along the gravel access road.

### ⓘ KEY AT-A-GLANCE INFORMATION

**LENGTH:** 3.5 miles

**CONFIGURATION:** Loop

**DIFFICULTY:** Easy

**SCENERY:** Gently rolling terrain in a hardwood forest containing laurel groves, a small pond, many fieldstone walls, bogs, and an excavated ruin

**EXPOSURE:** Good canopy cover throughout summer

**TRAFFIC:** Rather light, except on weekends

**TRAIL SURFACE:** Packed dirt with scattered rock crossings and root networks

**HIKING TIME:** 1.5 hours

**SEASON:** Year-round, dawn–dusk

**ACCESS:** No fee, leashed pets allowed, no bicycles

**MAPS:** Large map with blazed trails is painted on entrance kiosk; USGS Stamford

**FACILITIES:** None

**SPECIAL COMMENTS:** The dogwoods and mountain laurels explode with blossoms from late May to early June. Cross-country skiing is a popular winter activity. Horseback riding for GRTA (Greenwich Riding and Trails Association) members is allowed on designated trails.

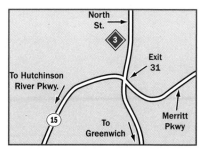

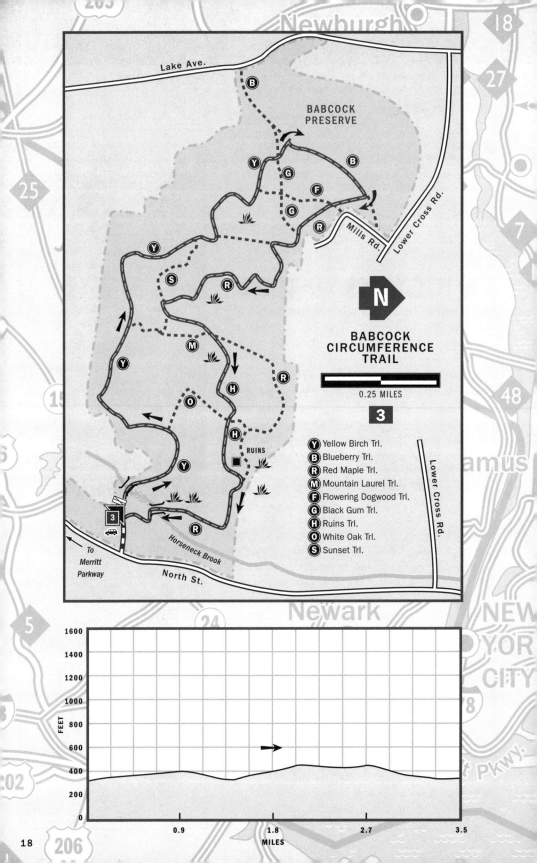

Lake Ave.

BABCOCK
PRESERVE

BABCOCK
CIRCUMFERENCE
TRAIL

0.25 MILES

**3**

Mills Rd.

Lower Cross Rd.

RUINS

Horseneck Brook

To
Merritt
Parkway

North St.

**3**

Lower Cross Rd.

Ⓨ Yellow Birch Trl.
Ⓑ Blueberry Trl.
Ⓡ Red Maple Trl.
Ⓜ Mountain Laurel Trl.
Ⓕ Flowering Dogwood Trl.
Ⓖ Black Gum Trl.
Ⓗ Ruins Trl.
Ⓞ White Oak Trl.
Ⓢ Sunset Trl.

FEET

1600
1400
1200
1000
800
600
400
200
0

0.9          1.8          2.7          3.5
MILES

To fall under the spell of this bewitching domain, try a 3.5-mile stroll around its perimeter, basically following the Yellow Birch Trail (YBT) on the way out and the Red Maple Trail (RMT) on your return. Begin at the kiosk in the parking lot, cross over the cable by the bridge, and stick to the yellow blazes along the old dirt-surfaced access road. Walk by a turnoff to the right, in about 200 yards, as the YBT narrows, levels off and passes into a moist, marshy zone. A bench to the side of the track beckons invitingly, with black birch and shagbark hickory trees flanking it. Remain with the main path as it then falls and rises over undulating ground, heading by the Mountain Laurel Trail (MLT) on the right. Ignore three succeeding left turns, as well as the orange-blazed Sunset Trail on the right. Walk straight ahead, through a dense patch of laurel, and once you have crossed a rusty chain-link fence, swing left, still on the YBT.

Even when the leaves are gone in late fall through early spring, the Babcock Preserve remains a lovely, secluded hollow.

Forty yards beyond the fence, the terrain becomes rockier, and at times the path has the feel of a well-eroded streambed. You'll quickly bottom out by a small bog and, once through there, face two successive spurs to the right, the second being the Flowering Dogwood Trail; like the earlier MLT, it's worth walking along when the trees are in bloom. The next option, also to the right, is the Black Gum Trail (BGT); it joins the YBT for a few paces prior to breaking off again to the right at the junction of two rock walls. Say goodbye to the yellow blazes here as you change over to the BGT. Don't get too comfortable, though, for the latter lasts a scant 20 yards before dead-ending at the Blueberry Trail, where you should roll to the right.

Stay with Blueberry as it slowly rises over a more open ridge, until a huge eyesore of a house looms left of the path, after maybe 300 yards. Shift to the right here onto the RMT (red blazes), and stay with it as it passes the Flowering Dogwood's far end. After grazing over a granite debris field and the BGT's reappearance, Red Maple bears to the left, drifting unpromisingly toward another house.

Fortunately for the sake of one's aesthetics, that vision proves to be a case of misdirection, as the red-blazed trace veers away from the house and through an overgrown patch of cat briar and fern-encrusted boulders. The RMT bends left at the next fork, threading through what is for now a less eye-appealing part of the forest. The scenery improves markedly, though, as you step once more through the chain-link fence, and the Red Maple drops down over a broad stone shelf into a rocky, roiling setting. This is one of the more rough-hewn parts of the preserve, a rock-pocked marshy area where you may need to rely on root- and rock-hopping to keep your boots dry—at least during the wetter months.

In the span of about ten minutes, you will pass a trio of trails to the right, with the first being the Sunset Trail (often flooded at this end) and the third being the MLT. Directly after the MLT, take a right onto the well-marked Ruins Trail (aqua blazes), which is also rather ragged and rocky. In a few minutes, you'll skip through a four-way intersection, still moving along the Ruins route, while the claws of cat briar climb closer on this increasingly narrow channel. (Long pants are advisable for this passageway.) As you drift by the overgrown wall that borders the left side of the path, look closely through the Japanese barberry for a pair of crumbly foundations, measuring roughly seven by ten feet. It is possible to enter the second, but keep in mind that timber rattlers may be dozing in the leaves by its base in warm weather.

A few yards beyond, the Ruins Trail rejoins the RMT, which leads back to the parking area. Forget about the slight spurs you'll encounter on the way there, but do stop, if it's not too buggy, by the bridge in the swamp to look for frogs and animal tracks in the mud.

▶ **NEARBY ACTIVITIES**

The Greenwich Audubon Center on Riversville Road, northwest of Merritt Parkway via Exit 28, offers educational walks, workshops, and many exhibits for all ages, and has a Leatherman's Cave on the grounds. Visit www.audubon.org/local/sanctuary/greenwich or call (203) 869-5272 for information.

Thirsting for something of a cultural nature? Try the Bruce Museum of Arts & Science on Museum Drive in Greenwich. Call for special exhibits at (203) 869-0376.

# BEAR MOUNTAIN DOODLETOWN CIRCUIT

## ▶ IN BRIEF

High country meadows, distant vistas, rugged mountain climbs, and the overgrown ruins of an old village are among the many highlights of this tiring yet delightful calorie-burner of a hike, which also features possible sightings of turkey vultures, hawks, goldfinches, red foxes, white-tailed deer—even black bears and rattlesnakes. No question: This is one of the more exciting moderate-length treks in the New York area, but a couple of challenging stretches are not for those of tender feet.

## ▶ DESCRIPTION

Bear Mountain State Park is, along with its contiguous neighbor to the west, Harriman State Park, one of the most popular nature preserves in the northeast, reportedly drawing more annual visitors than Yellowstone National Park. If not for the efforts of conservationists and wealthy area landowners, though, it might not have come into existence at all. Early in the twentieth century New York state authorities floated the idea of relocating Sing Sing Prison here. That was enough to galvanize E. W. Harriman, president of the Union Pacific Railroad, and others to donate

## ▶ DIRECTIONS

*By car:* Drive north on the New York State Thruway (I-87) over the Tappan Zee Bridge, taking Exit 13 onto the Palisades Interstate Parkway north. Leave the Parkway at Exit 19 to reach Seven Lakes Drive. Proceed for a half mile to the trailhead parking on the right, along a bumpy, partially paved road.

*By public transportation:* Take a ShortLine bus from Manhattan's Port Authority to the Bear Mountain Inn and arrange for a cab from there to the trailhead, just a few miles away.

## ⓘ KEY AT-A-GLANCE INFORMATION

**LENGTH:** 7 miles

**CONFIGURATION:** Loop

**DIFFICULTY:** Moderate/difficult

**SCENERY:** Mixed forest on steep, rocky slopes, gorgeous views from the Appalachian Trail, ruins of an old mining town, and the secluded Herbert Cemetery

**EXPOSURE:** Shady on slopes and in valleys, very open on ridges

**TRAFFIC:** Heavy on weekends, especially in summer

**TRAIL SURFACE:** Mostly packed dirt with some very rocky stretches, rooty in places

**HIKING TIME:** 3.5 hours

**SEASON:** Year-round, 8 a.m.–dusk, weather permitting; possible summer closures due to fire danger

**ACCESS:** No fee, dogs must be leashed, bicycling on paved roads, no mountain bikes

**MAPS:** At the Bear Mountain Visitor Center; USGS Popolopen Lake; New York–New Jersey Trail Conference, Harriman–Bear Mountain Trails

**FACILITIES:** Rest rooms and water at Visitor Center on Palisades Interstate Parkway, along with public telephone, book shop, and more

**SPECIAL COMMENTS:** Buy a trail map at the park office to reduce the likelihood of getting lost on the complex network of trails.

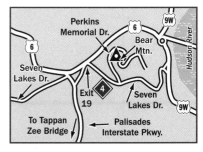

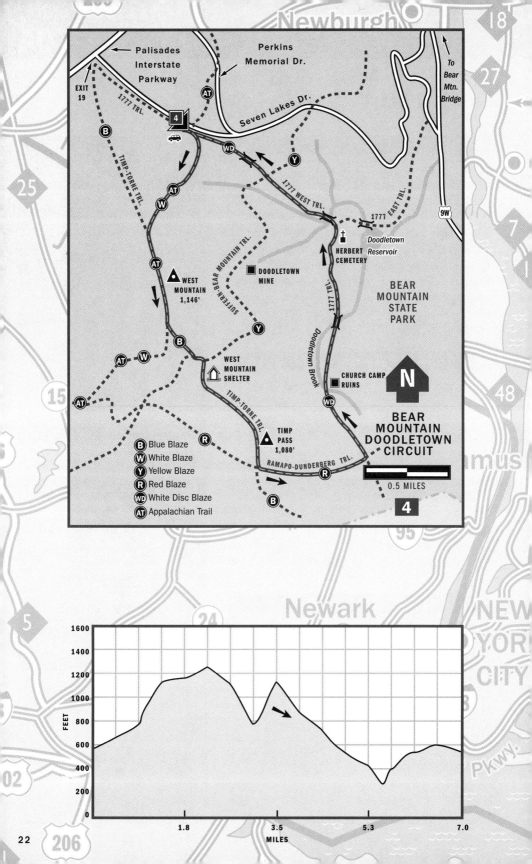

## Map Labels

Palisades
Interstate
Parkway

Perkins
Memorial Dr.

EXIT
19

To
Bear
Mtn.
Bridge

1777 TRL.

4

Seven Lakes Dr.

TIMP-TORNE TRL.

WD

Y

1777 WEST TRL.

1777 EAST TRL.

9W

7

Herbert
Cemetery

Doodletown
Reservoir

SUFFERN-BEAR MOUNTAIN TRL.

DOODLETOWN
MINE

WEST
MOUNTAIN
1,146'

1777 TRL.

BEAR
MOUNTAIN
STATE
PARK

Y

Doodletown Brook

N

WEST
MOUNTAIN
SHELTER

TIMP-TORNE TRL.

CHURCH CAMP
RUINS

WD

TIMP
PASS
1,080'

R

RAMAPO-DUNDERBERG TRL.

BEAR
MOUNTAIN
DOODLETOWN
CIRCUIT

R

0.5 MILES

B

4

### Legend

B Blue Blaze
W White Blaze
Y Yellow Blaze
R Red Blaze
WD White Disc Blaze
AT Appalachian Trail

### Elevation Profile

FEET: 1600, 1400, 1200, 1000, 800, 600, 400, 200, 0

MILES: 1.8, 3.5, 5.3, 7.0

money and land toward the creation of Bear Mountain–Harriman State Parks, which were jointly established in 1914 and today total more than 52,000 acres.

Nine years after the parks' inception, the first section of the Appalachian Trail was laid down in Bear Mountain, serving as a template for later additions to this historic long trail. During the 1930s, the CCC was active in the park, constructing shelters, rest rooms, vacation cabins, and roads, much of which remain intact today. It is not the period architecture, however, that draws people to the two parks like kids to ice cream. Fishing, boating, swimming, camping, picnicking, and horseback riding are just a few of the activities that make this a "something for everyone" sort of place.

Then there is hiking, and in Bear Mountain–Harriman you've got miles and miles of some of the best trekking terrain in the entire New York metropolitan region. Granite domes, rocky ravines, inspiring vistas, mellow meanderings through grassy forests, butt-busting climbs over mountain tops—whatever kind of hike you want— are available here. The Doodletown Circuit, a moderately strenuous loop of just over 7 miles, is a fine introduction to Bear Mountain's natural beauty and historic past. Begin the hike on the 1777 West Trail, to the left of the parking lot. Follow the white-disc blazes as the path climbs over rocky, fern-speckled ground through laurels, maples, and blueberry bushes before leveling off in a few minutes. At the first slight descent you'll leave the 1777, drifting to the right at an obtuse angle along an old grass-covered carriage lane. This meets, within a minute or two, the Appalachian Trail (AT), identified, as usual, by a long, white blaze. Remain with the AT as it rolls sharply right off the carriage lane in five minutes or so and heads steeply up a beech- and oak-punctuated slope. The ensuing brief downhill run into a boulder-filled ravine is just a teaser in advance of the most strenuous part of the hike, a prolonged exertion over stone-studded turf.

You'll want to catch your breath at the first false summit, a grassy plateau more than 300 feet above the trailhead that offers a clear vista of Bear Mountain Peak and the Hudson River. The views of both are even more commanding farther south along this

Whitetail deer now make their homes in what was once the thriving community of Doodletown, in Bear Mountain State Park.

rising dome of granite, as the well-beaten track tacks between scrub oaks and black birch saplings, climbing still higher up a talus slope. There is little in the way of real shade during this part of the hike, with the exposure growing as you hang a left at the junction with the Timp-Torne Trail (TT, blue blazes) and ascend a rocky knob that is more than 600 feet above the parking area.

Keep to the right of the oak growing off the knob and maneuver by a thicket of young birches on your way to still another granite shelf, this one overlooking the Palisades Parkway, a couple of colossal car lots, and the expansive hills of Harriman to the west. Continuing along the rocky ridge, which rises and falls and gives way momentarily to a lush, green saddle, you will enjoy an extension of those westward views. The trail eventually leads to West Mountain Peak at 1,146 feet of elevation. We once encountered a pretty hefty rattlesnake here, dozing by a rotted tree stump, so be careful where you step.

The TT diverges from the AT a short distance from there. Stay to the left on the TT, treading in the direction of the West Mountain shelter. If you packed a lunch, this is the place to unwrap it, as you are now entering a very appealing mountain meadow of scrub oaks and calf-high grass. Another such knoll follows in a moment, when the Suffern–Bear Mountain Trail (SBM, yellow blazes) joins the TT from the right. Cut through that second knoll on its right side, where the blue-yellow blazes are painted on the bedrock.

The path meanders quite a bit southward, then toward the east, before the TT and SBM diverge, with the TT bending acutely to the right (south), along the edge of a granite shelf. In sticking with it, you ramble by the West Mountain shelter, an excellent (and durable) example of the CCC's handiwork, and are rewarded with a clear view of the Hudson River. The going is fairly steep from there, descending over a debris field on the jagged side of the ridge. Just as the slope hits the skids—literally—with loose rocks offering little in the way of footholds, the trail swerves right toward a grassy saddle and safer steps.

The rest of the way, though, is hardly a cakewalk. But the downward direction adheres to a more moderate pace until it nears the bottom of the slope and doglegs first left, then right, hopping over a series of carriage roads. Did you manage to regain your wind on this downhill stretch? Good, because for the next 15 minutes it's back into low gear, grinding up another granite-strewn slope to the top of Timp Peak. Your left turn onto the Ramapo-Dunderberg Trail (RD, red blazes), lies just beyond its crest, though you should slow down long enough on the Timp to absorb the sublime views, first of the Bear Mountain Bridge and the Hudson to the north, followed by West Mountain and the rounded hills of Harriman to the west.

In 10 minutes of traipsing along the RD, the path meets the wide, well trammeled 1777, where you hang a left. The woods on either side of this easy, level, pebbly surfaced carriage lane (which was formerly known as Pleasant Valley Road) conceal many remnants of Doodletown. The first that you may notice is a poplar-shaded stone foundation, to the right of a confluence of streambeds. These are the remains of a dam and pool constructed by a church camp many decades ago.

Farther on is a series of old-growth maples—some with trunks measuring four feet across—where, not so coincidentally, a patch of pavement appears, as well as an old stone wall by the roadside. The surest indication that you are now in the heart of Doodletown is the appearance of newly installed interpretive signs marking where many houses once stood. Some residents held on until as recently as the 1960s; perhaps they were the ones who planted the irises that grow here, as well as the handful of spruce trees—conifers that are not native to Bear Mountain. The mounds and depressions on either side of the lane seem pregnant with ruins now concealed by vines and other vegetation. A driveway to the right leads to an open foundation, with several young maples rising from its core and old cooking pots littering the ground nearby. You might easily spend a couple of hours exploring the network of lanes that cut through these woods. Save time, though, for a brief side-trip to the Herbert Cemetery, on a narrow lane to the right, just after you pass two prominent pillars left of the trail. Many of the graves date to the early 1800s, with their headstones standing at odd angles like teeth badly in need of an orthodontist.

Returning to the 1777, proceed for another 100 yards, brushing by a bush of pink-flowering rose of Sharon, to the trail's departure from the carriage road—a left into an overgrown thicket. This is the start of 1777 West, which climbs, skips over a stream and by a ravine, finally meeting the SBM at a T. Keep to the left, now following the white discs of 1777 on the old Doodletown Road, an unpaved avenue lined with oaks. This stretch is an active birding area, where we have seen at various times goldfinches, robins, and a red-tailed hawk. The parking area lies about 15 minutes down the trail.

## ▶ NEARBY ACTIVITIES

This all-in-one park features several lakes where boating, fishing, and swimming are popular pastimes. Family picnics and barbecues go on all summer. In winter, skiing, sledding, snowmobiling, ice-skating, and ice fishing are permitted.

Hungry hikers can soothe their appetites in the snack bar or restaurant of the Bear Mountain Inn, a rustic lodge along US 9W, where a trailside museum and zoo are also located. For details, call the park office at (845) 786-2701.

# BLACK RIVER TRAIL

## KEY AT-A-GLANCE INFORMATION

**LENGTH:** 6.6 miles for the balloon, 7.8 miles for the one-way stretch from Cooper's Mill to the Willowwood Arboretum

**CONFIGURATION:** Balloon

**DIFFICULTY:** Easy start followed by moderate loop

**SCENERY:** Along the cascading Black River, grassy meadows and dark conifer forests succeed thick deciduous woods

**EXPOSURE:** Mostly shady with a few open road and meadow stretches

**TRAFFIC:** The farther you hike, the lonelier it gets

**TRAIL SURFACE:** A lot of dirt, but grass, pavement, rocks, and pine-needle carpet alternate

**HIKING TIME:** 3.5 hours

**SEASON:** Year-round, sunrise–sunset

**ACCESS:** No fee, pets must be on leash of maximum 6 feet long, no biking, no horseback riding

**MAPS:** At trailhead kiosk and Visitor Center

**FACILITIES:** Vault toilets, Visitor Center

**SPECIAL COMMENTS:** The Black River is a popular trout-fishing spot: fishermen—not bears—are commonly seen darting in and out of the bushes. And in spring, you may be so lucky as to find a pink lady's slipper orchid.

## IN BRIEF

Take a pinch of iron-mining history, combine that with a highly scenic river, add a few successional fields, a conifer-covered hillside, and the possibility of seeing wildlife, and what do you have? The makings of a tremendous hike along the Black River Trail. This one manages the neat feat of carrying you deep into a wilderness and back in time, all within the confines of a well-populated suburban community. A cabin ruin and hidden cascade add to the fun in a trek you are likely to savor long after its finish.

## DESCRIPTION

The folks at New Jersey's Morris County Park Commission are a modest lot. We conclude so, anyway, not from having met them—we haven't!—but because they manage one of the most beautiful trails most people have never heard of. That's the Black River Trail system we're referring to, as fine a parcel of real estate as you are likely to find in this part of the state. A good piece of this hike hugs the photogenic banks of the Black River, some of it passes through meadowlands rich in

## DIRECTIONS

Follow I-95/I-80 west across the George Washington Bridge. Leave I-80 at Exit 27 and drive south on US 206 for 8.1 miles. Turn right (west) on CR 513/SR 24 and continue for 1.2 miles to the large parking lot on the left, by Cooper Mill. If you have a shuttle car, park it first at the Willowwood Arboretum. From the intersection of US 206 and SR 24, proceed south on US 206 and drive 4.7 miles to Pottersville Road (CR 512). Make a right on CR 512, and after 1.2 miles, turn right on Lisk Hill Road. At the T, make a right on Union Grove Road. Continue 0.3 miles, and at the fork veer left onto Longview Road. The arboretum entrance is a half mile away on the left.

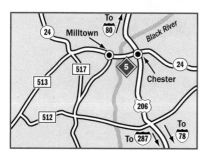

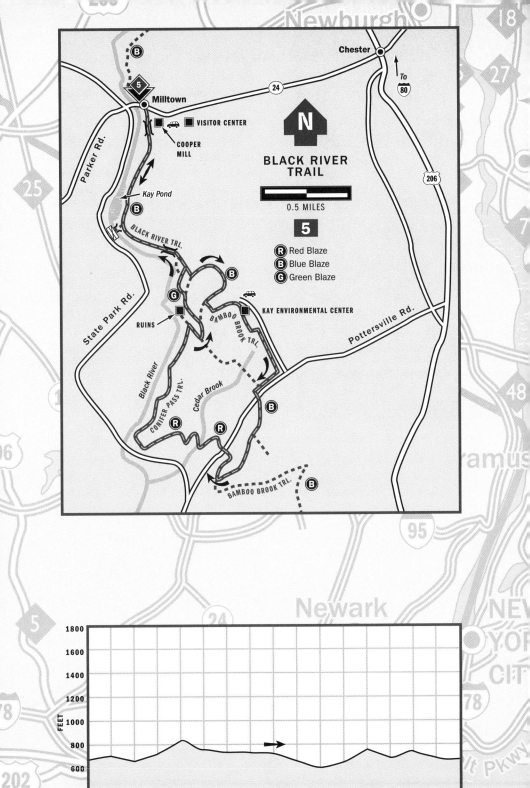

BLACK RIVER
TRAIL

0.5 MILES

**5**

R Red Blaze
B Blue Blaze
G Green Blaze

Chester

To
80

Newburgh

Milltown

VISITOR CENTER

COOPER
MILL

Kay Pond

BLACK RIVER TRL.

Parker Rd.

State Park Rd.

RUINS

Black River

CONIFER PASS TRL.

Cedar Brook

BAMBOO BROOK TRL.

KAY ENVIRONMENTAL CENTER

Pottersville Rd.

BAMBOO BROOK TRL.

The Cooper Grist Mill, built in 1826, is a prominent historic relic along the Black River Trail.

bird life, and a fair portion winds over a conifer-covered hillside. From dynamic cascades to a placid pond, from cabin ruins to a historic mine, there is hardly a dull moment on this relatively easy trek.

The entire length of this trail, from Chubb Park to Willowwood Arboretum, is 8.2 miles, one way. Thus, if you have an extra car, you might use it as a shuttle, leaving a vehicle at one end of the route and starting the hike at the other. Otherwise, we suggest a shorter loop of 6.6 miles, beginning at Cooper Mill. This solid limestone block construction, incidentally, is a remnant of the community of Milltown, which thrived during the nineteenth century. Don't bother to look for it on your Rand McNally: Milltown is gone, along with the blacksmith shop, distillery, sawmill, and general store that once shared the shoulder of the road with Cooper Mill. Iron mining was the local industry then, with the Chester Furnace, a mile to the north, producing 300 tons a week at its peak, and locomotives loaded with the stuff rattling through town every day. Miners netted three bucks a week in wages, and lived in a shantytown at the fringes of the community. The first mile of this hike showcases relics of that halcyon era.

Pick up the blue blazes of the Black River Trail at the mill. Chubb Park is to the north, through the tunnel that runs under SR 24/124. Your destination lies in the other direction, but take a moment to walk up the tunnel for a glimpse of the river on the other side of the road, where it is dammed above the mill. Having finished that detour, descend the wooden stairs behind Cooper Mill and cross the rivulet. A second short bridge ensues, which delivers you to a scenic swamp, where a stream slithers by skunk cabbage and irises toward the Black River. Maple, beech, black birch, and a mix of oaks shade the area around an array of granite boulders, while a couple of benches are ideally situated to soak up the serenity of this setting.

The path is clearly marked and very easy to follow as it swings left and parallels the gurgling river, tripping over a series of short bridges in the process. For the next half mile, the well-graded track overlaps the old Hacklebarney branch of the Central New Jersey Rail Road, which was constructed in 1873 to transport ore from the mines. Beyond a bit of gravel here and there, nothing is left of the tracks, but if you look closely to the right on passing the bog, you may see some terrapins and frogs among the ferns, violets, and jack-in-the-pulpits. Then there is Kay Pond, where the river is bottled up. Generations ago, this was the community swimming hole, but unless it is really hot, you would now be better off leaving it to the snapping turtles that lurk around the perimeter. The fenced-in building below the dam—originally a mill—was later converted into an electric plant.

Moving onward, the trail nears a chain-link fence where the overgrown, rubble-filled slope is all that remains of the Hacklebarney Mine. During its peak, from 1879 through 1892, the mine yielded around 20,000 tons of ore annually. It now produces birch trees, maples, and chokeberry. On departing that area, the hike heads into a wilder environment, with the rocky embankment to the left soaring 30 feet, and the river opposite crackling merrily along. Several additional short bridges and board-walks appear here, as the path hovers around an attractive bog. Finally, after passing concrete pilings that once supported a bridge, the track tapers uphill toward the east, leaving the water behind. The climb tops out at a fork in about 100 yards, with the blue blazes leading left, toward the Elizabeth Kay Environmental Center (EKEC).

In addition to the wild turkeys, red foxes, and coyotes that crisscross this hillside, remnants of walls prove that this hardwood forest was formerly open farmland. You may smell the sweet perfume of honeysuckle near the end of your ascent, part of a vast array of successional plants, like cedar, sarsaparilla, dogwood, and ash, that have resurfaced in what was formerly known as Hidden River Farm. Hidden River was purchased by Alfred and Elizabeth Kay in 1924, who maintained it as their summer retreat. Much of what they raised, including cows, chickens, pigs, herbs, miscellaneous grains and veg-etables, was shipped to their Florida residence. Eventually, the property was donated to Morris County, which converted the farmhouse into the EKEC.

Cross the grassy patch at the top of the hill and turn left at the intersection, moving toward the EKEC. Stay with the gravel drive 0.2 miles to the parking area, and once there, walk from the public telephone, marked with a blue blaze, to the far side of the house. Transfer to the Bamboo Brook Trail, straight over the aisle of mowed grass, and under a large maple by an orchard of flowering dogwoods. The path hits a T at a rail fence, where it jogs to the left, still blazed with blue. Go through the green wooden gate (it is usually open), emerging by a field speckled yellow with flowering lupin. In a moment, the trail lurches to the right, merging with the farm's entrance road. Bluebirds often cavort in the grassy meadow to your left, while butterflies favor the scrub growth over the fence. Remain on the driveway until it meets Pottsville Road and veer right there. Within three minutes blue blazes marking the entrance back into the forest appear on the left side of the road.

Even in an expanding neighborhood, where modest homes are being replaced with McMansions, there is a secluded feel to this lightly trafficked section of the woods. After a bit of meandering, the path arrives at a grassy breach in the trees, where deer frequently graze. A fork in the trail occurs a minute later, with the blue-blazed route continuing to the right. Hang with this track as it traverses an old forest lane, moving upward over increasingly rocky turf. In five minutes, that climb is done and—what else?—a descent commences. Partway down the hill, the Conifer Pass Trail (red blazes) forks to the right—take it, moving now in a west-to-northwest direction. There are a few knee-high stone cairns spaced out along the way to help guide you through the rocky terrain, and within four minutes, the path recrosses Pottsville Road.

On the other side of the blacktop, the hardwood forest evaporates as it is trans-formed, miraculously, into a wide, tilting plain of white pines. Ferns and false lilies grow by the feet of these silent giants, as well as Virginia creeper and barberry, while a piney scent, mingled with honey, often fills the air. The trail continues downward, swiveling from the west toward the south and then back to the west, ultimately hitting the trough at a pleasant little glade by Cedar Brook, which you hop over. It is uphill from there, steeply so for 60 seconds, with a leveling off among hardwoods and a fading complement of conifers. The descent that follows tapers toward the southwest before shifting northward. In a handful of minutes, as pines resurface with laurels, the path returns to the Black River.

In keeping to the right, alongside the dark, eddying water, you enter a fabulous part of the hike. Much of the thrill here derives from the finely chiseled rocky setting, one in which the river explodes by boulders and crashes over a series of erratics for a prolonged, voluptuous cascade. With the presence in June of pink lady's slipper orchids popping out of the peat up the slope to your right, all that is needed to complete the fairy-tale image is an elf sitting on a giant toadstool. You, too, may feel inclined to sit, with a rock by the dark river an ideal perch for immersing one's thoughts in the sound and fury of the scene. Gradually, the trail weaves away from the Black River, hugging the hemlock-covered hill, and swings right on a wide forest road. First, though, take five and stroll a few hundred feet to the left, to the stone foundation of an old cabin, its pinnacle of a chimney still intact. Hemmed in by rhododendrons and with the river bending just below, it is hard to imagine a more idyllic spot in which to build a retreat.

Back on track with the red blazes, walk uphill to the next junction at a slight leveling, and turn left. Keep left again in 250 feet, dropping off the dirt lane. Hemlocks are mingled with hardwoods here, with yellow penstemon speckling the forest floor. On reaching a ridge, the path tapers back toward the water, where the latter lustily crashes against protruding rocks, then resumes its upward trend. As the mountain laurels and pines recede, the track merges into a broad forest road, blazed green; continue straight on that (instead of the sharp right up the ridge). The land to the left of this hard, pebbly lane is posted as an "environmentally sensitive area." To hike the trails and bushwhack there, you'll need to obtain a permit at the EKEC or from the Morris County Park Police.

Stay with the green markings at the ensuing fork as they branch to the left, then switch to the unblazed trace on the right. This single-file forested path, overhung by beech saplings, oak, and tulip trees, merges in a moment with a wide track. A left turn there puts you back on the Black River Trail, the first leg of the hike. Cooper Mill is one mile ahead.

## ▶ NEARBY ACTIVITIES

You might start the hike with a guided tour of Cooper Mill, a restored gristmill that was a state-of-the-art operation when it was built in 1826. And consider ending the day at the Willowwood Arboretum, surrounded by rolling farmland, bisected by informal walking trails, and sporting 3,500 varieties of native and exotic plants. For detailed information on these facilities, call (973) 326-7600 or visit www.parks.morris.nj.us.

# BLACK ROCK FOREST PEAKS TO PONDS TRAIL

Historians report that Rome was built on seven hills. That's one more than Black Rock Forest can boast of, but then Black Rock also has half a dozen bodies of water, and it sees so few visitors that you are apt to have any or all of those features exclusively to yourself. Between the rock-scrambling to vistas and stream-hopping through swamps, you'll enjoy a great workout in a diversity of habitats that virtually guarantees wildlife sightings.

## ▶ DESCRIPTION

"Great crystals on the surface of the earth, Lakes of Light. If they were permanently congealed, and small enough to be clutched, they would, perchance, be carried off by slaves, like precious stones, to adorn the heads of emperors . . . ." It was Walden and White Ponds to which Henry David Thoreau referred, but his words seem just as applicable to the many radiant bodies of water within the Black Rock Forest Preserve. In fact, this park is so enchanting that after a few hours of tramping its high points and hidden dells, you may find yourself contemplating where to erect a cabin. Part of the reason this sanctuary is so captivatingly beautiful is its unique location between Schunemunk and Storm King Mountains, where it straddles two thriving ecosystems—the Hudson River basin and the Hudson Highlands. Additionally, while most of its 3,785 acres were set aside as

## ▶ DIRECTIONS

Follow US 9 north to Peekskill, then head west on US 6. Once over the Bear Mountain Bridge, enter the traffic circle and drive north on scenic route US 9W for 9.7 miles to Mountain Road. Make a right on it, and an immediate sharp right again, into a narrow tunnel leading to Reservoir Road. Continue straight for 0.1 mile to the parking area on the right.

## ⓘ KEY AT-A-GLANCE INFORMATION

**LENGTH:** 11 miles

**CONFIGURATION:** Balloon

**DIFFICULTY:** Very difficult

**SCENERY:** Half a dozen summits and half a dozen lakes, with a lot of rock-scrambling between gorgeous vistas and dizzying depths

**EXPOSURE:** No canopy on the barren summits, but largely shady elsewhere

**TRAFFIC:** Often light, but summer weekends may draw the brave

**TRAIL SURFACE:** A mix of dirt and rocks, with some pleasant grassy stretches

**HIKING TIME:** 6–7 hours

**SEASON:** Year-round, sunrise–sunset

**ACCESS:** Suggested donation $2 adult and $1 child, pets must be leashed, biking limited to members of the Black Rock Forest Mountain Bike Club

**MAPS:** Posted at trailhead kiosk; USGS Cornwall; New York–New Jersey Trail Conference, West Hudson Trails; Black Rock Forest map ($1) at kiosk

**FACILITIES:** None

**SPECIAL COMMENTS:** The wide, rolling woodland roads provide good cross-country skiing trails in winter. The forest may sometimes be closed due to fire hazard or deer hunting (which typically runs from late November through early December). Call (845) 534-2966 for the latest update or visit www.blackrockforest.org.

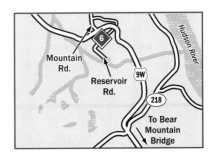

BLACK ROCK
FOREST
PEAKS TO
PONDS TRAIL

**0.5 MILES**

6

Y Yellow Blaze
W White Blaze
O Orange Blaze
R Red Blaze
B Blue Blaze
T Turquoise Blaze

early as 1928, the preserve's relative obscurity has resulted in a refreshingly unsullied domain. The miles of trails here, from broad forest roads to narrow woodland rambles, crisscross half a dozen peaks and a like number of lakes, with foot traffic surprisingly light throughout the year.

On leaving the parking lot, the red-blazed trail sinks down into a dark forest of hemlock, oak, maple, and tulip trees, with luminous ferns rising off the ground. Within half a mile the path hits bottom at a four-way intersection; continue straight and cross the bridge, now with blue markings. The stream to your left on the ensuing uphill grind is an auditory and visual delight that cascades noisily through several rocky constrictions. Ignore the sundry spurs as you plod along, and in ten minutes hop straight over the little arroyo and switch to the yellow-blazed track (the blue markings cross the wider stream on your left), still moving up the slope.

In another five minutes the yellow trail crests at a forest road. It proceeds straight on, up to Mount Misery, but you turn right, saving the Misery for later. Stay with this wide, pebbly lane for the next quarter mile, hanging a right with yellow and turquoise blazes at the obscure four-way junction shortly after you hear the stream noisily pouring off Aleck Meadow Reservoir. This narrow corridor through laurels and hemlocks leads directly to the reservoir. Follow the path counterclockwise below the earthen embankment of the lake, gaining meanwhile a good view from the concrete bridge of the water sluicing downhill over a rocky streambed. Just as you attain a level with the reservoir, where purple irises bloom in spring, the path veers right, heading upward among hemlocks, beeches, black birches, black gum trees, and innumerable boulders. This route, marked with a yellow rectangle (and the turquoise diamond of the Highland Trail), meets a T in three or four minutes and continues to the left. Then, in 60-plus seconds, it swerves to the right, trending steadily higher.

In less than a quarter mile, the surroundings evolve from hardwoods and mountain laurel, where wild turkeys are frequently observed, to a more Spartan, boulder-strapped environment. The final scramble up a steep rock face brings you to a sunny ledge, with views through spicebush to the south and of the Schunemunk range to the west. That's just an appetizer for Black Rock summit, 70 feet farther up the path, with its breathtaking panorama highlighted by the expansive Hudson as it flows under the Newburgh Bridge to Storm King Mountain, and Breakneck Ridge beyond the river. At 1,402 feet of elevation, Black Rock is not the highest peak you will climb today, but it may well deliver the most exciting vistas.

When you have had enough of this celestial setting, chase after the yellow blazes as the Stillman Trail (ST) departs the dome, down a series of natural steps, and swings left into the mountain laurels. In eight minutes, the ST launches left on the unpaved Hulse Road, only to jump right at a pipe gate by a four-way intersection of forest lanes. Leave the ST as it veers left immediately, remaining instead with Continental Road for 65 or 70 paces and then shift left on the Sackett Trail (SAC, yellow circles). This single-file track edges lower into a boggy, boulder-filled environment before meeting the grass-surfaced Hall Road. Steer left there, and continue on Hall Road at the succeeding four-way intersection, where the SAC forges to the right and the Compartment Trail (CT, blue blazes) branches left. In about a dozen minutes, the yellow blazes of the ST merge from the right. Stick with those as the ST breaks left, away from the road. In a few strides the blue blazes of the CT merge with the trail, as you begin a brief ascent.

On reaching the top of the hill, turn right at the four-way crossing, now adhering to blue and turquoise blazes. (The vernal pool to the left of the path is usually black with tadpoles in springtime.) Forget the traces that fork left through laurels to a rock ledge vista point; you'll get there soon enough. As the track circles to the left, leave it for the Split Rock Trail (SRT, white blazes), also on the left. The SRT hops back onto the plateau, where knee-high grass grows between the jutting rocks. This is the aptly-named Split Rock, elevation 1,400 feet, a fine vantage point from which to survey Sutherland Pond, directly below. Incidentally, among the skunk cabbage of the marsh just south of the pond are sundew, rare insect-eating plants. The SRT clings to this beautiful hunk of the Highlands for a minute or two, then departs the granite ridge, also leaving behind a cluster of pitch pine, sheep laurel, and spicebush.

Head straight across the forest road at the bottom of the slope, drifting uphill between Sutherland and Sphagnum Ponds (only the latter is fleetingly visible through the trees). Turn to the right in about a quarter mile on the Secor Trail (yellow markings), plunging into a nest of mountain laurel. Though initially overgrown, conditions improve as you gain elevation, with a fun scramble up a tilted shelf of granite occurring in a few minutes. The path snakes from this knob to another before coming to a fork with the Chatfield Trail (CFT, blue blazes), where you turn right. This peaceful, secluded half mile leg drops lower to a boggy pond, with fractured slabs of boulders standing like sentries below a great crag, and ends at a T. Go left on this white-blazed, meandering track and stride right in nine minutes on the spur marked with blue. This detour forges into a jumble of rocks, at which point you should scale the large, rounded Sisyphean boulder, the highlight of Eagles Cliff, at an altitude of 1,443 feet.

This vertigo-inducing aerie projects precariously out from the ridge and is so isolated you might actually see an eagle or (more likely) vulture roosting on it. The fabulous views swoop from the north to east to south, with Jim's Pond and Wilkins Pond serving as focal points below, while the denuded hill to the southeast, pocked with rusting military vehicles, is part of a West Point Military Academy training area. Wander down the orange-blazed spur to the left, along the length of this sensational ledge, and slip off the rocks in 300 yards. Trot to the left when the spur merges with a yellow-marked route, and pivot to the right as those yellow indications collide again with the white-blazed trail (WT). In eight minutes, a blue-blazed trace to the left, indicated by a cairn of stones, rapidly hits Spy Rock, a romantic nook shaded by a lone pitch pine. This is the highest point in the park, at 1,463 feet, but the views are limited. Moseying onward, the WT soon arrives at a staggered four-way intersection, requiring a dogleg first to the right and then left to carry you straight on. About four minutes beyond a yellow-blazed trace to the left (which leads over the rocky ridge to Arthur's Pond), the WT staggers right, off the forest road.

From initially losing elevation, this trail soon starts to churn upward, sputtering to the pinnacle of Rattlesnake Hill (1,405 feet) in about 15 minutes. This granite shelf is coated with pale green lichen, like barnacles clinging to the hull of a ship, and fringed with pitch pines. Visible through the latter is Bog Meadow Pond, where you may see people boating. Don't fret too much, though, about encountering the Rattlesnake Hill's namesake reptile: the most exciting animal we've encountered here is a scarlet tanager chirping musically at the setting sun. Walk directly across the dome and pass into the tangle of mountain laurel, with three slightly lower knobs succeeding this first one as the path keeps to the west side of the ridge. From there, a two-minute descent brings you to an intersection with a forest road, which the White Trail crosses diagonally. Then it is back to higher ground, meandering through an impressive spar of stony uplift. In little more than a minute, you near the top of the rise, with the boulders giving way to a grassy sward.

As with the previous peak, you may wonder about the name of this sun-exposed crest, Hill of Pines (1,410 feet), on observing that the two or three pitch pines growing here are greatly outnumbered by oak and spicebush. Justification for that moniker grows as the WT descends through an increasing number of hemlocks. The rocky trail, which doubles as a streambed in wet weather, swerves toward the northwest as it nears the bottom of the gulch, crossing a blue-blazed path when it reaches a natural rock garden, with a superabundance of boulders and stones littering the terrain. When the WT ends by the base of the next ridge, switch to a yellow- and turquoise-blazed track and bear to the right, instead of legging it straight up the lower part of the hill.

Pick your way carefully through this boulder field and gradually climb the steep heap of rocks known as Mount Misery. (In this case at least, there is no mystery surrounding the name.) You may have been higher today, but this ascent is probably the most arduous. Soon enough, though, the hard, eluvial turf changes to grass and a more gentle approach, delivering you at last to a very pretty knoll. There are great views to the west, including Aleck Meadow Reservoir and Black Rock Summit, where you were hours ago, as the trail lunges to the far edge of the peak and sticks with the ridge for several minutes. And then it is sharply downward, arriving in five minutes at the same crossing with the forest road you were at near the start of the hike. Continue straight with the yellow blazes, retracing your earlier steps back to the parking area.

## ▶ NEARBY ACTIVITIES

Give your feet a rest with a guided bus tour of the United States Military Academy at West Point. For details or parade schedules, call the Visitor Center at (845) 938-2638. The West Point Museum displays an impressive collection of bellicose objects, from uniforms to weapons, flags, and more. Call (845) 938-2203 for information.

# BLUE MOUNTAIN TWIN SUMMITS TRAIL

## KEY AT-A-GLANCE INFORMATION

**LENGTH:** 5 miles

**CONFIGURATION:** Loop with 2 spurs

**DIFFICULTY:** Easy/moderate

**SCENERY:** Rolling terrain with mostly deciduous forest, and panoramic views of the Hudson River from Blue Mountain and Mount Spitzenberg

**EXPOSURE:** Shady except for a small, open meadow area that the trail crosses twice

**TRAFFIC:** Heavy on summer weekends; light weekdays

**TRAIL SURFACE:** Dirt and heaps of rocks and pebbles

**HIKING TIME:** 2.5 hours

**SEASON:** Year-round, 8 a.m.–dusk

**ACCESS:** $4 in summer with Westchester County Park Pass, $8 without pass, dogs must be leashed

**MAPS:** At entrance booth; also at www.wmba.org; USGS Peekskill

**FACILITIES:** Rest rooms and water at picnic areas, public phone

**SPECIAL COMMENTS:** Many of the wooden, numbered navigation posts that are on the WMBA (Westchester Mountain Biking Association) map are missing on the trails. Remember that in addition to mountain bikers you also share this park with equestrians and fishermen. The latter, though, tend to stick to the ponds.

## ▶ IN BRIEF

The fun trails here meander so much you may be reminded at times of a roller-coaster ride. Its hilly terrain encompasses a pair of ponds, a number of bogs, boulders, and glacial erratics, as well as two significant peaks with views extending to the Hudson River and Tappan Zee Bridge.

## ▶ DESCRIPTION

Blue Mountain Reservation is a scenic, mountainous park of 1,583 acres, many of which are colored by glacial erratics, granite uplift, and dense groves of maples, black birch, and beech trees. Once part of the parcel acquired in 1677 by Stephanus Van Cortlandt that later became Van Cortlandt Manor, it is now managed by the Westchester County Parks Commission.

Considering the suburban sprawl that hems it in, the air at Blue Mountain smells relatively clean and pure. There are occasions, though, when your nostrils may detect a *soupçon* of scorch to the atmosphere, an igneous influence associated not with overcooked coffee, but with the burning of rubber on rock. This is, after all, one of the top spots for mountain biking in the New York

## ▶ DIRECTIONS

*By car:* Take SR 9 north to Ossining and proceed for another 9.5 miles to the Welcher Avenue exit. Turn right and drive straight for three blocks to the park entrance. Proceed beyond the tollbooth, past the Trail Lodge, to parking lot 3.

*By public transportation:* The Hudson Line of Metro North goes to Peekskill Station. From there, it is 1.5 miles to the park entrance. If you choose not to taxi, walk east on Hudson Avenue, turn right on Washington Street, and continue for about 1 mile to Welcher Avenue. Hang a left there and march straight ahead (Welcher becomes Lounsbury Avenue) into the park.

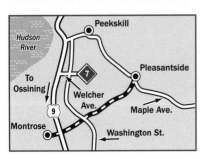

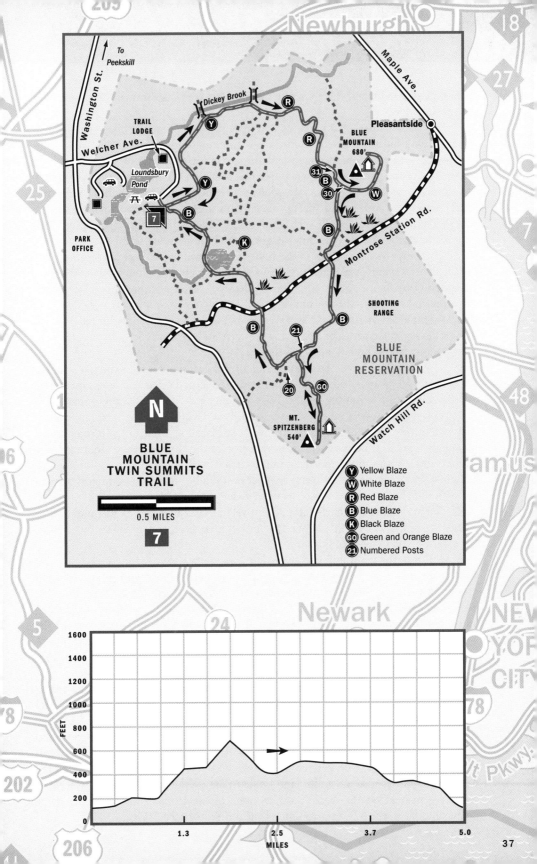

To Peekskill

Washington St.

Newburgh

Maple Ave.

Dickey Brook

TRAIL
LODGE

Welcher Ave.

Loundsbury
Pond

**Y**

**R**

**R**

Pleasantside

**BLUE
MOUNTAIN
680'**

**31**
**B**
**30**

**W**

**Y**

**B**

**7**

PARK
OFFICE

**K**

**B**

**B**

Montrose Station Rd.

**SHOOTING
RANGE**

**B**

**21**

**B**

**BLUE
MOUNTAIN
RESERVATION**

**20**

**GO**

Watch Hill Rd.

**MT.
SPITZENBERG
540'**

**N**

**BLUE
MOUNTAIN
TWIN SUMMITS
TRAIL**

0.5 MILES

**7**

**Y** Yellow Blaze
**W** White Blaze
**R** Red Blaze
**B** Blue Blaze
**K** Black Blaze
**GO** Green and Orange Blaze
**21** Numbered Posts

Newark

| | | | | | | | | |
|---|---|---|---|---|---|---|---|---|
| 1600 | | | | | | | | |
| 1400 | | | | | | | | |
| 1200 | | | | | | | | |
| 1000 | | | | | | | | |
| 800 | | | | | | | | |
| 600 | | | | | | | | |
| 400 | | | | | | | | |
| 200 | | | | | | | | |
| 0 | | | | | | | | |

FEET

1.3          2.5          3.7          5.0
MILES

metropolitan region, and there are often more bikers zipping through the woods than white-tailed deer.

The same features that make this preserve so popular among bikers should also appeal to avid hikers—namely a series of surging, rippling trails that link two mountain peaks, with a couple of large ponds tossed in for good measure. A 5-mile loop that connects the park's primary features like beads on a string begins at the northeast corner of parking lot 3, directly opposite the picnic area by the pond. Strike out on the rock-filled forest road that has been worn ragged by bikers and equestrians, and almost immediately you'll veer left onto the yellow-blazed side trail, a low, fern-dappled track that follows the outer edges of the boulder-filled forest.

Gradually the path tapers to the right, gaining nearly 100 feet in elevation during the first 15 minutes as it ascends into a small hamlet of hemlocks, where we spotted a wood thrush one August afternoon. When you arrive at a major fork, keep right (if you mistakenly take the left option you'll quickly come to a footbridge), jumping sharply right again in 100 yards. You've now exchanged yellow blazes for red and will enjoy an exaggerated series of zigzagging between the trees and rocks, bypassing three right options before branching off to the left.

Now the hiking becomes serious, and a good deal more fun, as the track snakes left around cyclopean boulders, creeps upward by a jagged ridge, and levels off among a mountainous, rocky setting. Pocket bogs are intersprinkled with stony substrate as the terrain rises and falls in quick succession. Post 31 indicates the next major junction, where you'll go right. Remain on this blue-blazed segment till you see post 30 (about 100 yards), which is a left-hand indicator for the climb up Blue Mountain. The chunky surface now underfoot is a nuisance but well worth enduring for the raw beauty of the surroundings as you maneuver past jumbo rocks and fat fingers of granite, with the climax being an unobstructed view over the Hudson from a broad, bald shelf. The mountain's pinnacle, at a deceptively modest 680 feet, is just a few yards farther up, near a stone CCC shelter. On our last foray here, the roofless structure was filled with myriad pieces of litter.

Return to the main trail and swing left, moving in a southbound direction. Bear right at the next fork, where the sight of open marshland lined with phragmites and other reeds signals your proximity to Montrose Station Road and a utility line that bisect the park. Parallel the marsh for 20 yards, then head left just prior to post 26 and cross this gravel road. The blue-blazed trail resumes on the other side of the street, trending slowly upward to a tree-covered ridge and, ultimately, Mount Spitzenberg. By the way, if you hear gunshots while walking here, don't bother to run for cover. The park operates a shooting range nearby.

Post 21, by a superannuated oak tree, marks the way to the left for the green- and orange-blazed spur to Spitzenberg's peak. Though even and wide at first, and overlapped by a number of animal traces, this leg gradually erodes into a scree-filled climb that peters out near the summit, leaving a final scramble up stone steps and washed-out rubble to the top. Another roofless shelter stands like a plaqueless monument atop this apex, with cedars, dogwoods, and flowering bottlebrush among the floral highlights. Ignore the graffiti and broken glass on the rocks underfoot and feast your eyes instead on the expansive panorama of the Hudson River looming large below and, far to the left, cars zooming over the Tappan Zee Bridge.

Backtrack to post 21 and point your dogs to the left. After walking downhill for 100 yards, bear right at post 20. Almost immediately, perhaps in 50 feet, you'll turn right again in a prolongation of the downward drift. In ten minutes, you'll recross Montrose Station Road as well as the marsh (the Hudson River is partly visible to the left), while adhering to the blue-blazed track. Within five or six minutes a glistening, gleaming pond will come into view; stay to the left (blue blazes still) for easy access to its south and southwest shores.

Cutting clockwise around the pond, you'll see many boulders ringing its perimeter, including one colossus that has been fractured by time and weather. The blue trail pulls away from the water by its northwest corner (the black-blazed trail to the right completes the pond circuit), leading downhill and back to the parking area.

## ▶ NEARBY ACTIVITIES

If you want to get closer to the Hudson River, George's Island is an attractive peninsula in Montrose, just a few miles south, and ideal for a shady riverfront picnic. For information, call (914) 737-7530.

# BUTLER OUTER LOOP TRAIL

## KEY AT-A-GLANCE INFORMATION

**LENGTH:** 3.5 miles

**CONFIGURATION:** Loop

**DIFFICULTY:** Easy

**SCENERY:** Lush, deciduous forest with a few stands of conifers, swamps, streams, rock outcroppings, and a few steep hills

**EXPOSURE:** Shady

**TRAFFIC:** Very light

**TRAIL SURFACE:** Dirt, rocks, and roots

**HIKING TIME:** 1.75 hours

**SEASON:** Year-round, dawn–dusk

**ACCESS:** No fee, no pets, no bicycles

**MAPS:** USGS Mount Kisco

**FACILITIES:** Undeveloped, but the Westmoreland Sanctuary across the street has rest rooms and water

**SPECIAL COMMENTS:** Bring binoculars and climb up to the bleachers of the Robert J. Hammershlag Memorial Hawk Watch to observe raptors during their fall migration, mid-August–mid-November.

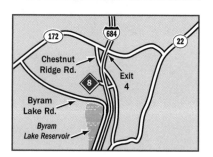

## ▶ IN BRIEF

*Boulders and bog crossings, hilltops and hemlocks,*
*Beech trees and pine groves, rock-hopping ravine*
*  romps,*
*Granite-strewn gorges and hawks flapping wings;*
*These are a few of our favorite things . . .*

## ▶ DESCRIPTION

On lacing up your boots and heading into the Butler Sanctuary, a Nature Conservancy preserve, you will hardly be traveling to Timbuktu. It may seem that way, though, for while it is a scant half mile from the Westmoreland Sanctuary, the bite-sized Butler sees very few visitors—none at all on some of the days we've trekked through. Sure, at a mere 363 acres, it can feel hemmed in by suburbia on three sides and I-684 on its fourth. But once you set off into the woods, into its deep ravines and thriving marshlands, you'll hardly be aware of the outside world.

The roar of traffic racing along nearby I-684 is, unfortunately, omnipresent as soon as you step out of your vehicle. Don't despair, though: Once over the initial ridge, you can lose the earplugs, as the sounds of "civilization" recede, eclipsed by the rustle of breezes among the birches and oaks and the squealing cries of hawks and kestrels soaring high overhead.

## ▶ DIRECTIONS

*By car:* Take the Hutchinson River Parkway north to White Plains, then I-684 north to Exit 4. Drive west on SR 172 for 0.3 miles. Turn left onto Chestnut Ridge Road and proceed for 1.2 miles, then hang a right across the bridge and park straight ahead.

*By public transportation:* Metro North's Harlem Line stops at Mount Kisco Station. It is less than 3 miles by taxi to the sanctuary.

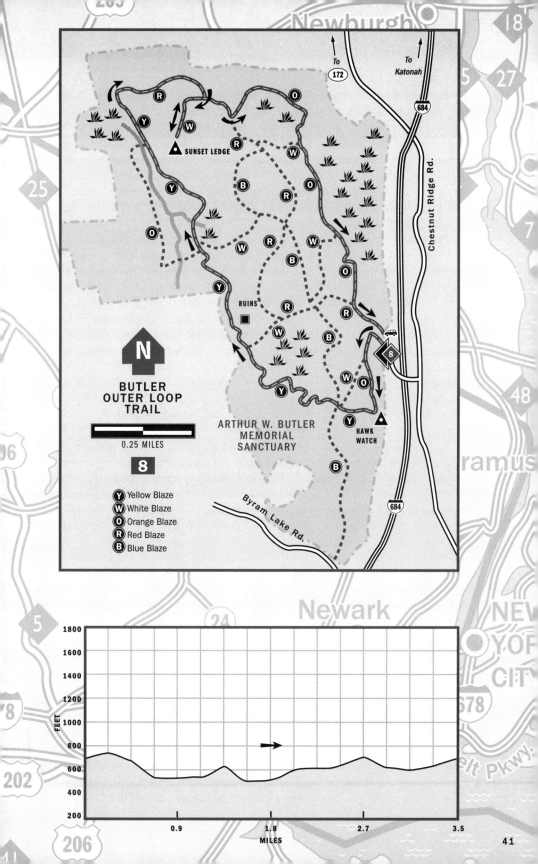

**BUTLER OUTER LOOP TRAIL**

0.25 MILES

**8**

Y Yellow Blaze
W White Blaze
O Orange Blaze
R Red Blaze
B Blue Blaze

SUNSET LEDGE

RUINS

ARTHUR W. BUTLER MEMORIAL SANCTUARY

HAWK WATCH

Byram Lake Rd.

Chestnut Ridge Rd.

To 172

To Katonah

684

684

To observe those raptors in flight during the autumn migration, a row of bleacher seats faces the open sky to the east. You can reach that and begin this hike by turning left, or south, at the dark-brown fence by the parking area and marching directly uphill along the orange-blazed trail. Even if you fail to see a raptor (the migratory period runs from mid-August through mid-November), you should be able to spot the weathervane-topped steeple of the nature center at the Westmoreland Sanctuary across the highway. The trail, changing from orange to yellow blazes, veers inland here (to the right), passing among cat briar, sugar maples, oaks, beech trees, hemlocks, and a handful of pines.

The yellow-blazed trail begins to undulate, shifting first downhill past a white-blazed route to the right, succeeded shortly by an intersection with a blue-blazed path. Remain with the yellow blazes as the trace then rises through a gap in an old stone wall, before descending steeply. This is an ankle-twisting stretch, where the trail narrows and involves a couple of rocky switchbacks, so be careful of your footing. A few well-placed stepping-stones by the fern-dappled marsh at the bottom are helpful in crossing the stream. Moving upward again, the track tops out by a series of granite boulders, offering a fine view over the swamp. With the hemlocks growing thicker here and animal trails adding to the confusion, you may have to be part bloodhound to sniff out the blazes. In a preserve this size, though, there is little chance of getting seriously lost.

As the trail briefly lingers on this higher ground, it swings slightly to the left and works along the saddle between two ridges, before descending 25 feet or so into a small gully. Atop the next rise, where the ground is covered in sedge grass and granite and maples dominate, are a couple of old rock foundations, relics from the 1800s when this area was open farmland. Staying with the sparsely placed yellow blazes, edge gently to the left of the ruins, keeping to the left, or west, of the rocky knob. The terrain tapers downward from here, becoming rather steep before leveling off at an overgrown swamp. If you are feeling bogged down, watch for a white-blazed turnoff to the right that can be used as an early bailout back to the parking lot.

The yellow-blazed track wends onward between two rock walls and a marsh made all the greener by the presence of skunk cabbage and ferns. As you start to grind uphill again, keep a sharp eye out once more for yellow markings, though if you have a decent sense of direction, moseying off the path won't pose any risks. The undulating continues, lilting by an orange-blazed spur to the left and a series of stones that are laid out like a narrow stretch of sidewalk to help ford a particularly moist patch of marshland. With a rugged, rocky cliff rising up 100 feet to the right, a talus slope at its base, and the low ground littered with boulders, this is the heart of the ravine. If the mosquitoes are not swarming too thickly, you might recline on one of the many lichen-crusted rocks and soak up the wild, rough-hewn atmosphere.

This trail terminates at the far corner of the sanctuary, next to a softly purling stream, its muddy banks festooned with oversized ferns. Roll right there onto the red-blazed path and begin the steady climb uphill. Don't let the effort distract you, though, from the surroundings; the last time we did this hike, we spotted a herd of seven deer snorting lustily through the oaks just below the ridge. The elevation gain over the course of 200 yards is perhaps 150 feet, though it may feel like more. Shortly after the crest is a side trail to the right, blazed white, that leads to Sunset Ledge, about a quarter mile away. The westward view from there is expansive, covering miles of hills, open sky, and a fair amount of freshly cleared land.

Back on the red-blazed route, the walking remains relatively level and easy all the way to a left-hand turn onto the path marked with orange blazes. Long pants are a good buffer against the swarms of mosquitoes that thrive in Butler, and such garb is almost essential to get through the thicket of briar that encroaches a lengthy part of this next stretch. Incidentally, that briar and blueberry bushes make this a popular area for foraging deer. As the trail descends, it parallels an old stone wall and a reed-rimmed swamp before coming to a vast network of rock walls that were once used for holding livestock.

Moving away from the swamp, you should see a white-blazed spur to the right, which runs back to the red-blazed track. Follow the orange blazes and in a fairly straightforward quarter mile a larger swamp appears left of you, with tulip trees thriving up the rocky slope to the right. The trail here threads over and around sundry stones and trees, requiring sharp eyes to find the elusive blazes. Drifting away from the marsh, the Swamp Trail meets a few white pines and straggly cedars before rejoining, at the top of a small hill, the red-blazed path. You will notice as you go left that the roar of the highway has reasserted itself. The hike is nearly over, with the parking lot only a couple of minutes ahead, just past the trail register kiosk.

## ▶ NEARBY ACTIVITIES

History buffs should enjoy the John Jay Homestead State Historic Site, which is the farmhouse—maintained with period-furnishings—where the first U.S. chief justice retired; it's on SR 22 in Katonah. For information, call (914) 232-5651.

# CALEB SMITH FULL CIRCUIT

## KEY AT-A-GLANCE INFORMATION

**LENGTH:** 3.3 miles

**CONFIGURATION:** Double loop

**DIFFICULTY:** Easy

**SCENERY:** Surprisingly secluded park contains fields, streams, and ponds, wetlands and upland forests, and gorgeous colonial-style nature museum

**EXPOSURE:** Mostly shady

**TRAFFIC:** Light to moderate and rather solitary on green loop

**TRAIL SURFACE:** Sandy with root network

**HIKING TIME:** 1.5 hours

**SEASON:** Year-round, 8 a.m.–sunset

**ACCESS:** $6 parking fee, no dogs, no bicycles

**MAPS:** At park office and posted at entrance kiosk

**FACILITIES:** Rest rooms, water, and public phone at park office

**SPECIAL COMMENTS:** The preserve is a popular winter venue for cross-country skiers and a great spot for fly-fishermen. Check out the newsletter for a calendar of nature programs.

## ▶ IN BRIEF

You don't have to be a big fan of the Colonial-era to enjoy Caleb Smith State Park—but it doesn't hurt. Wander beyond its historic house and first-rate nature center, though, and you'll be on your own—on a really fun hike, that is, through successional fields, pine barrens, swampy hollows freckled with wild flowers and skunk cabbage, with birds all around. Caleb Smith is a tranquil oasis in the heart of suburbia, with trails suitable for even the littlest Bigfoot in your tribe.

## ▶ DESCRIPTION

To stop by Caleb Smith State Park Preserve is to ingest a good-sized bite of Long Island history. The colonial house that now serves as a nature museum, with a rat snake in an aquarium and various child-friendly exhibits, was built by Daniel Smith in 1752. Smith's grandfather, Richard "Bull" Smythe, was a founding father of neighboring Smithtown, while his son, Caleb, became a thorn in the side of the British troops when they occupied Long Island during the Revolutionary War. Because Caleb, a graduate of Yale who was elected to the state assembly and also became a judge of common pleas, refused to take an oath of loyalty to King George, "he was shot at, roused

## ▶ DIRECTIONS

*By car:* Follow the Long Island Expressway (I-495) east to Exit 53. Take the Sunken Meadow State Parkway north to the junction with the Jericho Turnpike (SR 25). Continue east on SR 25 for 3.1 miles and turn left into the preserve. Make another quick left into the parking lot.

*By public transportation:* The Port Jefferson Branch of the Long Island Railroad goes to Smithtown Station. From there, a cab or bus ride on the S58 to the preserve only lasts about 1 mile.

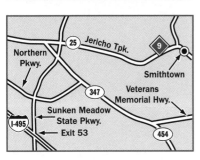

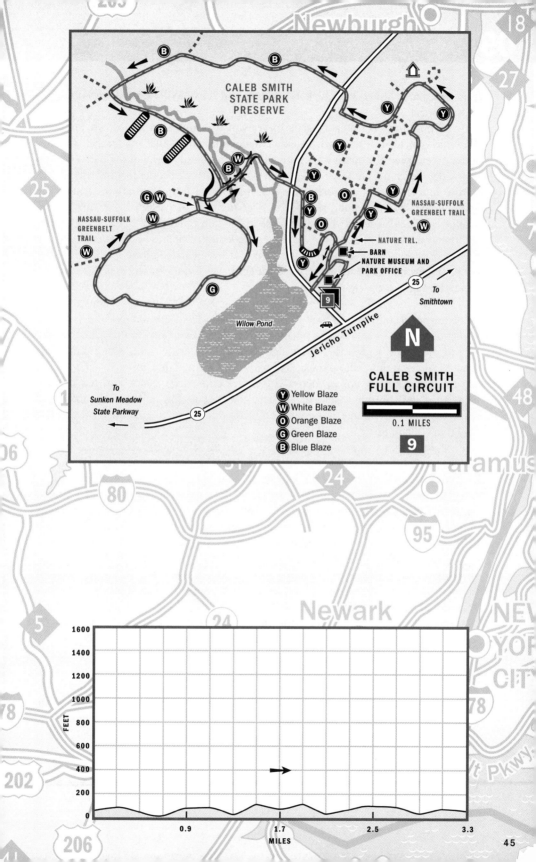

CALEB SMITH
STATE PARK
PRESERVE

NASSAU-SUFFOLK
GREENBELT
TRAIL

NASSAU-SUFFOLK
GREENBELT TRAIL

NATURE TRL.

BARN
NATURE MUSEUM AND
PARK OFFICE

25

To
Smithtown

Wilow Pond

Jericho Turnpike

To
Sunken Meadow
State Parkway

25

N

CALEB SMITH
FULL CIRCUIT

0.1 MILES

9

Y Yellow Blaze
W White Blaze
O Orange Blaze
G Green Blaze
B Blue Blaze

from bed, [and] lashed with hickory gads up and down Willow Pond," according to park records.

It shouldn't take hickory gads to get you to saunter up and down the pond these days, or to hike the park's shady circuit of trails, for that matter. Fair weather and a decent pair of walking shoes are all that is required. Many of the paths overlap firebreaks, and most are fairly wide, allowing two or three people to stroll abreast. To start a double loop of approximately 3.3 miles, head from the parking area to the Smith home, passing along the paved road in front of it. Once past this green, clapboard-sided structure, obey the black arrow that points to the left. Forget about the orange diamond blazes—those are for cross-country skiing—and focus instead on staying with the yellow discs inset with black arrows. Circle around to the left of the red barn, beyond the main house, and bear left at the fork (a half-mile cinder-surfaced nature trail lies to the right).

For the next couple of minutes, the level, grassy track is largely sun-struck, an exception to an otherwise shady hike. It slips by a few outbuildings and a pair of burlap-covered wigwams (Canada geese often nest in the vicinity in the spring) before drifting to the right, past the barns. Keep to the right at the fork, where the yellow discs break away from the orange diamonds, and swing left a moment later on the dirt forest road. Now among dense clusters of chokeberry, oaks, and red maples, many aged and sporting wrinkled, splintery goiters, you may notice a few birdhouses spaced out among the trees. Those are for wood ducks and owls, though presumably they don't cohabitate.

Shortly after the forest road crosses over the cinder-surfaced nature trail, it divides, with yellow blazes continuing to the right toward a pocket meadow with a lone conifer at its center. Hug the far right of that open space, and in several strides you will enter a corridor of cedars, at which point you should turn left. (Straight ahead is a white-blazed section of the Suffolk Greenbelt Trail.) The meadow is now on your left, faintly visible through the hedgerow of cedars and a smattering of black birch. Once by the field, hang a right at the slanted four-way crossing, onto the wood chip-surfaced turf. The track passes a couple of white pines as it tapers downhill, then abruptly loops to the right, regaining lost ground. Launch left at a little circle or roundabout, where a branch-and-leaf lean-to has been constructed off the trail; now back on an unpaved service road, strut straight with the yellow discs as the cross-country ski blazes skip off to the right. Hew to the right in another handful of paces, leaving the park road, as the dirt trail remains flat and wide.

Blue discs appear at the next intersection, and you continue straight with those, as the yellow ones split to the left. Steer right on this peaceful path just before it meets a patch of pavement, no more than 200 yards from the previous junction. The track cuts to the left, crosses the paved park road, and proceeds by cedars and white pines, ever so gradually losing elevation. This is one of the more appealing parts of the park, where a lowland swamp, decorated with ferns and skunk cabbage, colors the left side of the trail, and the ground, shaded by a mature mix of trees, rises to your right. Remain with the sandy blue-blazed route as it begins to climb and passes a couple of maverick, unmarked spurs, as well as a pair of disused stairs leading off to the right. On hearing a rustling among the oak leaves covering the ground here, you may conclude that an industrious squirrel is intently gathering acorns. Take a closer look: More likely what your ears have caught is the sound of a rufous-sided towhee scavenging for a smaller scale of seed.

In a little while, the Blue Trail (BT) breaks to the left, hopping over a serpentine swamp stream via a little bridge. You will take that path later, heaving right for now with the green and white blazes—the latter, incidentally, being a continuation of the Suffolk Greenbelt Trail (SGT). Ascend the erosion-control steps and scoot left at the triangular T, still adhering to the green-and-white markings. When the two colors diverge in 30 seconds of ambling, go with the green blazes to the left. You are now in an upland forest populated by cedars, many types of oaks, and a fair number of white pines—not to mention dense clusters of cat briar. As you move along, the rather sizable Willow Pond comes into view down to the left. The green circuit glides right at the slight Y, rejoining the SGT shortly at a T. Cruise right, and in five minutes pull to the left, bounding by spot where this miniloop diverged awhile earlier. Traipse down the steps to return to the BT.

Once more following the blue blazes, walk over the small bridge and, a few seconds later, another such span. The level track, flanked by ferns, garlic mustard, and skunk cabbage, soon swings to the right, where a third bridge appears. Turn right just after crossing the park road, as yellow discs now unite with blue, and stick with yellow as it veers off to the right in 100 yards. March right at the T, and a few additional paces should put you back by the wigwams and the open field. The Caleb Smith house and trailhead lie to the right, a couple of minutes away.

### ▶ NEARBY ACTIVITIES

If you cannot bear being on Long Island without catching a glimpse of the coast, Heckscher State Park is the place to be. Never mind the 1 million annual visitors, the Great South Bay is roomy enough for a cool dip, and there is a swimming pool as well. Camp or picnic, hike or bike; visit www.nysparks.state.ny.us/parks or call (631) 581-2100 to find out more.

# CAUMSETT NECK LOOP

## KEY AT-A-GLANCE INFORMATION

**LENGTH:** 7 miles

**CONFIGURATION:** Loop

**DIFFICULTY:** Moderate

**SCENERY:** Peaceful peninsula harbors woodlands and grasslands, salt marsh and rocky shoreline, freshwater pond, and old dairy farm

**EXPOSURE:** Very open in meadows and beach areas, some shady trails

**TRAFFIC:** Light to moderate, but sunny days attract many outdoors fans

**TRAIL SURFACE:** Grass, sand, and dirt

**HIKING TIME:** 3.5 hours

**SEASON:** Year-round, 8 a.m.–sunset

**ACCESS:** $6 parking fee May–October and on winter weekends and holidays

**MAPS:** At entrance booth; USGS Lloyd Harbor

**FACILITIES:** Rest rooms, telephone, and water at dairy farm complex

**SPECIAL COMMENTS:** The beautiful setting and the gentle terrain encourage people with baby strollers to take advantage of this expansive domain, which also accommodates horseback riders, bicyclists, and joggers.

## IN BRIEF

It's all downhill once you get past Caumsett State Park's most obvious landmarks, a dairy farm and stone manor house. Downhill *literally*, as the extensive trail system meanders among open fields and mature stands of hardwoods, reaching a physical low point by a series of bluffs abutting Long Island Sound. Abundant wildlife—including gray foxes—and a wealth of birds endow every step in this beautiful park with the possibility of surprise or discovery. Springtime, when blossoms color the trees and wildflowers carpet the ground, is our favorite time to visit.

## DESCRIPTION

Have you ever wondered what it would be like to have a few million dollars burning a hole in your pocket? To be as rich as Croesus, sitting on top of a golden heap? Well, stop wondering and get yourself over to Caumsett State Park. A trip to this peninsula—1,500 acres of meadows, marshes, forests, and farmland that extend dramatically into Long Island Sound—won't magically make you a millionaire, but it may help to visualize what a boatload of money can buy. When Marshall Field III, grandson of the founder of

## DIRECTIONS

*By car:* Follow the Long Island Expressway (I-495) east to Exit 49N. Take SR 110 north to Huntington and turn left (west) on SR 25A (Main Street). Very soon, make a right on West Neck Road, which becomes Lloyd Harbor Road. Continue straight into the park to the parking lot on the right.

*By public transportation:* Take the Long Island Railroad (Port Jefferson Branch) to Huntington. There are no buses to the park, so lighten your wallet with a taxi ride of about 8 miles.

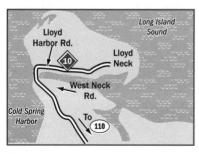

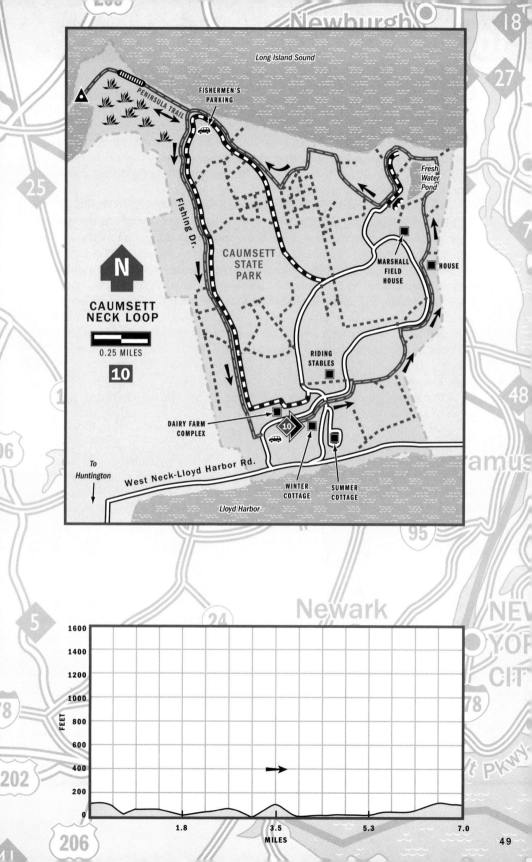

Long Island Sound

PENINSULA TRAIL

FISHERMEN'S
PARKING

Fresh
Water
Pond

Fishing Dr.

CAUMSETT
STATE
PARK

MARSHALL
FIELD
HOUSE

HOUSE

**N**

CAUMSETT
NECK LOOP

0.25 MILES

**10**

RIDING
STABLES

DAIRY FARM
COMPLEX

**10**

WINTER
COTTAGE

SUMMER
COTTAGE

To
Huntington

West Neck-Lloyd Harbor Rd.

Lloyd Harbor

1600
1400
1200
1000
800
600
400
200
0

FEET

1.8          3.5          5.3          7.0
MILES

Chicago's renowned department store, bought this spit of soil in 1921, he didn't have hiking in mind. With a fortune in his billfold and the collaboration of architect John Russell Pope, he created a self-sufficient community centered around a dairy farm, complete with 80 head of award-winning cattle, and a magnificent manor house modeled on those of Tudor England. True to the British tradition, visitors to the estate could indulge in hunting, skeet-shooting, fishing, polo, boating, tennis (both outdoors and in), and, of course, riding.

It is still possible to ride horses at Caumsett, which was acquired by the Empire State in 1961, but the egalitarian pursuit of hiking allows one to see the grounds under more serene circumstances. Caumsett, incidentally, was given its name by Field in honor of the Matinecock Indians who used to live here, and the word means "place by sharp rocks." From the parking area and entrance booth, proceed along the maple-flanked paved road in an east direction, keeping the dairy farm complex to your left. The Winter Cottage, a stone construction to the right that is a "cottage" only by the standards of a Vanderbilt or Field, appears just prior to a four-way intersection. Walk straight through the junction, passing the sprawling brick riding stables on your left. Remain with the paved road as it bends to the left, all the while showcasing the surrounding landscape, with mature plantings running the gamut from white pines, yews, and cedars to dogwood, forsythia, and honeysuckle.

The flora grows considerably wilder when you turn off the drive onto the unpaved lane to the right, opposite the horse corral. This easy, pebble-strewn track descends slightly for 100 yards or so before tapering to the left, with garlic mustard, chokeberry, briar, and black birch springing up along the grassy margins. After skipping the spur to the right that leads to an open field, the road appears to drift in the same direction, toward a low animal pen in that lush sward. Take the less-trammeled fork to the left here that maintains the straight direction, with the scrubby morass on either side of you growing ever thicker. Swing left again at the T by a vine-draped chain-link fence. The abundance of scrub growth provides great ground cover for birds, and to judge by the melodious jabbering that reaches one's ears, a number of sundry species take advantage of it.

After the sudden surge uphill hang a right, back on the main road. Remain with this as it swoops to the left and then straightens out. When you see a cinder drive, steer right on it. This seems at first to lead to a private dwelling, but as the driveway edges toward the house, on the right, the trail branches off to the left. (Pay no attention on making that turn to the trace that diverges to the right.) We have seen a gray fox treading stealthily among the wild violets and laurel here, as well as a great horned owl hooting above the magnolia trees (which blossom beautifully in early spring). On bearing left at the Y, this untamed setting segues to an open expanse of lawn, punctuated periodically with a few mature maples. As you approach the freshwater fishing pond, hew to its right side, following the unpaved lane.

Moseying counterclockwise around the pond, look for birds among the cedars, black birches, maples, and briar that ring its shore. At its north end, where auburn-colored phragmites rise above the water, the picturesque panorama encompasses not only the pond but also Long Island Sound and the rocky shoreline below the trail.

Stay with the sandy track as it parallels the Sound, yielding meanwhile a view to the left of the stately stone manor house high atop the grassy hill. In a couple of minutes, the path comes to a low bluff over the shore, with large-bodied oaks adding the allure of shade to an enticing area in which to laze or picnic. Cormorants often roost on the rocks that jut up above the water, and you may observe seagulls dropping shellfish on the stones in an attempt to open them.

From this enchanting spot, the trail veers sharply left and inland along a pebble- and sand-surfaced lane, where daffodils, vinka, and wild forsythia flourish in spring. Stick with this wide track as it arcs to the right and passes a small dam at the west end of the pond. Stride right two minutes later onto the dirt-and-grass path and persevere all the way back to the bluffs. The grass-topped overlook here is a mere 15 feet above the beach, with the rocks farther out crusted with seaweed. Stroll left along the bluff, cutting away from the water view in 150 yards, moving inland toward the knoll's grassy recess. The pebbly path resumes once you're by the large maple, winding southward uphill. On entering this small maze of trails, keep hard to the right at the first fork, and right again at the top of the slope. In about a minute this grassy lane merges with a sandy one, beside a superannuated dogwood tree. Amble to the right and continue along this route for roughly half a mile, all the way to the Fishermen's Parking Lot. Don't put away your birding specs, as we've spied a green-breasted warbler, blue jays, catbirds, a wood thrush, nuthatch, red-winged blackbirds, and even the elusive pileated woodpecker in this portion of the park.

Having reached the parking lot, march dead ahead to the hard sandy track that marks the start of the Peninsula Trail, a half-hour side trip. Here, fully exposed to the sun, you can enjoy great views of the Sound to the right (with a few intriguing erratics decorating the shore like the odd flotsam of a shipwreck), while to the left is a salt marsh where great and snowy egrets frequently fish. In a few paces, the firm surface of the path evolves to soft sand, and then boardwalk, succeeded by soft sand again, with any number of wildflowers and—surprisingly—prickly pear cacti springing up among the surrounding bayberry, cedar, and chokeberry. Although you may choose to wander along the shore to the end of the cove, the spur ends at the rotting wooden platform—the remains of docks used by Marshall Field III to land Coursande, his steam-powered yacht.

On returning to the Fishermen's Parking Lot, turn right on the dirt road. Remain with this route, which is known as Fishing Drive, for the next 2 miles, all the way back to the dairy farm. When the road has drawn within 200 yards of the farm and breaks to the left toward it, continue straight on the slightly rutted track, with open fields on either side of you. The trailhead parking lies a couple of minutes ahead.

## ▶ NEARBY ACTIVITIES

A guided tour through Theodore Roosevelt's home in Oyster Bay provides a fascinating portrait of how one of our country's great presidents lived. Sagamore Hill is a typical dark Victorian mansion, enlivened by T. R.'s personal belongings and collections. Call (516) 922-4447 for details.

# CHEESEQUAKE NATURAL AREA TRAIL

## KEY AT-A-GLANCE INFORMATION

**LENGTH:** 5.5 miles

**CONFIGURATION:** Loop

**DIFFICULTY:** Moderate

**SCENERY:** Sandy pine barrens, humid freshwater swamps connected by boardwalks, and lush hardwood forests boasting some of area's tallest trees

**EXPOSURE:** With the exception of a few marshland spots, trails are very shady

**TRAFFIC:** It can get rather hectic May–September, especially on weekends

**TRAIL SURFACE:** Dirt and roots alternate with sand and pebbles

**HIKING TIME:** 2.75 hours

**SEASON:** Year-round, 8 a.m.–dusk

**ACCESS:** Memorial Day–Labor Day, $5 weekdays, $10 weekends; free Tuesdays and rest of year; $50 parks pass gives access to all New Jersey state parks for one calendar year

**MAPS:** At park office and interpretive center; USGS South Amboy

**FACILITIES:** Rest rooms, water, and telephone at park office; nature interpretive center, campground, picnic areas, playground

**SPECIAL COMMENTS:** The attractive interpretive center is accessible by foot and offers educational exhibits as well as activities. Call (732) 566-3208 for information.

### IN BRIEF

Do you enjoy traipsing through cedar swamps and backwoods bayous while bounding over boardwalks? Cheesequake is well endowed in each of those categories, with plenty of raw, natural beauty left over to appeal to other tastes. The birding is great by its lake and marshlands. Then there are several notable forests, populated by stands of monumental oaks, tulip trees, and white pines. And the wide, swiftly flowing Cheesequake Creek is so alluring you may be tempted to bring a canoe.

### DESCRIPTION

For most people, Cheesequake State Park is little more than a green spot on the roadmap, with the Garden State Parkway cutting through it like a bull charging through a red-ribbon fence. On the way to or from the Big Apple, few motorists give the slightest thought to stopping. That's their loss, because this 1,274-acre park is extravagantly beautiful, partly because it straddles a transitional zone

### DIRECTIONS

*By car:* Follow I-95 south across the George Washington Bridge into New Jersey, switching to the Garden State Parkway south at Exit 11. Leave the parkway at Exit 120. Make a right on Laurence Harbor Parkway followed by another right on Cliffwood Avenue. At the T intersection, turn right on Gordon Road to the park entrance. The park office is on the right. For the trailhead parking, proceed straight to the next lot on the left.

*By public transportation:* From Penn Station, take the New Jersey Transit North Jersey Coast Line train to Aberdeen/Matawan Station. From there, an approximate 3-mile taxi ride will bring you to the park.

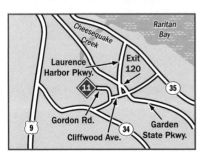

CHEESEQUAKE
NATURAL
AREA TRAIL

0.25 MILES

**11**

Y Yellow Blaze
G Green Blaze
R Red Blaze
B Blue Blaze

between two major ecosystems. Miles of trails (and a hefty amount of boardwalks) meander among pine barrens, a cedar swamp, marshlands, and open fields. In fact, there is so much eye candy in this diverse terrain that at the end of a day of hiking, many trekkers don't want to leave—so they set up a tent and camp.

Cheesequake's name, incidentally, is not a phonetic misspelling of some heavy sort of dairy-based dessert. Back in June 1940, when the preserve was first opened to the public, park officials plucked the word from the language of the Lenape Indians, who hunted and fished these grounds into the 1700s before being displaced by white settlers. The Lenapes were but the last in a long line of Indian tribes who found the Cheesequake (pronounced CHESS-quick) area inviting, with the earliest traces of occupation dating back 5,000 years.

The trailhead and map kiosk are to the far left of the parking area. Of the many overlapping and intersecting circuits within the park, the following 5.5-mile trek provides a broad overview of Cheesequake's natural attractions and varied habitats. Head out on the wide path and turn right at the fork, in 150 feet, onto the Yellow Trail (YT), where blueberry bushes and sassafras compose the understory and maples, mountain laurel, and various oaks provide shade. Bear left in a few paces at the slanted T, as the moss-sided track hugs a ridgeline that tapers toward Hooks Creek Lake. Enjoy the vantage point high over the water, then descend the wooden staircase. The YT continues to the left, near the bottom of the steps, but first hover a moment by the edge of the lake, which is attractively framed by a lone willow, cat-tails, and other reeds.

If you can resist the urge to cast out a line—the trout fishing is great in the spring, while perch and bass are the trophies in summer—return to the path and keep moving. A few pitch pines pop up by the side of a salt marsh, where you may spot cormorants, snowy egrets, and other shore birds partly concealed behind salt hay and cord grass. After pulling away from there, the path arcs to the right and hits a boardwalk, bringing you to a freshwater flood plain (another fine place for birding). Half a minute later, take the fork to the right to the interpretive center. In walking under the wooden archway, crossing a bridge, and steering toward the modern, wood-sided pavilion, you have exchanged yellow blazes for red and green ones. Pick up the Blue Trail (BT) to the right of the building, and stay with it along the spine of a sheep laurel–cloaked ridge. Those small platforms set within the cover of trees, by the way, are known as quail roosts, which are used, curiously, by bobwhites.

On descending back toward the marsh, the path meets a boardwalk, with a stream running by its side. Atop the stairs that follow, transfer to the right at the T, sticking with the BT as it breaks off from the red and green blazes. From this high-land stretch of turf, you gain a fine vista of the expansive marsh below. Enjoy it—you'll be brushing against marsh grass again momentarily. First, though, it is down another set of stairs, over a short bridge (with a murky, slow-moving stream barely eddying beneath), up some steps, succeeded by a descent. With the marsh now on either side of you, the track morphs into a 6-foot wide boardwalk, 2.5 feet off the ground. The highway is visible (but barely audible) far off in the distance, although you may find it more rewarding to scan the horizon—and underbrush—for birds. On our last foray here, we spotted seven great egrets on one side of the long walkway and a red-winged blackbird on the other.

Atop the next staircase the BT jogs right, overlooking the marsh, then left, adhering to the contours of a ridge. Ignore the traces as the path dips again toward the marshland, sticking with the blue discs that are posted among bayberry, holly, maples, black birches, and pitch pines, until they deliver you to an unpaved road. Slip under the wooden arch and hang a left, following the road for about six minutes, then veering right on the Green Trail (GT). (If you would like to detour to Perrine Pond, turn right on the unblazed service road that appears a couple of minutes prior to this.)

The path still clings to a ridge when it departs the gravel road, bobbing and weaving through an attractive setting of laurels, serviceberry, and pink flowering azaleas. In hilly terrain such as this, of course, it is only a matter of time before high ground becomes low, and sure enough, the trail soon drops down to a swamp speckled green with ferns and skunk cabbage. A boardwalk here stretches for a whopping 100 yards, ending at a wooden staircase. Tread up that, then down the steps that follow, onto the next boardwalk, surrounded suddenly, marvelously, by cedar trees. The walkway, which can be treacherously slick, snakes through this cedar swamp, where the water has been dyed orange by tree tannins leaching into the underlying soil. The planks end briefly—keep to the right at the fork—only to resume for a short spell longer. Then it is briskly uphill, back among laurels and oaks.

On hitting the park road, you have three choices: proceed directly across on the GT, swing right for Steamboat Landing, or left for an early bailout. The detour to Steamboat Landing is highly scenic and only requires about a half hour for the round-trip. As the conifers growing on the embankment to the left and right of the dirt road give way to hardwood trees, peer sharply to the left, about 70 yards in, for one of the park's largest white oaks. After coming abreast of a marsh, the lane forks: dogleg left around the barrier and lunge immediately right onto Dock Road. In three minutes, the unpaved lane dead-ends at a bend in Cheesequake Creek, by a confluence of streams, with the rotting pilings of an old steamboat landing 70 feet across the swiftly flowing water. There is a subtle, almost subliminal serenity to this delightful spot that makes it well worth visiting.

Back at the four-way intersection, venture right on the prolongation of the GT. As you shuffle along, check out the spectacular stand of white pines, concentrated primarily to the left. Too soon you leave that behind and ascend a slight slope that is well scarred with roots, followed by a wooden staircase—yet another example of the prodigious efforts at trail maintenance made by park staff and volunteers. The path dips again shortly and meanders over three bridges, then bends left at a faint fork. In time the path, which occasionally resembles a grooved toboggan run, approaches Museum Road, only to swerve right just before meeting it.

The ensuing segment of the hike showcases a few kettle-hole depressions to the right of you, and in the swamp to the left an impressive grove of tulip trees, many quite monumental in size. The GT soon arcs left toward the heart of that swamp and slips over 175 feet of boardwalk, jumping to the left at the end of the planks. With gigantic skunk cabbage leaves rising up from the mud and a thickly shrouded wetland to rival the swamps of Florida, you may not see many birds here; listen attentively while strolling over three additional boardwalks, though, and your ears might detect (along with the chirruping of frogs) the alien call of a red-bellied woodpecker or the hooting of a barred owl. After treading through a deeply rutted patch, look to the right for a giant beech tree, an icon among the many hardwoods in the area.

The group camping area is directly ahead when you pass under the wooden arch. Instead of entering it, go left on the dirt road, and in a couple of minutes scamper right under the next archway. The Red Trail joins Green here, as the path circumnavigates the backside of the campground, bending to the left as it approaches the second camping field. Ignore the spur to the right, which leads to the park office, bearing right instead a moment later on the gravel-surfaced Museum Road. Stay with that, and in two or three minutes you will be back at the parking area. Don't imagine, though, that you are finished with Cheesequake. Like many of the better hikes, this is one to experience in each of the four seasons.

### ▶ NEARBY ACTIVITIES

This park has a lot going for it throughout the year. In summer, it belongs to swimmers, boaters, campers, and picnickers; sledding and skiing are popular in winter. The variety of fall colors in the forests and marshes range from subtle to spectacular. And trout are stocked at Hooks Creek Lake in spring. For further details, contact the park at (732) 566-2161.

# CLAY PIT PONDS CONNECTOR

## ▶ IN BRIEF

It may be hard to believe, but many of Manhattan's buildings and sidewalks were once made from the clay drawn from the ground of this pocket-sized park. The nineteenth-century brick plant is long gone, replaced now by a fun series of lilting trails that loop by idyllic swamps and peaceful ponds, which serve as a backdrop for a colorful variety of birds and wildflowers.

## ▶ DESCRIPTION

Recent history notwithstanding, one of the most horrific events in New York's past occurred the evening of December 16, 1835, when a fire broke out in a downtown dry goods store. It was a bitingly cold night, and at a time when most structures were made of wood, gale force winds whipped the flames into an inferno, rapidly spreading the fire from block to block. With temperatures well below freezing, cisterns and wells were iced over, and what water the fire department could obtain quickly froze in their hoses. Only by dynamiting a broad break through the city was the blaze brought under control, after it

## ▶ DIRECTIONS

*By car:* Follow I-278 over the Verrazano Bridge where it becomes the Staten Island Expressway, and continue west for 6 miles to the junction with SR 440. Drive south on SR 440 for about 5 miles to Exit 3 (Bloomingdale Road). Turn left on Bloomingdale, followed by a right on Sharrotts Road, and a final right on Carlin Street. Proceed straight to the park entrance and parking lot.

*By public transportation:* From the Ferry Terminal, take the S74 bus to Sharrotts Road. Cross Arthur Kill Road and walk a quarter mile on Sharrotts Road, then turn left onto Carlin Street. The park lies straight ahead.

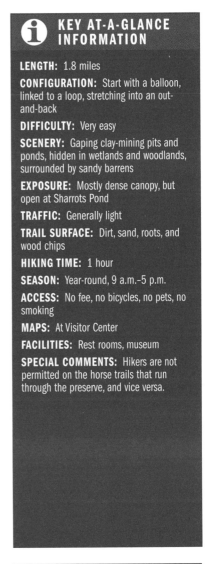

## ⓘ KEY AT-A-GLANCE INFORMATION

**LENGTH:** 1.8 miles

**CONFIGURATION:** Start with a balloon, linked to a loop, stretching into an out-and-back

**DIFFICULTY:** Very easy

**SCENERY:** Gaping clay-mining pits and ponds, hidden in wetlands and woodlands, surrounded by sandy barrens

**EXPOSURE:** Mostly dense canopy, but open at Sharrots Pond

**TRAFFIC:** Generally light

**TRAIL SURFACE:** Dirt, sand, roots, and wood chips

**HIKING TIME:** 1 hour

**SEASON:** Year-round, 9 a.m.–5 p.m.

**ACCESS:** No fee, no bicycles, no pets, no smoking

**MAPS:** At Visitor Center

**FACILITIES:** Rest rooms, museum

**SPECIAL COMMENTS:** Hikers are not permitted on the horse trails that run through the preserve, and vice versa.

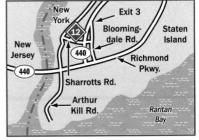

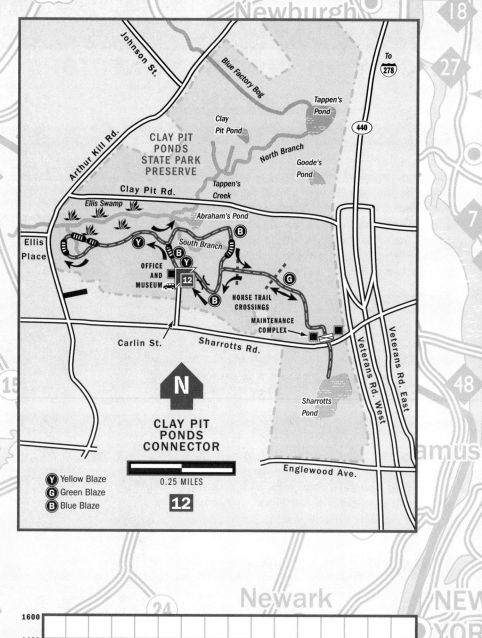

## CLAY PIT PONDS STATE PARK PRESERVE

**CLAY PIT PONDS CONNECTOR**

N

0.25 MILES

**Y** Yellow Blaze
**G** Green Blaze
**B** Blue Blaze

**12**

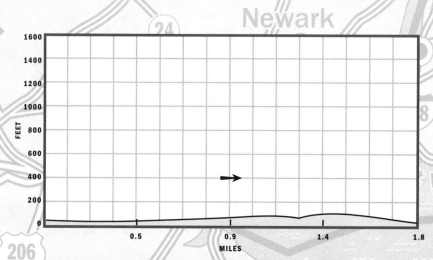

had raged for 15 hours and destroyed nearly 700 buildings, including the post office, Merchants' Exchange, and most of the financial district. In the aftermath of this disaster, the city restructured the fire department to reduce chaotic competition among volunteer outfits and implemented more stringent building codes to encourage the use of fire-resistant construction materials.

Enter German immigrant Balthasar Kreischer. Arriving at the Big Apple following the Great Fire (as it has come to be known), you might say Kreischer made his fortune from a wheelbarrow full of bricks. With wood out of favor, brick (along with iron and stone) became the material of choice for rebuilding the city, and Krei-scher's flame-resistant variety was considered to be among the best. What, you might ask, does all this have to do with Staten Island's Clay Pit Ponds State Park Preserve? Much of the clay for Kreischer's bricks was mined here, and by 1854, his gargantuan Staten Island brick factory stood on 700 acres of land. Near the end of the nineteenth century, over 300 people worked at that plant, churning out 3.5

Staten Island's Clay Pit Ponds State Park Preserve is an oasis of calm and beauty, where boardwalks lead through flourishing wetlands.

million bricks annually at its peak. Clay mining was largely finished by 1927, but it was not until 1976 that this 260-acre property was developed into a state preserve. You can still see vestiges of clay mining on this short, easy hike, which passes through a delightful mixture of habitats, ranging from wetlands and spring-fed streams to sandy barrens and open fields.

The trailhead is behind the nature center, a shingle- and clapboard-sided house with wisteria growing by its side. Pick up the yellow and blue blazes to the left of the picnic pavilion, on the bark-covered path. From initially overlooking a swamp, with a small stream beside you, the path soon descends through oaks, maples, sycamores, briar, birches, beech, and an occasional azalea, to a boardwalk, where skunk cabbage reigns. Shortly after that, the yellow and blue discs diverge; continue straight with yellow.

There is a fun lilt to the moss-sided track as it gently ascends and falls through this swamp. On strolling over another short boardwalk, bypass the spur to the right—that's where this miniloop comes to a close—and note the corrugated texture to the land around you, the lingering effects of clay mining. Any squealing of seagulls you may hear overhead is a reminder that the park, on the southwest side of the island, lies very close to the water. The ensuing boardwalk, shaped like an upside-down U, runs for 100 feet and passes beneath sweet gum trees, maples, and oaks. The dirt path alternates with a couple more segments of boardwalk, then rises to the right to reconnect this circuit with the outgoing route. A step or two prior to that is an appealing nook, to the left, where a bench is set under pin oaks, in front of a modest cascade.

Persevere along the yellow-blazed trail, swinging left at the close of the loop, and return to where the blue discs earlier branched off. Canter left there and cross the 20-foot-long span, beneath which creeps a slowly moving stream. The track bends abruptly to the right, paralleling that arroyo, with a bench and bird-viewing platform to the left, where Abraham's Pond is gradually silting up, becoming more of a marsh with every successive season. If you are lucky, you may observe a muskrat swimming among the cattails and yellow bullhead lilies. Keep straight at the trace to the left of a large, twin-trunked black birch, and stay to the right in 80 feet at another false junction. The scrub-filled bowl to the right is one more relic of when this locale was extensively mined for clay.

Three brief boardwalks follow, in the dips of the rolling trail, with a pocket meadow succeeding the last of those. Walk directly past the bench there by about 100 feet, stopping short of the tree cover opposite, and turn left on the green-blazed trail, an easy-to-miss spur to Sharrots Pond. Created late in 2002, this route is a work-in-progress, as evidenced by the porcelain toilet bowl abandoned beneath an oak tree just left of the shady, forested track. Farther on, the path glides through a pair of livestock barriers in crossing a horse trail, and repeats that same maneuver again in 100 yards. In rapid succession, it passes a luminescent field of ferns and a broken-up concrete foundation with a pair of old autos nearby, inexorably mulching back to their original elements, before meeting a barrier gate. Slip limbo-like under that and then swerve right with the meandering trail as it brushes by eastern cottonwoods, as well as some mounds of spent tires and cut-up logs. On continuing to bend right, you stride through another gate—usually open—and by a park maintenance building. On pavement now, roll to the right of the brown-sided house dead ahead, hop the pipe gate, and cross Sharrots Road.

A minute of walking on the gravel access lane delivers you to an open lawn-like field, with Sharrots Pond just beyond. Look for great lobelia around the banks of the water, as well as various types of bladderwort. If you are really lucky, you may also see an eastern mud turtle, which supposedly is found nowhere else on Staten Island. Herons, snowy egrets, and ringed neck ducks frequent this attractive pond, too. Backtrack from here to the pocket meadow where you jumped off the blue-blazed track, lunging left on it. In about 100 feet, the trail jogs right by a gate and descends a touch over erosion-control steps. With a sharp arc to the right, it emerges abruptly by a kiosk at the parking area.

## ▶ NEARBY ACTIVITIES

Time to let your body and spirit relax in the serenity of a Tibetan mountain temple. The Jacques Marchais Museum of Tibetan Art exhibits paintings and art objects from Nepal, Mongolia, and Tibet. It features a sculpture garden and a couple of ponds. For information, call (718) 987-3500.

# CONNETQUOT CONTOUR

## ▶ IN BRIEF

Critics carp that this is a long, arid hike without the payoff of vistas or dramatic scenery. They're missing the larger picture, one that starts with a nucleus of historic houses by a placid lake and loops through pretty pine barrens, enticingly lush fields, and swampy streams, achieving a rollicking climax by an active fish hatchery. Much of the time you'll be all on your own, with only birds, butterflies, and white-tailed deer for company.

## ▶ DESCRIPTION

Connetquot River State Park Preserve is one of the largest parcels of public land on Long Island, with hiking trails that go on for miles. You don't need to be a descendant of Bigfoot to get the best out of this varied terrain, though. All that is required, some insist, is a fishing rod or an appreciation for colonial architecture. No doubt about it: Angling and area history are as interconnected as the Yankees and the Bronx.

From the Secatogue Indians, who dubbed the river Connetquot, meaning "Great River," this

## ▶ DIRECTIONS

*By car:* Drive east on the Southern State Parkway to Exit 44 and continue east on Sunrise Highway (SR 27) for about 1.8 miles to the Pond Road Exit 47A. At the end of the ramp, turn left and cross the highway via the overpass, then enter the westbound lanes. After 1.4 miles, exit right into the preserve and park in the lot near the toll-booth on the left.

*By public transportation:* Board the LIRR train to Great River Station (Montauk Branch). From there, it is an easy 1.5-mile stroll to the park. Walk north along Connetquot Avenue, cross the bridge over Sunrise Highway (SR 27), and continue straight to the preserve entrance.

## ❶ KEY AT-A-GLANCE INFORMATION

**LENGTH:** 8.6 miles, with the possibility of several bypass shortcuts

**CONFIGURATION:** Loop

**DIFFICULTY:** Moderate

**SCENERY:** Mostly level terrain boasting sandy pine barrens, wavy grasslands, several streams, fish hatchery, and pond with an abundance of waterfowl

**EXPOSURE:** Very open along the fire roads in the first half, canopy cover in the second half

**TRAFFIC:** Quite light north of the fish hatchery; the southern part, with the main pond and the historic buildings, draws the most visitors

**TRAIL SURFACE:** Mostly sandy, some packed dirt, some grass

**HIKING TIME:** 4.5 hours

**SEASON:** October–March, open Wednesday–Sunday; April–September, open Tuesday–Sunday; 8 a.m.–sunset.

**ACCESS:** Call ahead for free permit at (631) 581-1005; $6 parking fee; no pets, no picnicking, no smoking

**MAPS:** At entrance booth and Visitor Center; USGS Bay Shore East

**FACILITIES:** Rest rooms, water, and public telephone at Visitor Center; rest rooms at fish hatchery; museum

**SPECIAL COMMENTS:** The Connetquot River is rated among the ten best fishing rivers in the country. Horseback riders share most of the trails.

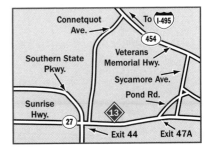

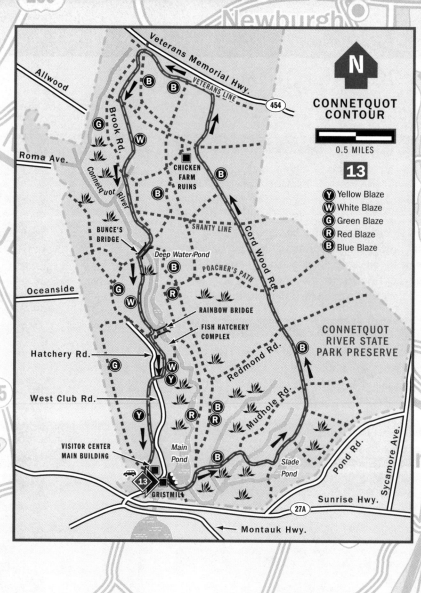

# CONNETQUOT CONTOUR

0.5 MILES

**13**

Y Yellow Blaze
W White Blaze
G Green Blaze
R Red Blaze
B Blue Blaze

CONNETQUOT
RIVER STATE
PARK PRESERVE

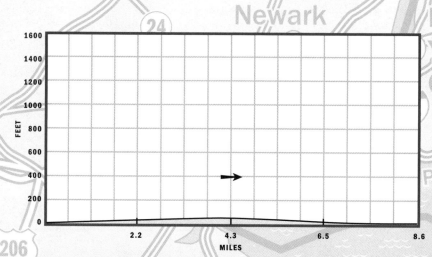

land passed to William Nicoll, sometime around 1684. He dammed a portion of the river and built a gristmill against the edge of the resulting pond. Fast forward to 1820, when Eliphalet "Liff" Snedecor leased a parcel of land abutting the millpond. Liff, who had a good nose for business, erected a tavern there, which soon became an important stagecoach stop. In little more than a decade, as the fishing grew in popularity, affluent sportsmen flocked to the tavern, with the result that it was easier to catch a fish than snag a room at the inn. Eventually, a number of Snedecor's most committed guests bought the tavern, along with 879 acres around it. Their group, incorporated in 1866 as the South Side Sportsmen's Club of Long Island, built a trout hatchery on the estate and continued to acquire land until their holdings totaled 3,473 acres. New York State purchased the property from the club in 1963 and opened it to the public ten years later. The pond, river, and affiliated streams are still considered among the top trout-fishing destinations in the Northeast.

When you have finished with fishing (or with poking around Snedecor's Tavern), proceed up the lane to the millpond. Keep to the left of the Oakdale Grist Mill, which was constructed around 1750, and walk over the dam. Although this hike rates a "moderate" because of its length, it follows level trails, with shorter excursions possible via an abundance of side tracks. Initially, the utility road sports both red and blue blazes. Stay to the left at the fork, walking between the old pillars. Outflow from the nearby pond results in swampy conditions on both sides of the track, with low reeds, skunk cabbage, and white flowering anemones thriving by the feet of chestnut oaks.

Turn right at the next fork, shortly after a viewpoint by the edge of the pond. Mink, ferrets, star-nosed moles, and even flying squirrels are among the mammals making their homes here, though you are more likely to see horses judging by the "apples" that punctuate the sandy surface of the trail. At the ensuing intersection, steer to the right, as pitch pines begin to grow in number. This wide, exposed forest lane is called Cord Wood Road (CWR, blue blazes), which you follow for an hour or so. It bends to the left at the Y, in about five minutes, and left again in another three minutes, then continues straight at the four-way crossing in an additional handful of minutes. Notice how the surroundings, cloaked in oaks and pines, have grown more arid as the CWR pulls away from the pond. Boggy hollows still spring up on the left from time to time, depending on the meanderings of various streams, and in early spring you may see wild violets and an occasional daffodil.

Ignore the side spurs, first to the right, then left, and hang with the wide CWR as it slips through a couple of four-way junctions. Skip, also, the grassy lane that appears to the left, just after a rather large park-like expanse. The succeeding intersection, in less than 0.25 miles, marks the site of the old chicken farm. The ruin—concrete debris, basically—lies several hundred feet to the left. Your route, though, is to the right, toward the grassy, pine-dotted plain. March straight ahead at the ensuing intersection, and within a couple of minutes, cars should be visible ahead of you, zipping along the road beyond the tree line. That signals the end of the CWT; veer left at the T, following the blue blazes onto Veterans Line (VL).

In 10 minutes, the VL starts to arc left, with the spur to the right leading to a gate by the road. As you swing around on the VL, the blue blazes break sharply to the left, while your direction is the middle path (more of a soft left). Leave that in four paces, seizing the narrow trace to the left. This shaded route, which bears the white blazes of the Suffolk Greenbelt Trail (SGT), runs through a wedge of pitch pines and scrub oaks sandwiched between a pair of wide, sandy, sun-struck trails. It is a pleasantly wild-looking stretch that fords, in roughly seven minutes, one of those sandy lanes. As you saunter along this flat turf, scan the overgrown understory for deer, and such butterflies as lavender-colored blue azures, yellow tiger, and black spicebush swallowtails.

The trail merges briefly with a wide loamy track and, in about 20 strides, breaks to the right, back under the cover of the forest. It intersects that sand trap once more, then merges with it. Remain with the sandy lane as you pass the blue-blazed connector to the left. Pursue the white blazes a few steps beyond that, branching to the right and crossing Bunce's Bridge. The SGT then moseys through a swampy area, where fishing spurs are grooved into the moss, and scoots to the left, snaking through a jungle of head-high sheep laurel and a handful of black birch. On skirting a picturesque bog, the path arrives at a fork, with the white blazes cruising left.

Stay with the SGT as it draws you by the bog and approaches Rainbow Bridge. Shift to the right there, moving away from the bridge, and in 20 yards the white blazes jog left onto the park road. Keep strolling straight toward the parking area as the road tapers to the right, just beyond the latrine. Yellow blazes join the white ones here and together parallel the road. Before continuing, though, make a side trip left to the fish hatchery, a small complex built in 1890, that still turns out a variety of trout in much the manner it did a century ago. The water here so often churns with flopping, hyperactive fish, you may be inclined to run for your tackle box. (We've also seen titmice, Canada geese, and guinea fowl in the vicinity.)

On leaving the hatchery, the trail hugs the left side of West Club Road. In a few minutes, though, it hops to the other side of the pavement and slips behind a thin curtain of oaks. Remain with this wide track as it brushes by the periphery of a series of open fields—developed by the sportsmen's club to attract game birds—all the way back to the parking area.

## ▶ NEARBY ACTIVITIES

From March through October, there is always something blooming at Bayard Cutting Arboretum State Park. Visit www.bcarboretum.com for a list of plant and bird species and their best viewing time. An elegant lunch and tea are served in the former Cutting Manor; for reservations, call (631) 224-3434, or contact the park directly at (631) 581-1002.

# CROTON POINT DISCOVERY TRAIL

## ▶ IN BRIEF

Hidden Hudson River access, sandy coves, and historic wine cellars are what this one is all about. Add an abundance of wildlife and a possible extension through a wildflower meadow, and this easy walk should make for memorable family fun.

## ▶ DESCRIPTION

When we first aimed our hiking togs toward Croton Point, we were, admittedly, skeptical. A partially paved trail that cuts through a campground and closes with a landfill-turned-meadow held all the allure of a dive into a deer tick–loaded leaf pile. Maybe even less. On closer scrutiny, though, we found it has a great deal going for it. For one thing, Croton Point, at 504 acres, lies on the largest peninsula of the Hudson River. In addition to the multitude of waterside vistas and waterfowl you would expect, within the confines of the park are the remains of a nineteenth-century brick-making plant, historic wine cellars believed to be the oldest in the Empire State, and a thick grove of conifers— largely spruce and Scotch and white pine. As an added enticement, there is also a great nature center with exhibits on flora, fauna, and area history.

Head toward the water as you leave the main parking lot, beyond the park office, keeping to the left of the large pavilion (which itself is just left of

## ▶ DIRECTIONS

*By car:* Take the New York State Thruway (I-87) north to Exit 9 (Tarrytown). Follow US 9 north for 10 miles and exit at Croton Point Avenue. Turn left at the end of the ramp, and left again at the light. The park entrance lies straight ahead. Proceed to the large parking lot by the waterfront.

*By public transportation:* Ride Metro North's Hudson Line train to Croton-Harmon Station. From there, walk about 0.5 miles south on Croton Point Avenue to the park entrance.

## ⓘ KEY AT-A-GLANCE INFORMATION

**LENGTH:** 2.5 miles; add 1 mile for the landfill meadow loop

**CONFIGURATION:** Loop

**DIFFICULTY:** Very easy

**SCENERY:** Rather level trail along riverfront, park roads, and lawns, with extensive views of Tappan Zee, its bridge, and bluffs across pebbly banks of the Hudson River

**EXPOSURE:** Open in beach and lawn areas at the start, partly shady in camping areas, no cover on landfill meadow

**TRAFFIC:** Hectic in summer and solitary late September–mid-May

**TRAIL SURFACE:** Sand, dirt, and gravel alternate with asphalt

**HIKING TIME:** 1.5 hours, depending on how successful you are at beachcombing

**SEASON:** Year-round, 8 a.m.–dusk

**ACCESS:** $4 with Westchester County Parks Pass, $8 without pass, dogs must be leashed

**MAPS:** At the park office

**FACILITIES:** Rest rooms and water at picnic areas and campground, public phone

**SPECIAL COMMENTS:** Bring binoculars for bird- and boat-watching.

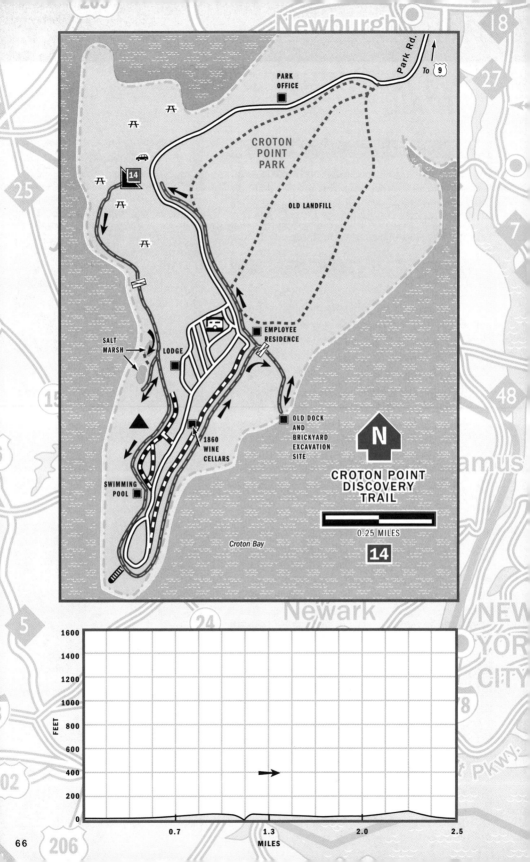

CROTON POINT
DISCOVERY
TRAIL

0.25 MILES

Nature Center Drive). Benches by the river's edge are ideally positioned for absorbing the breathtaking view of the Palisades across the way, as well as observing the Canada geese and groundhogs chomping on the grass nearer at hand. Go left there, sticking with the hard, sandy track used by maintenance trucks as it flows from the picnic area through a barrier gate to a tree-shaded, dirt-surfaced lane. Deer often graze among the wildflowers here, and in late summer, you may chance upon wild grapes—possibly descendants of those cultivated in the winery's vineyard more than a century ago. The depressions you see in the ground in this area (and elsewhere in the park) date from when clay was quarried for the brick factory.

In roughly 150 yards, the lane gives way to a gravel turnaround, the end of the tent camping loop. Look for a slight opening in the overgrown shrubs to the immediate right for a staircase of wooden pilings that leads down to a pair of ponds. Back on the main circuit, proceed through the campground (often frequented by fawn-furred cottontail rabbits), past the portable toilets and dumpster, staying left of the swimming pool, and by the basketball court. Just before the paved road loops leftward, a dirt path to the right slopes steeply down to the sandy point. There, among sassafras and eastern cottonwoods, with driftwood and weathered bricks by your feet, is a strikingly beautiful view of the bluffs across the way. Go ahead and test the water if you like, but for our money this isolated beach ranks higher as one of the Hudson River's most serene sunset spots.

Bear right on your return to the park road, continuing to the stop sign, where the trail goes left and away from the vacation cabins. Beyond the vine-choked hardwood trees now ranging to the right is the South Cove, with the remains of clay pits sandwiched in between. About 120 yards from the stop sign are the brick wine cellars, and if you are lucky—or you planned well by calling ahead—a few of these partly overgrown Romanesque vaults may be open for tours. Moving on, you'll soon arrive at a towering stand of white pines, many sadly succumbing to strangulation by vines (including flowering morning glory), and some notably large spruce specimens. This dirt track morphs back to asphalt at the next stop sign, by a brick-sided house. Follow the grass lane to the right and, stepping over the barrier, stroll through the ever-more-encroaching brush to the cove. You will pass a phragmite marsh along the way, and possibly wildlife (like the skunk and deer that we stumbled upon once), as the spur dead-ends by a large cottonwood, just left of a decaying dock. From this romantic spot, a sandy, secluded nook overlooking Croton Bay, you can feast your eyes on the tail end of the Palisades bluffs and, farther south, the Tappan Zee Bridge. Allow a few moments to beachcomb for sand-polished glass and oddly eroded bricks.

Back at the stop sign, stride straight by the employee residence to the next stop sign, where you'll meet the main road and the landfill meadow. Turn right at the wire barrier onto the meadow for a chance to see more wildlife and to add a mile to the walk. Otherwise, roll onward, on the right side of the road, back to the parking area.

## ▶ NEARBY ACTIVITIES

Croton Point Park has a campground, swimming pool (seasonal) and a nature center offering various programs. Overgrown nineteenth-century wine cellars can be toured. Call ahead (914) 862-8134 for the schedule.

At Van Cortlandt Manor, on South Riverside Avenue, costumed interpreters demonstrate crafts, and the eighteenth-century house is decorated in period furnishings. Call (914) 631-8200 for more information.

# DAVID WELD SANCTUARY TOUR

## KEY AT-A-GLANCE INFORMATION

**LENGTH:** 3.2 miles

**CONFIGURATION:** Out-and-back, connecting 4 loops

**DIFFICULTY:** Very easy

**SCENERY:** Splendid variety of habitats includes fields, swamp, deciduous forest, beach frontage, and kettle-holes

**EXPOSURE:** Open at outset, followed by shady canopy (except for some bluff viewpoints) and open at finish

**TRAFFIC:** Usually light, but popular on weekend afternoons

**TRAIL SURFACE:** Grassy, packed dirt, and roots

**HIKING TIME:** 1.75 hours

**SEASON:** Year-round, dawn–dusk

**ACCESS:** Free, no pets, only foot traffic

**MAPS:** Posted and handouts at kiosk

**FACILITIES:** None

**SPECIAL COMMENTS:** Glacial erratics are rare on Long Island, but this charming preserve has several sizeable specimens.

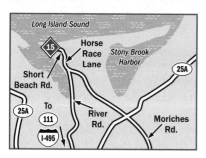

## IN BRIEF

Talk about bang for the buck: At the David Weld Sanctuary, you get bluff-top vistas of Long Island Sound, flowering fruit trees, a hardwood forest highlighted by colossal tulip trees, colorful swamps, a remote group of kettle-hole depressions, and even a few glacial erratics. All that and more, without being nicked for an admission fee!

## DESCRIPTION

David Weld and, in later years, his widow, donated much of this turf to the Nature Conservancy, which explains why it bears his name. History buffs might argue, though, that the preserve could just as well be called the Richard "Bull" Smythe Sanctuary. Smythe, after all, was one of the property's earliest owners, back in the 1600s. In truth, he held title to most of the acreage in these parts, including what is known today as Smithtown. Legend has it that Smythe made a deal with the local Indian chief for all the land that he could ride a bull around in one day. Waiting for the summer solstice, the longest day of the

## DIRECTIONS

*By car:* Follow the Long Island Expressway (I-495) east to Exit 56 onto SR 111 north. Drive for about 4 miles to the junction with SR 25 and SR 25A. Go straight across SR 25, then bear a quick left on River Road. Continue for 3.5 miles and turn left onto Moriches Road which becomes Horse Race Lane. After 0.4 miles make a left on Short Beach Road and proceed for 0.1 mile to the preserve entrance and parking area on the right.

*By public transportation:* Board the LIRR to St. James Station (Port Jefferson Branch). From there, a cab ride of about 3.5 miles delivers you to the sanctuary.

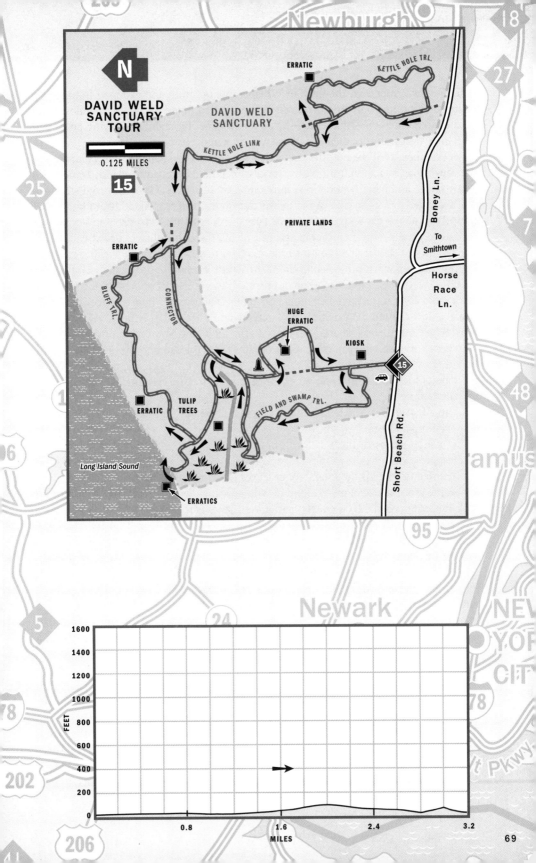

year, Smythe hopped on the back of Whisper, his pet bull, and galloped from sunup to sunset, stopping only briefly on what is now called Bread and Cheese Hollow Road for a simple lunch of—what else?—bread and cheese. By nightfall, Smythe possessed a 35-mile swath of prime real estate, as well as a new nickname.

Whether "Bull" or not, the fact is that the David Weld Sanctuary is a diamond in the rough, packing shorefront bluffs, successional fields, wetlands, glacial kettle-holes and erratics, and a hardwood forest into a modest 125 acres. From scattered stands of pines and red cedars to one of the tallest tulip trees on Long Island, from bluffs that rise 50 feet above the Sound to vestigial farms, this easy hike offers something for just about everyone over terrain that as recently as 1920 was largely a clear-cut pasture.

With the elevation all of 30 feet at the five- to six-car-capacity parking area, the highest you can expect to reach is about the century mark, found at the well-forested farthest end of this horseshoe-shaped preserve. To get to that spot, which is near the kettle-hole formations, while seeing the most that David Weld has to offer, walk straight in for about 70 yards to the kiosk, where a trail map is posted. Hang a left directly beyond the information board onto the Field and Swamp Trail, where eastern red cedars, sumac, and an assortment of fruit trees (blossoming beautifully in early May) contribute some texture—but not much shade—to the grassy meadow. Cottontail rabbits love to cavort here, which in turn attracts an occasional coyote, to judge by telltale trailside spoors.

In a few strides, the field undergoes a transition, as dogwood, chokeberry, briar, wintergreen, and other scrub interweave like a thick hedge maze around the path, while many species of birds twitter from the shady shelter of their branches. Soon maples and oaks are among the mix, and then, suddenly, you are in a hardwood forest. Those greens with the long, tender leaves growing amid the false lilies of the valley on the ground are ramps—a kind of wild leek that tastes wonderful when sautéed with butter and garlic. (Of course, gathering plants is a no-no in a nature preserve.) The scenery evolves still further when you turn right at the T, still on the Field and Swamp Trail. Skunk cabbage and marsh reeds line the fairly wide track, which is scarred by a fair share of roots, while a slow-moving stream putters along to the left.

This swampy swale continues even as you dart to the left at the Y. The rising ground to the right, though, is more densely forested, with a smattering of conifers outnumbered by beech, black birch, and oak trees. That lasts for all of a minute, until the next fork, where a left puts you squarely in the middle of a colorful swamp that is anything but dismal. Along the way, you may notice some tulip trees to the left that are truly gargantuan in scale, with the tallest, at 106 feet, being one of the largest on Long Island.

You may also notice the scent of brine increasing with every step you take. That is because this track, now called the Bluff Trail, is edging closer to—you guessed it!—a row of bluffs overhanging Long Island Sound. A spur to the left, just as the main route bends right, leads out to a grassy overlook of the water, as well as the beach below, where a couple of glacial erratics serve as dark pedestals for sunbathers. There is a fragment of a foundation stone in this triangular patch of grass, all that is left of a rustic retreat former resident Cornelia Otis Skinner once occupied. Skinner, a thespian and playwright, reportedly used the bungalow, which burned to the ground in 1987, to rehearse her monologues.

There is a scattering of a few more erratics as you stroll east along the Bluff Trail, in addition to some knobby oaks. If the weather is clear, you can see Connecticut from a bench a couple of minutes down the path. Be careful by the railing there, though, as the ground just beyond it is eroding quite severely. Moving along, the serpentine path winds through a tangle of briar and barberry, past yew trees, holly, and an enormous oak before finally drifting inland among cedars, maples, and jack-in-the-pulpits at ground level. Continue straight across the four-way intersection, shortly after a huge erratic, on what is now the Kettle Hole Link.

From an elevation of 20 feet at that junction, the trail makes an abrupt rush uphill, gaining in scant seconds 40 additional feet of altitude. Just shy of the crest, it scoots to the left, skirting the perimeter of an active farm where generations of debris have spilled onto the path behind a red barn, amounting to an agricultural archeologist's dream dig. After the track jumps right, onto a grooved surface, Kettle Hole Link ends at a fork, with the Kettle Hole Trail running both straight and left. We like to go left here, but it doesn't really matter which direction you take on this miniloop. Leftward, the route wends down a bit by a minor erratic, passing through the depression of a glacial kettle-hole. (Unlike those at the Westmoreland Sanctuary in Westchester County, the kettle-holes here do not contain water.)

The moss-sided path wanders over a corrugated landscape that is appealingly forested with silver-barked beech, black birch, and oaks. It arcs to the right a couple of times before hitting a T, where it continues again to the right. In a few minutes the loop is closed and you swing left at the earlier dogleg, back on Kettle Hole Link. Backtrack on that all the way to the four-way intersection at the bottom of the hill, where you should launch to the left. The last time we hiked this leg there were several trees down across it, but we had little trouble navigating through. In five minutes, this wide, smooth track meets a forest road, with a left returning you to the trailhead.

On the way there, though, make the short detour to the left, just after the David and Molly Weld monument stone. From swampy terrain limned with skunk cabbage and jack-in-the-pulpits, you are now entering a largely open, grassy area, so keep an ear up for cottontails. The landmark along this spur, listed on the map as a "huge erratic," lies to the right, tucked under some trees. A slanted, sedimented slab of slate-colored granite that rises some five to seven feet off the soil, the otherwise photogenic rock suffers, it seems, from a case of elevated expectations. At the conclusion of this side trip, swing left onto the grassy forest road. The parking area is dead ahead.

## ▶ NEARBY ACTIVITIES

Three separate buildings house very different collections of art and history in the Museums at Stony Brook. The permanent collections include American paintings, antique hunting decoys, and horse-drawn vehicles, but the changing shows are no less spectacular. Call (516) 751-0066 for current activities.

# DEVIL'S DEN CONCOURSE

## KEY AT-A-GLANCE INFORMATION

**LENGTH:** 8 miles

**CONFIGURATION:** Loop

**DIFFICULTY:** Moderate

**SCENERY:** Rolling woodlands, wetlands, gorge with gentle cascade, rocky ledge with splendid view of Saugatuck Reservoir, and several relics of lumber mills

**EXPOSURE:** Mostly shady, except for a few ledges and Godfrey Pond area

**TRAFFIC:** The farther out you go, the fewer people you encounter

**TRAIL SURFACE:** Packed dirt with rocky, rooty, and muddy stretches

**HIKING TIME:** 3.75 hours

**SEASON:** Year-round, sunrise–sunset

**ACCESS:** $2 donation suggested, no pets, no bicycles

**MAPS:** At the entrance kiosk; USGS Norwalk North

**FACILITIES:** No rest rooms or water; public telephone by Laurel Trail entrance

**SPECIAL COMMENTS:** The Den hosts many activities such as customized guided group hikes, and cross-country skiing and snowshoeing are permitted in winter.

## IN BRIEF

The extensive trail system of this sanctuary offers something for every level of walker, from tyros of the turf to foot-hearty highlanders. It slices through a rich variety of woodland habitats, showcasing a large pond and numerous streams, a rocky ravine, several granite-wracked gorges, high plateaus with expansive views of the surrounding hills, and even the ruins of a nineteenth-century lumber mill. Wild turkeys and white-tailed deer teem through these woods, and moist weather brings an intoxicating mix of mushrooms.

## DESCRIPTION

No one knows for certain how Devil's Den came by its menacing moniker. The Great Ledge viewpoint isn't guarded by a three-headed Cerberus, its streams don't flow with molten lava, and not a whiff of sulfur taints its air. On the contrary, when your lug soles start padding through the varied terrain, you will find yourself treading in hiker's heaven. Which isn't to say you'll feel like an angel at the end of this 8-mile hike. But with more than 1,700 acres to the preserve, encompassing hundreds of varieties of trees and wildflowers, dramatic ridgetop views, the ever-popular Godfrey

## DIRECTIONS

*By car:* Drive north on the Hutchinson River Parkway and continue as it changes to the Merritt Parkway. Take Exit 42, following SR 57 north for 5 miles. Turn right (east) on Godfrey Road, and in half a mile steer left onto Pent Road (the preserve is signposted), which leads to the parking lot.

*By public transportation:* Take Metro North's New Haven Line to Branchville Station. From there, grab a taxi for a ride of about 4 miles to the Den.

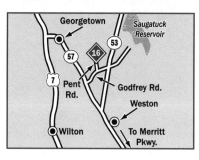

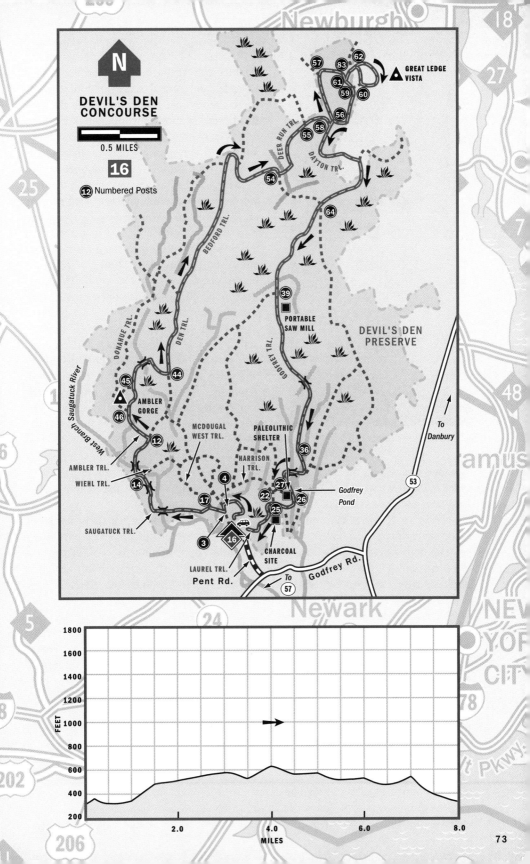

A springtime surprise, this pink lady's slipper orchid grows on the higher ledges of Devil's Den Nature Preserve.

Pond, a rocky ravine bisected by a picturesque cascade, and several scores of bird species, there's more than enough to elevate the spirits of even the most downtrodden of trekkers.

Numbered posts at most intersections simplify trail-hopping while minimizing the chance you'll get lost. Just remember to pick up a map at the kiosk before leaving the dogwood-, beech-, and hemlock-fringed parking area. We like to warm up briskly by starting with the Katharine Hill Trail to the right of the kiosk, a short but steep stretch that climbs past a multitude of mountain laurels before cresting on a rocky knob. This brief burst is by no means the only such ascent in the park, but it may be the most strenuous.

From that lichen-spattered granite aerie, the path drifts left, descends sharply over stone-studded turf, and bottoms out by a boggy stream. Follow the fern-flecked, granite-scarred gully for a few minutes to the trail's end at post 4. Turn left, and in a couple dozen steps, hang a right onto the McDougal West Trail, at marker 3. If you happen to be on this lush, marshy track in summer, look along the slick sides of the stream for scarlet gilia, one of the Den's more colorful wildflowers. As chunks of granite start to supplant the swamp, you'll turn left onto the Saugatuck Trail by post 17.

A series of short boardwalks help to ford a few of the swampier spots along this relatively level course, which, incidentally, tends to be prime mushrooming territory in early autumn—black chanterelles being among the choice specimens. The latter part of the track slants downward toward a more glacial, rocky environment, with oaks and birches pressing in upon the scene. Dawdle a moment on the bridge that shifts the path from the left side of the West Branch of the Saugatuck River to its right bank: The clear-flowing water often teems with trout.

Having set aside your figurative fishing rod, angle past post 14 (where the Wiehl Trail tacks back to McDougal) and across yet another bridge to marker 12, where you'll change over to the Ambler Trail (AT). Here commences a mildly strenuous ascent past laurels, only to level off by an eye-catching rock shelf to the right that rises 15 to 20 feet off the ground. Swing right at number 46, where you meet—and shun—the Donahue Trail, and enter directly into an even denser mass of mountain laurels, punctuated by an increasingly impressive display of granite. A brief side trip at post 45 leads to a blueberry-bordered vista point, with the rock shelf making a fine spot on which to pause and catch your breath.

Back on the AT, your ankles are in for a minor stress test as the route traverses a fair amount of shale and angular stones in one of the preserve's more enjoyable rock-scrambling spots. No sooner have you reached the ridgeline than the trail begins trending downward again, reaching a scenic climax at the Ambler Gorge. The great,

Devil's Den is a thriving woodland once again, after having been largely denuded to fuel charcoal kilns much like this during the nineteenth century.

gray-granite walls and rockslide of this ravine are truly sensational, and the seasonal cascade flowing through is sweet music for the eyes as well as ears. If you're a quiet hiker, you may find downy woodpeckers, yellow-shafted flickers, and other birds bathing in the water. In any case, remain vigilant for the elusive trail blazes here as well as for slick rocks near the stream.

The AT ends at pole 44, as you move left onto the Den Trail, which in turn morphs seamlessly after awhile into the Bedford Trail. It is 1.4 miles from that last number to post 54, where you should vault left onto Deer Run, a grassy area frequented by wild turkeys. Keep right at marker 55 in 0.3 miles, and then swing left in another five minutes at pole 58. In four steps you'll come to a fieldstone wall, with a left turn at marker 56 just beyond that.

This begins the first of two miniloops that reach a pinnacle at the Great Ledge, with its fabulous views over the Saugatuck Reservoir and surrounding hills. (Note that you'll want to adhere to the white blazes throughout these circuits; the yellow slashes date from an earlier era and are no longer valid.) At 0.35 miles, you'll take the right fork at post 57, which was partly obscured by a tangle of wild rose the last time we came through. If you hike here in late summer when the sedge grass is tall and the shagbark hickories have dropped their nuts, you're likely to see more deer and squirrels than hikers. Shuffling onward, roll left at number 61, the straighter of two options, then right at marker 83, 0.1 mile later. Make a left in about ten paces at post 62, and in approximately 30 yards you'll have to scramble over some rocks and roots and past some hemlocks before reaching, in a small knoll of oaks and white pines, the Great Ledge, with its panorama toward the east. This appealing, rocky plateau, which extends for 25 feet and also features a lower, smaller ledge, makes an ideal picnic spot. Look for pink lady's slipper orchids here in early June.

With the laurel canopy increasing in density as you mosey along the ledge to the south, you may have trouble finding the white blazes. Aim toward the south-southwest, over the rocky, mossy surface, until you reach post 60 down the hill. Bearing left there, you'll descend further into a marshy zone, where horned toads huddle among the ferns and mud. Keep left again at pole 59, as the rocky path snakes uphill among oaks, laurels, and pines, peaking atop a moss-covered dome. The view isn't so splendid, but the laurels, oaks, and pines lend an enchanting air to the spot.

Stay left a few minutes later on picking up post 56 again, and do the same at number 58. In 0.3 miles, transfer from the Dayton Trail onto Godfrey (GT) to the right. What starts as a subtle downward direction becomes, in roughly 40 yards, a rather steady descent into a beech-bespeckled swampland. The next post, 64, appears in five minutes, with the GT the middle of three options. Remain on that for another 0.6 miles, passing marker 39, until you reach the old sawmill site, notable for its rusty remnants of a nineteenth-century steam boiler and flywheel. Near the woods is the well-preserved foundation of a shed that may have housed the mill's boiler.

On concluding your explorations of the ruins and miscellaneous unblazed traces in this locale, return to the GT and proceed for another mile, sauntering right at post 36. With Godfrey Pond straight ahead, glide right at the T and spring over the bridge, where a crackling cascade plunges through the rocky gorge in springtime. A short uphill detour at post 27 showcases a high stone ledge: Its recessed pockets were used as shelters by Paleolithic hunters as early as 3,500 B.C.

Back by Godfrey Pond, continue counterclockwise and step up to the edge of the water when you reach the spill-off stream, near marker 26. Take a breather by the bench—and maybe a photo or two of the picturesque pond. Then go on to post 25 and turn right, moving down the graded slope to a bridge. Head left at number 24 and travel straight on until you reach the Laurel Trail at post 22, loping left there. The parking lot lies ahead, but preceding that is a re-created charcoal kiln—one of 40 such sites that once existed in the Den. The production of charcoal—used among other things for gunpowder, paint and ink, iron forging, and medicines—was a big business in these parts during most of the nineteenth century. Considering the volume of cut timber necessary for such endeavors, it seems a minor miracle that the Devil's Den is the wooded paradise we find it today.

### ▶ NEARBY ACTIVITIES

The handsome town of Ridgefield has a true gem on Main Street in the Aldrich Museum of Contemporary Art. Modern art is exhibited in an attractive white colonial building and a small sculpture garden. For information, call (203) 438-4519.

If you're game for more fun in the forest, consider heading up the road to the Trout Brook Valley Conservation Area, which lies just beyond the 60-mile cutoff mark for inclusion in this book. This handsome, hilly parcel consists of hardwoods, hemlocks, swampy streams, and granite ravines, making for a splendid and scenic hike. Take Exit 44 off the Merritt Parkway, head north on SR 58, turn left on Freeborn Road (shortly after crossing SR 136), and swing right onto Elm Drive. Maps are available near the trailhead and at www.aspetucklandtrust.

# FAHNESTOCK HIDDEN LAKE LOOP

## ▶ IN BRIEF

Relatively smooth, wide pathways make this a foot-friendly environment, one in which you may see an array of avians at any of three ponds and their related wetlands. Glacial erratics and rocky uplift lend extra *frisson* to the shady terrain, while an elusive air of mystery emanates from the overgrown remnants of nineteenth-century iron-mining operations.

## ▶ DESCRIPTION

Don't be put off by the fact that Clarence Fahnestock State Park is smack in the middle of densely populated Putnam County. In combination with the Hubbard-Perkins Conservation Area, Fahnestock measures 11,000 acres and is the largest preserve in the entire Taconic area. Admittedly, when most people think of this facility, its sandy-shored Canopus Beach comes to mind. Others, hooked on angling, view the park's many lakes and ponds as prime line-casting waters for pickerel, perch, bass, and trout.

Which is not to suggest that hiking in Fahnestock has all the appeal of a plunge into the Harlem River on a frosty November night. On the contrary, most of the park's many miles of trails, including a portion of the Appalachian Trail (AT), run through dense, under-trafficked forestland. What the setting may lack in the dramatic peaks and views of the nearby Hudson Highlands, it more than compensates for in seclusion, tranquility, and a sublime sort of beauty.

## ▶ DIRECTIONS

Take US 9 north about 10 miles above Peekskill, to SR 301 east (Carmel Cold Spring Road). Drive for 4.5 miles to a small parking lot on the left, by Canopus Lake. Additional parking may be found right by the Appalachian Trail crossing, 0.15 miles back down the road. The trailhead is on the right (south) side of SR 301.

### ⓘ KEY AT-A-GLANCE INFORMATION

**LENGTH:** 6.5 miles

**CONFIGURATION:** Figure eight

**DIFFICULTY:** Easy to moderate

**SCENERY:** Dense deciduous forest with laurel patches and conifers, talus slopes, rock outcroppings, lush wetlands, 3 bodies of water, iron mine pits, and a 0.75-mile piece of the Appalachian Trail

**EXPOSURE:** Thick, shady canopy in summer

**TRAFFIC:** Popular on weekends, otherwise light to moderate

**TRAIL SURFACE:** Mostly dirt with alternating rocky and sandy stretches

**HIKING TIME:** 3 hours

**SEASON:** Year-round

**ACCESS:** No fee, dogs must be on leash not more than 10 feet long

**MAPS:** USGS Oscawana Lake; New York–New Jersey Trail Conference East Hudson Trails

**FACILITIES:** No rest rooms or water on trails, but Canopus Beach in state park has both and much more

**SPECIAL COMMENTS:** Bow hunting for deer and turkey is permitted in season.

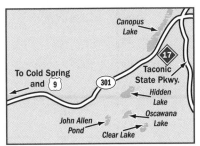

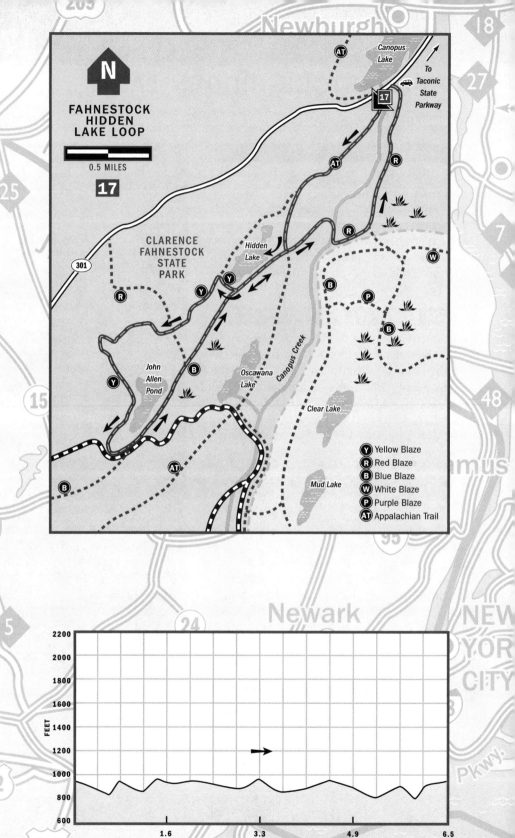

The 6.5-mile Hidden Lake loop is so secluded, in fact, you may have trouble finding its trailhead. From your parking spot by the edge of Canopus Lake, cross over to the south side of the street. Edge along the road to the west for a few yards until you see a barrier in the shadow of the woods. Slip by that and walk down the overgrown path to the fork. Keep right along a wide, well-trammeled track, where ferns decorate the rising ridge to the right, with glacial erratics and hemlocks scattered all around.

The AT shares this initial stretch, which is blazed white, as it flows from the dense cover of conifers to a more open array of oak, maple, and beech trees. The trail is well graded and slightly elevated from the forest floor—the curious effects of having been laid out over a defunct narrow-gauge rail line that was used in the nineteenth century to transport locally mined iron ore. Walking along this higher ground gives you an advantage in spotting wildlife, with wild turkeys among the more abundant of those that roam these parts.

In about half a mile, mountain laurel begins to crowd the path, making for a pretty pink floral display in early June. Follow the turnoff soon thereafter to the left, a rerouting due either to habitat restoration or flooded ground from work on the dam, depending on which of two signs posted there is correct. This short side spur covers rocky land, with a few downed trees to scramble over, before depositing you on the other side of the loop. Turn right there, leaving the AT as it drifts onward (the left branch brings you back to the trailhead), with blue blazes guiding the way.

This is a scenic stretch, enhanced by a partial view of the not-so-well-Hidden Lake to the right. Within ten minutes, though, you'll be venturing off it to the right, onto a yellow-blazed spur that was partly blocked by two large fallen trees on our last time through. They are easy enough to slide around, and in doing so you may see pileated woodpeckers, which favor such rotting timber.

Although short, the yellow-blazed track has the virtue of heading directly to the southwest side of Hidden Lake, in among knee-high sedge grass and wild grapes, where phragmites fringe the shore and lilies dot its jade green surface. When the water level is high, you'll need to rock-hop by the lakeside to get by. When it is low, the entire lake may indeed be hidden—by mud. Stay to the left at the next junction, back on the trail from which you were diverted earlier, with yellow blazes now marking the trees.

Moving toward the third cut-through, which you ignore; there is an impressively large boulder with two slender black birch saplings springing up against its side, as if they alone had checked it from tumbling farther down the hill. John Allen Pond rises into view just beyond the intersection. Perhaps 500 yards later, the grassy track bends to the right of a marshy gully, bends back again, and then the yellow blazes veer left off of the smooth railroad grade. Follow them into the thicket of mountain laurel. With that shift, a more wild forest unfolds, as large stones poke up through the surface of the path, which zigzags left and right past one large block of granite after another.

This leg connects momentarily to a second railroad bed, then spins by a couple of boggy spots and a series of slag heaps and mining holes. Some stepping-stones simplify a sticky stream crossing, but beware of that slippery moss. At the southwest side of the pond, where its overgrown edge is out of reach through a thicket, the trail jumps abruptly to the right, climbs over a moss-covered shelf of rocks and lichen-speckled talus, then swings toward the pond again. A couple of stone walls precede the next junction, where you stick to the left. The yellow-blazed trail ends in a few dozen yards, once by another group of slag heaps. Take a left onto the dirt-and-gravel road, and in roughly half a furlong, you'll see a blue-blazed path join this route from the right. Continue straight and do the same at the next fork, in maybe 100 yards. The jeep road circles around back toward the pond, and 50 feet from a walk-down access point to the water, the blue blazes lead you left, back into the forest.

From this overgrown, under-trafficked locale, the trail creeps below the concrete dam of the pond, where a few well-positioned stepping-stones ease the way through ground that is often muddy and slick from runoff. For a brief spell, you'll walk on top of a narrow leg of the dam, before returning to the darkness of the forest. Bear to the right of the enormous oak, which measures five feet in diameter, and as you encounter a second phragmite marsh, take a good look around. This area of aged oaks was formerly a hive of mining activity, its once-scarred ground now covered with grass and near a full recovery. If you have the time, you might wander off to the right once the path widens, to explore other such remnants of ore mining. Otherwise, steer left to complete the pince-nez loop.

Remain with this trail all the way back to the main road. For a time, you will be treading over rolling turf, though at no point during this hike is the elevation gain ever more than 50 feet. From a setting of rugged, glacial erratics, the environment evolves into fairly open grassy swathes, punctuated by a healthy sprinkling of oaks, birches and beeches. You should soon recognize the area you detoured through earlier, between the yellow-blazed option to the left and the intersection with the AT. Additional undulations ensue, with the narrow path corralled by pricklers and blueberry bushes.

After still more slag heaps and marshland, the main trail veers right at a fork deep within the hemlock canopy, then proceeds straight on through the next junction. A stream parallels the track for a spell as it gradually ascends past many eye-catching erratics and crests atop a ridge. Keep left there, rejoining a graded railroad bed. From there, Casey Jones, it's easy chugging, all the way back to the station.

## ▶ NEARBY ACTIVITIES

Canopus Beach is the place to relax after a hot hike, with boating, swimming, fishing, picnicking, and even showering among its amenities. Pick up a basic park map at the office, located a little farther east on the left (north) side of SR 301. The park is open in winter for ice and snow activities.

While in the area, plan to visit one of the grand mansions in the Hudson Valley area. Federal-style Boscobel dates from 1804 and is located on SR 9D near Cold Spring, overlooking the Hudson Valley. For information, call (845) 265-3638.

# FISHKILL RIDGE TRAIL

## ▶ IN BRIEF

When Walt Whitman penned, "a leaf of grass is no less than the journeywork of the stars," he might have been thinking of Fishkill. There is indeed a celestial atmosphere to its extended ridge, a sedge-sprinkled granite plateau of unsurpassed beauty and calm. The various vistas, while not heart-stopping, are nonetheless an added plus. Only the grueling grind up—an elevation gain of 1,000 feet over one mile—makes this an opt-out excursion for young children.

## ▶ DESCRIPTION

We hesitate to mention Fishkill Ridge in the same breath as the Hudson Highlands. The former, after all, at just over 1,000 acres, is but one quarter the size of the latter. And while the Highlands, a state park, is fine hiking terrain most any time, Fishkill, operated as a conservation area, allows hunting in late autumn, when hikers who value their health had best stay away—or color themselves like over-size pumpkins.

That Fishkill Ridge is often associated with the Hudson Highlands is certainly no coincidence, given its position at the north end of that range. Naturally, such geographic kinship blesses Fishkill with many of the same attributes that make its neighbor such a happy hiking ground, including rugged climbs to rocky ridges and craggy domes, awe-inspiring views of the Hudson River and surrounding hills, and a massive gain of elevation.

## ▶ DIRECTIONS

Take US 9 north about 10 miles past Peekskill, to the junction with SR 301. Continue from there, still on US 9, for 3.3 miles, turning left onto UHL Road (Old Albany Post Road North). Proceed for 0.25 miles to Reservoir Lane on the left, where the trailhead is located. Park on the shoulder of the Post Road, as there is no designated parking area. Additional parking may be found along US 9.

## ⓘ KEY AT-A-GLANCE INFORMATION

**LENGTH:** 5 miles

**CONFIGURATION:** Balloon

**DIFFICULTY:** Moderate

**SCENERY:** Rugged, steep trail ascends through hardwood forest to panoramic view of Fahnestock State Park, Hudson River, and quarry

**EXPOSURE:** Pretty shady all the way, with exception of highest ridges

**TRAFFIC:** Very light

**TRAIL SURFACE:** Mix of packed dirt, rocks, roots, and a couple of grassy patches; quite uneven at times

**HIKING TIME:** 3 hours

**SEASON:** Year-round

**ACCESS:** No fee

**MAPS:** USGS West Point; New York–New Jersey Trail Conference East Hudson Trails

**FACILITIES:** No rest rooms or water on trails

**SPECIAL COMMENTS:** Stellar viewpoints for leaf-peeping in autumn, but beware of bow hunters in big-game season.

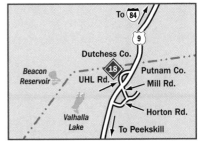

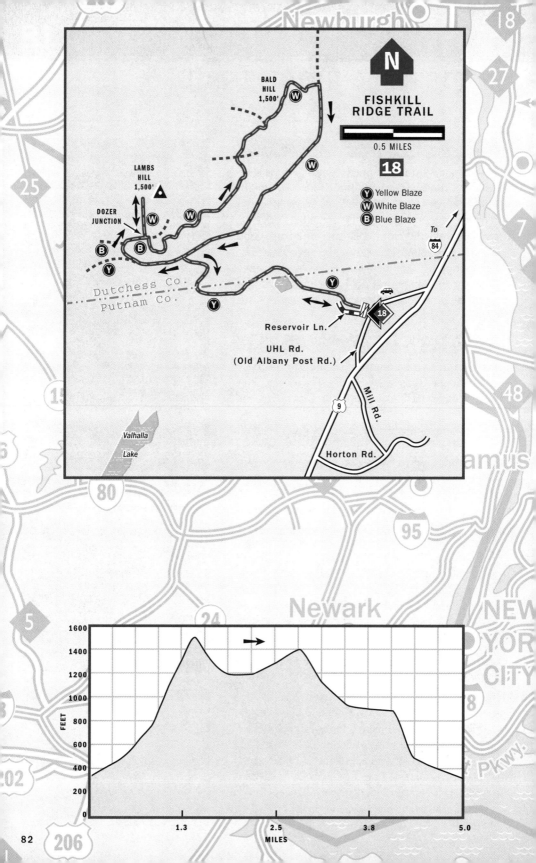

N

# FISHKILL RIDGE TRAIL

0.5 MILES

**18**

**Y** Yellow Blaze
**W** White Blaze
**B** Blue Blaze

BALD
HILL
1,500'

LAMBS
HILL
1,500'

DOZER
JUNCTION

Dutchess Co.
Putnam Co.

Reservoir Ln.

UHL Rd.
(Old Albany Post Rd.)

Valhalla
Lake

Horton Rd.

To
84

9

Mill Rd.

Newburgh

Newark

NEW YORK CITY

82

206

This last characteristic should not be underestimated. From the trailhead by Reservoir Lane to the highest point of the ridge, plan on climbing more than 1,200 feet, with most of that coming in the first fifth of a 5-mile loop. It is a grueling, stamina-draining ascent up a grooved track that bears more than a slight resemblance to a luge chute. The silver lining, of course, is that once you have gotten that out of the way, the remainder of the jaunt will be, well, like a walk in the woods.

On turning up Reservoir Lane, you may notice a yellow blaze posted on the vine-entangled telephone pole by the corner—welcome reassurance in this suburban neighborhood that you are on the right track. Hop the gate in about 200 yards, and beyond the small stream, the trail veers left into the woods. For five minutes, the steady ascent travels by ferns and dogwoods, maples, beeches, and black birch trees. A leveling off ensues, in which the path slips by the northeast side of a lily pond; then it is back to business, going steadily up the rocky track.

In another five minutes, the climb grows even more earnest, flying directly upward. While it is possible to immerse oneself in the grinding rhythm of such labor, try to keep an eye open for wildlife as you gain ground; we have seen frogs, toads, and a pileated woodpecker in the nearby bog, as well as white-tailed deer bounding over the higher reaches. If a breeze should waft by, you may notice an odd, eerie squeaking of maples and oaks rubbing against each other, somewhat like an orchestra's string section tuning up for a concert. And after periods of heavy rainfall, the entire forest becomes a fairy-tale land of colorful mushrooms.

To get from the bottom of the hill to the T intersection where the real loop begins requires 45 minutes of hardy hiking, with nothing that follows exacting quite the same exertion. This lower ridge is ringed with oaks, laurels, and tulip trees, while rocks and boulders are scattered everywhere. Stick to the left on the yellow-blazed route, which passes some towering granite outcroppings and a scree-covered slope, prior to arriving at an unblazed spur to the right. Steer right there, and in three minutes of steep uphill travel, the dirt track connects to another trail. Roll right on this now-rocky stretch, which is marked by blue discs, and remain with it for several minutes until you come to a rust-crusted bulldozer, near the top of the ridge.

Though long abandoned, the bulldozer is a vivid reminder of the threat of "development" that hangs over many a similar woodland. Don't let your feet grow too comfortable on this wide trail, though, for 15 paces beyond Dozer Junction, as the spot is known, is a short spur to the left—directly opposite the right turnoff to the Bald Hills. It should take you no more than ten minutes to navigate the circuitous path to Lambs Hill, a climb of 200 feet, where the grassy ledge, at 1,500 feet of elevation, delivers a fabulous vista of the Hudson River. The peaks of Storm King may bring you closer to the river, but we know of few other viewpoints that showcase its majestic, never-ending length so dramatically. This is the place for a memorable picnic or to sip a solitary brew while savoring the approach of a colorful sunset.

Return to the start of this spur and cross the wide trail (with Dozer Junction lying to the right), picking up the white discs that indicate the way to the twin Bald Hills. In a few uphill strides the chunky track draws you to a sun-struck stone terrace, a peaceful nook blessed with expansive views arcing from the northeast to southeast. A short descent over talus debris leads to a similar ledge, with a bird's-eye position over a quarry pond and a pocket of the Hudson River; the trail creeps from there in a northerly direction toward the Bald Hills. Much of this appealing plateau is decked with knee-high wild grass and fragrant blueberry bushes, while scrub oaks, shagbark hickories, a few tulip trees, and a fistful of cedars round out its rough-cut beauty. The Hudson is a little more visible from atop the next ridge, and the crest beyond yields an equivocal view of an active quarry and industrial site. You may encounter difficulties in locating the blazes along this section of the route, for most are painted on rocks and are easily confused with the many guano splotches deposited by birds. Similarly, don't be lured off track by the numerous animal trails that crisscross the grass up here. Simply remember that the path hews largely to the eastern fringe of the summit as it heads north, pressing onward through an intersection on the approach to the first Bald Hill.

With so many rocky, denuded peaks peppering one ridge, you may wonder how you'll identify the Bald Hills. Relax: The U.S. Geological Survey has rendered that child's play by implanting markers in the middle of their diminutive crowns. Immediately before the first, though, is a grass-covered access road. The white blazes share that wide, flat surface for a few yards, but as the lane loops to the left, the trail breaks right, still hugging the eastern line of the ridge. Both Bald ones top out at 1,500 feet of altitude, though with oak trees encircling the peaks like tonsured heads, the vistas are limited and thus a bit anticlimactic.

The descent that succeeds the second Bald Hill is surprisingly painless. True, you pass from tall, golden grass to hard, rock-impregnated earth, and from immovable boulders to a brief patch of ever-shifting scree. But it is seldom the tooth-grinding test of the lower joints that the march up might have led you to expect. Along the way is a crude hunters' platform some 15 feet off the ground. Shortly after that, the path bends right at a faint T onto the lower ridge, nearing the completion of the circuit. Twenty to twenty-five minutes of ease along this spacious lane should prepare you for the final stretch: a left down the yellow-blazed luge chute you ascended earlier.

▶ NEARBY ACTIVITIES

A historic and interesting attraction in this area is the Van Wyck Homestead on Snook Road, just before US 9 intersects with I-84 in Fishkill. Its displays of artifacts evoke Hudson Valley colonial life, with a special emphasis on the American Revolution. Call (845) 896-9560 for information.

# FITZGERALD FALLS TO LITTLE DAM LAKE APPALACHIAN TRAIL

## ▶ IN BRIEF

Near the start of this exciting trek lies Fitzgerald Falls, a waterfall so dynamic that you may wonder what could possibly follow as an encore. Don't worry: High drama is the norm for a wild stretch of trail that is generously peppered with rocky vistas and rugged gorges, in addition to a bayou boardwalk and romantic lake. Just remember to slip an extra apple into your day pack, because this hike requires plenty of stamina.

## ▶ DESCRIPTION

By most standards, an elevation gain of 650 feet hardly puts one at risk of a nosebleed. But when that feat is accomplished six times in a single outing—accompanied by corresponding losses in altitude—you may begin to wish that Tenzing Norgay had come along to carry your box of Kleenex. This out-and-back trek from Fitzgerald Falls to Little Dam Lake involves a heart-pounding effort in climbing three significant peaks. And

## ▶ DIRECTIONS

Follow the New York State Thruway (I-87) north over the Tappan Zee Bridge to Exit 15A (Sloatsburg) onto SR 17 north. For the shuttle option, drive one car about 8.5 miles north of Sloatsburg, then turn left on Old Orange Turnpike (CR 19). In less than 2 miles, make a right on Mombasha Road. Continue for a half mile to a small parking space on the right, where the white AT blaze is visible on both sides of the road. For trailhead parking, drive the second car back to CR 19 and make a right. After about 2 miles, turn right on SR 210/SR 17A and proceed for 2.5 miles, then swing right onto Old Tuxedo Road (which becomes Pennluna Road). Continue for 1.3 miles, then go right (north) onto Dutch Hollow Road/CR 5 (not Old Dutch Hollow). Drive 2 more miles to a small parking area on the right.

## ℹ KEY AT-A-GLANCE INFORMATION

**LENGTH:** 12.4 miles, 7 miles with shuttle car option

**CONFIGURATION:** Out-and-back

**DIFFICULTY:** Very difficult

**SCENERY:** Vertically zigzagging path takes in cooling falls, hemlock forests, challenging rock scrambles, peaceful lakes, and awesome vistas

**EXPOSURE:** Plenty of shade, except for grassy sanctuary and several bald summits

**TRAFFIC:** Often light, but AT has many faithful fans and thru-hikers

**TRAIL SURFACE:** A hearty cocktail of rocks, dirt, grass, and granite ledges

**HIKING TIME:** 6.5 hours

**SEASON:** Year-round

**ACCESS:** No fee, no bicycles, no horses, no motorized vehicles

**MAPS:** USGS Sloatsburg; Appalachian Trail Map Set #3, Hudson River to Greenwood Lake

**FACILITIES:** None

**SPECIAL COMMENTS:** You and your hiking boots had better be in good shape to accomplish 3 major ascents and descents in each direction.

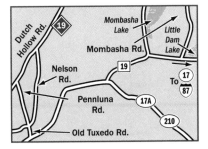

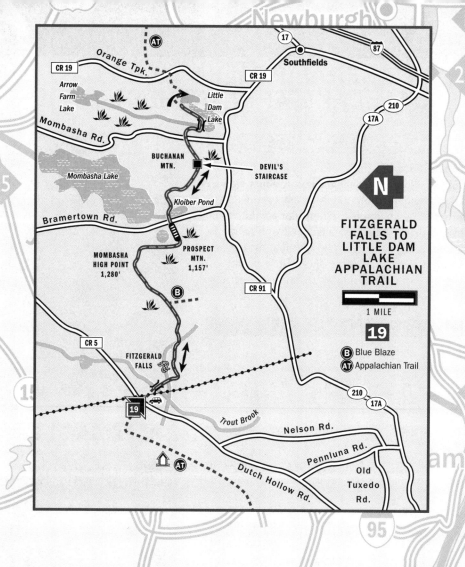

Southfields

CR 19
CR 19
Orange Tpk.
Arrow
Farm
Lake
Mombasha Rd.
Little
Dam
Lake

BUCHANAN
MTN.

DEVIL'S
STAIRCASE

Mombasha Lake

Kloiber Pond

Bramertown Rd.

**N**

# FITZGERALD FALLS TO LITTLE DAM LAKE APPALACHIAN TRAIL

1 MILE

**19**

Ⓑ Blue Blaze
ⒶⓉ Appalachian Trail

MOMBASHA
HIGH POINT
1,280'

PROSPECT
MTN.
1,157'

Ⓑ

CR 91

CR 5

FITZGERALD
FALLS

210

17A

**19**

Trout Brook

Nelson Rd.

Pennluna Rd.

ⒶⓉ

Dutch Hollow Rd.

Old
Tuxedo
Rd.

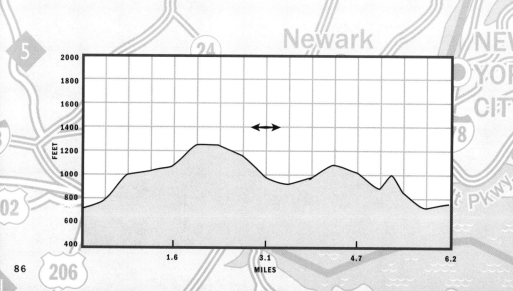

while the vistas from a couple of those birds' nests are the stuff that dream hikes are made of, some of the more terrestrial sights along the way have an even splashier impact.

The most obvious of those is Fitzgerald Falls, near the start of the jaunt. This sensational waterfall sets the tone for a highly scenic stretch of the Appalachian Trail (AT, white blazes), one so visually exciting and physically challenging that there is hardly ever a dull moment. The path initially descends off the east side of the road into a power-line break. On crossing that, it skips over a footbridge and enters a cool, dark hemlock forest. At first, the AT meanders uphill away from the stream, Trout Brook, only to snake back toward it. Do the easy hopscotch across the water, then bear to the left—not straight ahead, as the worn traces suggest. (Don't worry if you miss this turn, though; the blue-blazed spur circles around and rejoins the AT at the base of the falls.) More rock-hopping is required to make your way up the bifurcating Trout Brook, with a fine display of craggy trap rock to the left, before arriving at the foot of Fitzgerald Falls.

The Appalachian Trail goes right by Fitzgerald Falls, one of the most spectacular cascades in the region.

You may wonder on gazing up at this tremendous cascade—with its dramatically high pour-off producing a deafening roar and wafting clouds of mist—where the hike can possibly go from here. The answer, in a word: *up*. The trail scales a series of steps fashioned into the rocky bluff, just to the right of the crashing waterfall. This setting is nearly as thrilling seen from above, where the stream froths with whitewater as it approaches the edge. The AT grows steeper as it launches into the heart of the hemlock forest, its floor scored by lichen- and moss-coated rocks. Breaking up the climb are three fun stream fordings sandwiched around a crossing with a forest road after which the path hits a false summit by a tumbledown wall.

Gradually, the AT drifts out of the hemlock hamlet into a concentration of maples, with a nucleus of old walls running nearby. It may be a bit rocky underfoot, but the hiking is easier for the time being as the ground alternates between a gentle rise and a steady descent. About ten minutes into the latter, you bottom out and start gaining elevation again, with some seasonal arroyos percolating alongside the path. Indeed, the trail itself has come to resemble an ancient streambed—or a massive moraine field. The appearance of mountain laurel signals the advent of another steep climb, this time through a beautiful boulder-filled gorge. The culmination of that effort is a rocky knob, well shrouded in scrub oaks and blueberry bushes, with an AT register attached to a tree. When we last signed in, we read that a previous hiker had seen a black bear on the blue-blazed track to the right. A side trip 150 feet down that yields a great view to the west and south from a granite ledge.

If it is warm weather, you may hear what sounds like the chirruping of yellow-shafted flickers as you continue on the AT. That tuneless melody is actually the mating call of frogs in the vernal pond through the spicebush to the left. For the next few minutes, the path overlaps the rocky plateau, a composition of puddingstone and other conglomerates, as it climbs ever so slightly to the second knob. This granite dome is Mombasha High Point, which sits at an elevation of 1,280 feet—with more than half of those above the trailhead. Take a breather and enjoy the 360-degree panorama, with Mombasha Lake glimmering below to the east.

The descent that ensues (there's *always* a descent after such a viewpoint, isn't there?) begins rather tentatively, with a scramble over rocks by the edge of the ridge, but you gain momentum on exiting the boulder field and grove of pitch pines. In a dozen minutes, the path flattens out at the level of the lake and cruises straight through a four-way intersection. Ignore the unblazed trace to the left after the crossing, staying with the well blazed AT as it slides off a stone shelf and continues to lose elevation, passing meanwhile through a second four-way junction. You are now approaching an attractive swamp, with hefty boulders and thick clusters of laurel all around. A fun succession of wooden planks serves as an introduction to a lily pond. On departing this area of white birch, beech, maple, oak, and sheep laurel, a second, longer set of planks carries you to an open field of low-lying scrub. Described by some as a butterfly preserve, this sun-exposed expanse is no less attractive to a rich array of birds (come to think of it, birds *do* eat butterflies, don't they?), so you may want to keep your field specs handy.

The AT crosses the road here, hopping over a short bridge back into the forest. After fording a seasonal stream via a handful of stepping-stones, it is back into a climbing mode, this time steeply up the rocky, fern-flavored hill. In three minutes of chest-thumping effort, the slant grows less severe, until the fickle path starts to lose altitude, spinning into a laurel and hemlock hollow clenched within the jagged teeth of a watery ravine. To describe this primeval landscape of fractured and fissured granite as "dramatic" or "impressive" would be to damn it with faint praise. There will be plenty of time to think of your own superlatives as you pick your way, rock by rock, to the top of the bluff. Once that fun scramble is over, the ground levels off, as the AT hugs the edge of the ravine and overlooks the abyss. This idyllic setting, part of Buchanan Mountain, persists for several hundred yards, ultimately reaching a shelf at the south end of the peak with vistas extending far to the south and east. As beautiful as this spot is, the knoll off the path behind you is no less enchanting and provides the possibility of a private place in which to read, sketch, or woo your sweetheart, out of sight of other hikers.

Directly after that, another descent commences, steadily accelerating until you trough by a couple of seasonal streams. Look for jack-in-the-pulpits as you jump over those, and the two arroyos that follow during the next rocky ascent. If you took pleasure in the previous ravine romp, you'll love this one—it packs an exhilarating, ankle-challenging scramble up the Devil's Staircase, a rugged slope of rubble. This is a different chunk of the same Buchanan Mountain you were on a short time earlier, with a splendid view of Little Dam Lake from the crest. When you have regained your stamina and wearied of this wonderful locale, resume walking to the east, staying with the path on its downward trajectory. In seven minutes and a loss of 260 feet, the AT meets a road, slips over the blacktop, and proceeds into the woods.

The moss-sided track meanders from east to southeast, mildly descending, in five minutes, to a narrow footbridge. The swamp to the left is a haven for waterfowl, while Little Dam Lake to your right is favored by shutterbugs. No wonder, given the appealing look of the rock-lined lakeshore, attractively fringed with mountain laurel, hemlock, and scrub oak. The AT hooks to the left, through a clutch of laurel. For a moment the water is hidden, until the vegetation parts and you gain a view across the lake of the rising rock face on the nearby island. This is the turnaround point of the trek, although obviously you should feel free to explore the vicinity before doing so.

It will likely require 10 to 15 minutes of stiff climbing from the road to reach Buchanan's second crest, and an additional 15 minutes to hit its first peak. Remember as you scramble down their far sides, where the afternoon sun warms the rocks, to inspect the hidden nooks for rattlesnakes prior to placing your feet or hands. Some out-and-back linear hikes can seem tedious on the back half as you pass through familiar terrain. Not here, not with so stark a reversal of ascents and descents, and the efforts required to handle them. Even the sloping hemlock forest that you amble through on your approach to the top of Fitzgerald Falls assumes a special, almost mystical aura when seen in the waning light of day.

## ▶ NEARBY ACTIVITIES

At the Monroe Museum Village of Smith's Clove, visitors are submerged into the nineteenth century. Costumed interpreters demonstrate crafts, and exhibits include a natural history museum, schoolhouse, drugstore, and lots of Americana. Visit www.museumvillage.org or call (845) 782-8247 for details.

# GREAT KILLS CROOKE'S POINT LABYRINTH

## IN BRIEF

Calling all sun worshippers! You don't need to bake yourself on the beach, not while the fun, easy trails of this expansive park are so gloriously sun-struck. The Crooke's Point circuit lobs you from one shore area to another, with the agreeable mix of vegetation (including black cherry, bayberry, and yucca) lending a labyrinth-like feel to the jaunt. A sensational range of birds twitter and cluck from within that overgrowth, too, adding to the appeal of a fun, easy walk.

## DESCRIPTION

Great Kills Park, a unit of Gateway National Recreation Area, is not the place to go if you have a hankering to mosey meditatively deep in the wilds, with no sound to hector your ears but the buzzing of bugs and chirping of birds. Even if the weather is only halfway decent, people flock to Great Kills like pigeons to breadcrumbs. They come to jog, they come to swim, they come to roller-skate on the park's long paved road. You've got the sportsmen after saltwater fish, boaters out for pleasure cruises, model airplane hobbyists, baseball and softball players, soccer teams, kite-flyers, and seniors shuffling along the harbor-side promenade.

## DIRECTIONS

*By car:* Follow I-278 over the Verrazano Narrows Bridge where it becomes the Staten Island Expressway. Take the Hylan Boulevard Exit and proceed south for 4.7 miles to the park entrance on the left. Drive straight past the ranger station on the right to the beach center parking on the left, across from the marina.

*By public transportation:* From the Staten Island Ferry Terminal in St. George, take bus S78; or from Brooklyn, 95th Street and 4th Avenue, take bus S79 to the park entrance. The trailhead is about 1.5 miles ahead.

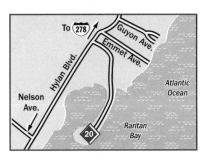

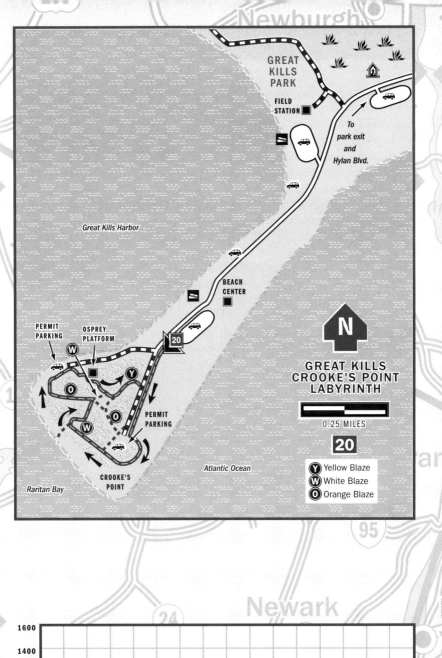

GREAT KILLS PARK

GREAT KILLS
FIELD STATION

Great Kills Harbor

To
park exit
and
Hylan Blvd.

BEACH
CENTER

PERMIT
PARKING

OSPREY
PLATFORM

**N**

GREAT KILLS
CROOKE'S POINT
LABYRINTH

0.25 MILES

**20**

W Permit
Parking

Y Yellow Blaze
W White Blaze
O Orange Blaze

PERMIT
PARKING

CROOKE'S
POINT

Atlantic Ocean

Raritan Bay

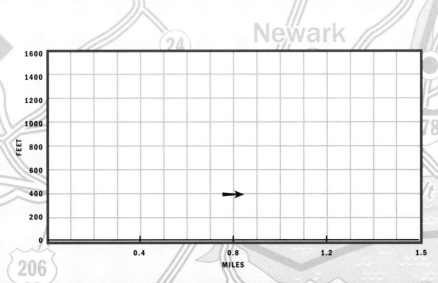

Great Kills also has three easy, level hiking trails, and while you are hardly likely to find yourself alone on any of them, they do draw fewer feet than most of the rest of Staten Island's most popular park.

Amateur ornithologists in particular will delight in the wonderful variety of birds that either nest or stop over here. The Blue Dot Trail, an out-and-back hike that parallels Hylan Boulevard behind a curtain of trees, is an especially active birding area. You can pick up its trailhead just west of the entrance parking lot. A new interpretive trail that winds by a freshwater pond and a wetland marsh actually follows an *old* route that was rediscovered in 2002 after park staff subdued a brushfire. This short loop begins behind the park police and ranger office, across the road from parking area A. Then there is Crooke's Point Labyrinth Trail, a nucleus of three paths that converge at the center of a scrub-covered spur of land that juts out into Raritan Bay. Though this small network resembles a labyrinth, the only way you are apt to get lost is if you have been baking in the sun too long.

The start of the Crooke's Point hike is in parking area G. Facing Nickol's Marina to the west, turn left and walk along the port side of the dirt-and-gravel access road. In six or seven minutes, the mouth of a yellow-blazed path appears to the right, well collared by coastal scrub. Stay with the park road, and when you arrive at the spacious fishermen's parking lot in a few dozen feet, swing left on the sandy spur to the beach. As you make your way toward the shore, check out the two fields that flank you for cowbirds, brown thrashers, and other birds nestling among the bayberry, yucca, and sumac. No bathing is allowed in this area of the beach, but with the aid of binoculars, you may be able to see Sandy Hook, to the southeast, on a clear day. Roll to the right when you reach the open shoreline, and in 40 yards cut back to the right toward the parking area. Proceed directly across the lot to the brown post marked with a white blaze at its top, and enter the trail behind it.

Pitch pines, black birch, black cherry, and flowering fruit trees are tightly interwoven along this shady corridor, contributing a bit of shade and a great deal of natural beauty to the setting. The fork to the left that occurs in a few minutes leads to the southwestern edge of Great Kills, with nothing but water beyond. Farther along the White Trail, you may have to do the limbo under a few low-hanging branches, before reaching a T. Veer left, now following orange blazes, and after three or four minutes of striding through a tangle of chokeberry, poison ivy, white birch saplings, and— once in awhile—yucca, you emerge at the west end of the peninsula. With a marina directly opposite across the bay, head down the sandy trail toward the water, angling right at the end of the parallel fences that protect the dune grass. Keep to the right, maneuvering through the small parking lot, and turn right again when you come to the far end of the yellow-blazed route you saw earlier.

Like the other two trails, there is a secluded, intimate feel to this track, due in large measure to the thriving, jungle-like nature of an undergrowth that constantly seems to be offering thorny embraces to passing hikers. A couple of minutes after it drifts under an osprey nesting platform, the path hits an intersection. Stay to the left with the yellow blazes, and in two more minutes, the trail returns you to the dirt-and-gravel access road. Go left there and retrace your steps back to parking area G.

If you are here between March 10th and August 1st, you may find the Yellow Trail barricaded to protect the osprey that nest on the platform visible just above the tree line. Should that be the case, after inspecting the nest with field specs or a spotting scope, backtrack along the shore to the orange-blazed route, and return to the junction where you left the white markings. Bear left there, now with orange and white blazes, and in 40 feet, as the orange blazes break off to the right, remain straight with the white markings. The yellow-blazed spur merges from the left in another 200 feet (feel free to venture up that as far as the barrier fence for a different angle on the osprey nest). Stick with Yellow all the way back to the access road, where you dart left and return to the trailhead.

## ▶ NEARBY ACTIVITIES

While you are waiting for the ferry in St. George to return to Manhattan, enjoy the vintage Staten Island Ferry Collection. Displays include scale models of historical ferries, period photos, nautical equipment, and drawings.

The Staten Island Institute of Arts and Sciences, also in St. George, documents Staten Island and its inhabitants as far back as the early eighteenth century through art, history, and a library. For details on both museums, call (718) 727-1135.

# GREAT SWAMP WILDERNESS TRAIL

## KEY AT-A-GLANCE INFORMATION

**LENGTH:** 3.8 miles

**CONFIGURATION:** Out-and-back over 2 loops

**DIFFICULTY:** Very easy

**SCENERY:** Level trail skirts open marshland, quiet canals, and shallow ponds

**EXPOSURE:** Canopy cover throughout

**TRAFFIC:** Usually fairly light

**TRAIL SURFACE:** Dirt and roots with a few grassy stretches

**HIKING TIME:** 1.75 hours

**SEASON:** Year-round during daylight hours

**ACCESS:** No fee, foot travel only, no pets on trails

**MAPS:** At refuge headquarters

**FACILITIES:** Rest rooms and water at refuge headquarters and Wildlife Observation Center

**SPECIAL COMMENTS:** The refuge headquarters is a good orientation point, with animal displays and checklists on fauna and flora.

## IN BRIEF

*Walk in a wilderness of swamps and bogs,*
*Under the beech trees or over moss logs.*
  *Admire the lily,*
  *On ground that's not hilly,*
*While looking for otters, turtles, and frogs.*

## DESCRIPTION

History records that, in 1708, what is now the Great Swamp and much of the land around it was purchased from the Delaware Indians for four cutlasses, a like number of pistols, 15 cauldrons, 30 pounds sterling, and a keg of rum. As you set off into the swamp and commence with involuntarily donating your blood to the swarms of mosquitoes that thrive in this muggy marsh, you may feel the Indians got the best of the deal.

## DIRECTIONS

*By car:* Follow I-95/I-80 west across the George Washington Bridge to Exit 41 and the junction with I-287. Proceed south on I-287 to Exit 30A, and south from there on North Maple Avenue. Bear left when it forks onto South Maple Avenue, continue past Lord Stirling Park, then turn left on Lord Stirling Road (which becomes White Bridge Road). Go left at Pleasant Plains Road. The refuge headquarters entrance is 0.4 miles ahead on the right.

To drive from the headquarters to the trailhead, backtrack to White Bridge Road, where you turn left. Continue for 1.1 miles, then hang a left on New Vernon Road. The trailhead parking is 2 miles farther on the right side.

*By public transportation:* From the New York Port Authority, take the New Jersey Transit train, Morris & Essex lines (Gladstone Branch), to Basking Ridge Station. From there, it is approximately 5.5 miles by taxi to the trailhead.

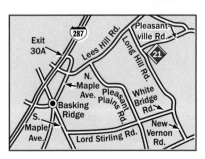

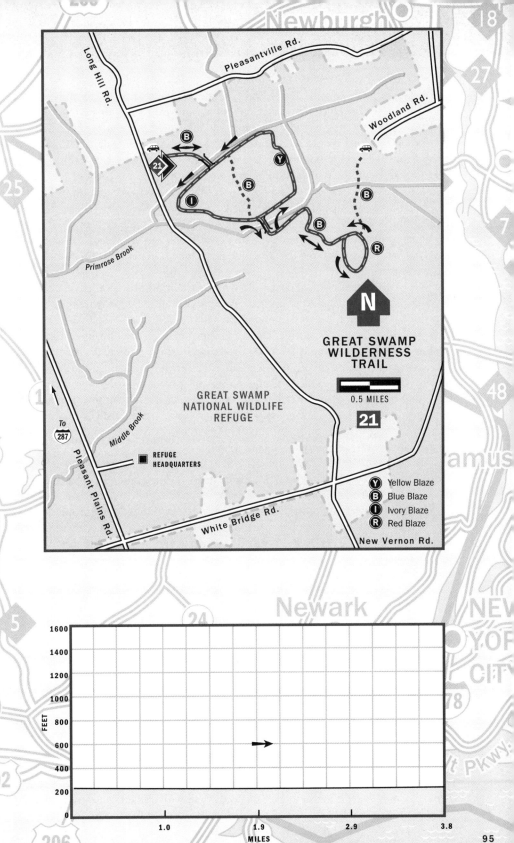

GREAT SWAMP
WILDERNESS
TRAIL

0.5 MILES

GREAT SWAMP
NATIONAL WILDLIFE
REFUGE

REFUGE
HEADQUARTERS

Y Yellow Blaze
B Blue Blaze
I Ivory Blaze
R Red Blaze

Come on, rub in some DEET and give the Great Swamp a chance: There is a subtle beauty to this place that grows on you as you stroll along its beech- and oak-lined trails. Peer intently beyond the ferns, cattails, and many mushrooms, and you may spot a frolicking river otter, red fox, coyote, or mink. The endangered salamander and threatened blue bog turtle also make their homes here, and 222 species of birds wing through the refuge at different times of the year.

A proposal in 1959 to build a jetport on this land spurred a grassroots effort to save the swamp, which brought about the purchase of 3,000 acres. That parcel was donated to the U.S. Department of the Interior, which has since increased the size of the refuge to just under 7,500 acres, with roughly half of that designated as wilderness. The level, easy trail we describe is one of four options that run through the wilderness area.

Take a good gander at the map posted at the trailhead by the car park. This double loop of 3.8 miles begins and returns on the Blue Trail (BT, blue blazes), switching off it three times along the way to investigate short side circuits. You'll be in a shady forest environment at the outset, among cedars, maples, and the more dominant beeches and oaks, the trunks of many coated with moss. Within ten minutes, the rather rooty path crosses two canals, and after the second sluice, bear to the right on the Ivory Trail (IT, white blazes). The forest opens up a tad on this 0.8-mile leg, and it is tempting to sit off to the side on a good-sized rock and wait for deer to come grazing through the knee-high grass. A small pond, farther along the IT, also offers the chance of seeing wildlife, and even the diminutive bog pots that pepper the sides of the path are active turtle and salamander habitats.

As the IT ends, the BT continues to the right and swerves over a wooden bridge, entering an area of white birches and, from spring through summer, a kaleidoscope of colorful wildflowers. If most of the blossoms are gone when you mosey through, console yourself with the multitude of mushrooms clinging to many of the downed logs. Beware of poison ivy, though, which grows abundantly in this sanctuary. Sputtering along, the BT leads by an appealingly wild, overgrown thicket that is reminiscent in some ways of a Florida swamp, lacking only cypress trees and alligators to complete the subtropical illusion.

In a few strides, you're out of Florida and back into a grassy grove of beech trees, ferns billowing by the ground, and a canal of murky water stewing silently to the left. The right fork by a fairly hefty beech marks the start of the red loop (RT, red blazes), which rejoins the BT in half a mile. As you move along that spur, you'll see cat briar, cattails, and maybe even a bobcat (but only if your imagination is lively). Otters near a phragmite marsh are a more likely sighting, if you pad the path with soft steps. The RT expires at a massive oak, where you turn left, back with the blue blazes. (The other direction takes you to the Woodland Road parking area.)

Within five minutes, you will see the earlier turnoff onto the RT, and shortly after that, recross the wooden bridge. Instead of turning left, though, which would bring you back toward the IT, veer right onto the Yellow Trail (YT, yellow blazes). This 0.9-mile segment meanders by a boggy patch, then straightens out and for perhaps 120 yards passes through a bower of oaks, aligned as if they had been planted to shade a carriage lane. A dense thicket succeeds that, with a small, grass-rimmed pond

60 feet to the right of the path. Silently follow the slight trace to the water's edge and you may spy wood ducks or other birds bobbing about the inky surface.

As the YT bends to the left, you'll encounter a more extended stretch of swampland, with bog pots and mossy roots serving as landmines on the trail. If you opted to wear boots instead of sneakers, this is where that decision pays off, as the ground can be very moist (downright muddy in spring). Keep right at the ensuing fork, cross through the narrow canal and over the bog pots, and proceed past the ivory spur. The trailhead is 0.5 miles ahead.

## ▶ NEARBY ACTIVITIES

The refuge is a great resource; it hosts an Outdoor Education Center off Southern Boulevard in Chatham as well as an Environmental Center on Lord Stirling Road. They introduce visitors to the area's geology and offer classes and guided tours. The Raptor Trust on White Bridge Road, a fascinating rehabilitation facility for birds of prey and other wild avians, is well worth a visit. Call the Refuge Headquarters for information at (973) 425-1222, or the Rehab Center at (908) 647-2353.

The Museum of Early Trades and Crafts in Madison is housed in a building listed on the National Register of Historic Places. Its many exhibits focus on New Jersey's rural past and the tools used by eighteenth- and nineteenth-century farmers and craftsmen. Call (973) 377-2982 for details.

# HARRIMAN HIGHLANDS TRAIL

## KEY AT-A-GLANCE INFORMATION

**LENGTH:** 11 miles

**CONFIGURATION:** Short-stemmed balloon

**DIFFICULTY:** Difficult

**SCENERY:** Fascinating mix of polished rock tables, blueberry and laurel patches, mysterious mines, marshlands, bald glacial ridges offering panoramic views, dense valley forests and sparse mountain vegetation

**EXPOSURE:** Shady in the valleys, open on ridges and grasslands

**TRAFFIC:** The higher you climb, the lonelier it gets, but for some reason there is always a lost hiker around Times Square.

**TRAIL SURFACE:** Very rocky and uneven: watch your footing!

**HIKING TIME:** 5.5 hours

**SEASON:** Year-round, 8 a.m.–dusk, weather permitting; possible summer closures due to fire danger

**ACCESS:** No fee, except for parking in major-use areas

**MAPS:** USGS Popolopen Lake; New York–New Jersey Trail Conference Harriman–Bear Mountain Trails

**FACILITIES:** No water or rest rooms on trail

**SPECIAL COMMENTS:** Like adjacent Bear Mountain State Park, Harriman is best explored with a detailed map (buy one at the park office) to reduce the likelihood of getting lost.

## IN BRIEF

How hardy are you? The answer to that question will determine how far you penetrate into this fabulous wilderness wonderland of rocks, meadows, and far-reaching vistas. Granite domes exuding a flavor of the far west are just one highlight. Others involve glacial gorges, mining ruins, a couple of laurel-fringed ponds, and beauty that never stops.

## DESCRIPTION

You don't have to be an über-hiker to enjoy hoofing it around the woods of Bear Mountain and Harriman state parks. Of the miles of trails that run seamlessly through their backcountry, there is a handful that are flat and relatively easy. We're not going to talk about those, though, because, frankly, that's not why we go there. These are parks where serious hikers and outdoors enthusiasts can take blister-busting treks to granite aeries, tromp from one end of a forest to another without

## DIRECTIONS

*By car:* Follow the New York State Thruway (I-87) north over the Tappan Zee Bridge to Exit 15A. Heading north on SR 17, drive about 9.5 miles through Sloatsburg and Tuxedo and ascend onto the entrance ramp for SR 17A/CR 210 on the left. Turn right at the stop sign in 0.1 mile onto CR 210. Follow it eastward for about 3.4 miles. A few parking spots are available on the left side of the road.

*By public transportation:* There is no efficient connection, but from the New York Port Authority terminal, New Jersey transit trains of the Port Jervis Line and ShortLine buses depart for Tuxedo. From there, you can pick up a taxi to cover the 6 miles to the trailhead on CR 106.

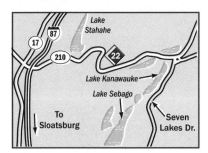

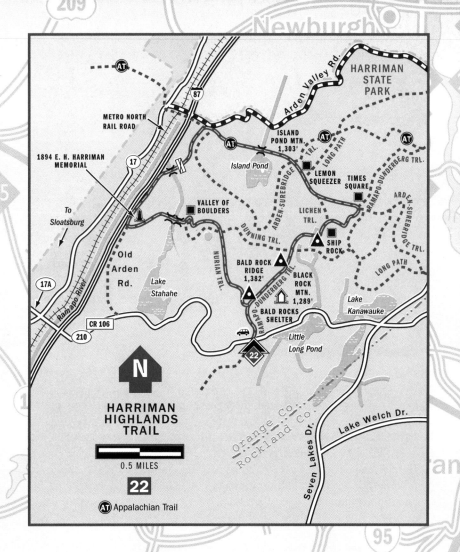

METRO NORTH
RAIL ROAD

1894 E. H. HARRIMAN
MEMORIAL

To
Sloatsburg

Old
Arden
Rd.

17A

CR 106

210

Lake
Stahahe

ISLAND
POND MTN.
1,303'

Island Pond

VALLEY OF
BOULDERS

NURIAN TRL.

DUNNING TRL.

LEMON
SQUEEZER

TIMES
SQUARE

LICHEN
TRL.

SHIP
ROCK

BALD ROCK
RIDGE
1,382'

BLACK
ROCK
MTN.
1,289'

BALD ROCKS
SHELTER

22

Little
Long Pond

Lake
Kanawauke

LONG PATH

ARDEN-SUREBRIDGE TRL.

RAMAPO-DUNDERBERG TRL.

Arden Valley Rd.

HARRIMAN
STATE
PARK

Orange Co.
Rockland Co.

Seven Lakes Dr.

Lake Welch Dr.

## N

## HARRIMAN
## HIGHLANDS
## TRAIL

0.5 MILES

**22**

(AT) Appalachian Trail

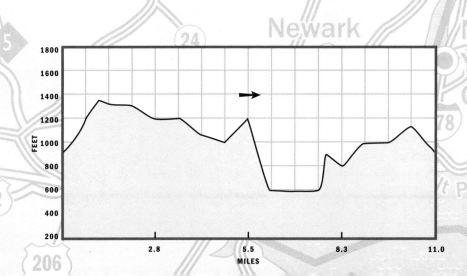

Glacial erratics scattered over granite domes endow Harriman State Park with a flavor of the high Sierras.

meeting another soul, and thread through serrated gorges that both humble and inspire at the same time.

The Harriman half of this dynamic duo of parks owes its name—and its existence—to E. W. Harriman, erstwhile president of the Union Pacific Railroad. He spearheaded the effort to preserve this area of the Empire State from developers who, among their other planned "improvements," wanted to relocate Sing Sing Prison to neighboring Bear Mountain. E. W. donated both money and land toward the creation of Bear Mountain and Harriman, which were jointly established in 1914 and today total more than 52,000 acres.

Look for the red-dot-on-white blazes of the Ramapo-Dunderberg Trail (RD) by the lower of the two small parking slots, and plan to stick with this for the first 2.5 miles of the 11-mile jaunt. For 50 yards, the RD tapers downhill near the road before swerving up and away to the left along a well-worn, rocky trace. In five minutes, you'll be among boulders and laurels, but even then the climb is just beginning. Ten more minutes of hearty exertion sends you through blueberry bushes, beech trees, maples, oaks, and many, many lichen-stained rocks, right to the top of the craggy ridge.

Well, almost. The final assault to the crest requires a bit of hand-over-hand clambering to surmount a few good-sized slabs of stone. That bit of fun concluded, you'll be rewarded with spectacular views from an unspoiled, grass-plumed plateau. Rest a moment in this rarefied atmosphere among the birch saplings and oaks before you proceed in a northerly direction along the RD. For several hundred yards, the path hops from one polished crest to the next, shifting first to the northwest, then northeast, succeeded by a hard move to the east. If there were snow-capped mountains beyond these rugged domes, one might mistake this perch for a granite throne high in the Sierra Nevadas. Unlike at the latter, though, bears breaking into cars is unheard of in this park.

A half-hour of steady walking delivers you to Bald Rock Ridge, the highest point in Harriman at an elevation of 1,382 feet, with a fine vista to the northeast of Black Rock Mountain. Persevere along the RD as it snakes by the left side of a backpacker shelter built in 1933, enduring evidence of the CCC's masonry skills. Also enduring are the scars of a wildfire, with numerous snags dotting the immediate surroundings. In a few minutes, you'll pass first the Dunning Trail and then, after several more dome-tops, the Lichen Trail. Perhaps 200 yards beyond the latter is a massive boulder, Ship Rock, that sails 20 feet off the ground. Such birds as yellow-shafted flickers, slate-colored juncos, and eastern bluebirds are attracted here by nearby pools of water.

The fire-scarred snags finally recede as the path skews downward to the left off the plateau, cutting through a cleft in a ridge. And before you know it, you're at Times Square, a major trail intersection where you will find boulders, laurels, and hemlocks rather than neon lights and yellow cabs. Before switching from the RD to the Arden-Surebridge (ASB, red-triangle-on-white blazes) be sure to double-check your bearings; we have encountered more perplexed people at this tricky crossing than anywhere else in the park. Take the immediate left, which is shared for quite a spell by the Long Path (green blazes, not blue, as some maps mistakenly indicate). Between this point and the other end of the Lichen Trail, you'll be zigzagging from the base of one rocky knob to another, keeping to the shade just off the ridgetop. Remain on the ASB all the way to the Lemon Squeezer, a jagged, clenched fist of a ravine where boulders perched precariously upon its rim, 40 feet above, seem ripe for rolling downward.

On sidling through the Squeezer and edging toward the left, the long white blazes of the Appalachian Trail (AT) emerge from the right. (If you are brimming with energy, consider a scrambling side trip in that direction to the top of the granite gulch to see the ruins of E. W. Harriman's summer cottage.) As the ASB veers away to the left, continue straight (or west), staying with the AT. That's Island Pond, a glacial kettle-hole, visible to the left as you descend from a grassy hillock; be patient, as the path is approaching the water in its own sweet way. Stroll north on hitting the carriage road, only to turn left in 40 yards or so, in the direction of the pond. The track rubs up against the pond's northern end, then ascends a grassy, rock-pocked ridge, yielding yet another view of the water.

This very pretty, pastoral area has recovered well from its time as a beehive of mining activity during the mid-to-late 1800s. Relics of that era remain in the vicinity, including a rusty water pump near a stone conduit and several slag heaps. That conduit, incidentally, which you cross via a short bridge, is part of an uncompleted spill-way designed and begun by the CCC in 1934; the rusty, steel-mesh cylinder on the ground just before it was reportedly used to separate varying sizes of gravel nuggets. From here, the AT crosses a gravel roadbed, darts briefly between some hemlocks, then meets another carriage lane, where it jumps left. In perhaps 90 yards, the AT leaves the level lane, heading right into a higher, rockier landscape. From atop that ridge, it's downhill all the way, over a lush, green, heavily tilted meadow, until you bottom out at the dirt-and-gravel Old Arden Valley Road.

Hang a left on the lane, which is no longer open to vehicular traffic, and remain with it for just over a mile to the memorial marker on the left shoulder. Its inscription reads, "This road was built in 1894 by E. H. Harriman to show the advantages of level roads in hilly countries," an ironic statement even then, coming from a rail-road magnate. (E. H. Harriman was likely E. W. Harriman's father.) Just 75 yards beyond that, on the same side of the road, is the turnoff, partly hidden by a rocky pour-off. Hew to the white blazes of the Nurian Trail (NT) back up the hill—the steep climb is not as bad as it first appears.

Having ascended two ridges, the path creeps into a hemlock-shaded gully, where more mining pits and concrete foundations are tucked among the many chunks of granite rising out of the ground. Go ahead and explore some of the old carriage lanes that loop labyrinth-like through the woods. In the end, though, keep to the left on the first one you encounter, passing a mess of cut logs piled over an old brick foundation, and in a couple hundred yards scoot to the right, off the lane, as the NT now heads east. High water in 2003 led to the installation of two log bridges that now eliminate the need to rock-hop over the twin streams in this grassy gully. The trace then leads via a few switchbacks to the top of the next ridge. You now overlook the Valley of Boulders, an eerie-yet-fabulous, talus-strewn depression, with cyclopean boulders and large oak trunks scattered around its basin.

Easy as this chaotic scene is on the eyes, it is a stress test for the ankles, out-doing the Lemon Squeezer as you work your way through it and up yet one more ridge. The Dunning Trail starts there (yellow blazes), and if you like, you may go right on that to a small, circular lily pond, rejoining the NT shortly after. Otherwise, remain on Nurian all the way back to where it meets the RD, at the crown of the first dome you conquered, five hours earlier. Your approach to this fork will be heralded by the NT swinging left at the base of the sizable monolith, up a few crude stone steps by a jumble of logs. This stretch calls for some dexterous scrambling before the white blazes end at a scrub oak and a junction with the RD. To return to the parking area, jog right 15 feet prior to that tree and stick with the RD as the path begins its descent.

## ▶ NEARBY ACTIVITIES

Haven't you had enough yet? After this nutcracker of a hike, you've earned a cold one. Try kicking back at Ramapo Valley Brewery, 122 Orange Avenue, Suffern, a restaurant that brews its own suds.

# HARTSHORNE WOODS GRANDEST TOUR

The rolling terrain of this densely forested county park provides a pretty fair workout over a modest amount of miles. Much of the land is covered by mountain laurel, which breaks into blankets of pink blossoms in early June. For far-reaching views of the Navesink River, consider visiting in late autumn through early spring, when the broad mix of hardwood trees is bare of leaves.

## ▶ DESCRIPTION

Take a stroll any day of the week along the 16 miles of trails in Hartshorne Woods, and you are likely to have company. Bikers, hikers, and even equestrians visit this 736-acre park with a regularity that a Metamucil consumer could only envy. As a well-kept secret, Hartshorne Woods ranks well below the secure, undisclosed locations to which some political big shots have been known to retreat. But then, a romp in this Monmouth County property is a lot more fun than bouncing off the walls of a concrete bunker.

If, on the other hand, bunker-hunkering is what makes you tick, Hartshorne has its share of such shelters, too. Its Rocky Point section was once a key piece in the Atlantic Coast Defense System,

## ▶ DIRECTIONS

*By car:* Follow I-95 across the George Washington Bridge into New Jersey and continue south, switching to the Garden State Parkway south at Exit 11. Leave the Parkway at Exit 117 for SR 36 east, and in roughly 11 miles, turn right onto Navesink Avenue. Proceed for half a mile to the trailhead parking on the left.

*By public transportation:* From Penn Station, the North Jersey Coast train stops at Middletown Station. Hop on New Jersey Transit bus 834 there, and ride it to Navesink Avenue.

## ⓘ KEY AT-A-GLANCE INFORMATION

**LENGTH:** 6 miles

**CONFIGURATION:** Double loop

**DIFFICULTY:** Easy/moderate

**SCENERY:** Rolling Monmouth hills covered by mixed forest, offering scenic glimpses of Navesink River

**EXPOSURE:** Almost completely sheltered

**TRAFFIC:** Heaviest on weekends, but plenty of visitors come to exercise midweek

**TRAIL SURFACE:** Mostly rock-filled dirt

**HIKING TIME:** 2.5 hours

**SEASON:** Year-round, 8 a.m.–dusk

**ACCESS:** No fee, pets must be leashed

**MAPS:** At trailhead kiosk; www.monmouthcountyparks.com

**FACILITIES:** Portable toilets at the trailhead, but no water

**SPECIAL COMMENTS:** Hartshorne means horn of the hart, or stag, and if you are lucky, you'll encounter not just an antler, but an entire deer.

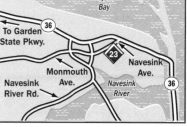

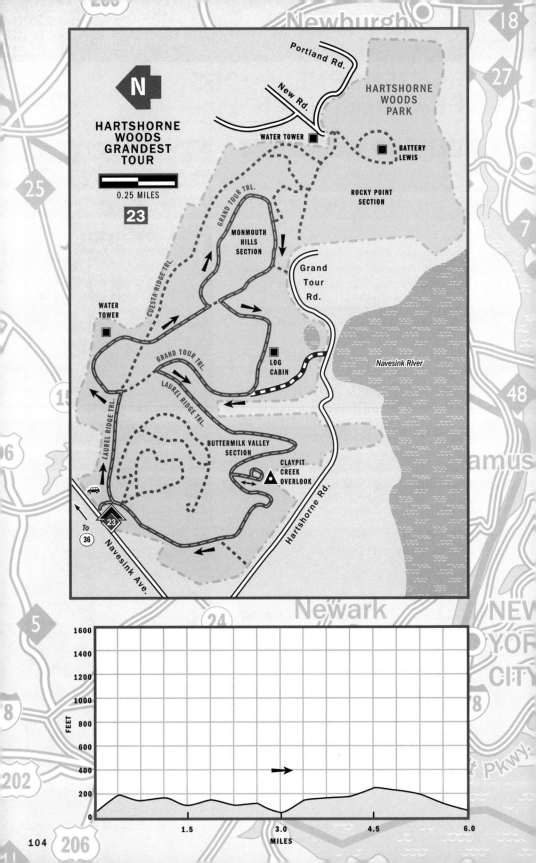

# HARTSHORNE WOODS GRANDEST TOUR

**N**

0.25 MILES

**23**

Portland Rd.

New Rd.

HARTSHORNE WOODS PARK

WATER TOWER

BATTERY LEWIS

ROCKY POINT SECTION

GRAND TOUR TRL.

MONMOUTH HILLS SECTION

CUESTA RIDGE TRL.

WATER TOWER

Grand Tour Rd.

GRAND TOUR TRL.

LAUREL RIDGE TRL.

LAUREL RIDGE TRL.

LOG CABIN

Navesink River

BUTTERMILK VALLEY SECTION

CLAYPIT CREEK OVERLOOK

Hartshorne Rd.

To 36

23

Navesink Ave.

| | | | | | | |
|---|---|---|---|---|---|---|
| 1600 | | | | | | |
| 1400 | | | | | | |
| 1200 | | | | | | |
| 1000 | | | | | | |
| 800 | | | | | | |
| 600 | | | | | | |
| 400 | | | | | | |
| 200 | | | | | | |
| 0 | | 1.5 | | 3.0 | 4.5 | 6.0 |

**FEET**

**MILES**

and paved trails there circle Battery Lewis, where artillery guns protected the Jersey Highlands and New York City during World War II. The other two sections of the preserve are more nature-oriented, with dirt and pebbly pathways flowing from swampy swales to oak- and laurel-laced heights, with occasional views of the Navesink River tossed in for good measure. Hartshorne, incidentally, is named for Richard Hartshorne, who, after spying this land from on board a ship in 1670, went on to purchase it from the local Indians. Some of his descendants still reside in the area.

This double loop encompasses the Monmouth Hills and Buttermilk Valley parts of the park. The most challenging aspect of the fairly easy, up-and-down tour is keeping to the correct trail, as blazes only appear at intersections—sometimes not even then—and the park map is unreliable. From the Buttermilk Valley trailhead on Navesink Avenue, go to the kiosk and take the Laurel Ridge Trail (LRT) to the immediate left. For five minutes, this wide gravel walkway slowly ascends through oaks and laurels before cresting and starting downward again. On bottoming out, lope left onto the Grand Tour Trail (GTT black diamond blazes). The moss-sided track persists down the slope for a bit, then shifts toward the east-southeast, gradually gaining ground.

The climb grinds on over the course of five to ten minutes, carrying you through a four-way intersection with a dirt road. The path crosses another old road as it reaches a ridge and beelines toward a water tower, and then spurts downhill through one more junction. After the rutted, rock-filled trail swoops to the left, swing left at the Y. You should now find yourself in a low bowl, one in which tulip trees, dogwoods, maples, and holly grow branch to branch with oaks and laurels. Bear right (or straight) at the succeeding fork, which delivers you to the opposite side of this depression, here hemmed in by thorny cat briar.

The Grand Tour veers to the right at the next full intersection, passing over hard, chunky ground and a small arroyo. When we last padded through, we spotted an inner tube clinging like an odd parasite to the cat briar, a reflection both of a mountain biker's bad luck and even worse trailside etiquette. On drifting around a bend into an open area, steer left at the fork and move toward the oak-covered ridge. Naturally, a descent follows, passing by a briar-choked marsh, then it is back uphill once more, with a glimpse of the Navesink possible off to your port side (left) through the trees. Shortly after that, also left of the path, is a log cabin, a group-rental facility, and just beyond you'll hit a T, with the hike hopping to the right.

Ten minutes of walking through a concentration of mountain laurels brings you to yet another fork. The right stem leads back to the trailhead; so unless you are feeling tired, head left into the Buttermilk Valley section of Hartshorne. This is another stretch of the LRT, though its namesake shrubs slowly give way to holly, oak, and birch as you climb the ridge. The Navesink is again visible from the crest, and then—too soon—it's back down the hill. The Claypit Creek Overlook spur, tucked among trees to the left, succeeds the next rise. The clay pit itself is hard to spot, but you will be rewarded nonetheless with even better vistas of the Navesink as well as Oceanic Bridge.

From that seven-minute side trip, Laurel Ridge begins a steep slide downward over a few log-supported erosion-control steps. A short spell of level terrain ensues, and then the final 15 minutes of the hike flows by a residential neighborhood—with all the sights and sounds that entails.

This Canada Goose has much to brood about in its secluded nest in Hartshorne Woods.

## ▶ NEARBY ACTIVITIES

Military history buffs should save some of their energy for a visit to Rocky Point, the southeastern section of the park. Its Battery Loop is a paved, 1.3-mile walk that leads to Battery Lewis, the largest of three still-standing World War II–era coastal defense facilities.

Otherwise: Time now to go get some seafood! Cruise down Shore Road or Bay Avenue in Highlands for a taste of the Jersey shore.

# HIGH MOUNTAIN SUMMIT LOOP

## ▶ IN BRIEF

The run up High Mountain is a great workout, vacuuming the air right out of your lungs. The view of Manhattan from the grass-and-granite graced peak is breathtaking, too, but there's more, including a small cascade, numerous stream crossings, a romantic pond, remote swamp hollows—even some Paleolithic rock shelters concealed in a ravine. And if that's not enough . . . well, you could always try a round of golf at the neighboring country club.

## ▶ DESCRIPTION

High Mountain Park, a 1,154-acre Nature Conservancy preserve, is a good news–bad news sort of place. First, the bad news: Many of the trails within this attractive sanctuary have been terribly eroded by ATVs and dirt bikes—so much so, in fact, that you will have to contend with large swaths of loose stones and a rutted maze of maverick paths. Now for the good news: This is one of

## ▶ DIRECTIONS

*By car:* Follow I-95/I-80 west across the George Washington Bridge. Leave I-80 at Exit 53 onto SR 23 north. After 1.3 miles, turn right onto Alps Road. Continue for 2 miles to the intersection with Ratzer Road and hang a right. Drive 1 mile, then make a left onto Valley Road. Proceed for 0.7 miles and swing right on Hamburg Turnpike. After 1 mile, head left on College Road and drive uphill for a mile, with the William Paterson University campus on the right. At the top, veer right into parking lot 6 (across from the trailhead sign on the left) at the recreation center; park at the top level, as close as you can to College Road.

*By public transportation:* Take the New Jersey Transit Main Line from Penn Station to Paterson. Brace yourself for a cab ride of about 5 miles.

## ℹ KEY AT-A-GLANCE INFORMATION

**LENGTH:** 6.1 miles

**CONFIGURATION:** Balloon

**DIFFICULTY:** Moderate

**SCENERY:** Rolling trail snakes through dense woodlands and lush wetlands that harbor endangered plants and a trap rock glade

**EXPOSURE:** Generous shade until the summit, which is very open

**TRAFFIC:** Often on the light side, but a favorite getaway of students from nearby campus

**TRAIL SURFACE:** Rock-packed dirt and a few grassy patches

**HIKING TIME:** 3 hours

**SEASON:** Year-round, dawn–dusk

**ACCESS:** No fee, pets must be leashed, no horseback riding

**MAPS:** Photocopy can be obtained at the campus recreation center; USGS Paterson; visit www.waynetownship.com or www.nynjtc.org

**FACILITIES:** None

**SPECIAL COMMENTS:** Heavy spring rains may transform trails into cascading streams.

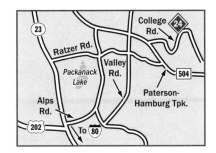

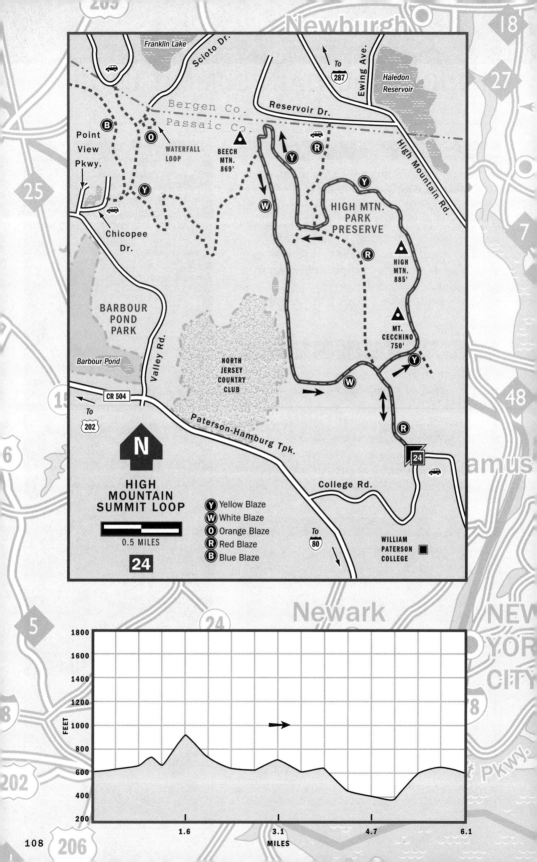

**HIGH MOUNTAIN SUMMIT LOOP**

Y Yellow Blaze
W White Blaze
O Orange Blaze
R Red Blaze
B Blue Blaze

0.5 MILES

24

Heavy rainfall transforms trickling cascades into a miniature Niagara at High Mountain Park Preserve.

the most beautiful parcels of land in the entire New Jersey Piedmonts, with the hike rising to a bald peak from which the Manhattan skyline is visible, and dropping down through a hardwood forest and fertile swamp. There are also several prehistoric rock shelters in the vicinity, though you may have trouble finding them. In more recent times, a few of the ridgetops here were used during the Revolutionary War to light signal beacons.

The only signals you need to think about these days are the trail blazes, beginning with red. From the upper left corner of parking area 6, return to the entrance drive and go to the other side of College Road. The preserve entrance is at the left end of the guardrail, indicated by a green sign emblazoned with "High Mountain Park" in gold lettering. Bear immediately to the right and march up the sloping forest road, where red blazes adorn the chestnut oaks and maples. Continue straight at the confluence of eroded traces at the fire lane turnaround, and ignore the many successive spurs that surface en route to the top of the hill.

High Mountain tops out at 885 feet, but you gain most of that elevation in the drive to the parking area. Even so, count on a steady ascent—especially after transferring to the yellow-blazed trail, a right turn that occurs in about 15 minutes. On leveling off, the wide track starts to lose ground, twisting by a handful of boulders as well as a smattering of white birches until it reaches a wetland. Use the stepping-stones if the stream level is high, and stay with the yellow blazes, dead-on, at the four-way intersection that ensues. Your ascent resumes when you cruise left at the T a minute later, with the path alternating between pebbles and bedrock. The terrain near the crest, colored by oak, black birch, sarsaparilla, and spicebush, is honeycombed with the deep ruts of long-gone dirt bikers, with all roads leading to the top.

Stick with the yellow markings as they bring you to the exposed peak of High Mountain, where buttercups grow between the cracks in the rock, and where the Manhattan skyline is visible on a clear day. The grooved stone under your feet, by the way, is an unusual form of basaltic trap rock, which is described by the Nature Conservancy as "globally imperiled." Moving along, glide right on leaving the vista point, and rejoin the forest road. For a brief spell, this feels like a garden path, as grass and trap rock line the way. Steer to the left of the large oak when you come to the lush opening in the trees, and follow the yellow blazes to the next rise, a protruding knob sitting like an enormous egg amid an oversize nest of colorful wildflowers. This is a wonderful section of the highland forest and a fun ramble through several pocket meadows, where the interplay of grass and rocks contributes to the eye-appeal. There is also a good chance of observing wildlife in the area.

Nothing lasts forever, of course, and soon enough a downhill stretch commences, drawing you back into the cover of the forest. From initially adhering to the rocky forest road, the trail soon darts to the left, narrowing to single-file within an overgrown corridor of maple, oak, and birch. Check out the spur to the right; it ends by a very scenic glade, where a cascade splashes against trap rock and a head-high glacial erratic abuts the stream.

On surging straight at the subsequent junction, the path hops over that same stream, with the water now placidly rippling by ferns and sassafras. A minute later, there is a four-way intersection with the red-blazed trail you were on earlier. Take the middle option, and hew to the right at the Y that materializes directly after, still with the yellow markings. The track meanders along a ridge for a spell, then shifts to the left at a fork with an unblazed forest road (the latter somewhat impeded by fallen trees). From there, you begin to lose elevation, bottoming out in a hemlock and cedar swamp where the trail veers sharply to the left. (The trace to the right, also sporting yellow blazes, ends at a road in a few dozen yards.) A steep climb succeeds that, capped by your merging left onto a forest road. In about a minute, this lane meets a junction with a white-blazed trail (WT), which you follow straight on, as the yellow markings branch off to the right.

The spring display of wildflowers on High Mountain is divine, but you pay for that pulchritude on this stretch, which resembles an active arroyo in wet weather. In spite of such soggy conditions, you are more likely to see deer and squirrels here than muskrats and otters. As you move downhill, ignore the forest road that appears to the right, emerging from a field of trap rock shale. The WT breaks right momentarily, departing the forest road for higher ground, only to return to the wide track in a few minutes. Soon the white blazes hop left, skipping over rocks to ford the wide stream. The serpentine path then swerves right, after bypassing a trace in the same direction, and arrives via a short spur (also to the right) at a romantic pond, with chestnut oak and black birch bracketing the idyllic scene.

Back on the main trail, bear right at the next fork, and rock-hop over the wash, staying with the blazes as they cut left and neatly avoid a golf course. Yes, you read correctly: For the next several minutes, the path skirts the perimeter of the North Jersey Country Club, circling by healthy cedars and oaks, crossing streams, and ducking behind a few impressive rock formations. As you drift away from the golf course, keep to the right at the fork, still with the WT. It's uphill from here, with a handful of stream crossings and a vine-covered cabin ruin thrown in for the sake of variety. Much of the ascent overlaps an old streambed, with its broken-up surface providing enough friction on the feet to encourage an appointment with Dr. Scholl.

Check out the bluff of trap rock to the left, which extends for more than 40 feet and rises an impressive 25 feet off the ground. That depression near its base may be the remains of a Paleolithic shelter. The WT ends at a fork a couple of minutes later, as you pick up red blazes and continue straight. In bypassing the yellow-blazed route that appears on the left, you have completed the loop. Remain with the red markings all the way back to College Road.

## ▶ NEARBY ACTIVITIES

In addition to Paleolithic hunters, mastodons once roamed High Mountain's verdant summit. The Bergen Museum of Art and Science in Paramus has two mastodon skeletons on display, as well as work by local and internationally known artists. For details, call (201) 291-8848, or visit www.thebergenmuseum.com.

# HIGH POINT DUET

## ▶ IN BRIEF

High Point State Park lies in the heart of black-bear country. Don't fret too much about that, though, as you are far more likely to encounter birds and butterflies on this rough-cut loop than any ill-tempered Smokey. There are also views galore from along the Appalachian Trail, access to a secluded lake on the back half of the hike, and a profusion of wildflowers throughout the spring.

## ▶ DESCRIPTION

Have you ever thought about getting high—*really high*? Just say yes, and slip your bunions into boots for a rousing hike in High Point State Park. The aptly named park achieves an elevation of 1,803 feet atop High Point Monument, making it the Garden State's tallest peak. The 360-degree panorama there extends to the Delaware River and the hills of Pennsylvania, the Catskill Mountains, and the fertile farmlands of northwestern Jersey. Our suggested hike does not summit High Point Monument, though you should save time for a side trip there. Which is not to imply that the following jaunt is devoid of views—far from it. More than half of the 10 miles of this trek overlap the Appalachian Trail (AT), with a number of fine vistas occurring en route. That's just for starters: The AT clings to a series of bluffs and rugged rock formations along the spine of Kittatinny Mountain Ridge, where wildflowers and wildlife sightings are all but guaranteed. White-tailed deer are among the more common of the woodland

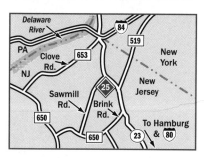

## ▶ DIRECTIONS

Follow I-95/I-80 west across the George Washington Bridge. Leave I-80 at Exit 53 onto SR 23 north. Continue approximately 11 miles north of Hamburg to the Visitor Center on the left. The trailhead parking is 0.1 mile earlier, also on the left side, by the maintenance building.

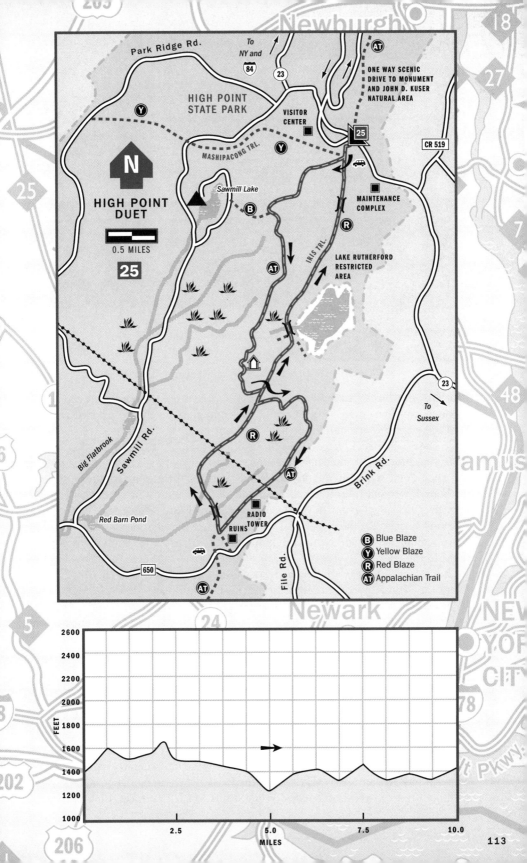

High Point State Park lives up to its name with stellar views across three states, as well as this vista of tranquil Saw Mill Lake.

denizens, but black bears roam these parts, too, as well as bobcats, raccoons, and possums. You may even hear the exotic chirruping of the elusive pileated and red-breasted woodpeckers and, in the lower swampy areas, the hooting of barred owls.

Time for a bit of history, though, before you set off. In 1888, Charles St. John built a vacation resort, the High Point Inn, on the edge of Lake Marcia, thus pinning the High Point name to this locale. When St. John later went bankrupt, Colonel Anthony Kuser and John Kuser, descendants of Swiss immigrants, bought the property. By 1911, High Point Inn had been refashioned into "The Lodge," to serve as Anthony Kuser's summer retreat. The Colonel had already consolidated all of the power companies in and around Trenton and was president of Southern Jersey Gas and Electric. He was so flush with cash that he ponied up $200,000 in seed money for the establishment of what later became 20th Century Fox, as well as $60,000 to finance a 17-month expedition to the Far East to study and draw pheasants. High Point became a state park in 1923, after the land was donated to New Jersey by the Colonel and his wife, Susie Dryden Kuser (whose father, United States Senator John Dryden, founded Prudential Life). Park officials later hired the Olmsted brothers of Boston—landscape architects and the sons of Frederick Law Olmsted, designer of New York City's Central Park—to beautify the preserve's grounds.

The influence of the Olmsteds is omnipresent as you drive the park roads, most obviously in the wide, swooping lawns that wrap around mature stands of trees. The responsibility for what you see on the trail, on the other hand, rests securely on the shoulders of Mother Nature. The trailhead is at an altitude of 1,400 feet, and your later elevations will vary from that by little more than a couple hundred feet. Thus, the greatest challenge you are likely to face is from the hard, chunky rubble that covers great passages of the AT. The trail at the kiosk, where a map is posted, is blazed with both red and yellow markings. When it hits the T, in 20 feet, turn left. In 150 yards, the yellow blazes break to the right, with the red markings shifting left just after that. The white-blazed AT continues straight, between the other two trails, with black birch, maple, various oaks, and a handful of shagbark hickory trees shading the area.

The AT is level for a spell, gliding over an old stone wall and paralleling a rocky bluff rising 40 feet high to the right. Soon, though, the trail ascends that ridge, a three-minute effort that culminates in a steep, lung-sucking scramble to the top. As is typical of these AT ridge walks, a dip ensues, succeeded by another rise, then a dip, and so on. In 20 minutes, the path brushes by a blue-blazed spur to the right, a connector to Sawmill Lake. Keep strolling on the AT, and in about a minute it rubs up against a broad bench of fractured granite, from which Sawmill Lake and the adjacent campground are visible. Approach this spot quietly and you may see a vulture or raptor perched on the rocks.

The AT tapers rapidly downhill, doglegging around a mound of glacial debris and slithering through a rock-limned gully between parallel ridges. The rocky upheaval underfoot resembles a cobblestone street in a war zone, but it improves when the track levels off and begins to climb. After an elevation gain of 150 feet, the AT passes among white birch and white pine on its way to a viewpoint looking out to the west. The path then jogs to the east side of the ridge, providing a glimpse of Lake Rutherford, a reservoir, a couple hundred feet below. The ghostly series of snags you see, by the way, are American chestnuts, killed off by a fungal blight that arrived in the U.S. a century ago.

Forget the trace that slices left to a view of the lake; there's a better vantage point dead ahead, on top of a rocky knob. For the next several minutes, the AT flanks an attractive shelf of granite that extends south from that node, a plateau that is enticingly easy to scramble up for more views of Lake Rutherford, or to just laze in the sun awhile. On passing the sign for the Rutherford Shelter, a backpackers' lean-to, the track skirts to the right of the stony ledge and drops downward over chunky ground. The Iris Trail (IT, red blazes) then merges from the left, overlapping the AT for a minute. Steer left on the AT when the two diverge, as the path descends to a swamp where white anemones, violets, and jack-in-the-pulpits preside in spring. More bog pots follow, with the track finally rising through blueberry bushes and pitch pines to a break carved into the forest for an underground pipeline. The AT continues directly across that opening, but first amble left to enjoy the rocky bird's-eye view, with what seems like all of rural Sussex County unfolding below.

Back within the shade of the trees, the path cruises right at a fork in roughly 100 feet and meets a staggered four-way intersection just beyond a trail register. The white blazes head directly across, while red blazes dodge both left and right. This is the turnaround point, where you leave the AT and transfer to the right on the IT. (A left on Iris brings you in 150 yards to the ruins of an old cabin, with little left except its crumbling foundation.) Unlike the AT, which is limited to foot traffic, Iris is a multipurpose track, shared by hikers, bikers, equestrians, skiers, snowmobiles, perhaps even people on pogo sticks, so a heads-up vigilance is called for.

The path descends for about four minutes before bottoming out at a low swamp. Skunk cabbage lines the grass-sided track here, along with Indian strawberry and violets. In June, you may stumble upon pink flowering lady's slipper orchids, too, and frogs croon from the muddy depths for most of the summer. Naturally, when it comes to hiking, what goes down must surge up again, and in a short time the trail rises to drier ground, where a network of mortarless walls serves as a reminder that most of this was once open farmland. At the pipe break, Iris doglegs right over buttercups and anemones for ten steps before swinging left, once more into the forest. (Several hundred yards to the east is the ridge you walked over earlier.) It then briefly reunites with the AT; remember to trot right in a few minutes with the IT when the routes split.

A loss of elevation follows, with Iris, well below the high bluff, meandering through a swamp. There among the ferns and other wetland vegetation, where tiger and spicebush swallowtail butterflies frequently flutter about, you may notice a few purple-flowering irises, justifying the trail's moniker. Shortly after, the red blazes jump to the left at a T with a forest road, and then lunge right in 150 feet at a Y. This wide, level track draws enticingly close to Lake Rutherford, arcing away to the left before you reach the water. On navigating an S-curve around a mound of angular boulders and a bridge crossing, the lake comes back into view. The path then rises to a two-tiered granite platform that overlooks the water by 40 feet. As shore-side spots go, this one ranks among the more picturesque. Proceeding from there, Iris hugs the contours of the reservoir for a spell, eventually gliding into a blueberry heath. Additional dips and climbs ensue, with the undulating terrain boasting a number of glacial erratics, many painted green with lichen. Once you have cruised over a small bridge—look for trout lily, trillium, and jack-in-the-pulpit in the spring—the IT arrives at the staggered four-way crossing where you first picked up the AT. Cut to the right with the red blazes, and return to the trailhead.

### ▶ NEARBY ACTIVITIES

Tucked into the northern part of the park is a scenic interpretive trail in an attractive sanctuary. The Dryden Kuser Natural Area encompasses a high-elevation cedar swamp, a variety of conifers, rhododendrons, and some endangered plant and animal species. Call (973) 875-4800 for more details.

Rest your feet in nearby Port Jervis, at the Gillinder Glass Museum, where you can admire the amazing art of glass-blowing. Visit www.gillinderglassstore.com or call (845) 856-5375 for more information.

# HOLMDEL BIG LOOP

For such a fully developed facility, Holmdel Park manages to pack a great deal of eye-catching scenery into its trail system. Hardwoods and pines, hills and bogs, and streams and wildflower meadows are all a part of what makes this walk so pleasant and diverting. A few sustained uphill stretches will get the hearts a-thumping in all but the most hardy of hikers, and with a petting zoo farm on park land, this is a can't-miss for the youngest trail-blazers in your crew.

▶ **DESCRIPTION**

That sound you just heard was a coin being flipped. When it boiled down to choosing between Holmdel and Tatum parks, with just 2.5 miles and the Garden State Parkway separating them, we were stuck. They are comparable in size, at about 350 acres each, and both are operated by Monmouth County. We found Tatum's Dogwood loop and Ramble of oaks and beech trees delightfully appealing. Holmdel, on the other hand, is endowed with a more exhaustive network of trails and features a hearty diversity of habitats. Our coin toss came up Holmdel.

Look for the kiosk by the southwest corner of the parking area; a map is posted on its back. We prefer this trailhead for its underdeveloped

**KEY AT-A-GLANCE INFORMATION**

**LENGTH:** 2.8 miles

**CONFIGURATION:** Loop

**DIFFICULTY:** Easy

**SCENERY:** Densely forested, undulating hills alternate with attractively landscaped open lawns, meandering streams, and secluded marsh

**EXPOSURE:** The middle mile traverses open fields, rest of trail is shady

**TRAFFIC:** Rather heavy on sunny weekends

**TRAIL SURFACE:** Dirt with some root-work at start, then cinder path, then back to dirt

**HIKING TIME:** 1.5 hours

**SEASON:** Year-round, 8 a.m.–dusk

**ACCESS:** No fee, pets must be leashed, no bicycles or horses on trails

**MAPS:** At covered kiosk by main entrance; www.monmouthcountyparks.com

**FACILITIES:** None at the trailhead, but rest rooms and water at main entrance, along with picnic area, playground, shelter, vending machines, and public phone

**SPECIAL COMMENTS:** Fishing in Lower Pond is a popular summer activity, with ice-skating, hockey, and sledding among the wintertime sports.

▶ **DIRECTIONS**

Follow I-95 south across the George Washington Bridge into New Jersey, switching to the Garden State Parkway south at Exit 11. Leaving the Parkway at Exit 114, head right (west) on Red Hill Road, and in 0.5 miles, turn right on Crawfords Corner Road. Drive for 1.8 miles to Longstreet Road; turn left and proceed for 0.2 miles to the trailhead parking on the right (at the Program Center entrance). The main entrance is a little farther south on Longstreet Road.

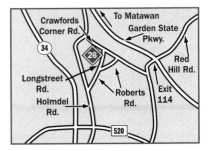

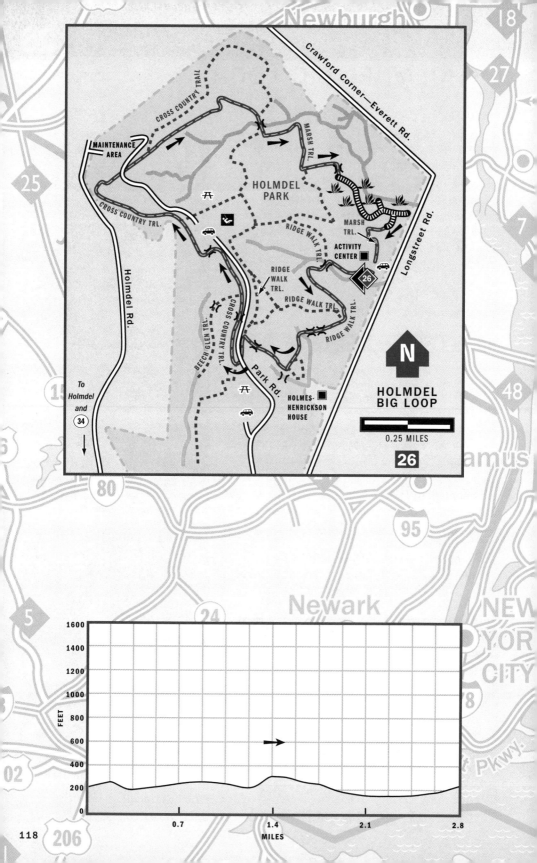

HOLMDEL
BIG LOOP

0.25 MILES

26

access directly into the park. By contrast, the main entrance, a few blocks down the street, is a nucleus of activity—particularly on weekends—what with all sorts of traffic buzzing around its arboretum and Longstreet Farm. This last-named is a Victorian-era "living farm," complete with a restored farmhouse, petting zoo, and costumed volunteers.

Proceed into the beech- and pin oak–accented forest, skimming by the viewing platform and stream to the left. Head over the bridge, and persevere along the path as it undulates up three successive ridgelines, with a left at a T occurring midway through that climb. Another left follows in a few minutes, after you have entered a thick stand of pines. All of this is a part of the Ridge Walk Trail, a roly-poly circuit that embraces a good chunk of Holmdel's densely forested backcountry.

From that turn, the path, now covered with cinder, tilts a touch downward, fording a little leaf-choked wash. Toward the left, through the birches and oaks, is the lush meadow of the picnic *platz*. On crossing a second bridge, the trail begins to rise, passing a spur blazed with a picture of a lady's slipper orchid. You may indeed see wild orchids down that little loop, especially if the weather has been wet and warm, but oaks, birches, and beech trees are a more certain bet. Trending downhill again from the crest, hang a right just before the small bridge, and stay with the meandering track as it leads over another bridge, this one nestled among wild rhododendrons.

Once across that span, spin sharply right and march on up the slope. Make a left when you come to the T, and walk 40 yards along the park lane to the exercise station. Traverse the road there, and hop right onto the Cross Country Trail, now rolling north. For the next several minutes, the path parallels the road, only to open up by a paved turnaround and expansive parking lot. You might want to don dark glasses or increase your pace to a jogging trot, if only to get by the upcoming less-attractive stretch more quickly. Keep to the left side of the lot in a northwest trajectory, threading from there to an area of open fields.

This is the far north end of Holmdel, with a residential neighborhood overlooking the park and a scrubby wildflower meadow by your side. The trail arcs sharply to the right by a fistful of white pines, spruce trees, and sumac, in addition to a couple of birdhouses. Flowing now in an east-northeast direction, the cinder track meets once more a paved access lane and begins a slight descent toward an open field. The Cross Country Trail circles this exposed expanse of grassland (pretty fair Frisbee golf territory), exiting the area on the lowest side of the sward, to the right.

On returning to the shade of the woods, take a left directly after fording the bridge, and in four or five minutes, this sandy track veers hard to the right. Watch out for the ankle-wrenching roots that may be hidden under slippery beech leaves on the ensuing uphill stretch. From the ridgetop, the path drifts leftward and down, into a leafy, soggy gully. Bear left at the post for the Marsh Trail, and in a couple of minutes, cross the footbridge and continue to the left. A boardwalk follows, meandering like a backwards S by a juicy bog. In warm weather, you should be able to spot snakes, turtles, or frogs here. A turnoff to the left is for a small oak-encircled viewing platform where you might quietly wait for birds to land in the marsh grass and green briar. If you can tiptoe through the tulip trees quietly enough on the second spur to the left, you may surprise some birds by a pool where stream runoff accumulates. All there was the last time we looked was a pair of 55-gallon drums embedded in the sand.

On the main trail once more, go over a couple of wooden bridges, and when you come to a slanted T, take the acute right and start trucking up the hill. In three easy switchbacks, you will be at the top, with the Program Building of the activity area to the right, and the trailhead parking straight ahead. And if your Vibram still itches with unspent energy, why not spin over to Tatum Park?

## ▶ NEARBY ACTIVITIES

In addition to the ornamental and fragrant Holmdel Arboretum, this park also contains historic Longstreet Farm, where interpreters in period costume illustrate the area's agricultural past. For information on both, call (732) 946-9562.

Tours of the 1754 Dutch-style Holmes-Henrickson house, just outside the park on Longstreet Road, are offered from May through September. For details, call (732) 946-3758.

# HUDSON HIGHLANDS
# BREAKNECK RIDGE LOOP

### ▶ IN BRIEF

Stupendous views, rock-scrambling, and strenuous climbs are a good part of what this thrilling jaunt is about, with a special accent on strenuous. This is one of the more memorable hikes in the Highlands, with a colorful finish by the remnants of an old estate and dairy farm—ruins far more extensive than the average ghost town. For many, this is the Holy Grail of highland trails, but don't try it without sturdy hiking boots and plenty of water.

### ▶ DESCRIPTION

Many hikes are so mild in nature, so undemanding of one's physical strength and capacity for endurance, that we think of them as woodland walks or streamside strolls, nothing to break a sweat over. Then there are the hugely challenging calorie-burners, the ones where the elevation gain is measured in four digits, not two or three; rocks are to be summited, not side-stepped; and no matter how much water we've brought along, it

### ▶ DIRECTIONS

*By car:* Take US 9 north, about 4.7 miles past Peekskill, to the junction with SR 403 (Garrison Road). Turn left and drive 2.2 miles to the junction with SR 9D, where you head north (right). Proceed for 4 miles to the village of Cold Spring and SR 301 east, and continue straight through the intersection for 0.7 miles to a small parking lot on the right. There is additional parking across the street, next to the Little Stony Point Bridge.

*By public transportation:* Metro North's Hudson Line stops in Cold Spring Station; in less than a mile you'll be climbing. Walk up Main Street, turn left on Fair Street, then left again on SR 9D. The trailhead is a short distance away, across from Little Stony Point Bridge.

### ❶ KEY AT-A-GLANCE INFORMATION

**LENGTH:** 9 miles, 8 miles without the spur to Bull Hill

**CONFIGURATION:** Figure eight

**DIFFICULTY:** Quite difficult

**SCENERY:** Rugged trail crosses two elevated, forested ridges, yielding stunning views of Hudson River and mountains on either bank, and passes extensive ruins of a dairy farm

**EXPOSURE:** Medium protection, tree canopy not very dense; many open areas on ridges and slopes

**TRAFFIC:** This is a popular hike, though seldom crowded, especially on higher peaks

**TRAIL SURFACE:** Mostly dirt and rocks, some rock scrambling, 0.5 miles of pavement at finish

**HIKING TIME:** 6 hours

**SEASON:** Year-round; best views are from late fall through early spring, but snow and ice in winter can make trail surface treacherous

**ACCESS:** No fee, dogs must be on leash not longer than 10 feet

**MAPS:** USGS West Point; New York–New Jersey Trail Conference East Hudson Trails

**FACILITIES:** No rest rooms or water on trails

**SPECIAL COMMENTS:** Bow hunting for deer is permitted in season.

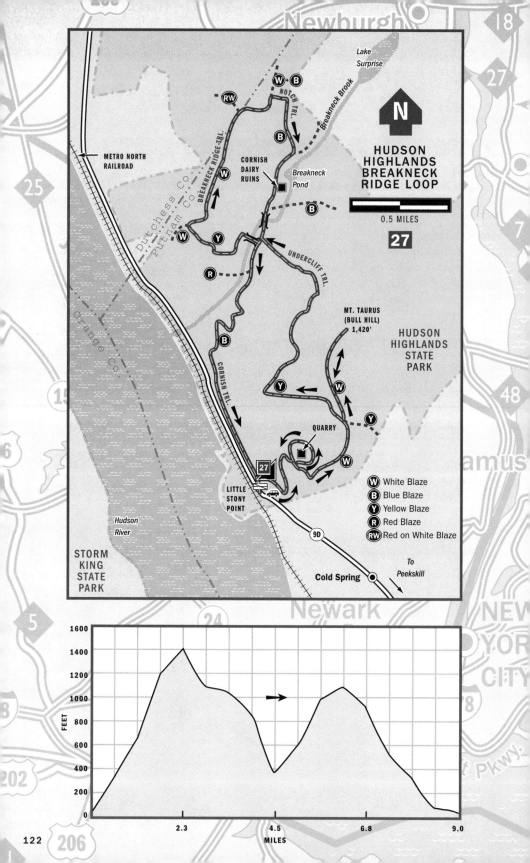

**HUDSON
HIGHLANDS
BREAKNECK
RIDGE LOOP**

0.5 MILES

**27**

MT. TAURUS
(BULL HILL)
1,420'

HUDSON
HIGHLANDS
STATE
PARK

METRO NORTH
RAILROAD

Dutchess Co.
Putnam Co.

BREAKNECK RIDGE TRL.

NOTCH TRL.

Breakneck Brook

Lake
Surprise

CORNISH
DAIRY
RUINS

Breakneck
Pond

UNDERCLIFF TRL.

CORNISH TRL.

Orange Co.

QUARRY

LITTLE
STONY
POINT

Hudson
River

STORM
KING
STATE
PARK

9D

Cold Spring

To
Peekskill

W White Blaze
B Blue Blaze
Y Yellow Blaze
R Red Blaze
RW Red on White Blaze

Newburgh

Newark

**FEET**

1600
1400
1200
1000
800
600
400
200
0

2.3        4.5        6.8        9.0

**MILES**

122

never seems enough. Hudson Highlands, a relatively undeveloped park of 4,000 acres, features just such a monster hike, a strenuous haul in which you are less likely to finish up with a spring to your step than a stumble down the slope. If you're at all like us, you'll love every minute of it.

On leaving the diminutive parking area, step around the gate that bars the quarry road and keep right, following the white blazes up the sandy slope. Even with vegetation growing thickly around the trail, and a number of dogwoods, oaks, and shagbark hickory trees in the vicinity, the sun exposure is intense and a hat should be considered mandatory summer apparel. The climb is steady for the first ten minutes, brushing by slag heaps from bygone quarrying, before arriving at the quarry itself. The path continues by the crater's right rim, but take a moment to tour the hollowed-out core—and catch your breath!—while observing a recovery in progress, as sumac, cottonwoods, oaks, and cedars rise up from the knee-high grass that covers this damaged ground.

The going gets steeper on resuming the trail, but with the elevation gain comes a series of false summits where you can rest and enjoy striking views of the town of Cold Spring below, the Hudson River beyond, and the rising rocky profile of Storm King across the water. If it is a warm day, you may share that panorama with plenty of lizards sunning themselves on the pale slabs of stone littering the area. Indeed, the higher you get, the greater the quantity of rubble, with the climax being a scramble over rocks to a plateau that rests about 650 feet above the trailhead.

On rising another 250 feet through blueberry bushes and sassafras, the path forks, with yellow blazes launching leftward and white blazes pointing to the right. Don't be put off by the low-swooping turkey vultures: Opt for the right leg, which leads to the crown of Mount Taurus. For a brief spell, the way doesn't seem so strenuous, hopping over shelves of buff-colored granite, darting between black birch trees and scrub oaks, even descending a bit. Then, all too soon, the bill comes due, and it's back up the mountain, leap-frogging over melon-sized chunks of stone from one false summit to another (with limitless views at each). Yet more scrambling over a slanted rock face finally yields the top at 1,420 feet of elevation. The laurel- and oak-sprinkled setting of Taurus, also known as Bull Hill, is an ideal spot in which to swap some real whoppers with your companions.

For vistas that are no less enchanting and to get on with the hike, return to the Undercliff Trail (UT) at the aforementioned yellow-blazed turnoff. Although it is a couple hundred feet lower, the UT offers several stellar vantage points, including a spectacular view from a rocky knob-outpost, a towering perspective of Route 9D and the tunnel to the north, Storm King over the river, and of course the Hudson itself. The verdant plateau beyond is Breakneck Ridge, beautifully tree-covered and looking deceptively easy to reach. Shuffling onward, the stone-studded path finally enters a touch of shade cast by oaks that loom larger and taller.

In less than half an hour, the UT starts a seriously steep descent down a talus slope, switchbacking through maples and laurels, creeping in the general direction of Breakneck Ridge. Stone steps in strategic places help make this drop more foot-friendly than you might otherwise expect, before hitting a grass-topped carriage lane with a surface smooth enough to push a baby carriage. As you proceed downward at a more gradual angle, listen for the rat-a-tat-tat of pileated woodpeckers, which are often heard drilling into the beeches and birches coloring this part of the park.

Cross the seasonal streambed, near a small grove of hemlocks, swing left on a larger carriage road, blazed red, and then roll right and ford the wooden footbridge. You've lost 800 feet since descending from Mount Taurus—no bull!—and are about to regain a good portion of that. Did you enjoy that strenuous stretch to the last peak? Let's hope so; some hikers maintain that this next bit is even tougher, an assertion we're not inclined to argue with. All we know is if it were any steeper, you'd probably need rappelling ropes to make your way up. Switchbacks help, wending their way through the moraine field, and when a series of boulders appears to block further progress, the makeshift trail somehow snakes to its left, sparing you—for now—the need to scramble. Another 40 yards and you'll be facing the vertical side of a large knob, with a fine glimpse of Taurus behind your back.

On moving forward under the limbs of wild dogwoods, another angular escarpment surfaces. It is possible to climb over the rocks there (beware of rattlesnakes sunning themselves on the upper reaches!) to the pitch pine-dotted ledge above for a moment of off-trail solitude in a rough-hewn, wildly beautiful spot. There are even faded orange blazes that lead up there and beyond. Ultimately, though, it is the yellow markings to the left of this grand protrusion to which you want to adhere, avoiding the oblong blocks of granite and sharp-edged rocks as the path switchbacks downward through another moraine patch. Having dodged a couple of oversize boulders, you'll begin to climb again, surmounting a steep talus slope and threading through a few more switchbacks. At the base of the next bluff—a dramatic protrusion of dark gray rocks—below a hanging garden of ferns and weeds, are the remains of a crude rock shelter.

The yellow blazes expire abruptly just north of that, once you've passed through a rocky notch. This is the start of the Breakneck Ridge Trail (white blazes); stay to the right as the strenuous, rocky climb grinds on. Yet one more igneous crag follows near the crest, with a fun hand-over-hand scaling of stones required to reach its dome. The worst—or best, depending on your outlook—of the ascent is finished, so rest a moment and enjoy the sublime views and serenity of the setting. The wrinkled promontory directly across the wide, rollicking Hudson is Storm King Mountain, with the extended ridge of Schunemunk Mountain looming beyond it. That spot of land near the east shore of the river is Pollepel Island, where the largely-intact ruin of a five-story castle, built in Scottish baronial style early in the twentieth-century, still stands.

From this stage onward, Breakneck is just a name (rather than an actual hiking risk) as it flows from one rising knuckle to the next along the spine of this ridge, with low, grassy saddles in between. The highest point, at the third pinnacle, tops out at 1,150 feet. Once the fourth rise is behind you, the inevitable descent begins, dropping 60 feet over rock fill in a matter of seconds.

Not so fast, though, for from that minor gully there is another peak. Ignore the spur to the left and remain on Breakneck. The ridge is almost level for a change as it draws gradually to this last summit, one that yields a splendid 360-degree panorama, with Lake Surprise beaming brightly to the northeast. Shifting downhill, hew to the right in about 150 yards at a junction with the Notch Trail (blue blazes).

The Notch heads lower immediately, at first over rocky ground, but soon giving way to an easier, hard-earth surface. The forest is denser here, and the use of blazes not too generous, so some hard squinting may be in order to find the blue discs. In roughly 20 minutes—and a loss of 500 feet—the path hits a T with a carriage road, Breakneck Pond lying just beyond. Veer right onto the pebble road, which leads in a few minutes to the impressively large ruins of the Cornish Dairy, consisting of a number of stone-block and concrete structures scattered on both sides of the lane. This is a fun area to explore, but as always in such locales, be cautious about entering ruined buildings.

The blue blazes make a sharp left up another carriage lane (circling back eventually to Mount Taurus), but you should saunter straight ahead as the road trends downward, serenaded for a spell by the pleasant tinkling of Breakneck Brook. Eventually, after crossing the brook on a narrow bridge, you'll walk by the Undercliff Trail (to the right and left) and the bridge (to the right) you used earlier on the way up to Breakneck Ridge. When the trail diverges, perhaps 100 yards beyond a derelict pump house, stay to the left on the blue-blazed route.

From there onward, an enticing network of grassy lanes cuts through the forest. Simply adhere to the main drag, which imminently turns to asphalt, and you'll be fine. Though this section of the park lacks the views and raw beauty of the higher elevations, its upside in spring and early summer is so rich an explosion of wildflowers that paisley looks drab by comparison. Because of the lush vegetation, white-tailed deer often graze the area. We once saw a black racer snake, too, curled up on the path, in no hurry, apparently, to race anywhere. Shortly after you encounter the round foundation of an old cistern, the ruins of the estate's greenhouse appear cloaked among the bushes to the right. Several yards beyond that is the prize, the remains of the stone mansion itself, partially overgrown by a tangle of rhododendrons. When the paved lane reaches the pillared gate by Route 9D, slice left on the trail leading into the overgrowth. You'll be back at the trailhead in five minutes.

## ▶ NEARBY ACTIVITIES

This hike is plenty for one day, but experiencing a sunset on Little Stony Point by the Hudson River, just across the road, will jump-start your revival.

Did the glimpse of the castle on Pollepel Island pique your interest in this state-owned land? Kayak and boat tours there run from May through October. Call the Bannerman Castle Trust, (845) 831-6346, or Hudson River Adventures, (845) 220-2120, for details. See also www.bannermancastle.org.

# JAMAICA BAY WEST POND TRAIL

## KEY AT-A-GLANCE INFORMATION

**LENGTH:** 1.8 miles

**CONFIGURATION:** Loop

**DIFFICULTY:** Very easy

**SCENERY:** Views of coastal marshlands along level, gravel trail flanked by exotic plants and circling a brackish pond populated with waterfowl

**EXPOSURE:** Mostly open, but some shady trees on east side in North and South Gardens

**TRAFFIC:** Very popular on weekends

**TRAIL SURFACE:** Packed dirt covered with gravel

**HIKING TIME:** 1 hour, more for serious birders

**SEASON:** Year-round, sunrise–sunset; can get breezy in winter

**ACCESS:** Free, but must obtain permit at Visitor Center; no bikes, no smoking

**MAPS:** At Visitor Center

**FACILITIES:** Rest rooms and water at Visitor Center, water fountain by bird blind near South Garden

**SPECIAL COMMENTS:** Sunsets can be gorgeous. Bring good binoculars or a spotting scope to watch abundant and fascinating bird life. If you want to hike the East Pond across the road, wear watertight shoes and go when the tide is low. Inquire ahead at (718) 318-4340.

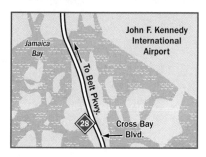

## ▶ IN BRIEF

This hike is for the birds—and for those who love to observe them in all their curious shapes, plumages, and idiosyncrasies. The richest sightings are during the spring and fall migrations, when the ponds and surrounding marshlands teem with waterfowl, but this is a refuge of calm worth visiting throughout the year. Among its huge array of exotic plants is an abundance of colorful wildflowers that bloom from spring through early autumn.

## ▶ DESCRIPTION

On the surface of a New York area map, it is easy to overlook Jamaica Bay Wildlife Refuge. In spite of its prime position east of Brooklyn and south of Queens, Jamaica Bay's near proximity to JFK Airport evokes images of ambling with one's ears stoppered against sonic boom, while the sandy soil constantly quakes from crisscrossing jet traffic. Who would willingly walk in such cacophonic conditions?

Well, serious birders, for one. The fact of the matter is that the flyovers are not as frequent—nor as nasty—as you might think, with many more birds soaring through the air than 747s. The

## ▶ DIRECTIONS

*By car:* From Brooklyn, take the Belt Parkway east and exit onto Cross Bay Boulevard (Exit 17) south. Drive over the North Channel Bridge and proceed for 1.5 miles to the signposted refuge entrance on the right. Access the trail through the Visitor Center.

*By public transportation:* Take the "A" New York City subway line to Far Rockaway or Rockaway Park and exit at Broad Channel Station. Walk west to Cross Bay Boulevard, then north (right) for about 0.5 miles to the refuge entrance on the left.

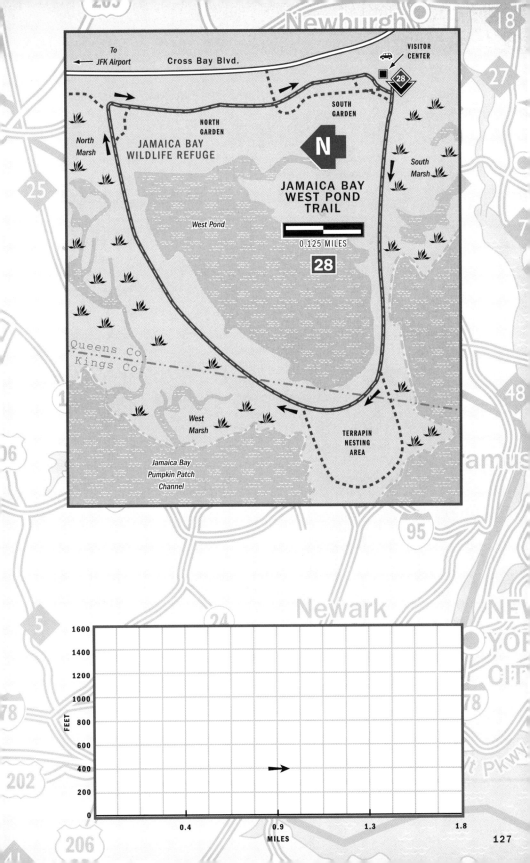

refuge was established in 1951 by the New York City Parks Department, which promptly created two freshwater ponds and transformed what was then barren land into a veritable garden. In 1972, the National Park Service assumed management of the 9,155-acre refuge, under the umbrella of the Gateway National Recreation Area, which has two other units within the metropolitan region. Since then, more than 325 species of birds have been identified in the park.

The West Pond is the more accessible of the two principal bird-watching zones, with a 1.8-mile gravel path circling it. Throughout the year, feathered creatures of all stripes, shapes, and colors can be seen by its shore and in its water, as well as on the surrounding marshlands. But if you are one of those who knows a booby from a bunting and a grackle from a grosbeak, you should consider timing a visit to coincide with major avian activity. The park service notes that evenings in late March are ideal for observing the mating behavior of American woodcocks, a multitude of southbound migrators starts appearing in mid-August, and autumn months are ripe for seeing songbirds, raptors, and warblers.

Once through with the obligatory registering at the Visitor Center, pick up the start of the West Pond loop behind the building. Right away you'll arrive at turnoffs to the Upland Nature Trail and the South Garden Trail. If you choose to travel in a counter-clockwise direction, start with the South Garden Trail. It flows in a meandering fashion first into Upland and then the North Garden Trail before emerging at the northeast corner of the West Pond circuit. A left at that point completes the tour around the pond and marshes.

We prefer to travel in a clockwise manner, bypassing those two side spurs. The path is wide and level, with viewpoints spaced out between thriving stands of winged sumac and a wondrous array of wildflowers, including the yellowish-orange gaillardia, purple loosestrife, blue vervain, purple gerardia, evening primrose, salt marsh flea bane, goldenrod, rose mallow, and—perhaps the biggest botanical surprises—prickly pear cactus and flowering yucca. Clearly, this preserve is as much fun for amateur botanists as it is for birders.

Look left toward the South Marsh and you may see such salt-loving waterfowl as snowy and great egrets, yellow-crowned night herons, and possibly an osprey up on the nesting stand. Gil Hodges Memorial Bridge is also visible off in the distance. In a few dozen yards, the vegetation cloaking the trail opens up more, offering greater views of the phragmites-flanked West Pond. So many birds are drawn to its brackish water that you might more easily count the leaves on a tree as put a number on them. The Terrapin Nesting Area spur is farther on to the left (closed during the diamondback terrapin's breeding season—typically midsummer through mid-September). Continuing along the loop, the North Garden appears on the right, notable for its invitingly grassy grove of mature willow oaks, cedars, and sweet gum trees.

By all means explore the North Garden trails, since landscaping along the main path becomes less attractive as it parallels the noisy Cross Bay Boulevard back to the parking lot. The North Garden, on the other hand, while offering no further views of the West Pond or saltwater marshes, is a peaceful, less trammeled oasis. Many of its trees (as well as those in the South Garden), including white birches, cottonwoods, American holly, white pines, and trees of heaven, were planted by the refuge's first supervisor, Herbert Johnson, back in the 1950s and early 1960s.

Now somewhat overgrown, there is a small warren of trails threading in and out of the thicket, leading, eventually, to a tiny bird pond, complete with a viewing blind. This is a fun area of the park to wander around while listening attentively to all sorts of little critters crackling noisily in the underbrush. And since the North Garden, Upland Trail, and South Garden are interconnected, with the West Pond on one side of you and the main path on the other, there's no real chance of getting lost. Just keep moving southward, and soon enough you'll be back by the Visitor Center.

## ▶ NEARBY ACTIVITIES

Fort Tilden and Jacob Riis Park have bathing, beaching, and golfing facilities. Breezy Point is another birders' paradise. All three locations are to the southwest of Jamaica Bay.

# JENNY JUMP MOUNTAIN LAKE TRAIL

## ▶ IN BRIEF

Only when the trees are bare of leaves will you be able to enjoy the superb view of Mountain Lake from the trail high above. That's not a problem on the remainder of this lightly-trafficked circuit, a mildly arduous uphill grind into a beautiful forest. Granite boulders and rocky uplift, reminders of the last Ice Age, are naturally interwoven with a heavy helping of hardwoods, including oaks, beeches, maples, and tulip poplars. Bears range throughout these hills, as do wild turkeys and other birds.

## ▶ DESCRIPTION

To reach Jenny Jump State Forest, you will have to travel through some of the prettiest farmland in the entire Garden State. Moravian immigrants were attracted to this lush, fertile area, the Kittatinny Valley, in the latter part of the 1700s, probably because the rolling hills reminded them of the Old Country. Although a smallpox epidemic and financial difficulties led the group to disband in 1808, many of their solidly built limestone buildings (as well as a few of their sturdier wooden structures) still survive in the neighboring communities.

## ▶ DIRECTIONS

Follow I-95/I-80 west across the George Washington Bridge. Leave I-80 at Exit 12 to Hope. Drive 0.9 miles to a blinking intersection light. Turn left (north) on CR 519 and continue for 1 mile to Shiloh Road. Make a right and proceed for 1.1 miles to State Park Road on the right. The park office—which has maps—is 0.8 miles away. For the trailhead, backtrack on State Park Road 0.8 miles and make a left on Fairview Road. At the T-intersection, swing left on CR 611, and after 1.5 miles, head right on CR 679 (Mountain Lake Road). Proceed for 2.9 miles, and veer right onto Lakeside Drive North. The parking lot is 0.4 miles ahead on the right.

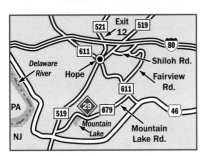

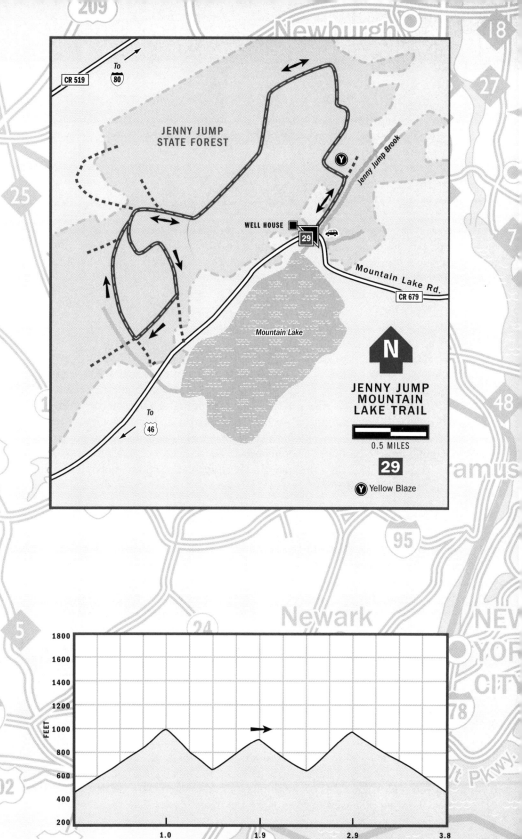

JENNY JUMP
STATE FOREST

CR 519

To
80

Jenny Jump Brook

Y

WELL HOUSE

29

Mountain Lake Rd.

CR 679

Mountain Lake

To
46

N

JENNY JUMP
MOUNTAIN
LAKE TRAIL

0.5 MILES

29

Y Yellow Blaze

Also surviving is the legend of how this mountain range acquired its unusual name. In 1747, Sven Roseen, a Swedish missionary, recorded that a girl named Jenny was picking berries on a high ridge when a band of Lenape Indians approached. Her father, spying the natives and fearing the worst, called out to her to jump, which she supposedly did. Perhaps Jenny's tragic end is also responsible for how Ghost Lake came by its moniker, as well as Shades of Death Road, which leads to it. You can walk to Ghost Lake via the Summit Trail—if the specter of this locale's eerie past doesn't spook you. This is a popular out-and-back trek that brushes by an old cabin ruin midway out. The Mountain Lake Trail, on the other hand, is haunted by far fewer hikers, making it the ideal circuit for individuals looking to jump into a solitudinous stroll in an attractive woodland. The 3.7-mile circuit has the added attraction of being high above Mountain Lake, though views of the water are only possible from late fall through early spring, when the leaves are off the trees.

The trace that leads into the forest by the map kiosk peters out in a few dozen yards by a concrete ruin overgrown with poison ivy. The real trailhead is 150 feet farther up the road, just shy of the fieldstone well house. Follow the yellow blazes inland, passing at the outset a boggy stream to the right. The impressive granite outcroppings you see here were deposited by the Wisconsin glacier 21,000 years ago as it moved south from Canada. The rich range of trees, such as tulip, maple, birch, oak, and beech, are of a more recent vintage, having sprung up on former farmland in the last century. Of the same era are a couple of cement and cinder-block foundations adjacent to the stream, where ferns, mayapple, meadow parsnip, anemones, and wild geraniums contribute to the peaceful setting.

From wide and easy, the trail rapidly resembles an old riverbed, with enough rocks and stones underfoot to build a fair-sized fortress. Swing left at the fork, still with yellow blazes, as the path pulls away from the water and begins a long, steady climb. The last time we did this route, there were a number of fallen trees across the track; they were easy to navigate around but reinforced the notion that not many bipeds bother with this hike. In addition to the obvious benefit of solitude, this absence of interlopers seems to draw wildlife—including an occasional black bear, but especially birds—into the open. A pair of Baltimore orioles and a scarlet tanager are the highlights among the many birds we've encountered here. This meandering loop hits many false summits during its ascent, while shifting from a west direction to the southwest, then north, and northwest, and back toward the south again.

After about 15 minutes of treading uphill, a steady descent ensues, with the path bottoming out by a diminutive orchard of mayapples. Bear left as the trail forks during the uptick that follows, and ignore the subsequent unblazed trace that soars uphill to the right. Within seconds, the track, currently edging in a southeast direction, arrives at a Y—stay to the left. As it lurches from east to south, the path encounters a couple of cedars and some fragrant honeysuckle (frequently attracting tiger and spicebush swallowtail butterflies), and an overgrown spur branching to the left. The main trail swerves right just beyond this and forks, with the straight-on option leading down to the lake. Take the hard right that churns up the stone-filled hill, a continuation of the steep undulations that compose this hike. You may see (or hear) wild turkeys in this vicinity, and the view of Mountain Lake is superb when the trees are bare.

On reaching the rotting hunter's platform mounted on the trunk of a black birch (five minutes from the last intersection), hang a right on the trace. Now moving toward the northwest and still uphill, you pass a lone pine tree, with the track leveling off a moment later. Hook right at the T on an old forest road, where you can enjoy a great ridgeline view over the lower forest. As you begin to descend, bypass the overgrown spur to the left, sticking with the wide track until it meets a triangular T, where you should turn left. This completes the little loop part of the hike, putting you back on familiar turf. Just remember to bear to right in a few minutes at the next fork, and adhere to the earlier route to bring this excellent cardiopulmonary workout to an end.

## ▶ NEARBY ACTIVITIES

If you are a stargazer and in the area on a Saturday evening in summer, the observatory site of the United Astronomy Clubs of New Jersey may offer an otherworldly type of attraction. Visit www.uacnj.org or call (908) 459-4366 for details.

In charming Hope, some stores and banks provide brochures for self-guided walking tours among the town's Moravian architecture. For more details, call (908) 459-5011.

# JOHNSONBURG SWAMP TRAIL

## IN BRIEF

To paraphrase Justice Lewis Powell's sentiment on pornography, when it comes to limestone, we may not be able to describe it, but we know it when we see it. You will, too, after a journey through Johnsonburg Swamp, where a healthy portion of the hike overlaps limestone cliffs, ridges, and outcroppings. Scenery ranges from deer-inhabited grassy fields to dark forests to a sublime view of Mud Pond from High Rocks. In between, you'll find no end of birds and wildflowers, perhaps an elusive salamander or two, and, of course, plenty of limestone.

## DESCRIPTION

Johnsonburg Swamp is a botanist's paradise. Its soil is rich in dolomite, providing a nourishing environment for such rare plants as leathery grape fern, hoary willow, white-grained mountain grass, ebony sedge, and the carnivorous lesser bladderwort. It may require the keen eye of a specialist to spot these species, but that should not detract from your pleasure in visiting this unusual preserve—not if you enjoy wandering through open farmland and a secluded hardwood forest, where colorful wildflowers and a range of wildlife proliferate. And certainly not if you have any interest in scrambling over High Rocks, a remark-

## DIRECTIONS

Follow I-95/I-80 west across the George Washington Bridge. Leave I-80 at Exit 19 and remain in the right lane. At the end of the ramp, cross over CR 517 onto CR 667 and drive north for 0.25 miles, then turn left onto CR 612. Proceed for about 5 miles to the intersection with CR 519 and make a right, followed by a left on CR 661 north. At the junction with SR 94, head right (north) for 0.2 miles to the Frelinghuysen School parking lot on the left.

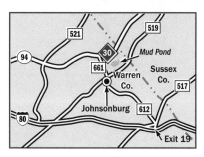

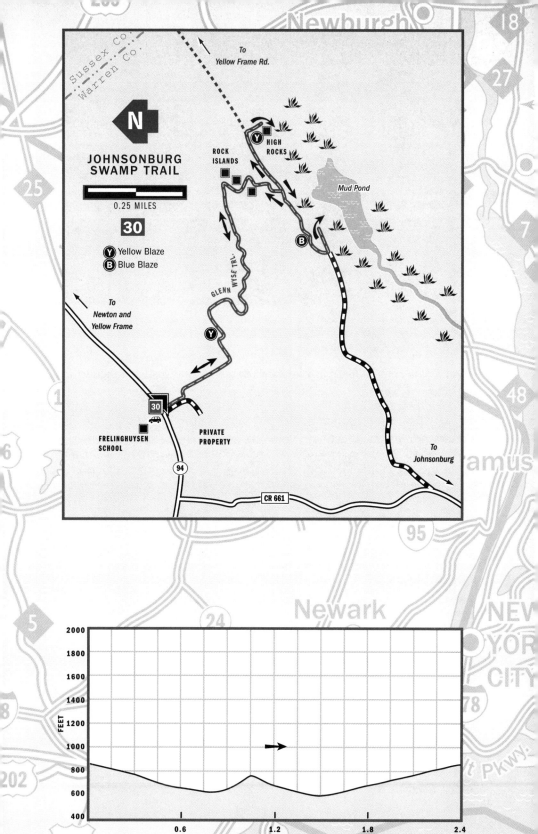

**JOHNSONBURG SWAMP TRAIL**

0.25 MILES

**30**

Y Yellow Blaze
B Blue Blaze

To Yellow Frame Rd.

Sussex Co.
Warren Co.

ROCK ISLANDS

HIGH ROCKS

Mud Pond

GLENN WYSE TRL.

To Newton and Yellow Frame

FRELINGHUYSEN SCHOOL

PRIVATE PROPERTY

94

CR 661

To Johnsonburg

The croaking of frogs is audible even from High Rocks, an eagle's nest overlook of the Johnsonburg Swamp.

able limestone bluff, which yields a dramatic view of Mud Pond and the surrounding swamp.

The trailhead for this 450-acre Nature Conservancy property is directly across the street from the Frelinghuysen School, down the paved driveway of, ironically, a real estate developer. Keep to the left of that taupe-colored, single-story building, as the lane turns from macadam to gravel and continues between open fields. Shift left on the grass path in about 250 feet, at a fork. Follow the yellow-and-green blazes between two rock walls, still moving in a southward direction with a scrub-covered wall on your right, and a field opposite. At the southwest corner of this grassy area, the track arcs to the left, leading to the east end of the open expanse. Stroll to the right there, entering another field as you pass by a maple tree and an overgrown wall, and then swing left to complete the dogleg. Sarsaparilla and other scrub flank both sides of the track, to which you adhere for approximately 260 feet, until the trail bends south, or right. By the way, if you have ever wondered what successional forests looked like before they became overgrown with trees and shrubs, this maze of meadows provides a pretty fair illustration.

Remain with this downward slope for 175 feet, then swerve right into yet another field. The path slices left again in a gap between the scrub bushes and tapers toward the southwest, under a power line. (Our hearts skipped a beat when we nearly stepped on a couple of large rat snakes tussling under the long grass on our last trek here.) In 30 steps, the track jumps left, or east, and in a few strides more, there is a sign for the Glenn Wyse Trail to the right. Head in that direction as it enters, in a dozen paces, a steeply slanting woodland, one densely forested with cedar, white pine, maple, birch, oak, and tulip trees. If it has been raining recently, you may find white-capped morels, a delicacy, near the base of the cedars. And try gently lifting a log or two off the forest floor to see if any of the nine species of salamander that live in this sanctuary are hiding underneath.

The trail descends on a diagonal, minimizing elevation loss (as well as making for an easier return trip), and crosses a seasonal arroyo at the base of the ravine. The eye-catching rock island to the left, soaring 45 feet up with a maple growing out of a cleft in its side, is covered with colorful columbines in early spring. As the trail approaches a less dramatic series of stony uplift, it wanders slightly left (still south-bound) away from a low field on the right. Stay on the right margin of the rising terrain, and you should soon observe the next yellow blaze. The serpentine path slithers left from there, circling south by a large stratified mound and edging uphill. It crests atop a limestone ridge in a couple of minutes, where the shale-like layers of dark stone lie exposed underfoot and among the rising ground around you. As the trail veers south, it comes abruptly to a T, with yellow blazes heading left and blue ones to the right. Go left for now, through a saddle between heavily etched fins of limestone, where mayapple, yellow asters, and jack-in-the-pulpit thrive.

In roughly four minutes, the path hits a low post marking the spur to High Rocks, to the right. Take that trace and climb over the bluish black rock—being careful to avoid the plethora of poison ivy—to enjoy this splendid outpost 250 feet above the amoeba-shaped Mud Pond. The latter, a limestone sinkhole, is a thriving beaver habitat, and with binoculars you should be able to spot one or two of their lodges on the water's periphery. The dominant hill far beyond is Jenny Jump Mountain. Nearer at hand, rumor has it that there are six small caves hidden somewhere within the eroded recesses of this formation, but we have yet to find them.

Back at the post, you may turn right and pursue the yellow blazes for a half hour as they take you out of the forest and into open pastureland, ending, finally, at Yellow Frame Road. If you turn left there, walk 0.7 miles to the next corner, turn left again, and in another 0.7 miles you will be back at the school. We find it more rewarding, however, to skip that leg and instead return to the intersection with the blue blazes, following those along the ridge to the west. From atop this limestone shelf, there are splendid vistas of the marsh at the near end of the pond, where cattails and chokeberry add texture to the scene. The blue blazes peter out in three minutes, but the worn track goes on, dropping down to a level with the marsh. Hop over the rocks on the left and lope left on the forest road. Its turnaround point is a few yards ahead, with access to Mud Pond just beyond. This is a great nook in which to lie low with your spotting scope handy, scanning the surroundings for hummingbirds and waterfowl, as well as turtles sunning themselves on partially sunken logs. Lavender flowering bugleweed (in the mint family), grows in abundance here, along with wild geraniums. When you have finished exploring the area, retrace your steps back to the trailhead.

▶ **NEARBY ACTIVITIES**

The middle of the Delaware National Scenic River marks the border between Pennsylvania and New Jersey along its 40-mile course in the Delaware Water Gap National Recreation Area. You'll need more than an afternoon to explore this magnificent park, but you can also tour it by car and take in its waterfalls, rural scenery, and historic Millbrook Village. Visit www.nps.gov/dewa for more details.

# MERCER LAKE TRAIL

## KEY AT-A-GLANCE INFORMATION

**LENGTH:** 2.9 miles

**CONFIGURATION:** Out-and-back with loop in middle

**DIFFICULTY:** Very easy

**SCENERY:** Bogs and canals surrounding a pretty lake make for fun water crossings and bird sightings along well-forested, level trail

**EXPOSURE:** Very few open spaces, except along lakeshore

**TRAFFIC:** Popular biking park, thus you will seldom be alone on trails

**TRAIL SURFACE:** Dirt, mud, some root-work

**HIKING TIME:** 1.5 hours

**SEASON:** Year-round, dawn–dusk

**ACCESS:** No fee, pets must be leashed

**MAPS:** USGS Princeton; www.angelfire.com/nj2/smart17/maps.html

**FACILITIES:** Seasonal water and rest rooms at trailhead, also public phone, picnic area, and playground

**SPECIAL COMMENTS:** Be alert to mountain bikers and deer zipping through the woods. At the lake you may witness a regatta or fishing tournament.

## IN BRIEF

While Mercer County Park is known primarily for its athletic facilities, there is more than enough in the natural realm for hikers to trip over. Stream crossings, lake access, a colorful forest of second growth hardwoods—even an overgrown ruin—make this a breezy, entertaining walk.

## DESCRIPTION

Mercer County Park is a well-endowed, multipurpose facility, decked out with 18 basketball courts, 7 soccer fields, 12 softball fields, miscellaneous tennis courts, picnic areas, a marina, and, of course, Mercer Lake itself at the center of the property. Subtract all that from its 2,500 acres, and Mercer still has some space left over for a number of trails, with those in the less groomed northern portion of the park providing the illusion of being further out in the wilds than they really are.

Puttering along its pleasant pathways through swamplands and hardwood forests, out to the edge of the trout-stocked lake and back, you'll probably see an abundance of birds—but hardly any other hikers. Which is not to suggest the track will be yours alone. On the contrary, you may meet a number of individuals, but nearly all will very likely be members of the fat-tire set, propelling themselves over Mercer's wide, flat trails atop mountain bikes.

## DIRECTIONS

Follow I-95 across the George Washington Bridge into New Jersey and continue south on the New Jersey Turnpike (I-95). Take Exit 8 and proceed east on SR 33 for about 5 miles to the junction with CR 641 (Windsor Road). Turn right and drive 3.5 miles to Dutchneck-Edinburg Road across CR 535. The park's east entrance is 0.3 miles ahead on the left.

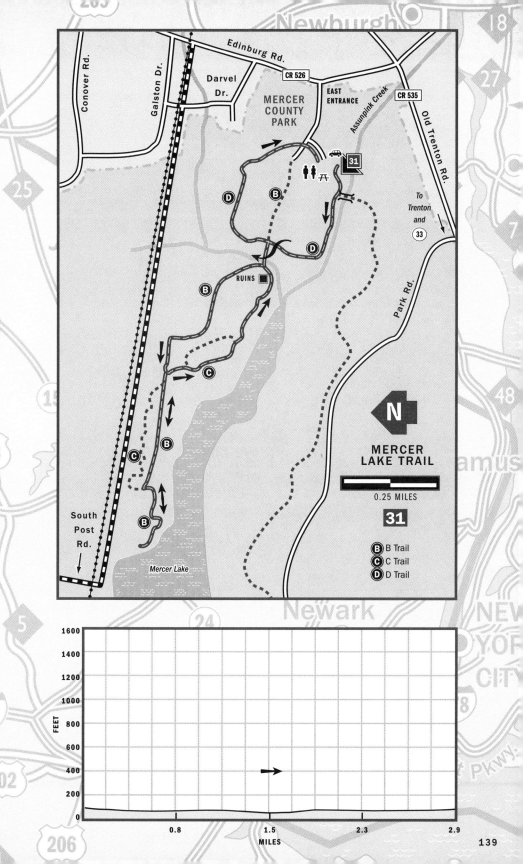

MERCER
LAKE TRAIL

0.25 MILES

**31**

Ⓑ B Trail
Ⓒ C Trail
Ⓓ D Trail

From the east entrance parking area, head to the left of the rest rooms and picnic area. Bear right at the staggered fork, just past the covered picnic pavilion, onto a trail blazed with a black D over a diamond (to the left is a bridge which leads, via a strip of pavement, to the southern section of the park). The right path parallels a canal for a spell, part of a system of streams that sluices through the forest and helps nourish a diverse plant community, including, right at the outset, maples, sycamores, shagbark hickories, tulip trees, various oaks, sweet gum, cat briar, and poison ivy. The extensive ground cover in particular is favored by birds, with goldfinches, cardinals, blue jays, slate-colored juncos, and yellow-shafted flickers among the many that ply this patch of parkland.

On walking through a small, leaf-filled canal (occasionally wet in springtime), turn left onto the B Trail, where another, wider canal awaits. With water flowing through this one pretty much year-round, rock-hopping is probably the only way to get across with dry shoes. Keep right at the wishbone fork and continue along the somewhat straight lane, which is graced by cedars, cottonwoods, and birches, as well as ubiquitous oaks. In roughly 250 yards, the moss-rimmed track veers sharply right, reaching another fork in a couple of minutes. Launch left, and in a moment or two you'll hit a stream crossing, where several small branches have been stretched over the water to form an impromptu—if slightly unsteady—bridge. Stay straight on the other side, and ignore the alphabet soup of blazes that fly from one letter to another in rapid succession.

When you hit an intersection by a tri-trunked oak, with a large yellow boathouse looming through the trees just ahead, swing left toward the lake. Five minutes puts you by a phragmite marsh and the water, half exposed to the sun, with knee-high grass all around and possibly a couple of pheasants frolicking in the underbrush. Find a rock, sit down, and enjoy this peaceful nook for a few minutes; if you brought along Walt Whitman or Emily Dickinson, this is the place in which to pull them out and say hello.

That poetic interlude concluded, return to the tri-trunked oak, retrace your steps over the makeshift bridge of the previous stream and hang a right, again toward the water, on a C-blazed track. As it meanders through a thicket of scrub oak and willow, steer right at the T, then, after a gully of a canal, go right again at the wishbone fork. Emerging from the clench of cat briar, the trail brushes up against the side of a wide, grape-green tributary, where mallards like to fish. It meanders by the stream for a few seconds, then presses inland, passing more cat briar, an old tire, a car melting into the muck, and the concrete ruins of a couple of homes slowly being swallowed by the swamp. Who knows; with a stout shovel and a bit of time, you might come up with Jimmy Hoffa. March right at the next T, back onto the B route in the direction of the trailhead.

Rock-hop once more over the previously forded canal, meeting in three minutes the D Trail, which runs right and left. Instead of returning directly to the right, lope left to extend the loop. This leg of the hike leads into an attractive, oak-dominated forest, one in which you may have to sniff like a spaniel to stick to the trace. Although it heads away from the lake, there are still several swampy spots to sidestep, with a few stretches all the muddier from the steady fat-tire traffic squishing through. The trail ends within 120 yards of the rest rooms, with the parking area adjacent.

## ▶ NEARBY ACTIVITIES

Ready for some cultural enrichment? Try the enchanting Grounds for Sculpture in Hamilton, with works by American and international artists. The beautifully landscaped domain, formerly the New Jersey State Fairgrounds, also has a cafe and restaurant. Call (609) 586-0616 for information.

The first harbingers of spring at Mercer County Park are the lustrous leaves of unfurled skunk cabbage.

# MIANUS RIVER GORGE TRAIL

## KEY AT-A-GLANCE INFORMATION

**LENGTH:** 5 miles

**CONFIGURATION:** Out and back

**DIFFICULTY:** Easy/moderate

**SCENERY:** Undulating trail winds through old-growth and succession forests along cool slopes of gorge, past cascades and lush quarry

**EXPOSURE:** Very shady canopy throughout

**TRAFFIC:** Popular on weekends

**TRAIL SURFACE:** Packed dirt, some rocky and rooty stretches

**HIKING TIME:** 2.5 hours

**SEASON:** April–November, 8:30 a.m.–5 p.m.

**ACCESS:** Donations encouraged, no pets, no bicycles

**MAPS:** At entrance kiosk; USGS Pound Ridge

**FACILITIES:** Water pump and rest rooms near entrance

## ▶ IN BRIEF

Great gorge and reservoir vistas, old-growth hemlocks, an intricate network of nineteenth-century farmstead walls, glacial erratics, and granite outcroppings highlight one of the better short treks in the region. Mianus is at its best in springtime, when the streams and cascades are most watery—but its cool, well-shaded paths also offer a welcome respite from the heat of summer.

## ▶ DESCRIPTION

Hold the snickering, please. Contrary to what some wits might suggest, Mianus River Gorge owes its peculiar sobriquet to Sachem Myanos, leader of a local band of Mahican Indians that reportedly summered on the sandy shores of Long Island Sound in the late 1600s, using the gorge as their hunting grounds during colder months. That white-tailed deer still roam these woods (along with the occasional red and gray fox, raccoons and, every so often, a polecat) owes less to the dietary discretion showed by the Mahicans and their white supplanters than to the ongoing efforts of the Nature Conservancy and the Mianus River Gorge Preserve, who jointly manage the domain.

Though Mianus, at 738 acres, is hardly a mighty oak, it has grown quite a bit from the littlest of acorns, when the Nature Conservancy created it in 1955 with an initial purchase of just 60 acres. Before a decade elapsed, this woodland

## ▶ DIRECTIONS

Drive north on the Hutchinson River Parkway and continue as it changes to the Merritt Parkway. Take Exit 34 and head north on SR 104 (Long Ridge Road). In 7.5 miles, turn left onto Millers Mill Road, and left again, after the bridge, on unpaved Mianus River Road. The parking lot is 0.5 miles ahead on the left.

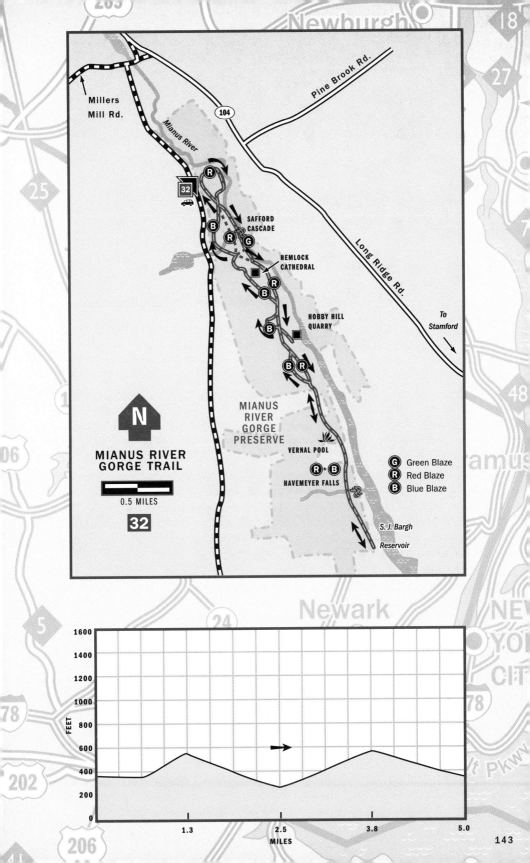

Ancient walls marking where farms once stood traverse the dense woodlands of Manus River Gorge.

habitat was recognized by the federal government to be of such significance that it was designated the country's first Natural History Landmark. That status stems in part from a remarkable concentration of old-growth hemlocks, some dating back 350 years, which is clustered along some of the steeper slopes of the gorge. More accessible features include rocky outcroppings jutting high above the river, superb views of the S. J. Bargh Reservoir, a seasonal waterfall, an eighteenth-century mica and quartz quarry, and an intricate series of solid stone walls.

Trails fall into three color groups—red, blue and green—that overlap over the course of a relatively easy out-and-back hike of 5 miles. Maps are available at the kiosk, though you are unlikely to get lost if you bear to the left throughout the walk. Take a moment prior to setting off to peruse the picture display on stone walls, a useful backgrounder on Mianus's many mortarless walls that run throughout the woods. These are relics from the nineteenth century, when most of the trees in this area were cleared for farming and pasture land.

Begin on the red trail to the left of the kiosk. It and the subsequent paths are very well maintained, ranging from a wood-chip surface initially, to hard-packed earth later on. Protruding rocks pose the only real hazard, one that is fairly typical of this sort of rolling, up-and-down, glacier-wracked terrain.

Once past a couple of aged cedars and a few sugar maples, you come directly to a shade-sheltered bench by an appealing overlook of the Mianus River, some 40 feet distant. For the first half mile or so of the hike, the trail meanders past beech trees, hemlocks, and an occasional oak, sticking fairly close to the river. Roughly halfway along that distance, after a slight ascent, is a grassy patch to the right; it's a piece of pasture in succession, slowly being swallowed by the resurgent forest.

Yet another reminder of this area's bygone agricultural era follows, as you descend again toward the water. Look for a tree with a "4" mounted on it by a stepping-stone "bridge" that fords a seasonal tributary. That marks the spot where farmers

Trillium, trout lily, marsh marigold, and mayapple are among the spring gems you may see glittering in the understory of Mianus River Gorge.

routinely rode their wagons across the river, with the old lane they used still faintly discernible uphill to the right.

A short series of ascents and descents ensues, culminating at yet another great view into the gorge. Then, on turning left onto the green spur, the trail drifts steadily lower past numerous hemlocks until it meets a rather still section of the river. Though buggy in the spring, this is a peaceful glade, with skunk cabbage and ferns coloring the mossy bank, and a large stone wall running through the woods on the opposite side of the water. We once came upon a pileated woodpecker here, noisily knocking its beak into a fallen beech.

The Safford Cascade, to the right in roughly 100 yards, is generally active only from springtime through early summer, when a stream of water crackles photogenically down the rocky hillside, and dragonflies flit about in the moist spray. (Even when the cascade is dry, though, the moss-covered stepping-stones can be surprisingly slick.) A few paces beyond is a fork, with the right option retreating to the trailhead, and left, or straight ahead, joining the red trail for the continuation of the hike.

This begins one of the few sustained uphill stretches in the preserve, with the path threading toward the Hemlock Cathedral, home to most of the old-growth conifers, and yielding one more overlook of the river. Predictably, it descends from there, reaching in a couple of minutes the Rock Wall Breach, the narrowest point in the gorge, where glacial ice sculpted this sharp bend in the river more than 15,000 years ago.

The trail now meanders uphill, passing in the process several fine specimens of mature beech trees and a growing number of granite boulders, many mottled green with lichen. Keep to the left at each of the succeeding two intersections, as an increasing amount of mica specks glitter on the humus-laden path—a sure sign that you are approaching the Hobby Hill Quarry. A well-marked spur to the left ends, in perhaps a furlong, at the quarry, where ferns and lianas protrude like a hanging garden from the carved-out rock wall.

Back on the main trail, proceed on red as the undulating route brushes by a series of well-preserved stone walls. On heading through a rather open stretch of such hardwoods as maple, oak, and black birch, the path veers toward the gorge, dropping down a few feet in elevation to Vernal Pool, a boggy spot marked by a "10." Throughout Mianus, such wetlands are rife in spring with trillium, trout lily, mayapple, and marsh marigold, and in early summer you may find frogs, horned toads, snapping turtles, and eastern ribbon snakes in the vicinity.

A spur to the left appears a few minutes later, once you have climbed a bit, going out to a fair view of the reservoir. The laurel-fringed mound of granite there, shaded by oaks and hemlocks, is a choice place to rest or have lunch. A sign cautions that this is a "deer tick research area," a warning that would be no less applicable to the entire Northeast. It is probably a bluff meant to discourage bushwhacking down the embankment to the water, though the prevalence of poison ivy should prove a sufficient deterrent.

Goldfinches occasionally bathe in the small pool below Havemeyer Falls, which is just ahead via the next spur. The stream that makes up this scenic splasher is reputedly the healthiest tributary in Mianus's 37-square-mile watershed, though it is often dry by late summer. With a bit of rock-scrambling, you can easily reach the bank of the Bargh Reservoir. Not too many years ago, the falls marked the hike's turnaround point. Additional land acquisitions, however, have extended the route by nearly a quarter of a mile, right to the rocky shore of the reservoir. The elevation there is just under 300 feet, lower than the trailhead by a mere 50. Post 15, nearly halfway back, is the highest point, where the elevation tops 550 feet. The return along the blue trail follows much the same route as the red, with a few side branches providing the illusion that you are on a loop rather than a straight track.

## ▶ NEARBY ACTIVITIES

Finished the five miles at Mianus and you're still hot to trot? The Henry Morgenthau Preserve is in the vicinity, with a short trail to the pristine Blue Heron Lake. You can reach that by turning left (north) on Long Ridge Road on leaving Mianus, hanging a right when Long Ridge hits SR 172. Continue east for about 1.5 miles, where the entrance and a small parking lot are to the right.

You might add another mile or so to your trekking total with a stop at the Bye Preserve, a Nature Conservancy unit just north of the Connecticut state line on the east side of Route 137. Beech, black birch, and a variety of oaks are the predominant trees along the small ravine at the heart of this peaceful pocket-park.

# MUTTONTOWN MYSTERY TRAIL

## ▶ IN BRIEF

You don't have to be a fan of obscure Albanian history or murder mysteries to enjoy wandering the woods of Muttontown, not with such an appealing variety of habitats tucked into the domain. A vast network of trails and old estate lanes weaves through swampy swales, miniature savannas, a rhododendron jungle (that transforms in July into a fairyland of pale pink blossoms), some glacial deposits, and even a few ghostly ruins. Of course, if you do have a thing for unsolved mysteries, so much the better.

## ▶ DESCRIPTION

Thumb through the brochures at Muttontown's nature center, and you will learn that the 550-acre preserve runs the gamut of habitats, from open fields and lowland swamps to rolling hills, kettle ponds, and upland forests. One pamphlet talks about the variety of animals in Muttontown, with raccoons, red foxes, star-nosed moles, and masked shrews among its denizens. Another brochure boasts of the birds that nest here, including flickers, rose-breasted grosbeaks, bobwhites, and bobolinks. There is even a brief

## ▶ DIRECTIONS

By *car*: Follow the Long Island Expressway (I-495) east to Exit 41 onto SR 106 north. Continue on SR 106 for 4.1 miles to the intersection with SR 25A (Northern Boulevard). Go left, and after 0.1 mile, turn left again onto Muttontown Lane. Drive 0.2 miles—through 2 stop signs—to the preserve entrance on the right, and veer left at the fork to the parking area.

By *public transportation*: Take the Long Island Railroad (Port Jefferson Branch) to Syosset Station. From there, a cab ride of about 4 miles will bring you to the preserve.

## ⓘ KEY AT-A-GLANCE INFORMATION

**LENGTH:** 3.3 miles

**CONFIGURATION:** Loop

**DIFFICULTY:** Very easy

**SCENERY:** Six different habitats, including wet woodlands, rolling fields, kettle ponds, and upland forests, as well as mysterious ruins

**EXPOSURE:** Sheltered at start, then exposed in fields, followed by more tree cover

**TRAFFIC:** Light to moderate, except when school groups are exploring grounds

**TRAIL SURFACE:** Grass, sand, roots, pebbles, and plenty of mud in spring

**HIKING TIME:** 1.5 hours

**SEASON:** Year-round, 9 a.m.–4:30 p.m.

**ACCESS:** No fee, no pets, no bicycles

**MAPS:** At Visitor Center

**FACILITIES:** Rest rooms and water behind Visitor Center

**SPECIAL COMMENTS:** Bridle paths and cross-country skiing trails wind through the preserve.

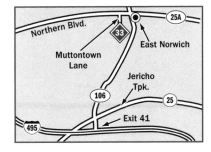

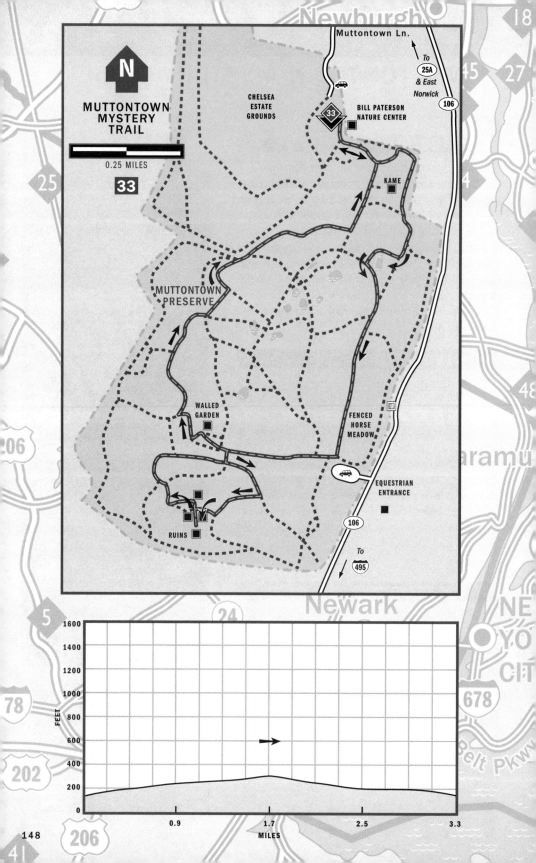

N

MUTTONTOWN
MYSTERY
TRAIL

0.25 MILES

33

CHELSEA
ESTATE
GROUNDS

Muttontown Ln.

To
25A
& East
Norwick

106

33

BILL PATERSON
NATURE CENTER

KAME

MUTTONTOWN
PRESERVE

WALLED
GARDEN

FENCED
HORSE
MEADOW

RUINS

EQUESTRIAN
ENTRANCE

106

To
495

Newburgh

Newark

148

Within the deepest recesses of Muttontown Preserve are the ruins of a lavish palace, once owned by a deposed Albanian king.

account of how the preserve came into being, with 400 acres purchased from the estate of Lansdell Christie, 100 acres donated by Alexandra McKay, and a 20-acre lot given by Mrs. Paul Hammond. What you won't find is any mention of the ruins of Knollwood, the international intrigue surrounding King Zog, rumors of hidden treasure, and a murder mystery that is still unsolved.

To call Knollwood an estate would be to injure it through understatement. Built in 1907 by Charles Hudson, a venture capitalist, Knollwood was a 60-room granite palace that combined such myriad architectural flourishes as Italian Renaissance, Greek revival, and Spanish Churrigueresque. Lying at the center of what is now the Muttontown Preserve, Knollwood was purchased in 1951 by Ahmed Bey Zogu, better known as King Zog of Albania. Zog, who had a penchant for poker and perfumed cigarettes (reportedly smoking an average of 150 a day), became president of Albania in 1925 and proclaimed himself king three years later. Not all of his subjects were delighted by this turn of events, so to consolidate power, Zog put each of his four sisters in command of an army division, while his mother ran the royal kitchen—just to make sure his food wasn't tampered with. Still, Zog was almost gunned down by two assassins in 1931, and by 1939, after Italy invaded Albania and defeated its army in two days, he "retired" to England, bringing with him a fair balance of his country's bullion. It was during a visit to the US in 1951 that King Zog saw Knollwood and purchased it with—so it was rumored at the time—"a bucket of rubies and diamonds," to the tune of $102,800. Such tales can take on a life of their own, and although Zog reportedly never lived at Knollwood, treasure hunters, convinced that his booty was hidden within the domain, climbed over the walls and vandalized the establishment beyond repair. In 1955, the estate was sold to Lansdell Christie, a mining tycoon, who four years later razed the mansion to the ground.

More recently, in November 2001, six men were practicing orienteering in Muttontown when one saw a glint of sunlight beneath a tree. That reflective matter turned out to be bone—part of a human skeleton curled up in a fetal position below a light layer of leaves. The authorities were summoned, and after an extensive forensic examination, the corpse was determined to belong to a woman of approximately 35 years, 5'1" to 5'3" in height. The victim—she had been murdered, the police concluded—was missing a top front tooth, as well as the metal or plastic denture that would have filled the gap. With few clues to go on, the case remains open.

You won't require a deerstalker cap and a pal named Watson to follow the scent in this beautiful sanctuary—sturdy-soled walking shoes and the park map should more than suffice. Pick the latter off the rack on the back porch of the Bill Patterson Nature Center abutting the parking area. Turn around there and face the woods: The trail to the right is the shorter interpretive path, while left—your direction—leads into the larger part of the park. In spring, the trails may be a bit soft—downright muddy in spots—but that inconvenience is more than balanced by a colorful collage of wildflowers, including grape hyacinth, blue penstemon, mayapple, periwinkle, wild violet, and anemone, that sparkle on the ground like precious jewels.

The trail bends to the left, initially following the contours of a chain-link fence. Bear left in a few seconds at the wide fork, and right at the next junction, exchanging the dirt track for a grassy path. Ignore the trace to the right as you cruise higher through a cluster of white and black birch trees, maples, cedars, and pines on the way to a T. Hang a right there, and a hard right again in a dozen steps, when you reach the boundary fence. Keep to the right at the pipe gate, in something like 70 feet, and swing left in 100 yards at the ensuing intersection. Now in an area of flowering dogwoods, oaks, and an occasional fruit tree, steer right at the Y, marked by a rare trail blaze, and after striding 175 feet, go right at the subsequent fork. Soft soil and the sound of frogs signal that you are in the vicinity of a lowland swamp, even if trees conceal it from view. Hop left at the T, onto a three-person-wide track, and in 150 feet the shaded lane yields to a wide, grassy field.

As you march to the right, look sharply for bluebirds flitting about the meadow. Stay with this open stretch for several minutes, passing the post by the recessed field to the right, skipping the spur to the left, and holding to the right side of the rail fence until you see the kiosk by the equestrian parking area. Turn right directly after that onto the broad dirt lane, bypassing the spur to the right that appears almost immediately. The easy walking along this maple-shaded carriage road lasts for several minutes, until it begins to bend toward the north, whereupon you glide left on a narrower path. This route enters a labyrinth of trails where much of the fun derives from exploring off the beaten track. Saunter left at the four-way intersection, and then—in a couple of minutes—right at the fork. From an overgrown estate road overhung with aged apple trees, you are now on a narrower track sided by rhododendrons and ivy. The forest grows wilder as you break to the right at the next fork, with yews dwarfed by a handful of Cyclopean pines and beech trees.

And then—suddenly—you are standing among the ruins of Knollwood, with two raised, columnar temples flanking a low, rising stair. As you stroll first south of the stairs to the overgrown bunker, then retrace your steps and head north between the two temples, try to imagine what this looked like half a century ago when it was lavishly landscaped with reflecting pools and formal gardens, marble fountains, Greco-Roman statues, and ivy-filled urns. Stick with the trace that extends north above the stairs; it leads to an imposing wall. A baroque gargoyle fountain leers from its center, with symmetrical staircases—now collapsed—rising on either side. This is all that remains of the mansion itself. The trail resumes to the left as you face this crumbling edifice, swooping around its far side. Dart left at the T with the asphalt-covered lane, reentering a forest of rhododendrons. Stay with this until the four-way intersection (you met this same crossing from the opposite direction on the way to the ruins), where you venture left and, in 75 feet, left again at the T. Take the middle of three choices at the upcoming junction; it brings you to the front of what is listed on the map as a walled garden. This is yet another remnant of the Knollwood era, an imposingly large enclosure with a stucco-covered wall that measures about eight feet high and a football field long.

To continue, cut left of the garden wall; when you near its far end, bear to the right. Roughly 100 feet after it arcs to the left, the trail comes to a fork marked by a post. Roll right there on the overgrown track and adhere to it for 0.25 miles, turning left when you reach the wide dirt trail by a scrub-filled bowl. Go left once more at the T, having passed a dogwood-fringed field, and in a couple of minutes hang a right. Stride straight on by the merging traces and an open field, as the dirt underfoot changes to sand and the chain-link fence from the start of the hike reappears on your left. Launch left at the T and left again at the Y that follows. (A minute later there is a moderately steep spur to the right that ends by a kame, or glacial deposit, sitting at an elevation of 220 feet.) On jumping to the left at the succeeding fork, you are now on familiar turf, backtracking along the first leg of the hike.

## ▶ NEARBY ACTIVITIES

Planting Fields Arboretum State Historic Park, in Oyster Bay, was landscaped by the Olmsted brothers of Massachusetts, whose father designed Central Park. It includes impressive greenhouses, stately gardens, woodlands, and lawns, as well as Coe Hall, a Tudor Revival mansion open to the public. To learn more, visit www.planting fields.com or call (516) 922-8600.

# NORVIN GREEN'S HEART

 **KEY AT-A-GLANCE INFORMATION**

**LENGTH:** 9.3 miles

**CONFIGURATION:** Loop

**DIFFICULTY:** Difficult

**SCENERY:** Abandoned mines, waterfalls and cascades, gnarly laurel forest, and stellar 360-degree panoramic views revealing New York City skyline

**EXPOSURE:** Very shady, except on bald peaks

**TRAFFIC:** Often light, but good weather brings out students and nature-lovers

**TRAIL SURFACE:** Rock-filled dirt, some grassy and rooty stretches

**HIKING TIME:** 5 hours

**SEASON:** Year-round, 9 a.m.–dusk

**ACCESS:** No fee

**MAPS:** At kiosk by Weiss Ecology Center; USGS Wanaque; New York–New Jersey Trail Conference, North Jersey Trails

**FACILITIES:** Nature center, water, rest rooms, and public telephone at Weiss Ecology Center

**SPECIAL COMMENTS:** Rain-fed streams may make some water crossings tough. Remember to bring a flashlight if you want to go spelunking in the old mines.

## ▶ IN BRIEF

If you're considering venturing into Norvin Green, you had better dust off your sturdiest hiking boots. This is a challenging hike into an undeveloped, seriously rugged locale. Your resourcefulness in fording multiple deep-water stream crossings and steep climbs (along with an even steeper descent) will be rewarded with mountaintop vistas, majestic waterfalls, spectral erratics, a couple of historic mines, as well as nonstop natural beauty.

## ▶ DESCRIPTION

Are you a child at heart? Do you enjoy being out in the rain, walking through puddles without an umbrella? Does wrestling with a dense, tangled overgrowth deep in a backwoods wilderness fill you with joyful thoughts of playing explorer? If the answer to these questions is an unqualified yes, then Norvin Green State Forest is just the place for you. Don't be misled by the fact that many of its trails coincide with old logging roads; this is an undeveloped park where rugged is the byword, and raw natural beauty the reward. So how does parading through puddles relate to the price of pitch pines, you wonder? A typical trek in Norvin Green involves fording numerous streams without the benefit of a bridge, wading on occasion through swift-moving, knee-high water. This

## ▶ DIRECTIONS

Follow I-287 over the Tappan Zee Bridge and take Exit 57 (towards Ringwood) onto Skyline Drive. Continue to the intersection with Greenwood Lake Turnpike (CR 511) and make a left, followed by a right in 1.7 miles on Westbrook Road. Drive 1.9 miles, then make a left onto Snake Den Road. Proceed 0.6 miles to the parking area on the right. Parking is also available at the Weiss Ecology Center, 0.2 miles ahead.

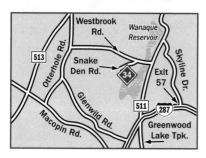

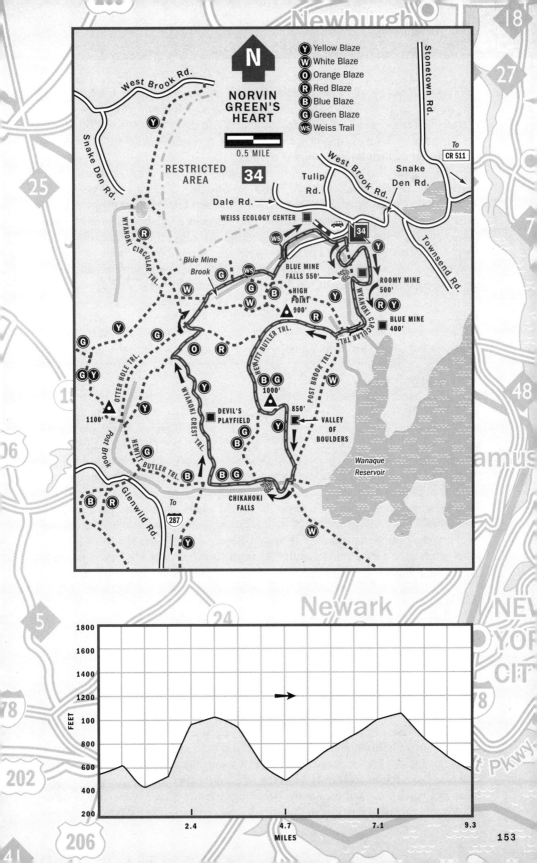

thrilling walk on the wild side involves two such crossings (one by a delightful water-fall), as well as 1,400 feet of elevation gain and loss, culminating in a view of Manhattan from atop a bald dome. Seasoned hikers will enjoy this preserve throughout the year, but we favor visiting in spring, when the forest is freckled with flowers and the challenge of high-flowing water is greatest.

The trailhead is 200 feet east of the parking lot on Snake Den Road, directly opposite the turnoff for Ellen Street. Turn right into the woods on the Wyanokie Circular Trail (WCI, red dot over white-circle). For the first few minutes, the pine-shaded path is pinched between private residences. Those are left behind soon enough, though, as you enter into the Highlands environment of granite-studded rolling hills. Head to the right with the yellow blazes when they fork off in five minutes. This circuitous spur slithers uphill over grass and bedrock, amid a canopy of black birch, oak, and mountain laurel. On reaching a ridge, it dips downhill and then climbs a second ridge, followed once more by a drop in elevation, this time to a purling stream. Rock-hop over that, then scamper up the next slope—the highest ridge yet—staying with the grassy track as it meanders to the top of Blue Mine Falls. This is a pretty setting, at 550 feet of elevation, where the great cascade tumbles into a jumble of oversize boulders, with a number of flat stones on which to sit and relish the watery atmosphere.

Just as the yellow-blazed path encounters a mammoth erratic, it intersects with the WCI. Stick with the yellow markings for now, moving across the junction and back toward higher ground. It is steep going for a few minutes, but it's worth the effort for the views to come atop a rocky knob, where chestnut oak, maple, cedar, and a sizable fin of granite bracket the hills to the west. The yellow blazes shift to the right on leaving this extended bedrock, tracing a line south along the rolling contours of the hill. With a rocky plateau ahead, the track suddenly swerves right, down a steep slope of scree, with a couple of back-filled mine shafts carved into the side of the granite bluff. On hitting the base of the headland, the path approaches the entrance to the Roomy Mine, named after Benjamin Roome (not for the spaciousness of its main entrance), a nineteenth-century surveyor. Iron ore was excavated here from 1840 to 1857 (and for a short spell in 1890), with the tunnel extending more than 100 feet. Outside of spring, when water often floods it, this shaft can be explored with the aid of a flashlight.

Swing left on the WCI when the yellow-blazed route reconnects with it. The main path bends to the right by a bridge, while the Blue Mine lies straight onward, a few yards beyond the broken-up concrete platform. In spring, the broad Blue Mine Brook flows into the yawning orifice of the mine, as frogs and birds bathe in the eddying current. Water has often inundated this historic operation, forcing its closure many times since it was initially opened in 1765. Known variously over the years as the London, Whynokie, and Iron Hill mine, the bluish hue to its iron ore is responsible for the name by which it is now identified. Across the wooden span, a steep ascent lifts you from an altitude of 400 feet to a little over 900. Along the way, the WCI encounters a maverick campfire ring and a squatter's lean-to, where lilies of the valley perfume the air in May. Hold to the left shortly after that, as the yellow blazes break away on a spur, and then to the right when a white-blazed trace surfaces on the left. We once spooked a grouse in this area that was concealed in the grass by the base of a gargantuan birch; it was only too happy to return the favor, stopping our hearts for a moment with its abrupt flutter of wings.

A field of boulders, succeeded by a stand of dead chestnut trees, signals the imminent end to this uphill march. To merely say that High Point summit is granite bedrock partly clad in grass, fringed with knee-high ferns, blueberry bushes, and such wildflowers as Indian strawberry and goats beard, is to do its beauty an injustice. Even with a cluster of spicebush and pitch pines at the periphery, the view here at 900 feet is spectacular, a 360-degree panorama that takes in I-287 to the south, and the New York City skyline beyond that, with the Empire State Building clearly discernible. Your (reluctant) descent from this idyllic dome begins at its northwest side. In about a minute, the Hewitt Butler Trail (HB, blue blazes) merges from the right and for several minutes overlaps the WCI. Continue straight on the HB when the red-dot blazes tack to the right.

The subsequent summit, though 100 feet above High Point, lacks the latter's dramatic vistas. Nonetheless, it is a highly picturesque plateau, with a ten-inch-wide vein of quartzite running through it, and globular glacial erratics, somewhat like misshapen Michelin men, scattered throughout. It requires a fun hand-over-hand scramble up a 35-foot long slab of granite to reach this knoll, which extends quite some distance to the south. Cruise left at the fork onto the yellow-blazed track, which persists along this delightful, sun-struck shelf for five minutes or so before finally losing elevation. A rocky knob partway down the slope faces to the south, providing another opportunity to view the Wanaque Reservoir and the Big Apple from afar. In springtime, fuchsia-yellow penstemon and rare moccasin flowers add a touch of magic to this jagged, antediluvian environment. From there, the sharp descent grows more earnest, with the path snaking by one sentinel stone after another, part of a valley of boulders that rolled off the high bluffs eons ago.

Old faded markings lead over the rocks, but fresh yellow blazes reroute the path westbound, a hair shy of the boulder field and down the moraine-filled, grassy slope. This is an underused segment of trail, and you may have to limbo under some fallen trees and detour around others. A series of seasonal stream crossings coincides with the ongoing elevation loss, with no shortage of rocks to skip over. The yellow blazes end at a slanted T with the Post Brook Trail (PB, white blazes) and a rusty chain-link fence. Slice right, then right again in two minutes at the four-way intersection. The imminent crossing with Post Brook, a tributary to the Wanaque Reservoir, is not so easily handled. By late summer, the water level should have receded enough to allow for rock-hopping, but wading is often required. While you strip off your boots and socks, don't forget to scan the stream bank for moccasin flowers, which thrive in this moist, shady habitat.

As you slosh west away from the stream, ignore the numerous traces branching right toward the water: Additional aquatic adventures lie ahead. Bounding over the next stream, five minutes distant, is facilitated by an abundance of rocks (a staff for balance comes in handy here). Then, with the roar of splashing water as a prelude, you're at Chikahoki Falls. At first glance, the PB appears to expire at this explosive waterfall, separated from it by the wide-flowing, seasonally bifurcated Post Brook. A second inspection suggests that the trail leaps the left fork of this runoff and strikes up the opposite embankment. Hold on—the white blazes actually cut right just prior to the cascade, through its broad, deep right fork. Within half a minute of wading across, the dirt path draws to the top of Chikahoki Falls, where a thrilling series of lesser cascades churns Post Brook into a succession of whitewater.

The PB ends as blue and green blazes merge from the right. Stride straight on, jumping over the following confluence, and in five minutes turn right on the Wyanokie Crest Trail (WCR, yellow blazes). Whether you spell it Wyanokie, Whynokie, or Wanaque, by the way, its root is Winaki, a local Indian word meaning "land of sassafras." Sassafras does indeed grow throughout the Highlands, but your eyes are more likely to light upon the endless array of boulders—and the streams that flow by them. There are several such seasonal water breaks during the upcoming mile, as the path gains 500 feet, with rock-hopping sufficient to get by all of them. At one stage, just after a modest cascade, the WCR itself appears to be an ancient streambed, with nothing but rounded, wobbly rocks to walk on. Keep the stream to your right, and in a few hundred yards, the path exits this Devil's Playfield, winding through mossy ground for a pleasant—if fleeting—change. At the base of a massive granite escarpment, the WCR resumes climbing, crossing the shoulder of the rise and sparing you the steepest assault. Only at the third such plateau does the track drift right and surge up the higher end of the bedrock, passing meanwhile among a silent vigil of eerie, oblong erratics. Look for orange paint on one such knee-high rock, which indicates your exit to the right off the WCR.

This short, orange-blazed connector traverses the crest of the hill, hugged closely by blueberry, laurel, chestnut oak, and black birch. It ends in three minutes, at which stage you should hew to the left, back on the red-blazed WCI. In an additional five minutes, the path tapers off the shady ledge toward a wetland and collides with a four-way intersection. Hang a right on the Otter Hole Trail (OH, green markings) and proceed downhill on this old logging road, remaining with the green blazes for the ensuing half-hour until you arrive at a washed-out bridge. The OH doglegs left, then rock-hops to the right over the wide Blue Mine Brook. Instead of crossing here, though, walk onward on the Weis Trail (W, green "W" on a white square), paralleling the water and with a rickety bridge 150 feet ahead.

Having braved that wobbly span, the W is now flanked on either side by rivulets. Not for long, though: You'll have to stretch to get over the flow on your right, and then jump left at the T. A bridge makes the succeeding crossing easier, as the W veers right immediately after that (the track to the left has been closed) and meanderingly approaches an attractive cascade. (Some damming work was underway on our most recent visit, which may result in minor changes to the trail layout.) The W lunges left just shy of the cataract, in the process delivering a glimpse of Highlands Natural Pool, to which some of this stream water is being diverted. Continue by the entrance to this water park to the edge of the athletic field. Keep to the right, along the south side of the field, and follow the pine-shaded track back to the road. The parking lot lies 100 yards beyond.

## ▶ NEARBY ACTIVITIES

True rockhounds should sniff out a side trip to Franklin's Mineral Museum, where mines, minerals, ores, and fossils are featured. For information, call (973) 827-3481.

# PELHAM BAY
# HUNTER ISLAND LOOP

## ▶ IN BRIEF

Giant beech, birch, and tulip trees lend welcome shade to this tranquil oasis within a tennis-ball lob of one of the area's more popular beaches and sports complexes. Close proximity to a lagoon, the bay, and a salt marsh make this a birding paradise, especially during the spring and fall migrations, so don't forget to bring your binoculars.

## ▶ DESCRIPTION

In the mood for a trivia question? Name the Big Apple's biggest park? Hint: It consists of land the city acquired in 1888 and now totals 2,766 acres, including 13 miles of shoreline. If you guessed Pelham Bay Park, you may be ready for an appearance on Jeopardy.

Of the 28 estates that once lined Pelham Bay, only the Bartow-Pell Mansion (circa 1840) remains. Which is not to suggest that this coastal park is largely undeveloped. On the contrary, visitors with a penchant for play can indulge in a panoply of pursuits, including tennis, basketball, golf, beach-bathing, even horseback-riding. Oh,

## ▶ DIRECTIONS

*By car:* Take I-95 north to Exit 8B (Orchard Beach/City Island) and follow the signs to Orchard Beach for approximately 2.5 miles until you reach the large parking lot on the right. Drive straight across the lot, and park by the tennis courts. Orchard Beach lies directly beyond.

*By public transportation:* The New York City subway's 6 train goes to Pelham Bay Park Station, where the Bx29 City Island bus will take you to the City Island Traffic Circle. Walk from there to Orchard Beach. Memorial Day–Labor Day, the Bx12 and the Bx5 (weekends only) run to Orchard Beach.

## ℹ KEY AT-A-GLANCE INFORMATION

**LENGTH:** 2 miles; add half mile for Twin Islands Nature Trail

**CONFIGURATION:** Horseshoe loop

**DIFFICULTY:** Very easy

**SCENERY:** Saltwater marshes with views of Long Island Sound on one side and a deep, lush forest on the other

**EXPOSURE:** Mostly shady trails; exposed when exploring shoreline

**TRAFFIC:** On summer weekends, most people remain on Orchard Beach

**TRAIL SURFACE:** Gravel and dirt

**HIKING TIME:** 1 hour

**SEASON:** Year-round, dawn-dusk

**ACCESS:** Free admission; Memorial Day–Labor Day $5 parking fee

**MAPS:** At Orchard Beach nature center during summer

**FACILITIES:** Several rest rooms along Orchard Beach boardwalk, concession stands in summer, picnic areas, tennis courts, golf course, playground, athletic field

**SPECIAL COMMENTS:** Bring insect repellent May–September, when mosquitoes reign.

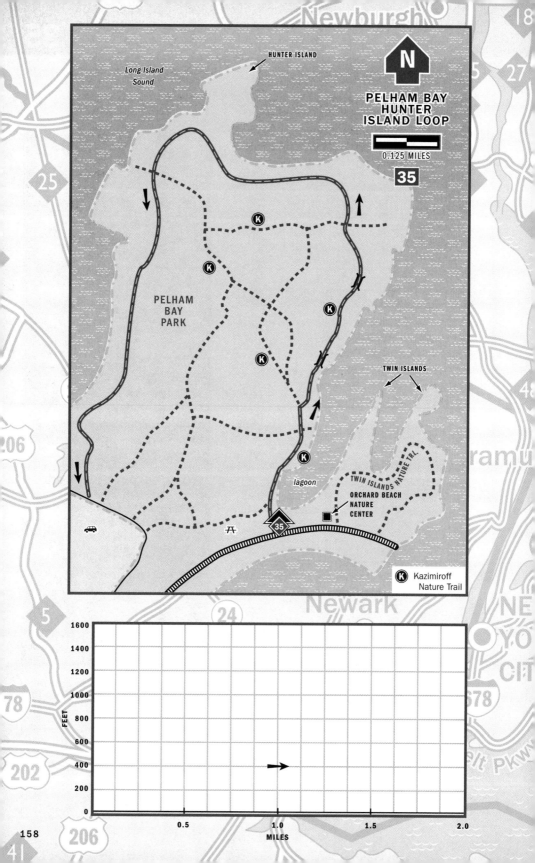

**N**

## PELHAM BAY
## HUNTER
## ISLAND LOOP

0·125 MILES

35

HUNTER ISLAND

Long Island
Sound

Ⓚ

Ⓚ

PELHAM
BAY
PARK

Ⓚ

Ⓚ

Ⓚ

TWIN ISLANDS

Ⓚ

lagoon

TWIN ISLANDS NATURE TRL.

ORCHARD BEACH
NATURE
CENTER

35

Ⓚ Kazimiroff
Nature Trail

| | |
|---|---|
| 1600 | |
| 1400 | |
| 1200 | |
| 1000 | |
| 800 | |
| 600 | |
| 400 | |
| 200 | |
| 0 | |

FEET

→

0.5          1.0          1.5          2.0
MILES

did we overlook hiking? There is that, too, with the excellent—if unchallenging—Hunter Island 2-mile loop just off Orchard Beach.

Start at the northeast end of the parking lot and stroll toward the water. No, this is not going to be a sandy beach walk; when you hit the concrete boardwalk, turn left and go to the Orchard Beach nature center, at section 2 of the beach, where you can pick up an interpretive brochure. Retrace your steps along the boardwalk (about 100 yards) to the first opening in the outer barrier, opposite section three. Take the gravel path there and move inland, passing en route the lagoon by the nature center. Steer to the right of the picnic area, and in a jiffy, you'll be standing in the shade of oaks, birches, black locust, and shagbark hickory trees, with beggar squirrels scrambling around by your feet.

You may have observed that Hunter Island is actually not an island. It *was* until 1934, when the New York City parks commission filled the water between it and the mainland with rocks, effectively extending the peninsula. A similar stunt was pulled on nearby Twin Island, 13 years later. Nonetheless, the contrast between the calm of this peaceful retreat and the rollicking sounds of the picnic-parties and beach-bathers beyond is sharp enough to feed the illusion of being on a distant speck of land.

The first leg of this easy, level hike overlaps the Kazimiroff Nature Trail, and the brochure you picked up at the nature center is pegged to its numbered posts. Don't get too carried away with the reading, though, or you may miss the great white egrets and other waterfowl that fish and nest in the weeds and shallows of the surrounding marshes. Actually, there is little chance of that, as the abundance of spurs to water and marsh viewpoints makes bird sightings almost as common as the swarms of mosquitoes that hover over hikers like cumulus clouds.

Toward the center of Hunter Island, a tangle of sassafras, silver-bark beech, and black birch—many aged and goitered—lend an air of seclusion to this part of the park. Feel free to dart inland and explore the rat's maze of interlacing trails; with water on three sides of the peninsula, you'll have to work hard to get lost. For the easiest water access, though, hang around the perimeter, sticking to the right at almost every major junction. Head through the first such intersection, which occurs just as you encounter a cluster of mature tulip trees. Bear right at the next fork, brushing by a massive oak and over a pair of long wooden bridges. At the four-way crossing, continue straight as the path descends perhaps 12 feet over a large stele-like stone, then bends left, yielding glimpses of a salt marsh and the north end of the bay.

March onward through the intersection that appears right after a superannuated tulip tree; the left leg returns to the Kazimiroff, while the trace to the right leads to water access and a picnic table amid the sandy marsh. The trail circles to the left, then parallels the lagoon and begins a great stretch for watching birding and boats—have your binoculars handy. Remain walking in a southward direction, by majestic oaks and a few mature cottonwoods, while keeping the cordgrass and water to your right. The odd popping sound of tennis balls indicates the trail's imminent end by a cluster of white birch trees and picnic tables at the north side of the parking lot.

Abundant waterfowl and the briny scent of the sea add to the pleasures of Pelham Bay Park.

## ▶ NEARBY ACTIVITIES

The Bartow-Pell Mansion Museum and Gardens, on Shore Road within the park, showcase upper-crust country living of the 1800s. The nine-acre estate includes plush period furniture, art collections, and a carriage house. For information, call (718) 885-1461.

If you feel like donning a tourist's hat, plan to explore City Island. All sorts of art galleries, antiques, and craft shops, as well as many popular seafood restaurants, are wrapped up in the picturesque atmosphere of this quaint fishing town.

# RAMAPO–RINGWOOD RALLY

You know those western hikes in which miles go by with only the cacti or an occasional butte lending variety to a uniform landscape? This trek is cut from different cloth, with so much diversity spilling out of it you'll hardly feel the hours slip away. In addition to six scenic lakes, towering bluffs, no end of streams, glacial erratics by the bushel, and a number of memorable ruins, these woods are inundated with wildlife (including black bears), birds beyond count, and a spring flower display a horticulturalist would envy.

## ▶ DESCRIPTION

As with numerous other hikes in the Highlands of New Jersey, there are so many trails tattooed into the hills of the Ramapo Mountains, it is sometimes hard to know where to begin. Many of these are logging roads that date back to the previous century, when steel was mined extensively from Ringwood Manor to the north, Ramapo Lake to the south, and west beyond Norvin Green State Forest. During that era, this heavily forested country was denuded of trees, and the smelting forges, where oak, maple, and pine trees were reduced to ash, belched streams of smoke into the atmosphere nearly around the clock. Rock crushers, too, worked all day reducing boulders to stones in the process of separating ore from tailings, while their earsplitting racket resounded throughout the region.

## ▶ KEY AT-A-GLANCE INFORMATION

**LENGTH:** 14 miles

**CONFIGURATION:** Loop

**DIFFICULTY:** Very difficult

**SCENERY:** Challenging trails snake through lush forests, past babbling brooks, placid lakes, and humid swamps, over many rock outcroppings and ledges yielding splendid views

**EXPOSURE:** Lush canopy sometimes interrupted by open, grassy spots and bald summits

**TRAFFIC:** Light to moderate; in summer, Boy Scouts will cross your trail; Ramapo Lake circuit is hugely popular on weekends

**TRAIL SURFACE:** Mix of dirt, grass, roots, and lots of rubble underfoot

**HIKING TIME:** 7–8 hours

**SEASON:** Year-round, 8 a.m.–8 p.m.

**ACCESS:** No fee

**MAPS:** At Darlington County Park, 600 Darlington Avenue, Mahwah, (973) 327-3500; www.co.bergen.nj.us; USGS Wanaque; New York–New Jersey Trail Conference, North Jersey Trails

**FACILITIES:** None, but first parking lot, 1 mile earlier, has kiosk with posted map, public phone, and portable toilet

**SPECIAL COMMENTS:** Nearby Campgaw Mountain County Reservation and Ramapo Valley County Reservation offer great camping. Permits can be obtained at Darlington County Park (see above).

## ▶ DIRECTIONS

Follow I-287 over the Tappan Zee Bridge and take Exit 57 (towards Ringwood) onto Skyline Drive. After 0.1 mile, the first parking lot appears on the left. Proceed another mile to the second parking lot on the left, across from the Camp Tamarack sign.

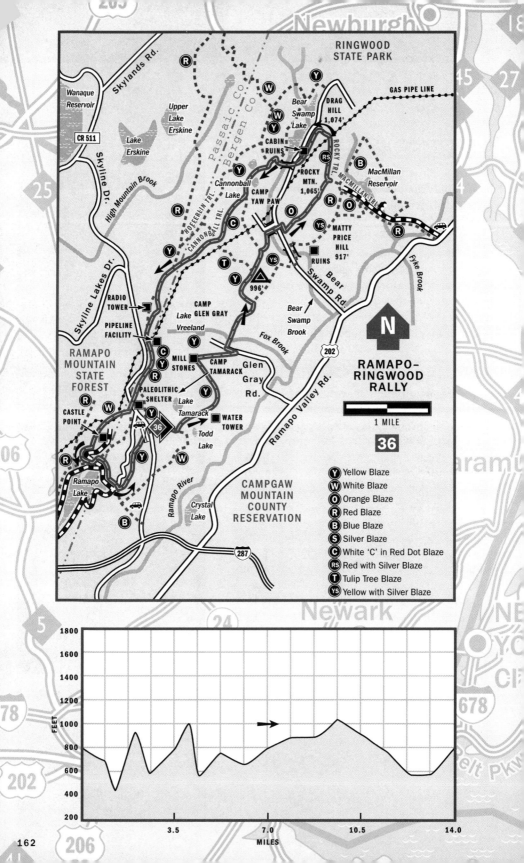

RINGWOOD
STATE PARK

GAS PIPE LINE

Wanaque
Reservoir

Skylands Rd.

CR 511

Upper
Lake
Erskine

Lake
Erskine

Bear
Swamp
Lake

DRAG
HILL
1,074'

High Mountain Brook

Skyline Dr.

Passaic Co.
Bergen Co.

CABIN
RUINS

ROCKY
MTN.
1,065'

RS

B

MacMillan
Reservoir

ROCKY TRL. MACMILLAN TRL.

Cannonball
Lake

CAMP
YAW PAW

O

MATTY
PRICE
HILL
917'

YS

Fyke Brook

JOEFERLIN TRL.

CANNONBALL TRL.

C

R

O

RUINS

T

YS

996'

Bear Swamp Rd.

Skyline Lakes Dr.

RADIO
TOWER

PIPELINE
FACILITY

CAMP
GLEN GRAY

Lake
Vreeland

Bear
Swamp
Brook

Fox Brook

202

RAMAPO–
RINGWOOD
RALLY

RAMAPO
MOUNTAIN
STATE
FOREST

MILL
STONES

CAMP
TAMARACK

Glen
Gray
Rd.

N

1 MILE

36

CASTLE
POINT

PALEOLITHIC
SHELTER

W

Y

36

Lake
Tamarack

WATER
TOWER

Todd
Lake

Ramapo Valley Rd.

Ramapo
Lake

B

Ramapo River

Crystal
Lake

CAMPGAW
MOUNTAIN
COUNTY
RESERVATION

287

Y  Yellow Blaze
W  White Blaze
O  Orange Blaze
R  Red Blaze
B  Blue Blaze
S  Silver Blaze
C  White 'C' in Red Dot Blaze
RS Red with Silver Blaze
T  Tulip Tree Blaze
YS Yellow with Silver Blaze

By contrast, the most you are apt to hear these days, once the roar of traffic is behind you, are the dulcet notes of nature, including the territorial chirpings of birds and the siren songs of cicadas and crickets eager to find a mate. In a forest so filled with history and reflecting the myriad beauty of the Jersey Highlands, something worth photographing is always just around the corner. On one path or another, you may stumble upon a Paleolithic rock shelter or an abandoned swimming pool filled with wildflowers, frogs and turtles sunning themselves by a lily pond, an ancient outhouse perched precariously on the edge of a granite dome, deer grazing in a grassy meadow, or a black bear gorging on blueberries. The following hike, interspersed with ponds and lakes, a number of ruins, and far-reaching vistas, serves as a colorful introduction to the Ramapo Mountains.

This towering cistern is part of a sprawling ruin atop Castle Point, along the Ramapo-Ringwood loop.

From the large parking area, turn around and walk to the opposite side of the road. Look for three white blazes of the Todd Trail (TT) on the telephone pole by a speed-limit sign, and head into the woods there. You descend initially over moss-padded bedrock through a setting of maple, chestnut oak, black birch, dogwood, and flowering azalea. In a couple of minutes, the TT levels off by a seasonal stream, darts around a large protruding slab of granite, and forks to the right, resuming its elevation loss. On hitting the bottom of this gully, the track meanders back toward higher ground, meeting in ten minutes a slanted T with a forest road. Stay with the TT as it shifts first to the right, then left at a Y in 60 feet, succeeded immediately by a second right. Cruise left off the grassy forest road in another 80 feet onto a yellow-blazed trail (YT). That brings you quite rapidly to Todd Lake, an attractive lily pond surrounded by sheep laurel, dogwood, and ferns, where you shadow the shoreline clockwise to a fragmentary ruin of an old cabin (where we once surprised a pair of water snakes and a lizard sunning themselves on the rocks).

Moseying along, the YT rises to a grassy plateau graced by the presence of a powder-blue water tower, only to drop away moments later, losing ground as it approaches a seasonal stream and minor cascade. The yellow markings are clearly visible along this stretch, as they lead higher up the hillside, cresting by a sign for the historic "Millstones," where such stones were quarried and carved decades ago. There are two discarded efforts to the left of the path, near the emergence of a white-blazed route, and another circular stone—the finest of the trio—lies to the right as you begin to descend. The YT, now also bearing white tags, forks left when it meets a carriage road, and seconds later darts across the paved Glen Gray Road.

On dropping off the pavement, the path swings left by the old Tulip Springs Tent Site, dating to 1917, and parallels the road briefly before bending toward Fox

Brook. It is an uphill march again, once you hop past that rocky creek, with the yellow and white routes diverging in about three minutes. Steer right with the YT and continue upward, passing by an enormous erratic just as the track arcs to the left. In ten minutes of steady walking, the trail levels off on the ridge and threads through a colorful area of rocks and ruins, including a ramshackle outhouse—use it only if you must! Forge onward past the cabin foundations by the stream, and swing right at the slanted T with the grass-covered logging road. In 20 yards the YT breaks to the left, near the corroded framework of a collapsed fire tower, once more striking upward. At the false summit there are additional cabin remnants, barely discernible at ground level, but the real prize—a clear view of the Manhattan skyline to the southeast—awaits at the top of the crest.

Don't fret if haze or fog curtail the vista, for even without that New York eyeful, this remains, at 996 feet above sea level, an enchanting lichen-crusted shelf, decorated with knee-high grass, scrub oaks, and a smattering of chestnut snags. When you have had enough of the rarefied atmosphere, continue along the YT, which is joined at the summit by the MacMillan Trail (MT, orange markings). The Old Guard Trail (OGT, green tulip tree leaf on white blaze) appears a minute later on the left and can be used as a cut-through to the Cannonball Trail (CT, white "C" on red) if you want to slice 3 or 4 miles off the hike.

After fording a rocky debris field and a colorful seasonal runoff, the YT/MT shifts left onto a carriage road. In about 60 seconds the MT breaks to the right—follow it. Now trending downhill, this rocky route encounters a log cabin, its tarpaper roof now collapsed, and a pair of appealing streams, only to emerge on Bear Swamp Road. Go right on that and right again once you have walked over the wooden car bridge. In two minutes you should fork left with the orange blazes back into the forest, entering a colorful clutch of high granite ridges topped by scattered cedars. This isolated area of striking rock formations ends too soon when the MT, having dropped down to a small stream, cuts sharply to the right toward MacMillan Reservoir. Your direction is over the trickling tributary to the left, on the red and silver-blazed Rocky Trail (RT). Before shuffling off on that, however, you might venture five minutes farther on the MT for a view of the picturesque lake.

That bit of sightseeing over, proceed along the RT as it gains nearly 200 feet over the next two-thirds of a mile. On leveling off, hold to the left side of the boggy wetland, then cross the pipeline break where it is patched with an elbow of pavement. Scoot left at the Y, back on Bear Swamp Road, with Bear Swamp Lake beyond the trees to the right.

In hugging this side of the lake for 0.4 miles, you might pop down to the right and explore the ruins of lakeside cabins (be on the lookout for rusty nails, reclusive rodents, and slumbering snakes). The paved drive of one leads to an intact slate patio, right by the water; the house, however, looks as though it was blown apart by a bomb. Farther on, a substantial stone foundation bristles with columbine in the spring. Cross the bridge by the dam pour-off and turn left on the CT, passing in the process yet another ruin, its chimney pointing skyward like a petrified snag.

Stick with this path for 5 miles, all the way back to Skyline Drive. It is well marked and wide for most of that distance, overlapping old logging roads. It bypasses a couple of traces to the right, then bends right at a fork, en route to a small pond where purple irises bloom in spring and bullfrogs bellow throughout the summer. We spooked a wild turkey here once, its wings banging noisily against the close-growing birch trees as it struggled to take flight. The trail glides by a log cabin, an outpost of Camp Yaw Paw, and then swerves right, near the concrete dam of that shallow pond. Vigilance is your watchword for the ensuing 20 minutes, as the CT is intersected by a handful of paths, including the far end of the OGT. Fork to the right about 300 feet beyond a towering A-frame (just after a 4-way junction), and lunge right again in another three to four minutes. Shortly thereafter, the path arrives at an open-topped, rectangular concrete tank, apparently an old bathing pool that now swims with lavender geraniums in May.

It is uphill from here, through a grassy woodland—a favorite haunt of white-tailed deer—before meeting a small seasonal cascade that skips noisily from one stone to another. Jump to the right once you get through that rocky zone, making for the ridge. The CT merges shortly with the Hoeferlin Trail (HT, yellow blazes) and continues straight, crawling over the granite bedrock of the ridge, where spicebush and penstemon thrive, before tailing off to the left. Note the two rusty trucks, circa 1945, below the slope: one upside down, the other with a tree indenting its roof. About a minute beyond the radio tower—100 yards away atop the ridge—the track joins the utility road leading to that tower. Dogleg left here and swing right in a few paces, pursuing the blazes back into the forest. Stride through the four-way intersection, ignore the trace that appears moments later, and cut right out to Skyline Drive, bypassing the two fenced-in gas outlets of the pipe-line cut. Hug the near shoulder of the road for 15 yards and then hop the metal gate and return to the shade of the woods. In about five minutes, the HT bounds to the left, and you may follow it to the parking area if you are ready to quit. (In doing so, look for the Paleolithic Indian shelter around to the right on dropping off the rocky bluff.)

Still with us on the CT? Great, because in addition to the lovely Ramapo Lake, a thrilling bit of drama awaits at Castle Point, not far ahead. When the CT crosses Skyline Drive, transfer to a white-blazed trail by the "Slow" sign, 150 feet down the road to the left. There is a decent view to the west from a rock shelf, and then the path descends into a laurel-choked wetland, fords a serpentine stream, and lurches to the left of a phragmite marsh. Next the trail swings left on a gravel track, reunites in a second with the gas-line cut, and starts up the hill. Just as the break threatens to become really steep, the path springs to the left by an easily missed, overgrown post. Blazes are hard to see, but in about three minutes, the trace slips to the left off this well-beaten track and continues over bedrock and grassy ground. Turn left at the T under a string of power lines, and branch to the right in a few paces, leaving the wide cut. Near the top of the hill, the trail jogs left by an arrow painted on a rock, finally achieving the summit in another minute.

The views of the hills to the east—and especially of the Wanaque Reservoir, west of you—are wonderful. No less eye-catching, however, is the crenelated gray-stone tower that dominates this granite dome, where cedars and sycamores provide nominal shade and columbine and penstemon grow from the fractured bedrock. This muscular monument measures 30 feet high and a good 15 feet wide, but it is not the castle to which the name Castle Point refers. No, in spite of its medieval appearance, this is merely a cistern that once held drinking water for a nearby estate. The trail plunges south on the ridge, brushing by pitch pines, lilies of the valley, and, in a couple of minutes, an overgrown swimming pool, with a rickety set of stairs daring you to enter its weed-choked depths. Enough of these architectural hors d'oeuvres; the main course, the burned-out ruins of a colossal, three-story fieldstone mansion, is just ahead. Now completely overgrown, this "castle" was built by William Porter (no relation to the master of short stories known as O. Henry; *this* Porter was a stockbroker) in 1909–1910, but he died in a freak car accident just before his estate was finished. Porter's widow lived in the house, known alternately as Foxcroft, Oakland Castle, and Van Slyke Castle, until her death in 1940. Her heirs sold the property, and by the early 1950s, it reportedly became tied up in a drawn-out divorce. Unoccupied, the mansion proved too tempting a treasure for trespassers and by the end of the decade it was set on fire by vandals.

When you have finished exploring the ruins, proceed south, keeping to the east—or left—side of the ridge. The trail hops over the wall here (look for a blaze on the rocks), just shy of a large dead pine. (Don't forget to enjoy the great view of the lake below before you start scrambling down the rocky slope.) Stay with the white blazes as they fork right, and in one minute, head right on the forest road. This lane arcs sharply to the east as it approaches Ramapo Lake and continues clockwise around its shore. The north end of the lake is a glacial depression formed during the last ice age, between 12,000 and 15,000 years ago, while a stone dam has helped to amass the remainder of the water. It is a very pretty setting, with yellow-flowering lilies on the surface, rocks around the shore, and a trickling cascade on the left.

As the road bends left on approaching the dam, look for yellow blazes. Leave the pavement in a minute, when those blazes dive into woods to the right, and pivot at once to the left, now paralleling the road. Gradually the trail delves deeper into the forest, climbing uphill toward the east. Hang a left at the T, ignoring the pair of traces that succeed that, and then go right at the fork, still with yellow markings. A bar gate appears shortly beyond the pond on your left, with the parking lot, and the end of hike, a few stumbling steps farther on.

## ▶ NEARBY ACTIVITIES

Still have some stamina left? Skylands Manor and the New Jersey Botanical Garden, both within Ringwood State Park, make a wonderful combination of a Tudor-style mansion in a flowering environment. Gothic Ringwood Manor, also on the park grounds, contains nineteenth-century American paintings and furniture. For information and guided tours, call (973) 962-7527.

# ROCKEFELLER MEDLEY

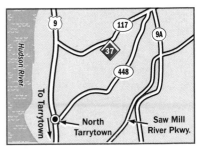

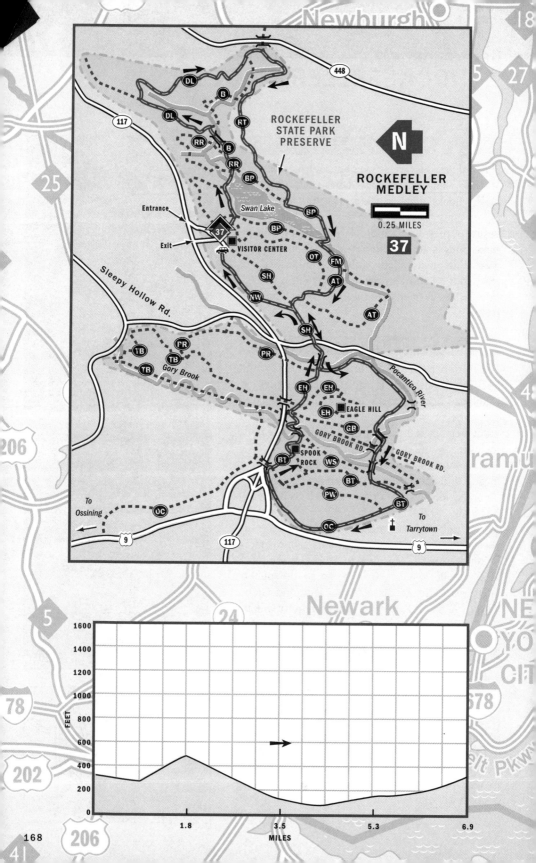

ROCKEFELLER STATE PARK PRESERVE

ROCKEFELLER MEDLEY

0.25 MILES

37

Swan Lake

Entrance
Exit

VISITOR CENTER

Sleepy Hollow Rd.

Gory Brook

EAGLE HILL

Pocantico River

GORY BROOK RD.

GORY BROOK RD.

SPOOK ROCK

To Ossining

To Tarrytown

boots to survey this realm. Almost all the trails are graded carriage lanes, and thus the most challenging obstacles you are likely to contend with are pebbles on the path. That said, this is one dazzling domain, laced with more than enough loops to put in a long, enjoyable workout.

Stop by the modern Visitor Center, uphill from the parking area, and pick up a map. Trails are extremely well signposted, but a map is necessary to get the most out of this sprawling park. Continue onward to the pastoral Swan Lake, where lilies dot the water and oaks thrive by its cattail-lined shore, and you'll probably see more people jogging, strolling, and sunning themselves than over the remainder of this 6.9-mile jaunt. Follow the left side of the lake, and just after fording its grass-covered dam, hang a left onto Old RR Bed. You may be relieved to observe that the well-groomed look of the lake area, with the lawn snipped just so, does not carry over to the undulating forestland beyond the water. In fact, as you move right onto the Brook Trail, wildflowers, ferns, and sassafras begin to vie for space with the strip of grass that flanks the gravel- and sand-surfaced track.

Your next turn is to the left, between two bridges, loping uphill on David's Loop among dogwoods, birch, beech, and tulip trees. Hilly and nearly a mile long, this is one of park's more secluded—and prettier—pieces of trail. It ends back on Brook, where you jump left onto the Ridge Trail. Also about a mile in length, the Ridge runs by fairly open grasslands that evoke the times when farms still operated in these parts. For a while it is also within earshot, alas, of Route 448, picking up a disturbing amount of traffic noise before wending away to the right.

Eventually, the Ridge dead-ends back at Swan Lake; bear left on the Brothers' Path, then right at the subsequent four-way crossing in perhaps 125 yards. Keep right at the ensuing junction, where a conduit flows off the lake, then pivot sharply left, leaving Brothers' Path for the Farm Meadow Trail. This parallels a small creek for a bit, until you cut right onto the Ash Tree Loop. The circuit is soon joined from the right by the Overlook Trail, to which you switch in a few moments as it bends away to the right. Tack left when Overlook meets the Old Sleepy Hollow Road Trail, and stay with the latter across the pavement (look out for cars!) and over the bridge, until it slams into the Pocantico River Trail. Lope left there.

This 0.75-miles stretch by the scenic, meandering river is especially enjoyable in spring, when the water level is high. There is a modest cascade maybe 100 yards below the bridge, with a number of viewing spots atop the retaining wall from which to gaze at the purling water. You might also choose to leave the path and sit on a rock by the river, sandwich or sketchpad in hand. At the finely wrought Romanesque bridge—one of several such structures in the preserve—canter to the right and persevere along

From hardwood forests to gurgling streams, the beauty of Rockefeller State Park can often be captured from its many graceful bridges.

Pocantico until it eventually hits the Gory Brook Road Trail. Veer left past the bridge, then stride straight ahead, bypassing the concrete span at the intersection with the abandoned road. At the next junction, hew to the right over the moss-covered bridge, marching forward at the succeeding fork.

You are gamboling along Witches Spring, with a steep, overgrown hillside rising up over your right shoulder, a moist, boggy thicket off to your left. In heading through the ensuing exchange, you'll be transferring to the Big Tree Trail and trending more steeply upward, with a thick grove of pines off to the side. Shift left at the subsequent intersection, shortly after a partly hidden cemetery, arriving in a matter of seconds at the Old Croton Aqueduct Trail (OCA). Roll right and stick with the OCA for roughly 0.75 miles.

The most appealing part of the OCA is where you first meet it, with a 20-foot high, solid section of the aqueduct's old wall towering over the trail. There are few further ruins to enliven this leg, though, and the path draws uncomfortably close to the cacophonic US 9. No matter, for in 15 minutes you fork right back into the preserve, while the OCA drifts off to the left, over a bridge and US 117.

Once within the park, turn left on the Big Tree Trail, where the trees are no more impressive than those you saw earlier on David's Loop, and left again at the T. Continue downhill and circle to the right, keeping an eye out on that side of the path for Spook Rock, a gray, oblong erratic streaked with black varnish. Whether this sarcophagus-like stone resembles a ghost that's gone to sleep, an ogre lying on his back, or whatever, depends upon your imagination—and, just possibly, the sounds emanating from the forest at that particular moment.

Ambling onward down the hill, step left at the first fork, and ditto at the base of the triangle. You should now be in the boggy area of Witches Spring Trail, passing over a bridge and then swinging left onto Gory Brook (once more) at the top of the rise. Make a right a few seconds later and remain on Eagle Hill until it hits Pocantico, where you go left briefly, then right, recrossing the bridge at the end of Old Sleepy Hollow Road Trail, and then hopping over Sleepy Hollow Road itself. This is familiar ground—a retracing of your earlier steps until you meet the somewhat overgrown Nature's Way on the left.

Nature's Way is the only trail in Rockefeller that is restricted solely to hikers. While it is a pity that only a half mile is so designated in a park this large, and that it runs *ear*fully close to the busy US 117, Nature's Way does have its pretty points. It arcs by locust trees, hemlocks, and Tarzan vines that hang invitingly from broad-limbed white pines. A granite outcropping just off trail adds to the rustic charm of this path, as did the three white-tailed stags we encountered on a recent visit. The hike ends at the overflow parking area, with the main lot just ahead.

## ▶ NEARBY ACTIVITIES

This area is quite rich in Rockefeller-themed cultural attractions. The Kykuit Rockefeller Mansion in Pocantico Hills features a magnificent art collection, antique carriages, and automobiles, as well as terraced gardens overlooking the Hudson River. Call (914) 631-9491 for information.

Philipsburg Manor in Sleepy Hollow (on US 9) is a Dutch-style stone manor house with eighteenth-century furnishings and a working gristmill. Call (914) 631-8200 for information.

Highlights of the Lyndhurst Estate in Tarrytown (also on US 9) include oil paintings, Tiffany glass, silk rugs, and trompe-l'oeil ceilings and walls. Call (914) 631-4481 for details.

The Union Church on Bedford Road (Route 448) is open to the public and contains stained glass windows by Chagall and Matisse. For tours, call (914) 332-6659.

# SANDY HOOK HIKING TRAIL

## KEY AT-A-GLANCE INFORMATION

**LENGTH:** 9.6 miles

**CONFIGURATION:** Out and back

**DIFFICULTY:** Moderate

**SCENERY:** Dunes and beaches, salt marshes and maritime forests, historic lighthouse and fort

**EXPOSURE:** Mostly exposed, except for a few stretches through holly forest

**TRAFFIC:** Summer weekends attract hordes of beach-lovers, but only a fraction visit the trail

**TRAIL SURFACE:** Mostly sandy, but paved in Fort Hancock area

**HIKING TIME:** 5 hours, maybe less with a good tailwind

**SEASON:** Year-round, dawn–dusk

**ACCESS:** $10 beach parking Memorial Day–Labor Day; seasonal beach pass $50; pets must be leashed

**MAPS:** USGS Sandy Hook; National Park Service map at Visitor Center

**FACILITIES:** Rest rooms, water and public phone at Visitor Center, seasonal rest rooms and beach showers in Fort Hancock area and at beaches

**SPECIAL COMMENTS:** Be sure to come before 10 a.m. on summer weekends; when the parking lots fill, the park closes until space frees up. In spring and summer parts of the beaches may be closed to protect nesting shorebirds. On weekends the lighthouse offers tours.

## IN BRIEF

Beach dunes, huge holly trees, saltwater marshes, coastal defense ruins, a nineteenth-century fort, and even a historic lighthouse combine to endow this long, level jaunt with an interdisciplinary appeal. The icing on the cake comes in two flavors: a striking view of Manhattan from an observation deck near the Hook's end, and the many waterfowl and migratory birds that pass by at various times of year.

## DESCRIPTION

Of the 2.5 million people who visit Sandy Hook every year, less than a fifth of them ever make it off the beach. No question, this barrier peninsula is blessed with extraordinary ocean vistas along its 7 miles of sandy shore. But to limit yourself to sunbathing, salt spray, and splashing surf is to miss the greater part of what Sandy Hook is all about.

## DIRECTIONS

*By car:* Follow I-95 across the George Washington Bridge into New Jersey. Continue south and switch to the Garden State Parkway south at Exit 11. Take Exit 117 off the Garden State Parkway onto SR 36 east. Drive for about 12 miles to the park entrance, then proceed north to the parking lot by the Spermacetti Cove Visitor Center.

*By public transportation:* From the New York Port Authority, take the New Jersey Transit 834 bus, which stops close to the park entrance; or from Penn Station, take the New Jersey Transit North Coast Line train to Red Bank Station. The New Jersey Transit 834 bus runs from there to Highlands, New Jersey. The most scenic option by far is the ferry, with service between Manhattan and Sandy Hook operating in summer months. Call the park for information at (718) 354-4606.

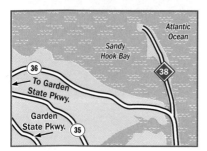

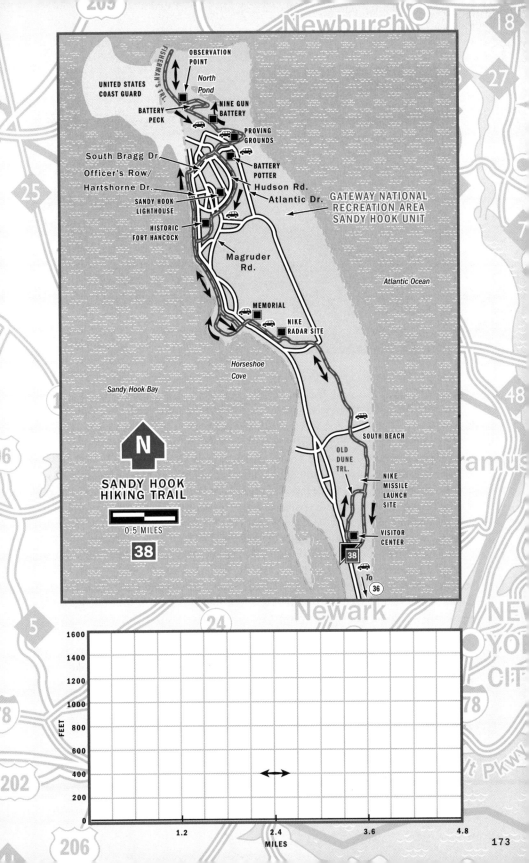

OBSERVATION
POINT

North
Pond

UNITED STATES
COAST GUARD

NINE GUN
BATTERY

BATTERY
PECK

PROVING
GROUNDS

South Bragg Dr.

BATTERY
POTTER

Officer's Row/
Hartshorne Dr.

Hudson Rd.

Atlantic Dr.

GATEWAY NATIONAL
RECREATION AREA
SANDY HOOK UNIT

SANDY HOOK
LIGHTHOUSE

HISTORIC
FORT HANCOCK

Magruder
Rd.

Atlantic Ocean

MEMORIAL

NIKE
RADAR SITE

Horseshoe
Cove

Sandy Hook Bay

N

SANDY HOOK
HIKING TRAIL

0.5 MILES

38

SOUTH BEACH

OLD
DUNE
TRL.

NIKE
MISSILE
LAUNCH
SITE

VISITOR
CENTER

38

To
36

FISHERMAN'S TRL.

173

Hard surf, historic battlements, and 7 miles of beaches are all part of a visit to the Sandy Hook peninsula.

A unit of Gateway National Recreation Area, the 1,665-acre Sandy Hook is, essentially, an elongated sandbar that extends from the north end of New Jersey's coast up toward Coney Island. But what a sandbar! With salt marshes, a maritime forest—including one of the densest concentrations of American holly on the Atlantic coast—and great diversity of plant life, it is also a critical stopover point in the Atlantic Flyway, as birds of all feathers flock to it during spring and fall migrations. And because of Sandy Hook's strategic position at the mouth of New York Harbor, it has played a role in guiding ships and protecting the city since 1764. The lighthouse built then is still in use; it's our nation's oldest such beacon. Near it is Fort Hancock, an aggregation of dozens of gun batteries and buildings which defended the harbor from 1895 through 1974.

This visually exciting linear hike takes in much of Sandy Hook's historic and natural attributes. It is level and easy, but the sun exposure for much of its 9- to 10-mile length is fairly extreme. Pick up a Fort Hancock walking tour pamphlet at the Visitor Center and strike out on the Old Dune Trail there. Right from the get-go, the peninsula's plant diversity is on display, with red cedar, holly, scrub oak, black cherry shrubs, bayberry, black gum, and even prickly pear cactus thriving in the sandy soil.

In a few minutes, the winding track opens up to a view of the ocean. Remain north through the four-way intersection to post 11, which relates to the Nike missile site that was once within the nearby rusty chain-link fence. The Sandy Hook Hiking Trail leaves the Old Dune loop here and runs along the right side of the fenced-in compound, which now shelters a pair of old dumpsters and a derelict trailer. To the right is the ocean, where tankers and other ships often cruise the waves farther out.

From there, the path flows along the tops of the dunes, cutting through the fragile grass; try to walk gently so as not to damage the plants. Once past another fenced-in depot, the trail swings away from the giant clamshells and driftwood of the beach and back into a cedar grove. In a couple of minutes, it passes a paved access road to South Beach, with a pillbox and bunker to the right—leftover defenses from World War II.

The subsequent stretch is one of the few shady points of the walk, slipping through a thick, jungle-like entanglement of vines, very tall holly, sumac, cat briar, and phragmites. Bear left at the sandy fork, and in five or eight minutes a fenced-in bunker appears, succeeded by additional ruins a few paces later. At the next paved access road, dogleg left and then right to stay with the path. Keep an eye out for the blue-blazed gray posts, which run the length of this hike.

Had enough of military ruins yet? Let's hope not, since many more compounds await along the loamy ground, including another fenced compound where the Nike radar station tracked Soviet jets. Only a series of elevated platforms remain of the former, indicated by a signboard on the installation's west side. Traverse to the northwest corner of the parking lot there, almost directly under some power lines, and edge right to the grassy pocket-park memorial for James Champion and Hamilton Halliburton.

From their memorial mast, the path cuts to the road and after 300 yards crosses to a walkway wending west, out to Horse-

Built in 1764, the Sandy Hook lighthouse is the oldest such beacon still functioning in the country.

shoe Cove and an overlook of the salt marsh. If you don't see an abundance of cavorting waterfowl here, you'd better have your eyes checked! Move north by the rotting pilings of an old pier and, to your right, cement foundations of the shipyard. The National Park Service intends to clean up all the debris here, but in the meantime be very careful where you step. The trail bends to the right by a couple of large concrete hulks that have been colorfully-tattooed with graffiti, despite a sign warning people not to approach them.

Enjoy the ensuing patch of sandy shore, for soon you'll climb up to the park road, turn left, and remain with pavement right into Fort Hancock, due north. Although the military has used the Hook since the War of 1812, most of the sand-colored brick buildings of the fort date from the early 1900s. Stroll up the west side of Officers Row to the Rodman Gun, where Hartshorne Drive meets South Bragg, and strut right onto the latter. The next blue-blazed post is 200 yards ahead on the north side of the road. From there you'll take a right on Atlantic Drive, cross the road, and enter the proving ground where cannons were tested, or "proofed," prior to being put into action.

This spur flows for perhaps 150 yards by a number of old foundations, then veers left, leading into a gravel parking area. March north alongside the cordoned-off Nine Gun Battery, a ghostly concrete structure with a labyrinth of rooms and cells. The trail continues at the north end of the lot, past similar batteries. When you reach the interpretive sign about warblers, by Battery Peck, go right and struggle through the sand dunes to a rail fence, then loop left to the observation deck. From atop that post, which overlooks North Pond, you can clearly see the Verrazano-Narrows Bridge, and, just beyond, the Manhattan skyline. The Coast Guard facility nearer at hand is off limits to the public. From the base of the observation deck, shift left to rejoin the trail and retrace your steps to South Bragg Drive. Before doing so, however, you might venture out on the Fisherman's Trail (1 mile round-trip) to the end of the Hook.

Back by South Bragg, head left onto Hudson Road, passing Battery Potter and the brick power plant, one of the oldest edifices of the fort. As the street angles to the right it runs smack dab into the lighthouse. This tower was originally built on the tip of the peninsula, but an accumulation of tide-swept sand over the years has extended Sandy Hook more than a mile northward. Who knows, someday it may reach Staten Island. Pick up Magruder Road at the lighthouse and stick with it to the Nike missile at the fort's entrance. Return from there by your earlier route, and at post 11 on the Old Dunes Trail, go left along the beach to complete the loop.

## ▶ NEARBY ACTIVITIES

The illuminating Twin Lights Historic Site State Park in Highlands, a double lighthouse, features a commanding view from its north tower, and its museum documents the works of inventor Guglielmo Marconi and the Life Saving Service. For details, call (732) 872-1814.

# SCHUNEMUNK MOUNTAIN RIDGE LOOP

## ▶ IN BRIEF

Some hikes balance a number of attributes, providing a razzle-dazzle of experiences. Then there is Schunemunk Mountain. After a grueling gain of 1,300 feet right at the outset, you'll enjoy several miles atop a double ridge, with nothing but views to distract you. Views north to the Catskills, west to Kittatinny Ridge, east to the Hudson, and to the south—well, you get the idea: For views better than this, you'd have to sprout wings. The autumn leaf-peeping is heaven-sent, and for sensational highland scrambling from one pudding-stone knob to another, this one is hard to top.

## ▶ DESCRIPTION

Remember the fable about the grasshopper and the ant? Good, because the tiring, knee-buckling haul up the slope of Schunemunk Mountain is best approached with the steady pluck of a pismire, rather than the short-lived, "be happy" attention span of a leaf-eating locust. The 1,300-foot vertical gain at the outset of this hike is indeed draining, but once that is out of the way, you'll have several miles of ridgetops to ramble

## ▶ DIRECTIONS

*By car:* Follow the New York State Thruway I-87 north across the Tappan Zee Bridge. Take Exit 16 and drive north on SR 32 for 7.4 miles. At the sign for the Black Rock Fish & Game Club on the right side of the road, turn left on Pleasant Hill Road, followed by an immediate left on Taylor Road. Proceed 1.6 miles and go left onto Otterkill Road. The parking lot is 0.8 miles farther on the right side.

*By public transportation:* Take the Metro North Railroad Port Jervis line to Salisbury Mills–Cornwall Station. From there, a cab ride only lasts about 2 miles.

## ⓘ KEY AT-A-GLANCE INFORMATION

**LENGTH:** 10.5 miles

**CONFIGURATION:** Balloon

**DIFFICULTY:** Difficult

**SCENERY:** Steep ascent leads to double ridge, separated by a brook and a swamp, yielding several 360-degree vistas on top of conglomerate bedrock, surrounded by dwarf growth of pitch pine and oak

**EXPOSURE:** Shady ascent, exposed ridge loop

**TRAFFIC:** Popular venue in spring and fall

**TRAIL SURFACE:** Rock-studded dirt, some grassy patches, and bedrock

**HIKING TIME:** 6 hours

**SEASON:** Year-round, sunrise–sunset

**ACCESS:** No fee, no motorized vehicles

**MAPS:** Posted at trailhead kiosk; USGS Cornwall; New York–New Jersey Trail Conference, West Hudson Trails

**FACILITIES:** None

**SPECIAL COMMENTS:** Wear good hiking shoes with decent traction. Binoculars will help in identifying distant landmarks and soaring birds. In winter, blazes and cairns may be snow-covered.

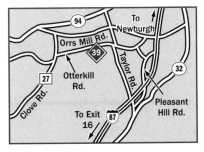

**Y** Yellow Blaze
**W** White Blaze
**R** Red Dot on White Blaze
**B** Blue Dot on White Blaze
**K** Black Dot on White Blaze
**D** Turquoise Diamond Blaze
**T** Turquoise Blaze

N

SCHUNEMUNK
MOUNTAIN
RIDGE LOOP

1 MILE

39

SCHUNEMUNK
MOUNTAIN
SUMMIT
1,664'

MEGALITHS

WESTERN
RIDGE
TRL.

To
Exit 16

along, with views that never stop and only a modest amount of additional exertion required.

Geologists enthuse about how the rocky substrate of Schunemunk is far younger than the underlying base of the Hudson Highlands, and that its uplifted fins of rock are compressions of shale and sandstone dating to the Ordovician and Silurian eras. The brittle layer of conglomerate that crowns this formation is more eye-catching still, being stained reddish-mauve in places—most notably along Schunemunk's summit ledge—by an iron-based hematite and larded with eggs of quartzite, compressed and fossilized sand from the beaches of an ancient sea. That this puddingstone is an extension of the Devonian strata is probably only of interest to specialists. What you should keep in mind, though, is that during an outing on May 22, 2002, one hiker was killed and two others injured when a rockslide occurred on the hill they were bushwhacking up. We suggest therefore that you stick to the blazed trails and think twice about bringing bantamweight walkers on this challenging trek. Timber rattlers, hidden within the folds and crannies of the rocks, are another hazard you may encounter in the 2,400-acre preserve, which became a state park in 2001.

This sensational jaunt begins 0.1 mile east of the parking lot, as you near the railroad trestle. Head into the forest on the worn trace and proceed uphill under the cover of maple, oak, black birch, box elder, and hemlock. Stay with this moss-sided Trestle Trail (TT, white blazes) as it breaks to the right in a minute and soars straight up the slope. The TT levels off for a spell in a thinly treed, appealingly grassy area, only to resume its sharp ascent in a few minutes. A half-hour's effort should put the worst of this climb behind you, with a trace to the right delivering a glimpse of the valley below. The next spur, to the left, brings a fair piece of the Hudson River into view, with Storm King rising up to the east, and the sculpture garden of its namesake art center visible in the lowland.

Moving along, the slope, which is crowded by blueberry bushes, continues to rise for three more minutes until the TT ends at a junction with the Barton Swamp Trail (BST, red dot on white blazes). Turn right and climb up the face of the slanted rock, clinging to the blazes as they flow over the north end of this conglomerate platform, arriving soon at a four-way intersection. Proceed straight onward, now on the Long Path (LP, aqua markings), hugging the rocky western ridge of the twin-crested Schunemunk Mountain, which is creased down the middle, like the crown of a fedora, by the cool, shady Barton Swamp. Schunemunk, incidentally, is a Lenape Indian word that means either "ancestral fireplace," or "excellent fireplace," depending on the translator; if you tackle this sparsely-treed hilltop in summer, the word takes on a cruel irony.

Traipsing along this western rim, which is a couple hundred feet lower than the eastern ridge to the south, you are at eye level with vultures and hawks. You're also enjoying no end of spectacular vistas as the trail zigzags around stunted pitch pines—some more than a century old—and mountain laurel, with innumerable blueberry shrubs (rich with berries mid- to late-July) covering the ground. Keep going straight at the junction with the Sweet Clover Trail (SCT, white blazes), on the left and at the subsequent crossing with a forest road, adhering to the rises and dips of the puddingstone plateau. Its general trend is toward the southwest, but occasionally the LP pulls a surprise by darting to the right, to the edge of the ridge.

Continue dead ahead on meeting the turn-off to the left for the Western Ridge Trail (WRT, blue dot on white blazes)—unless you would like to cut a mile or two off the hike. Bear right in another 90 seconds as the BST reappears, also merging from the left. We had the spit scared out of us here once by the sudden slithering of an eastern fox snake, which we briefly mistook for a venomous rattler. A few cairns mark the route over the broad bedrock.

Gradually, the LP arcs to the southwest, dipping down into Barton Swamp, a shady notch of hardwood trees and vernal streams. Lope left on reaching the forest road, and left again in 30 seconds at the T. Hang a right in ten yards, now leaving the wide lane, and proceed through the swamp, hopping over the moss-sided Baby Brook to the base of the talus slope. The first time we did this, we looked hopefully to the left and right before realizing that the trail does not indulge in any sidewinding or switchbacking. That's right: The LP surges straight up, over the steepest part of this sandstone and shale debris. Happily, a false summit surfaces as a rest stop about six minutes up the rock heap, and in another minute, you should reach the shoulder of the bluff, with a five-foot-high step to the next level. The edge of the east ridge is just a short scramble from there.

Follow the cairns over the slanting slab of conglomerate to the junction with the Jessup Trail (JT, yellow markings), turning left on the latter as it flies higher up the rock. The views are superb when you reach the top, spanning every direction but northeast. Save your film, though: The best is yet to come. The JT, which is over-lapped here by the Highland Trail (HT, aqua diamonds), continues to gain ground as it scales another cataclysm of boulders, with the fractured rocks giving way to a bald knob. A stunning, prolonged platform of conglomerate succeeds that, and then the clearly marked blazes drift higher, meandering from one side of this extended shelf to the other, always sticking—like stink on a skunk—to the highest part of the ridge.

A few minutes later, the JT comes to the modest peak of Schunemunk, identi-fied by a marking on the rock that notes where a fire tower once stood. From this attractively barren spot, 400 feet above the base of the talus slope you maneuvered through half an hour earlier, you can see the Catskill Mountains to the north, and even the needle-like monument at High Point State Park, far away in northwestern New Jersey. A second painted inscription, a minute's walk from the first, indicates the way to the Megaliths, north over the bedrock. In less time than it takes to boil a quail egg, square white blazes draw you to this fascinating, spectacular formation, where colossal slabs of conglomerate have fractured and dropped off of the main plateau, resembling a major section of an interstate highway after an earthquake.

Back on the JT, the yellow blazes are a bit more faded from this stage onward. Heave to the left in about five minutes as the path bends that way on meeting the Dark Hollow Trail (black dot on white squares). The HT breaks off a score of minutes later, as the Jessup, joined now by the SCT, moseys straight along, arriving shortly at a rocky node. Are you tired of vistas yet? This backdrop of the Hudson River is cer-tainly a bell-ringer, but if you are here in early to mid-June, try scanning the pitch pine– and laurel-shaded ground, too, for pink lady's slipper orchids.

Having descended a slanted rock, the SCT branches off to the left, and shortly after that, the JT finally leaves the ridge, departing this wonderland of puddingstone.

On a clear winter day, the northern view from Schunemunk Mountain's colossal Megaliths stretches as far as the Catskills.

When the JT veers right at the buggy Baby Brook, you should proceed straight with the red dots of the BST. This leads to the last climb of the day, a rugged assault on the splintered side of the west ridge, atop which you jog right, again on the white-blazed Trestle Trail. Stroll quietly during the leisurely descent back to the road and you just might spy a wild turkey or white-tailed deer, both of which roam these woods.

## ▶ NEARBY ACTIVITIES

For a closer look at the colorful shapes you admired from Schunemunk ridge, plan to explore Storm King Art Center in Mountainville. Modern sculptures by internationally renowned artists are exhibited in a splendidly landscaped outdoor environment. Visit www.stormking.org for detailed information, or call (845) 534-3115.

# SHARK RIVER CIRCUIT

## ⓘ KEY AT-A-GLANCE INFORMATION

**LENGTH:** 3.5 miles, add 3 miles for Pine Hills Trail extension

**CONFIGURATION:** Loop

**DIFFICULTY:** Easy

**SCENERY:** Rolling trail meanders through marshlands and dense mixed forest, with 0.75-miles stretch paralleling Shark River

**EXPOSURE:** Protective canopy all the way

**TRAFFIC:** Very popular with locals

**TRAIL SURFACE:** Dirt, sand, and roots

**HIKING TIME:** 1.75 hours

**SEASON:** Year-round, 8 a.m.–dusk

**ACCESS:** No fee

**MAPS:** At trailhead kiosk

**FACILITIES:** Rest rooms and water across street in developed area of park; also picnic area, playground, and public phone

**SPECIAL COMMENTS:** Bring insect repellent to this swampy area in late spring and summer. Fishing is permitted in the pond across the street, and ice skating takes place there in winter, when a warming fire often burns in the shelter. Visit www.monmouthcountyparks.com for information.

## ▶ IN BRIEF

Boardwalks, wildflowers, and sandy riverbanks make this fairly flat walk a hands-down winner for young children. Hardened hikers, too, should enjoy the illusion of being out in the wilds, as much of the loop passes through an overgrown bog and woodland.

## ▶ DESCRIPTION

For much of the hike in this Monmouth County park you will hardly be aware of the river. And even while walking along its sandy banks, enjoying the shade of birch trees, oaks, and white pines, we doubt very much you'll see any sharks. Tempted to test that by dangling your toes in the copper-hued water? By all means, be our guest. Who knows, you might come up with a snapping turtle.

Follow the Shark River 4 miles east, and you will arrive at the Atlantic Ocean. Along the way, you may find—if you are very lucky—fossilized shark teeth from the Eocene and Myocene eras. We suggest leaving the wading, though, to paleontologists, directing your attention instead to the trails. The 725-acre Shark River Park, which opened in 1961, features several fairly easy loops that dart through an eclectic—and attractive— mix of forest, bog, and riverside environments. And with the ocean so near, it is not unusual to hear the whistling of seagulls soaring overhead, or to smell the briny odor of salt spray in the breeze. The greatest challenge you may face, though—

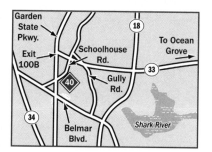

## ▶ DIRECTIONS

Follow I-95 across the George Washington Bridge into New Jersey and switch to the Garden State Parkway south at Exit 11. Take Exit 100B off the Garden State Parkway onto SR 33 east and drive a half mile, then turn right onto Schoolhouse Road. The park entrance and parking lot are on the right; the trailhead is on the left.

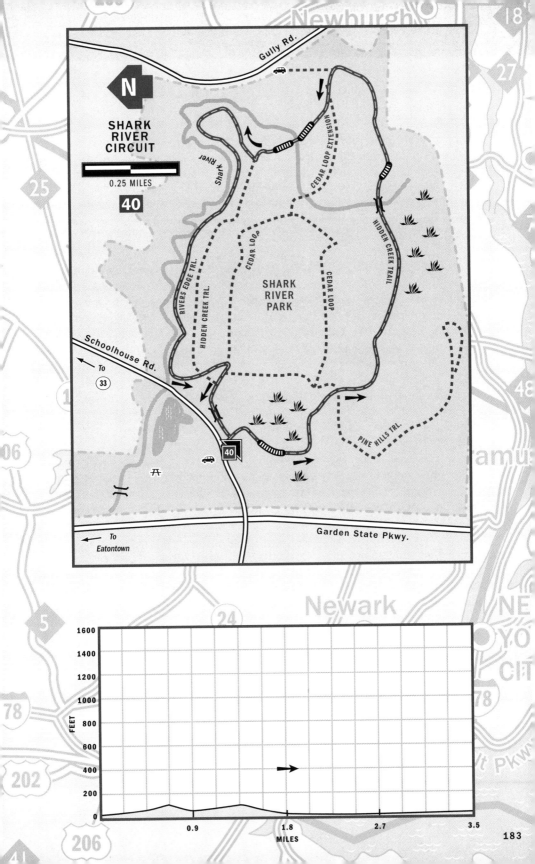

aside from shark-spotting—is the spotting of trail indicators, which are only posted at major intersections.

The trailhead is across the street from the parking area and picnic grounds. Pick up a map at the kiosk there and enter the forest, taking an abrupt right at the split-rail fence onto the Hidden Creek Trail (HCT). Immediately on descending into an appealingly ragged-looking bog, there are a couple of phragmite-flanked boardwalks, both of which could use extensions since they often have pools of mud that precede and follow them. The path widens a bit from there and starts to climb. As it does, keep to the left on a faint trace; what looks to be the main route splits in two farther on, with both of those legs petering out.

In addition to a mix of oaks, tulip trees, laurels, and holly, cat briar grows lustily along this stretch, reaching shoulder height in many places, and from springtime through summer, wildflowers are as much a part of this swampland as raccoons are in campground trash bins. Look for carnivorous pitcher plants here, too. Within ten minutes of treading along the rolling turf, you'll arrive at a four-way crossing, with the HCT continuing onward. (If time allows, though, try the side trip to the right along the Pine Hills Trail, a 1.5-mile stem to an inviting stand of conifers.) After a couple of log puncheons, the trail hits a long wooden bridge, with a bench by its far side. A boardwalk succeeds that, and then gradually the HCT begins to climb to higher ground.

For a short spell, you'll travel through level terrain, with just a sprinkling of pebbles underfoot. Don't deviate from the main trail at the next two intersections, nor as it later tapers left and descends mildly. When it spits you out at an open field, jog toward its far left (northwest) corner, where the HCT resumes by the wooden fence. The trail veers left here, bypassing a staircase, which is in disrepair. A 50-foot stretch of boardwalk at the bottom of the slope helps navigate the gummiest parts of this boggy network of streams, and several shorter spans ensue. Stop for a moment at the bench overlooking the creek—which is no longer hidden—to enjoy the miniature cascade.

At the top of a modest hill is a T; bear right on Rivers Edge Trail (RET). When, in a moment or two, this wide track meets a fork, you should edge to the right, or straight, and climb down to the riverside, once again staying clear of the decaying stairway. As its name implies, the RET parallels the Shark River, swimming first one way, then another. The russet cast to its water, by the way, is derived from iron oxide and tree tannins leaching out of the soil.

Just outside the park, beyond the river, is a concrete bunker that blights the view. Once that is behind you in a few dozen steps, you might take advantage of an isolated rock from which to sit quietly and wait for passing wildlife. In any case, stick to the right, skipping the many spurs that drift back to the HCT. One turn to look for, though, is a right leading down a slick staircase, arriving again at the river, and a little plank that crosses it. If there are young kids in your party, this is the place for them, what with the sandy riverbank so enticingly near.

You'll eventually ascend a stairway and find yourself back on an open swath of the HCT, looking very much like a carriage lane with a few maples and eastern cottonwoods lending variety to the forested mix. Remain straight until reaching a T, then head right onto the Cedar Trail. In about 45 yards, at the next post, hang a left, and after a couple of minutes among close-growing laurel, you'll emerge by the trailhead.

Tall phragmites are a year-round presence flanking the boardwalks in Shark River Park, where you may spot plentiful birdlife, but very few sharks.

## ▶ NEARBY ACTIVITIES

Some beach resorts have a way of evoking a certain soulful nostalgia. Ocean Grove, with its picturesque Victorian architecture, is just such a community. Breathe deeply the briny air while strolling along the boardwalk, and maybe take in a pipe-organ concert or one of the frequent religious and cultural summer programs held in its Great Auditorium. For more information and a schedule of events, visit www.ocean grovenj.com or call (800) 388-4768.

# SOURLAND MOUNTAIN TRACK

 **KEY AT-A-GLANCE INFORMATION**

**LENGTH:** 6.7 miles, including spurs to Devil's Half Acre and Roaring Rocks; 4 miles without spurs

**CONFIGURATION:** Loop with 2 spurs

**DIFFICULTY:** Moderate

**SCENERY:** Lush second-growth hardwood forest, bisected by a few streams and Texas Eastern Pipeline, boasts fantastic boulders and discrete vernal ponds

**EXPOSURE:** Very shady, except when crossing pipeline route

**TRAFFIC:** Light to moderate; can be busy on weekends

**TRAIL SURFACE:** Dirt, some roots, and many, many rocks and boulders

**HIKING TIME:** 3.5 hours with spurs, 2 hours without

**SEASON:** Year-round, sunrise–half hour after sunset

**ACCESS:** No fee, pets must be leashed, no horses

**MAPS:** At trailhead kiosk; www.park.co.somerset.nj.us; USGS Rocky Hill

**FACILITIES:** Portable toilet and emergency phone near parking lot

**SPECIAL COMMENTS:** Hunting is not allowed, but poachers have been known to encroach on the undeveloped area. Plan to wear orange during hunting season.

## IN BRIEF

Are you familiar with that kids' game, Scissors, Paper, Stone? This hike abbreviates that to Stones. You'll be stepping over egg-sized stones, fist-sized stones, stones like bocce balls, and some that are larger than cantaloupes—really *big* cantaloupes. Don't worry . . . boardwalks and bridges carry you over the worst of those, preventing this from becoming a prolonged exercise in ankle-aching agony. Meanwhile, the many winding streams, bird-filled stands of cedars, and easy bushwhacks to a pair of thrilling boulder cataclysms add up to an excellent, memorable outing.

## DESCRIPTION

If you have spent any time in the Watchung Mountains, the geology of Sourland Mountain should seem familiar: Both are made up of an unusual gray diabase known as trap rock. Sourland is so flush with it that the locale once boasted a quarry, with much of its substrate being carved out and paved into roads or crushed for use as railroad gravel. Sourland is also rich in history; during the Revolutionary War, John Hart, who had signed the Declaration of Independence, successfully eluded British troops in these hills. The German immigrants who later farmed this region, though, were responsible for its name, dubbing the mountain "Sorrel" land, for the russet-red color of its soil.

## DIRECTIONS

Follow I-95/I-80 west across the George Washington Bridge to Exit 41 and the junction with I-287. Proceed south on I-287 to Exit 17 onto US 206 south. Drive about 7 miles, then head west on CR 514. After 2.8 miles, turn left onto East Mountain Road. Continue for 1.9 miles to the park entrance on the right. The parking area is straight ahead.

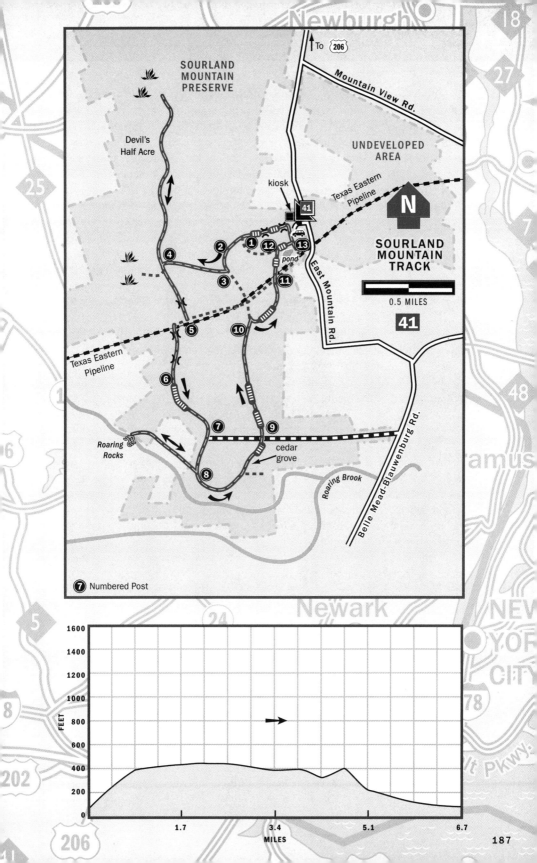

After you stub your toe a few times in this wilderness of rocks you may feel that *"fels"* land or *"stein"* land would have been more appropriate monikers for an area where the surface stones appear to occupy more space than the top soil. Don't let the thought of a bruised big digit deter you from visiting this Somerset County park, though—unless you're a member of the Barefoot Hiking Club. Hikes, like ice cream, come in many flavors; while some prefer vanilla or chocolate, others enjoy rocky road. It is in large part the rocky road of so many boulders and rocks that makes Sourland Mountain Preserve such a fascinating—and exciting—place in which to walk. Most of its 2,600 acres are undeveloped, but intrepid bushwhackers will find a number of traces branching away from the main loop that lead to enchanting boulder fields and secluded streams.

The hike begins beyond the covered kiosk at the edge of the woods. Head into the forest, where maple, oak, beech, and tulip trees compose the canopy, and bitter-sweet, barberry, chokeberry, jack-in-the-pulpit, garlic mustard, and mayapple compete for root room among the litter of stones. A bridge and the first of many boardwalks help in fording a boulder stream and seasonal water flow. Keep to the right after those, and in a couple of minutes, the path swerves over another bridge, followed by a second boardwalk. Ramble right at the fork a few seconds later, indicated by post 1, and strike up the hill, bearing right at post 3. You gain about 250 feet in elevation over the ensuing several minutes, until the track tapers downhill and starts to swing left by marker 4. The hike continues in that direction, but if you are feeling adventurous, you may want to investigate the trace forking to the right.

There are currently no official blazes along this meandering path, which sneaks into the undeveloped section of the sanctuary. With mountain bikers having indulged in some trail building, however, the risk of straying far afield is not too great—at least not for the first mile. In a matter of minutes, the track enters a highly dramatic boulder field, where a number of colossal stones seem poised to tumble down the hill. The serpentine route surges west from there, then back toward the north, bounding over a second congregation of boulders. Much of the path now overlaps bedrock, requiring an extra effort to determine its subsequent moves. Look for the rock ramps that mountain bikers have constructed with the flair of the CCC to ease their travels over the larger mounds of diabase. In 20 to 25 minutes of navigating through this obstacle course, you should find yourself surrounded by boulders in the heart of a ridge of rocks known as the Devil's Half Acre. Some trees here bear faded white blazes dating from an earlier era, but only skilled bushwhackers should consider journeying further. In any case, the boulder field soon evolves into a rock-filled swamp, where the white markings are farther and farther apart, and the challenges to your ankles increase with every step. If you are searching for a reason to extend your adventure beyond the Devil's Half Acre, though, we've seen a handful of the rare and beautiful *Orchis spectabilis* flowering about 100 yards to the west, in the middle of the secluded swamp.

The trek resumes back at the fourth post, with the loop cruising toward the south. The spur to the right that surfaces in a minute or two is also worth checking out. It leads, in just 150 feet, to a large mound of rocks perched dramatically by a stream-laced swamp. If you have lathered on bug spray, this gorgeous nook is a great place to nosh on a sandwich in solitude or blow a few bars on your harmonica. The main route proceeds southbound, gradually losing elevation as it hops over a stream, then recrosses it via a bridge. Shortly after that, the path emerges under the open sky of a forest cut for the Texas Eastern Pipeline (yes, you read correctly). The trail doglegs right by 35 feet, and then lurches left back into the cover of trees. You may, however, first feel inclined to walk to the left up the pipe-cut for a fine view of the eastern hills.

The succeeding bit of trail is marked by numerous bridge and boardwalk crossings. This is an area of vernal pools and seasonal streams, a habitat that nurtures such amphibians as wood frogs, gray tree frogs, and spotted salamanders. Post 6 pops up in about 20 minutes, as the path shifts sharply left by the preserve's boundary fence and descends steeply and ruggedly over rocky turf. Turn right at post 7 a few minutes later, with the ground finally leveling off in a shady bower of beech and birch. The open gate in the chain link fence at pole 8 provides your next bushwhacking opportunity. Head to the right there, venturing onto 3M property. The path—hard dirt well packed by the tread of many feet—ascends to a fork, with the left leg bringing you to Roaring Rocks, a tremendous cataclysm of boulders concentrated around Roaring Brook.

This rousing setting trumps the view you'll have later of Roaring Brook from a spur off the main trail. That trace appears in about half a minute after your resumption of the loop. Carrying on from there, the path enters a cedar forest and continues straight at post 9. As you stroll over the ensuing series of boardwalks, listen attentively for melodious birdcalls. You may not see the flickers, rufous-sided towhees, red-bellied woodpeckers, wood thrushes, bluebirds, and mockingbirds that nest in these trees, but you can't miss their rich range of twitterings, tubular notes, and deep vibratos. Glide right at post 10, descending first over chunky ground, succeeded by more wooden spans. Cross the clear-cut of the pipe break, just after post 11, and hang a right at post 12. The path materializes on the far side of a diminutive pond (where the frog population surges in summer), with the parking area to the left.

## ▶ NEARBY ACTIVITIES

The Delaware & Raritan Canal State Park at Blackwell Mills attracts lovers of history as well as the outdoors. In the nineteenth century, steam tugboats and mules delivered freight along this corridor, and many historic buildings, bridges, and locks still exist. Visit www. state.nj.us or call (732) 873-3050 for information.

From October through May, the 11 greenhouses of Duke Gardens in Somerville display gardens and climatic conditions of different countries. For a guided tour, call (908) 243-3600.

The Old Dutch Parsonage and the Wallace House, both state historic sites in Somerville, may slake your appetite for history with their wide array of period furnishings. Call (908) 725-1015 for information.

# STERLING RIDGE TRAIL

## KEY AT-A-GLANCE INFORMATION

**LENGTH:** 10.2 miles

**CONFIGURATION:** Out-and-back

**DIFFICULTY:** Difficult

**SCENERY:** Ironworks relics at entrance of cool hemlock forest, followed by rugged mountain ridges with stellar highland views, leading to 1922 fire tower

**EXPOSURE:** Shady start succumbs to exposed slopes and ridges

**TRAFFIC:** Rather solitary

**TRAIL SURFACE:** From packed dirt to densely rocky with a few grassy patches

**HIKING TIME:** 5.5 hours

**SEASON:** Year-round, sunrise-sunset

**ACCESS:** No fee, pets must be on leash no longer than 6 feet

**MAPS:** At Visitor Center; USGS Greenwood Lake; New York–New Jersey Trail Conference, Sterling Forest Trails

**FACILITIES:** None

**SPECIAL COMMENTS:** The park hosts a great deal of activities: snowshoeing, ice fishing, boating, hunting. Call (845) 351-5907 for information.

## IN BRIEF

"Alone far in the wilds and mountains I hunt," wrote Walt Whitman, in an example intrepid hikers might like to emulate here. Not to bag some of the rich range of wildlife that runs through these woods. No, the quarry to set your sights on consists of a thriving second growth forest, boggy lowlands, fabulous vistas, and ridgetop rambles. Further explorations into the unsullied domain, which includes dramatic ruins of eighteenth- and nineteenth-century ironworks, are possible via a number of unblazed paths.

## DESCRIPTION

Just 35 miles from Central Park is one of the wildest, least-developed parcels of land in the entire metropolitan area. You want to see bobcats,

## DIRECTIONS

*By car:* Follow the New York State Thruway I-87 north over the Tappan Zee Bridge, taking Exit 15 and continuing on SR 17 north for about 3 miles. Just before Sloatsburg, turn left (west) on Sloatsburg Road/CR 72 (which changes to Ringwood Pompton Road/CR 150), and drive 6.6 miles to Greenwood Lake Turnpike/CR 511. Hang a right on CR 511 and persist for less than 4 miles to a grassy triangle on the right, by East Shore Road/CR 162. Park in the gravel lot to the left. For the Visitor Center, continue north on SR 17 to the junction with SR 17A. Turn west and drive 1.4 miles, then go left on Long Meadow Road (CR 84). Proceed 3.5 miles and hang a right on Old Forge Road. The Visitor Center is 1 mile ahead on the left.

*By public transportation:* Take the New Jersey Transit bus 197 from the New York Port Authority Terminal to the trailhead by the junction of the Greenwood Lake Turnpike and East Shore Road in Ringwood.

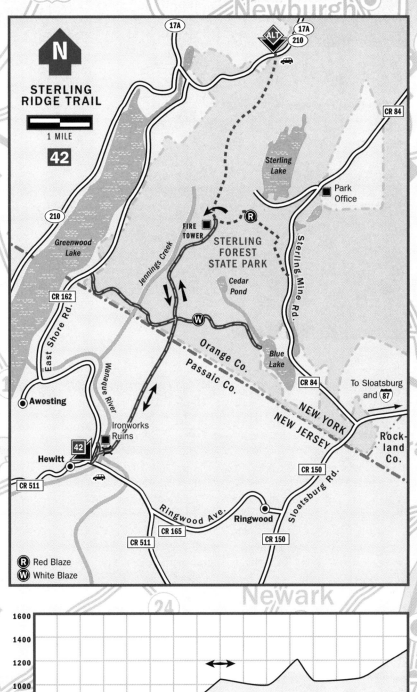

**STERLING RIDGE TRAIL**

1 MILE

**42**

N

Sterling Lake

Park Office

CR 84

17A

ALT 210

17A

210

Greenwood Lake

FIRE TOWER

R

STERLING FOREST STATE PARK

Cedar Pond

Sterling Mine Rd.

W

Jennings Creek

CR 162

East Shore Rd.

Orange Co.

Passaic Co.

Blue Lake

CR 84

New York / New Jersey

To Sloatsburg and 87

Rock-land Co.

Awosting

Wanaque River

Ironworks Ruins

Hewitt

42

CR 511

Ringwood Ave.

CR 165

CR 511

Ringwood

CR 150

Sloatsburg Rd.

CR 150

**R** Red Blaze
**W** White Blaze

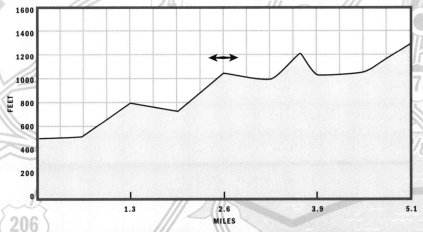

This serene swamp marks the start of a strenuous ascent into the highly scenic Sterling Forest.

black bears, coyotes and rattlesnakes? They're all there, as well as red-shouldered hawks, red-bellied woodpeckers, red foxes, red-faced butterflies and, well, of course, white-tailed deer. And if you like to mix a little history with your hike, there are the sprawling ruins of a Civil War–era iron foundry to look forward to, with foundations dating back to the American Revolution.

This is Sterling Forest we're talking about, one of New York's newest state parks, an undeveloped preserve of nearly 20,000 acres. It wasn't always so. In 1702, the land was purchased from the Iroquois by the Earl of Stirling. Iron ore was soon discovered there, and as mining grew in importance, the trees of the forest—needed to fire the forges—dwindled proportionally. By 1885, when the property was bought by the Sterling Iron and Railway Company, hardly any trees remained. Left largely fallow, the land renewed itself, with the open fields succeeded by the dense forest you see today.

There are a couple of ways to approach the linear Sterling Ridge hike. If you want to cover its entire 9-mile length, plan to leave a car at one trailhead (on the south side of Route 17A, for example) and shuttle in a second vehicle to its other end. Or, lacking a shuttle car, try hiking in as far as the fire tower (roughly the halfway point), then out again over the same ground. The more interesting terrain, arguably, lies south of the tower, and it is also the more rugged. Think twice before bringing young children on this hike.

Walk from the gravel parking area across CR 511 toward East Shore Road. Look for a dead tree, partially engulfed in a patch of sumac and poison ivy, tattooed with a blue-on-white blaze. The trail starts there, heading directly under a mantle of maples. Within moments, it scoots by a few concrete foundations and slag heaps, followed in five minutes by the substantial remnants of an ironworks. At the intersection just after that, keep to the left (make a mental note of this junction for your return), and you will quickly come to another ruin composed of large gray stone blocks, shored up with beams on one end. The path shifts right there and passes a couple of benches set in a nook overlooking a peaceful pond. Just upstream is a grassy meadow, with the mother lode of ironworks ruins off to the side. These massive stone buildings once housed foundry furnaces and the waterwheels to power them. Take five to explore the area, where an unblazed trace leads up the river to more ruins and a cascade with a seven-foot drop.

Back at the meadow, the trail cuts right over a wooden footbridge and then bends left, beginning a steady uphill trend into the forest. Walking along this old road requires little effort initially, as maples are gradually displaced by hemlocks and the music of the river serenades you. Ignore the initial spur to the right, but go right at the next fork, where yellow blazes color the left option. And so begins the workout, as the track climbs steadily to a high ridge, veers left over a chunky streambed, and continues the ascent up a rocky slope of scree. On approaching the stone plateau where a couple of cedars cling to the Spartan ground, scan the surrounding brush for wild turkeys, which often frequent this area. Linger a moment, too, to enjoy the vista to the south, where the pond you brushed by earlier is so distant it might as well be a drop of dew.

The climbing resumes via switchbacks around a craggy escarpment and a handful of shagbark hickory trees. A few dozen yards beyond is a bulging granite dome, 650 feet above the trailhead, with clear views over the hills to the west. This is the first of a series of interconnected ridgetops, and quite possibly the prettiest. Think about snacking on a sandwich here among the long golden grass, in the shade of scrub oaks and sumac—you're going to need the energy! Moving onward along the grassy path through maple, oak, and birch, in ten minutes you'll see a discreet white tag on an oak indicating the state line "separating" New Jersey from New York.

Roll straight through each of the ensuing unblazed junctions and enjoy the next half mile or so of fairly level, easy strolling. Then it is back into the saddle with a steep, sun-exposed climb up another 75 feet to the highest point of the ridge. The views west from this pine-encircled rocky tor are memorable, though the expansive Greenwood Lake remains hidden by lower tree cover. There are two more scrub-pine plateaus after this, with a carpet of blueberry bushes between them, and then an odd, altar-like erratic, tucked under a hemlock.

Dropping into a boggy gully, the stone-spiked, mossy trail slices first through laurels and oaks, then hits a thicket of rhododendrons prior to scaling another loose rocky embankment. This shelf is, like the previous, 725 feet above the road, and it extends for 200 yards before the path descends to a largely defoliated hemlock hollow. Steer to the right at the intersection there, and march right through the following junction. Perhaps 100 yards ahead and to the right is a high, rising series of rock fingers or granite tendrils. For a route that has yet to pursue any shortcuts and that hasn't seen a peak it didn't summit, the next move could hardly be a surprise. That's right: Up and over the steepest section of those rocks. Having put that behind you, keep an eye out for blazes as you dogleg first right, then left on crossing a forest road. The fire tower is just ahead.

At 5 miles out, the fire tower is the turnaround point of the hike. This 65-foot structure was built in 1922 and is still in service, as is the adjacent warden's cabin. Before retracing your steps back to the road, consider climbing the tower for a view that extends all the way to Manhattan on a clear day. Closer by, you can survey the lovely land through which you've just journeyed, aware that it was slated until relatively recently to be "developed" into 15,000 homes.

▶ **NEARBY ACTIVITIES**

Long Pond Ironworks on the Greenwood Lake Turnpike has several remnants of the ironmaking industry from the eighteenth century, as well as a museum. Call (973) 657-1688 for details.

Skylands Manor and the New Jersey Botanical Garden, both within Ringwood State Park, are a wonderful combination of a Tudor-style mansion in a flowering environment. Gothic Ringwood Manor, also on the park grounds, contains nineteenth-century American paintings and furniture. For information and guided tours, call (973) 962-7527.

# STILLWELL WOODS STROLL

## ▶ IN BRIEF

Venturing into Stillwell Woods involves a compromise. In all probability, you will share the terrain with joggers, bikers, and perhaps even an occasional deer tick. You'll also be among a bevy of birds in a beautiful setting that undulates like a roller coaster from high hardwood forests to a low, soggy swamp. With suburbia pressing on every border, this attractive domain is a welcome walk on the wild side.

## ▶ DESCRIPTION

Stillwell Woods County Preserve is directly across a busy street from Syosset High School, wedged within a suburban neighborhood that appears, at certain times of day, to be bursting at the seams. At various points on the hike, you may hear dogs barking, power mowers buzzing over lawns, motorcycles roaring along Route 108—even the rumble of the LIRR commuter train as it rattles

## ▶ DIRECTIONS

*By car:* Follow the Long Island Expressway (I-495) to Exit 44 onto SR 135 north. Drive 1 mile, then turn right on Jericho Turnpike (SR 25). In less than 1 mile, turn left onto South Woods Road. Proceed for 1.3 miles, passing Syosset High School on the left, and turn right into Stillwell Woods Park. Parking is available alongside the ball field.

*By public transportation:* Take the Long Island Railroad (Port Jefferson Branch) to Syosset Station. From there, grab a cab for a 2-mile ride, or walk. Head right (north) on Jackson Avenue and veer right onto Cold Spring Road. In less than 0.5 miles, go left on Syosset Cold Spring Harbor Road and walk about 1 mile to South Woods Road. Turn right and proceed to the park entrance on the left.

## ⓘ KEY AT-A-GLANCE INFORMATION

**LENGTH:** 3.2 miles

**CONFIGURATION:** Loop

**DIFFICULTY:** Easy

**SCENERY:** Rolling trails surround a large, grassy field, harboring wildflowers, cottontails, and abundant bird life, including pheasants

**EXPOSURE:** Shady canopy with some open field passages

**TRAFFIC:** Light on weekdays, especially before 5 p.m.

**TRAIL SURFACE:** Grass, sand, dirt, and pebbles

**HIKING TIME:** 1.5 hours

**SEASON:** Year-round, sunrise–sunset

**ACCESS:** No fee

**MAPS:** Posted at trailhead kiosk; Long Island Greenbelt Trail Conference; Sal's Snappy Dogs hot-dog stand on Jericho Turnpike (SR 25) between South Woods Road and Woodbury Road

**FACILITIES:** Seasonal portable toilets in adjacent sports field

**SPECIAL COMMENTS:** Highly popular mountain-biking area on weekends and evenings; be vigilant on blind turns.

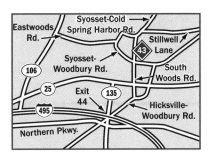

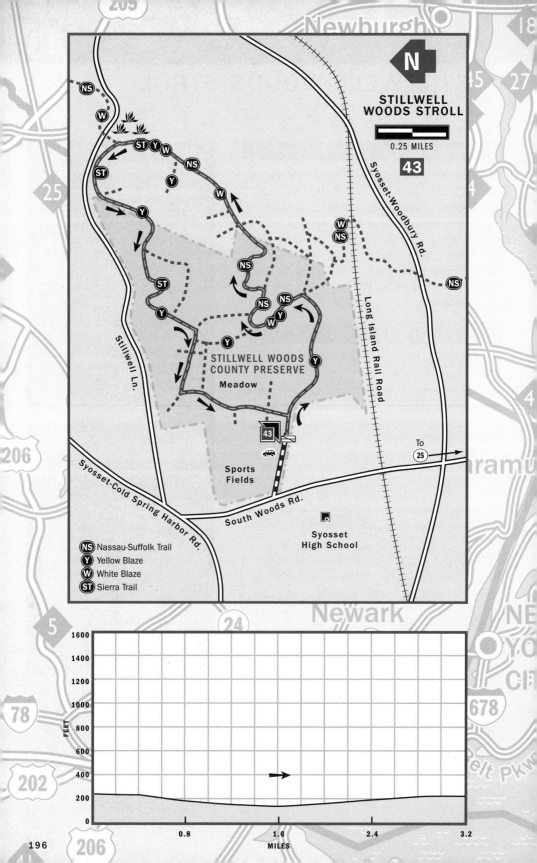

# STILLWELL WOODS STROLL

0.25 MILES

**43**

**NS** Nassau-Suffolk Trail
**Y** Yellow Blaze
**W** White Blaze
**ST** Sierra Trail

STILLWELL WOODS
COUNTY PRESERVE

Meadow

Sports
Fields

Stillwell Ln.

Syosset-Cold Spring Harbor Rd.

South Woods Rd.

Syosset
High School

Long Island Rail Road

Syosset-Woodbury Rd.

To
25

down the nearby tracks. So, you may wonder, with such a cacophony intruding upon the peace of the park, why bother to visit it? Would it suffice to tell you that this secluded nook is a rough-cut patch of nature, with beautiful, varied terrain that ranges from grassy fields dappled with wildflowers—where you may encounter ring-necked pheasants, among many other birds—to a surprising undulation of hills and shady ravines? Probably the most convincing way to answer that question is for you to slip on your boots and see for yourself.

Head east on the maintenance road to the far right of the ball fields. Slip by the yellow barrier gate, checking the trail map at the kiosk in the process. Walk with the painted yellow dots straight onward, passing a few maverick trails (there are many throughout the preserve, worn into the soft soil by bikers and—more of a problem in the past than presently—dirt bikes and ATVs) as you approach a large, open field. Take the right fork there, edging by the south side of the meadow, which is bordered by sumac, cedars, and an occasional white birch. When you reach the end of the field, in about eight minutes, shift left to its east margin, now moving north in an area frequented by cottontail rabbits. The white blazes of the Nassau-Suffolk Greenbelt Trail (NSG) merge with the yellow dots here, with both colors running concurrently until they jointly leave the field at its northeast corner. At this point, currently on a wide dirt-and-pebble track, you steer right, sticking with the white markings. Keep right at the next Y, and left at the one that soon follows.

From sun-exposed terrain that was initially quite flat, the mossy ground—now dense with blueberry bushes, pin oaks, and mountain laurel—begins to pitch a bit, first descending, then rising, dropping again, followed by another short ascent, and so on. Proceed straight through the four-way crossing atop one such crest, and at the succeeding junction where the soil is badly scarred by dirt bikes, dart right with the white blazes. Farther along on another plateau, a bench is appealingly set under an oak tree. The NSG swoops right there before snaking to the left through a second-growth forest of oaks, laurel, and white and black birch trees. Shortly after, the Sierra Trail (ST, yellow diamond blaze) joins this route from the left, with its yellow blazes painted beside the white ones. The ground is creased by numerous mountain-biking spurs here, but with the trail markings clearly evident, you don't have to worry much about straying from the main path.

Eventually, the loamy track descends to a thriving, verdant swamp, where the noise of cars speeding down Stillwell Lane may reach your ears. The yellow and white blazes diverge by a maple tree; follow the yellow markings to the left. (Unless, that is, you care to extend your hike 1.4 miles north on the NSG to its entrance into Uplands Farm Sanctuary.) A rather steep climb ensues, making up for your loss of elevation on the way to the swamp. As the ST hits a laurel-enclosed crest, a rutted bike track merges in from the left, only to cut off to the right in two or three minutes. Skip the other maverick spurs that appear shortly too, remaining with the yellow blazes as they glide right at the triangular fork. In less than a minute, the path veers left over concrete rubble and erosion-control corduroy steps, shifting left at the bottom, and left once more at another triangular T. At the top of a slight rise, among white pines and mountain laurel, the yellow blazes draw you to the right, and right again at a T in 200 feet.

On walking an additional 150 feet along this wide dirt track, with red cedars and flowering dogwoods on either side of you, the painted yellow spots slip to the left on a side spur. Instead of turning with them, continue straight ahead to the yellow plastic mountain-biking blaze, about 70 feet distant. Cross the four-way intersection there and bear left at the next fork (the right option rejoins this route momentarily). The trail bends left toward a large stand of conifers, with another track merging from the left just after that. Take the left fork of the Y that follows, and then, a couple of minutes later, cross the wide fire road. This final leg is a bit overgrown, snaking through the underbrush for a minute before dead-ending at the fire road you started on. The trailhead is to the right, 250 feet away.

### ▶ NEARBY ACTIVITIES

It may be hard to imagine now, but three centuries ago, there were many farm villages on Long Island. The Old Bethpage Village Restoration project has relocated and reconstructed several buildings and their equipment in a central location. Costumed guides provide explanations and demonstrations in farmhouses and homes, a church and an inn, a blacksmith shop, and a store. For detailed information, call (516) 572-8401 or visit www.oldbethpage.org.

# STOKES SELECT

## ▶ IN BRIEF

For fear of overselling a park, we normally resist assigning it too many superlatives. But in Stokes we're stumped: This solitary, mountainous jaunt is so darn beautiful we can't help but beat the drum for it. It's a strenuous outing that alternates between lowland bogs and high-country terrain, providing several hours' communion with an extended patch of unspoiled nature. In spring, Kittatinny Ridge brims with wildflowers, while the autumn display of colors seen from this, New Jersey's highest natural point, is pure hiker heaven.

## ▶ DESCRIPTION

There are few animal sightings quite so exhilarating as an encounter with a bear. And in Stokes State Forest, visitors are constantly reminded that stumbling upon a black bear in the backcountry is a very real possibility. Though the odds are slim—these shy creatures are likely to scoot into the cover of the forest at the first sound of your approach—just the chance of seeing an *Ursus americanus* in the wild adds an extra *frisson* of danger to the hike. Not that this gem of a trek needs any gilding—not with the heart-stopping panorama atop Sunrise Mountain, and certainly not with much of your mileage accruing along the scenic Kittatinny Mountain Ridge, which explodes with wildflowers in the spring.

## ▶ DIRECTIONS

Follow I-95/I-80 west across the George Washington Bridge. Leave I-80 at Exit 34 onto SR 15 north, continuing to US 206 north. Drive about 4 miles north of Branchville and turn right onto the park road (Coursen Road). The park office is on the left. For the trailhead, proceed straight 1.8 miles, toward Stony Lake. At the T-intersection, turn right on Kittle Road and drive 0.25 miles to the trailhead parking.

## ⓘ KEY AT-A-GLANCE INFORMATION

**LENGTH:** 9.1 miles

**CONFIGURATION:** Loop

**DIFFICULTY:** Difficult

**SCENERY:** Marshes and wildflowers in lowland hardwood forests; stunted tree growth on mountain ridges; panoramic view of rural Sussex County atop Sunrise Mountain

**EXPOSURE:** Very little exposure, even on mountain ridges; only two open viewpoints

**TRAFFIC:** Light to moderate, but Swenson Trail is favored by mountain bikers and cross-country skiers

**TRAIL SURFACE:** Dirt, roots, and endless rocks

**HIKING TIME:** 4.5 hours

**SEASON:** Year-round

**ACCESS:** Memorial Day–Labor Day, $5 weekdays, $10 weekends; free rest of year; $50 parks pass gives access to all New Jersey state parks for one calendar year

**MAPS:** At park office; USGS Culvers Gap; New York–New Jersey Trail Conference, Kittatinny Trails

**FACILITIES:** Rest rooms, water, and public phone at park office; picnic area near trailhead

**SPECIAL COMMENTS:** This park offers great camping—and fishing—near a trout-stocked stream and lake. In winter, bring your cross-country skis, snowshoes, or ice skates.

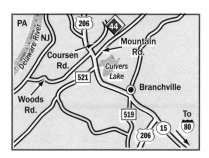

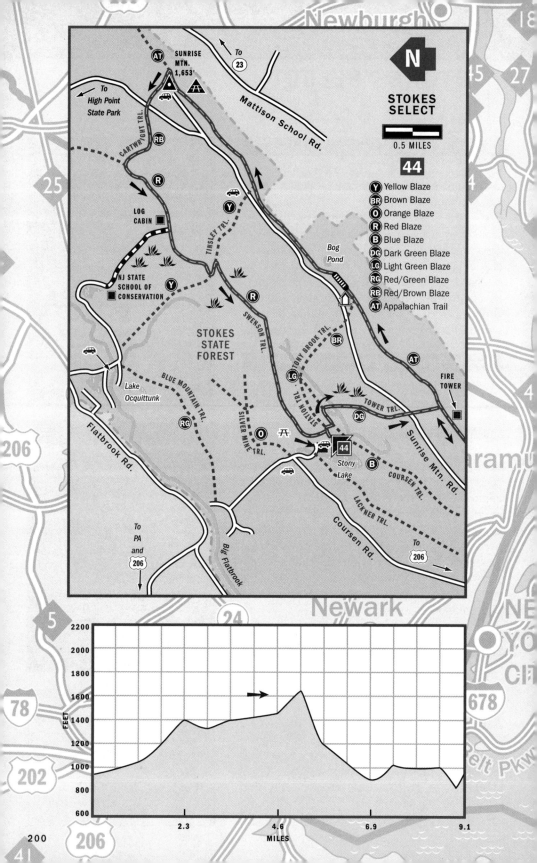

Glacial debris appears to be heading downhill on the Cartwright Trail, at Stokes State Forest.

As you tramp over the trails, it may seem hard to believe that most of this beautiful park's 15,482 acres were completely denuded of trees as recently as a century ago. The damage began with the arrival of Dutch and English settlers who, on displacing the Lenape Indians in the early 1700s, carved large swaths of farmland out of the forest. The remaining trees came down in later decades, used up as firewood and charcoal. It is only from 1907, when an initial parcel of 5,432 acres was purchased by New Jersey, that Stokes underwent a renaissance. All that is left now of the old homesteads are ruins and rubble, largely overgrown by vast stands of oak, birch, beech, maple, and hemlock.

Your hike commences at the kiosk to the right of the paved parking area by Stony Lake. Six different colored blazes share the forest road initially as it plugs steadily upward away from the trailhead. The red markings of the Swenson Trail, your return route, break to the left within 100 yards, and a few steps later, the green-blazed Station Trail forks left, too. Hew to the right as the path narrows, and head left at the T. There is an old cabin foundation off the track to the left, in the middle of a stand of white pines, with your turn to the right on the Tower Trail (TT, dark green blazes) occurring just before that. Vestigial walls tumble through the swamp here, but in spring, your eye will more likely be attracted to the abundance of wildflowers, including mayapple, star-shaped anemones, irises, violets, periwinkles, false lilies, jack-in-the-pulpits, and skunk cabbage.

For a couple of minutes, the rocky track remains rather level, sloshing through one wet spot and then another, past white birch, shagbark hickory, some ash, as well as oak and maple, before grinding sharply upward. In slightly less than ten minutes and a gain of 200 feet in elevation, the path levels off and cuts through a couple of seasonal streams. When it meets Sunrise Mountain Road, the TT shifts diagonally across the pavement to the right, with the steepest part of the climb still ahead. Don't let the exertion or the pebbly granola underfoot distract you from checking out the glacial deposits left and right of the trace, as well as the impressive bluff formation you are ascending. Near the crest, as you enter a concentration of mountain laurel,

Built by the CCC during the mid-1930s, Sunrise Mountain Shelter, at 1,653 feet, provides a bird's eye vista of the farmland surrounding Stokes State Park.

some fun hand-over-hand rock scrambling is necessary to reach the top of the granite ledge.

The TT ends at a slanted **T** with the Appalachian Trail (AT), as the hike continues to the left. Take five, though, to catch your breath. It is possible to climb the fire tower dead ahead of you, though the hatch at the top is usually locked. Anyway, no extra height is necessary to enjoy the splendid views of the hills to the north and west, with Stony Lake far below looking no larger than a puddle. And in spring, this bald plateau is colorfully peppered with pink penstemon. Having finished your breather, walk northeast on the AT, staying with the white-blazed route for approximately 3 miles. Although the AT clings to the meandering Kittatinny Mountain Ridge at an average elevation of 1,400 feet, most of the year vistas are rather limited, due to the extensive scrub vegetation. Still, the forested scenery is quite appealing, with sheep laurel, service berry, and flowering azalea adding a welcome contrast to the mix of hardwoods, and occasional bog pots providing fertile ground for wildflowers and amphibians.

Your first glimpse of Sunrise Mountain comes shortly beyond the yellow-blazed fork of the Tinsley Trail to the left. At an altitude of 1,653 feet, it appears to tower above the surrounding ridge, but after a minor descent, the climb to its peak is accomplished in little more than two minutes. The massive stone picnic shelter that crowns this knob like an oversize tiara was built by the CCC in the latter half of the 1930s, while a U.S. Geological Survey crew later added the low obelisk. The stupendous panorama, meanwhile, has been provided by Mother Nature, with views extending in every direction but north, where the horizon is partially obscured by trees. While you are scanning the surrounding countryside for recognizable landmarks, you may see raptors and vultures soar by at eye level.

The AT zips over a fin of rock on the east side of this ridge, descending momentarily toward an adjacent parking lot just off Sunrise Mountain Road. The spur to the right, as you near the lot, leads to a sun-struck rocky shelf, where two benches face the east, overlooking the lush farmlands of Jersey. The AT then drops down over a stone staircase and skirts to the right of the parking area. Aim your eyes left shortly after that, scanning the shrubs for the brown-over-red blaze of the Cartwright Trail (CT). The start of this trace is badly overgrown, making it all too easy to miss your turn. Much of the next mile is over wild, untrammeled turf, contributing a healthy dose of natural beauty to what, for us, is one of the most delightful parts of the hike.

On gliding directly over a rising mound of bedrock (not to its right, as it first appears), the CT zigzags downward into a grove of pitch pines, descending abruptly from there into an avalanche of rubble and glacial erratics. Cross Sunrise Mountain Road and continue into the dense forest, where an occasional fallen tree or broken limb may require minor bushwhacking to proceed. In ten minutes, the CT tapers downward over a chunky moraine field that doubles as a seasonal streambed. With blazes hard to see here, your best approach is to move due west, holding to the left of the streambed. The trace ends at a T with the Swenson Trail (ST, red blazes), by a grave-like mound of stones. A cross sticking out of the top of that tumulus has the word "Cartwright" scrawled on it, tersely explaining, finally, what became of Adam.

Scoot to the left and remain with the ST all the way back to the trailhead, a distance of about 3 miles. The path swings through a boggy patch en route and hopscotches over a couple of seasonal streams, pulling up in a dozen minutes to a cabin. Stay straight, cruising to the left of the bog ponds, as the track begins to ascend into a rocky environment. Within five minutes of leaving the cabin, the ST hits the Tinsley Trail, whereupon Swenson jumps left, part of a delayed dogleg that is completed in about 100 seconds when it breaks to the right, leaving the wide track. Some rockhopping over streams ensues; part of a swampy precinct that attracts an abundance of birds (and bugs). The wandering trail finally enters into a concentration of laurels and white pines before merging with the main route. The trailhead is straight onward, a three-minute stagger away.

The fun may not end with the unlacing of your boots. Seconds after driving away after our last hike here, we had to hit the brakes as a 450-pound black bear abruptly lumbered out of the woods and shuffled across the park road. It was a humid summer afternoon, and he seemed in no hurry, but the forest had swallowed him up before we could extricate a camera from our pack.

## ▶ NEARBY ACTIVITIES

A great, short alternative hike is a foray into the Tillman Ravine Natural Area at the southwest end of the park. The fun out-and-back trail is 2 miles long and snakes downhill along the cascading Tillman Brook, in a dense grove of hemlocks and rhododendrons. Several species of endangered plants and animals exist in this cool, shady environment. Call (973) 948-3820 for details.

# STORM KING SUMMIT TRAIL

## IN BRIEF

Few hikes manage to blend a rocky, mountainous setting with dynamite views, while still being easily accessible by a major highway. Storm King is one of those, delivering a quick payoff in panoramas nonpareil of the majestic Hudson River and surrounding hills from a series of rough, romantic granite domes. Its handy proximity to US 9W makes this short circuit immensely popular, but there is enough viewing space atop the many domes for everyone to have a blast.

## DESCRIPTION

The newspaper reports were alarming . . . frightening, even. Fire crews summoned to douse the wildfires that swept through Storm King State Park in 1999 made an explosive discovery: The ground was pregnant with live munitions dating back to World War I, when the neighboring West Point Military Academy used the area for artillery practice. Miraculously, generations of hikers have roamed these hills without triggering a detonation; even so, this revelatory bombshell forced state authorities to close the park for three years while the Army Corps of Engineers toiled to clear the ordnance. Much of Storm King's 1,900 acres are now open again, including the best vista points, but bushwhackers should note that only a 25-foot wide band of turf on either side of the trails has been screened for shells. That margin of

## DIRECTIONS

Follow US 9 north to Peekskill, then head west on US 6. Once over the Bear Mountain Bridge, enter the traffic circle and drive north on scenic route US 9W for about 9.4 miles to a large, open parking lot on the right, on a hilltop in a bend of the road. If you come to Mountain Road, you have gone too far.

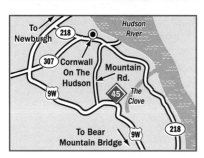

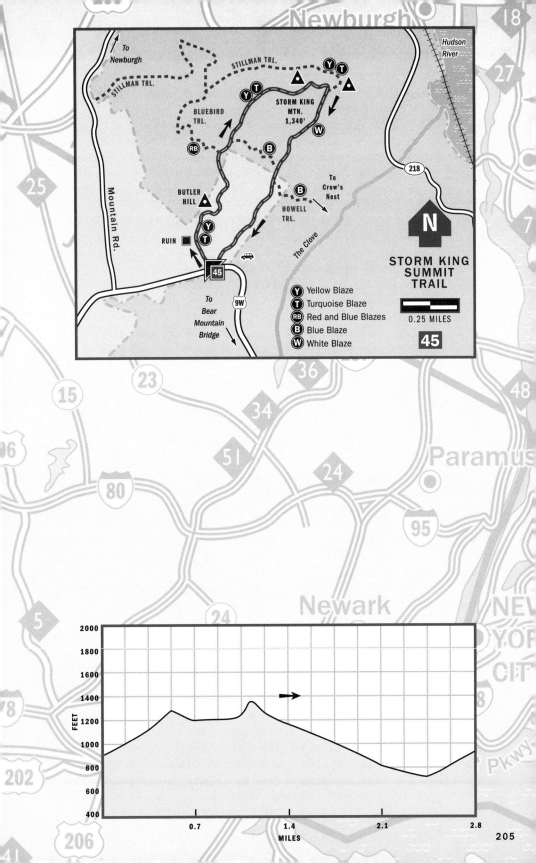

To
Newburgh

STILLMAN TRL.

STILLMAN TRL.

Hudson
River

Ⓨ Ⓣ

Ⓨ Ⓣ

BLUEBIRD
TRL.

STORM KING
MTN.
1,340'

Ⓦ

ⓇB

Ⓑ

BUTLER
HILL

To
Crow's
Nest

Ⓑ

HOWELL
TRL.

The Clove

218

Ⓨ
Ⓣ

RUIN

45

N

9W

To
Bear
Mountain
Bridge

STORM KING
SUMMIT
TRAIL

0.25 MILES

45

Ⓨ  Yellow Blaze
Ⓣ  Turquoise Blaze
ⓇB  Red and Blue Blazes
Ⓑ  Blue Blaze
Ⓦ  White Blaze

**FEET**

2000
1800
1600
1400
1200
1000
800
600
400

0.7          1.4          2.1          2.8
**MILES**

safety should more than suffice to enjoy this short loop, which is highlighted by several outstanding overlooks of the Hudson River.

Walk to the far left (or north end) of the parking lot and look for yellow and turquoise blazes as you near the highway. Enter the woods there and scramble up the slanted bedrock, under a mantle of maple, oak, and sheep laurel. This jaunt gets going with a jolt, like a morning gargle of Turkish coffee, zigzagging up a steep slab of granite. In five heart-pounding minutes, as you near the crest of the first hill, the ruins of an old cabin appear, with three stone pillars aligned in front of the foundation. This is all that is left of Spy Rock House, the summer home of Edward Lasell Partridge, a Big Apple physician who was a member of the Palisades Interstate Park Commission during the first half of the last century. In that position, Partridge helped lead the drive that preserved much of the Hudson Highlands.

The trail shifts to the left of the ruin and circles behind it toward the east, losing a touch of elevation before darting into a jumble of rocks. In a few seconds, the upward trend resumes, scaling the ridge through the cleft between two boulder-wracked peaks, passing among mountain laurel, black and white birch, scrub oak, and pitch pine in the process. Catch your breath at the first knob of this bald dome (a.k.a Butter Hill), 358 feet above the trailhead, while absorbing the great view of the western hills, as well as the neighboring Black Rock Forest and Route 9W to the south. Next up is Butter Hill's peak, three minutes farther to the east and 50 feet higher. Spicebush borders the summit, but not enough to interfere with the stellar 360-degree panorama, highlighted by the Hudson River flowing like a small sea from beneath the Newburgh Bridge to the north, growing larger and wider as it approaches Storm King.

On leaving this sun-exposed crow's nest, the narrow path glides north along the rocky ridge, arriving at a fork in a couple of minutes. Bear right with the yellow-and-turquoise blazes, ignoring the Bluebird Trail (BT, red/blue markings), and in a moment you will pass the Howell Trail (HT, blue blazes) on the right. The track treads through fairly level terrain for several minutes, with Storm King peak dead ahead and the attractive granite and scrub-oak setting common to the Hudson Highlands all around. After jogging slightly right—then left—by a stand of hemlocks, the path starts to gain ground, grinding upward over bedrock. The following plateau is more tree-covered, most notably by chestnut oaks and pitch pines, but the view north of the Newburgh Bridge is no slouch.

Continuing east toward the Hudson River, you drop into a saddle between the last rise and Storm King peak. That lull is finished in about one minute, when you come to—and must scale—a large, slanted rock face. The vista spot above that opens up in a few paces to a magnificent image of the Hudson flowing directly toward you, with an extension of the Highlands hulking dominantly across the river. Look closely, and you may see boats, like little specks of foam, puttering around on water far below. You should also be able to spot Pollepel Island, about a thousand feet off the far shore. During the Revolutionary War, colonists anchored 12 wooden bulwarks in the rocks beneath the rapidly flowing water between Pollepel and Plum Point, on the left bank of the river. These emplacements were connected by an enormous wooden chain and topped with steel spears, a *chevaux-de-frise* intended to puncture the hulls of

British ships sailing up the Hudson. The gambit failed, as the British used flat-bottom barges to maneuver up river, where they burned the town of Kingston to the ground in 1777.

If you brought field specs along, take a closer look at Pollepel Island. Rising high out of the scrub growth is the grandiose ruin of Bannerman Castle, dating from 1901–1918. Designed by Francis Bannerman, an arms dealer, partly as a summer home, and in part to house the munitions he purchased as military surplus from the federal government, the five-story baronial estate promptly fell to ruin after being acquired by the Taconic Parks Commission and New York State in 1967. Attempts are now being made by the Bannerman Castle Trust to stabilize the edifice and restore some of its paths, with boat trips there from Newburgh offered periodically during the summer.

The environment becomes more corrugated as you shuffle along on Storm King Mountain, with additional viewpoints enticingly accessible through the laurel and beech saplings along the way. The most dramatic vista, moments away, is actually a bit lower than several of the earlier ones. No matter—from this jutting spar of a rocky perch, you have a dizzying glimpse of the choppy Hudson River as it eddies and swirls beneath you. When Persian poet Omar Khayyam penned the words, "a jug of wine, a loaf of bread—and thou, beside me singing in the wilderness," it is hard to believe he didn't have this locale in mind, even though the new world of North America was still five centuries away from being "discovered." When you have had enough of the celestial visions, as well as the wine and bread, carry your song and sweetheart onward, down to yet another rocky vantage point as the track loops southward.

In a few minutes, the descent accelerates and the path meets a junction, with the yellow-turquoise markings shifting left on the Stillman Trail (which connects with the BT in a bit), while white blazes branch to the right. The circuit continues with the white blazes, but if you are not yet tired of breathtaking vistas, venture left by a couple hundred yards to a final, uncluttered overlook of the river. Back on the white-blazed track, the rocky landscape persists, with the bluffs towering above you to the right particularly notable. On hitting a rocky ledge, with fleeting views of Route 9W to the west and a sliver of the Hudson south of you, the white route snakes downward to lower and quite rocky ground. The white blazes disappear as the HT merges from the right, with the latter's blue markings now showing the way. In another five minutes, a spur to the left materializes. This is the connector to the Crow's Nest, recently reopened after being cleared of live ordnance by the Army Corps of Engineers. The blue markings fork off here, but you should proceed straight on the unblazed track.

This path overlaps an old forest road, with a retaining wall supporting its left side. As it begins to rise, the boulder field peppering the slope above draws closer, until the moraine and jumbo rocks are all around—a colorful clutch of chaos, frozen in place. That is succeeded momentarily by a rusting refrigerator and a couple of tires to the left of the trail, which unofficially mark the imminent end of the hike. Storm up the steep hill ahead, then hang a left at the crest by the low, long erratic. Out in the open of a grassy berm, the parking lot is a few paces to your right. On approaching that, note the plaque that bears the following inscription: "Freedom Road, the

Don't take a stick to this piñata! Its magnificent papier-mâché construction holds hundreds of hornets, not candy.

route traveled by the 52 American hostages from Stewart Airport to West Point after their release from captivity in Iran, January 25, 1981."

> ▶ **NEARBY ACTIVITIES**

After this Highlands intro, you can continue your explorations in the Museum of the Hudson Highlands in Cornwall-on-Hudson. Displays feature natural and cultural history, as well as changing art exhibits. Call (845) 534-5506 for additional information.

Did the glimpse of the castle on Pollepel Island pique your interest in this state-owned land? Kayak and boat tours there run from May through October. Call the Bannerman Castle Trust at (845) 831-6346 or Hudson River Adventures at (845) 220-2120 for details. See also www.bannermancastle.org.

# SUNKEN MEADOW TO NISSEQUOGUE RIVER TRAIL

## ▶ IN BRIEF

Birds and bees, beaches and trees, from boardwalks to bluff tops, Sunken Meadow packs a rich range of nature into a short stretch of trail. This serene, scenic hike offers extended contact with Long Island Sound and the Nissequogue River, passes fleetingly through an isolated upland forest, and culminates at an eerie old lunatic asylum, where the palatial grounds are landscaped with flowering fruit trees, dogwoods, and daffodils.

## ▶ DESCRIPTION

The official title of the domain from which this hike begins is Governor Alfred E. Smith/Sunken Meadow State Park. Like the cumbersome nature of that *nom d' état*, the initial impression you may have on arriving here in summer is of one vast ocean of cars, of a parking lot without end. Scratch beneath the surface of that paved expanse, though, and what you will find—beyond fabulous views of Long Island Sound—is a great hike that offers some of the best birding in the region and a pastel palette of wildflowers in spring. From sandy bluffs overlooking the Nissequogue River to an eerie amble through the grounds of an old lunatic asylum, this out-and-back jaunt, while neither strenuous nor overly long, is nonetheless the sort that leaves a lasting impression.

## ▶ DIRECTIONS

*By car:* Follow the Long Island Expressway (I-495) to Exit 53 onto the Sunken Meadow State Parkway. Proceed 7.3 miles north on the Parkway to the park toll booths, then continue for 1.2 miles to the Visitor Center and the parking lot straight ahead.

*By public transportation:* The Port Jefferson Branch of the Long Island Railroad stops in Kings Park Station. A 2.5-mile cab ride will bring you to the park.

## ⓘ KEY AT-A-GLANCE INFORMATION

**LENGTH:** 5.5 miles

**CONFIGURATION:** Out-and-back

**DIFFICULTY:** Easy, level start, then moderate

**SCENERY:** Boardwalk views of Long Island Sound, bluff views of Nissequogue River estuary, tidal flats, and rolling hardwood forests

**EXPOSURE:** Shady, except for boardwalk section at start and end

**TRAFFIC:** Can be pretty intense weekends, and very popular with morning joggers

**TRAIL SURFACE:** Sandy stretches, dirt, and roots

**HIKING TIME:** 2.5 hours; more if birding or exploring Kings Park

**SEASON:** Year-round, sunrise–sunset

**ACCESS:** $6, $8 Memorial Day–Labor Day when life guard is on duty

**MAPS:** At Visitor Center; Long Island Greenbelt Trail Conference; USGS Northport

**FACILITIES:** Rest rooms, water, and public phone at Visitor Center; picnic areas, play fields

**SPECIAL COMMENTS:** Bring binoculars for birding or for the views, and a swimsuit for a dip in the Long Island Sound. Part of the walk includes the grounds of the former Kings Park Psychiatric Center—a defunct lunatic asylum. Most buildings are closed to the public.

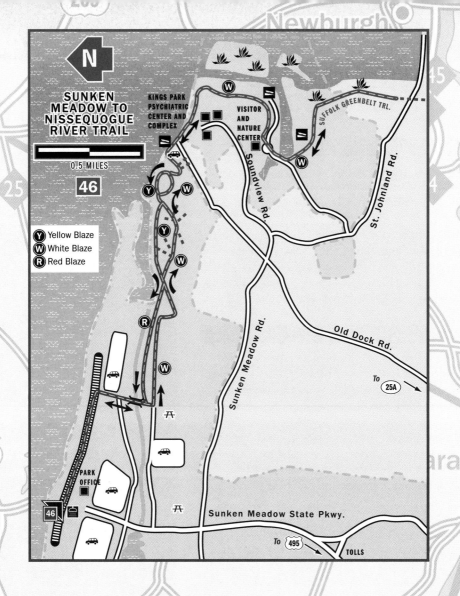

## SUNKEN MEADOW TO NISSEQUOGUE RIVER TRAIL

0.5 MILES

46

Ⓨ Yellow Blaze
Ⓦ White Blaze
Ⓡ Red Blaze

KINGS PARK PSYCHIATRIC CENTER AND COMPLEX

VISITOR AND NATURE CENTER

SUFFOLK GREENBELT TRL.

St. Johnland Rd.

Soundview Rd.

Old Dock Rd.

To 25A

Sunken Meadow Rd.

PARK OFFICE

Sunken Meadow State Pkwy.

To 495

TOLLS

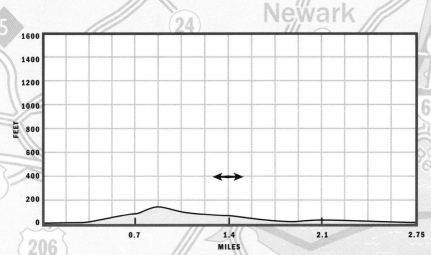

To start, stroll from the main parking area (lots 1 and 2) through the bathhouse pavilion, and turn right onto the boardwalk. With the gentle waves of Long Island Sound lapping at the sand to your left, stick with the wide wooden boardwalk for five minutes, until you reach a paved path to the right. Take that conduit, and in 200 yards, after passing parking lot 3 and shuffling over a bridge (great white and snowy egrets, loons, cormorants, and Canada geese often skim across the reed-rimmed water below), hang a left at the T, where you meet the picnic grounds. Still on macadam, you may notice the white blazes of the Suffolk County Greenbelt Trail (SGT) underfoot. Although the SGT connects Sunken Meadow to the Atlantic Ocean and Heckscher State Park 36 miles to the south, this particular trek runs only 2.8 miles before returning.

The track shifts to the right in a couple of minutes, moving uphill and away from a cedar-lined fence. It proceeds more steeply after encountering a pair of concrete benches by an apple tree, with the pavement being replaced by bark. The conclusion of this short burst puts you atop a row of bluffs, where oaks, chokeberry, and briar limit the elbow room. Ignore the red-blazed spur on the left and keep to the right on the SGT as yellow blazes fork left a few paces later. Directly past a chain-link fence are three trails, with the SGT the righthand (more straight, actually) option. The ensuing intersections appear in quick succession, with the SGT's white blazes evident throughout. Taken in sequence, you should scoot left at the slanted T, left at the next fork (in about 100 feet), then right at the following junction and, almost immediately, another left.

Now in the open atop the bluffs, the Sound should be visible (unless there is fog) straight ahead, with the far end of parking lot 3 coming into view in a few strides. Bear to the right at the fork, as the sandy track scuttles along the bluff, where pitch pines, oaks, cedars, and cat briar do little to obstruct the fine water vistas. For a brief spell, yellow and white blazes run concurrently, until the white markings abruptly swing to the right, back into an overgrown nest of briar, white birch, and oak. The Atlantic flyway overlaps the area, and this lovely, untamed spot is often alive with the chirping and twittering of an abundant assortment of birds.

On looping back to the bluffs, the SGT merges once more with yellow blazes and branches to the right, traipsing by a few unblazed spurs while providing views of the Sound and a few brackish marsh ponds below. After a marina parking lot materializes to the left, the white blazes veer inland and dive into a tangle of thorny plants. Dart left at the fork that occurs a minute later, and go left again in a yard and a half, descending over a set of steps to the marina's parking area. Cut directly toward Long Island Sound to the far side of the lot, where you should swerve to the right along the sidewalk. Do a beeline by the boat launch, cruising to the left of the Old Dock Inn (note the white blaze on the telephone pole there). A dogleg left—and then right—around the rail fence delivers you to the sandy beach, where the Nissequogue River converges on the Sound, and a bevy of boats often shuttle around. Continue on this colorful strip of shore for about 300 yards, until the white blazes signal a break to the right, up a sandy mound and a piling-supported staircase.

Oaks and birches shade a bench up on this high ground, and with a commanding panorama of the Nissequogue and the marina, you could do a lot worse for a lunch spot. The SGT exits to the left of the bench, holding mostly to the edge of the bluff as it snakes by orange lilies, periwinkles, grape hyacinth, fruit trees, cedars, dogwoods, and daffodils. You may also see a number of slender, vertical bat houses mounted on an occasional maple. When the path, which features more curves and clefts than a Victoria's Secret catalog, hits a T, dog it to the left, then step to the right at the next fork.

Not long after that, a handful of boarded-up brick buildings appears through the trees to the right. At first glance, these spooky structures look vaguely like a decommissioned military installation, or maybe an old school. Close, but no cigar. What you are moseying by was once the Kings Park Psychiatric Center, better known by county residents as the local loony bin. Established more than a century ago to aid shell-shocked veterans of the Spanish-American War (and later expanded to accommodate World War I GIs), Kings Park held 9,300 inmates at its peak in 1954, and consisted of 150 buildings. The number of patients dwindled in later years, and in 1996 the hospital was finally shuttered. Happily, much of the compound and surrounding land have been preserved as Nissequogue River State Park, which came into being in 1999.

The SGT skirts the property for five minutes, until it descends gradually toward a duff-colored concrete building, its windows covered with green boards, and then heaves to the right. The park Visitor Center lies straight ahead, with exhibits inside on native plants and animals, in addition to a history of Kings Park. Plan to linger here for a walking tour of the former institution. It is hard not to be impressed by the sheer scale of this sprawling complex, and by the vaguely spectral nature of all the decaying, moldering edifices.

Rejoin the SGT on the sidewalk in front of the Visitor Center. In about 200 yards, its white blazes tack left, off the concrete and in among maples, pines, and a number of derelict buildings. Pivot left when the track meets a paved road (which leads to a marina), and in 50 feet saunter to the right among a snarl of chokeberry. With broken-up asphalt underfoot, the marina, now on your left, is largely obscured by brush, while to the right are several boarded-up structures. Additional ruins follow, including, after the ground begins to undulate, a greenhouse—with some of its glass panes still intact. The overgrown marshland to the left is fringed with reeds, and this combination of water and concealing cover makes it an excellent birding area.

When the SGT meets St. Johnland Road, it pulls to the left and crosses the thoroughfare. This is the turnaround stage of the hike, the point at which you backtrack to Sunken Meadow. Once on the bluff, beyond the Old Dock Inn and above the marina parking lot, you might try a change of pace with the yellow blazes as they diverge to the right from the SGT. Ignore the many ruts that have been burned into the soil by mountain bikers, and in a couple of minutes the yellow blazes reconnect with the white. Then, in a matter of several strides, go with the red blazes as they surge right. This initiates a steady descent from the bluff, drawing you under pitch pines, by a few ponds (swans brood in the adjacent marsh during the spring), back toward parking lot 3. Instead of marching off in that direction, though, remain straight with the level trail as it hugs the left side of the canal. Enjoy the birding here, but remember to glide right at the bridge, where you reunite with the white blazes.

The delicate flowers of phototonic mayapple lie protected beneath their parasol leaves, deep in the woods of the Sunken Meadow to Nissequogue River Trail.

With the boardwalk once again underfoot, you are nearing the end of the hike. As rich as its earlier portions were for birds, the beach area is prime people-watching turf. And given the right temperature, the water ain't so bad for swimming, either.

## ▶ NEARBY ACTIVITIES

What would Long Island be without a Vanderbilt mansion? This Spanish Revival–style building in Centerport, furnished with original period pieces, houses a marine museum and planetarium. For guided tours and information, call (631) 854-5555; for the planetarium, call (631) 854-5544.

# SWARTSWOOD SPRING LAKE TRAIL

## ℹ KEY AT-A-GLANCE INFORMATION

**LENGTH:** 3.8 miles

**CONFIGURATION:** Loop

**DIFFICULTY:** Easy

**SCENERY:** Secondary succession forest with ponds of various sizes, impressive old growth hemlock community, and wetlands habitat

**EXPOSURE:** Balanced between shady and partially exposed

**TRAFFIC:** Moderate to heavy on weekends, light during week

**TRAIL SURFACE:** Grass and dirt

**HIKING TIME:** 1.5 hours

**SEASON:** Year-round, sunrise–sunset

**ACCESS:** Memorial Day–Labor Day, $5 weekdays, $10 weekends; free rest of year; $50 parks pass gives access to all New Jersey state parks for one calendar year

**MAPS:** At park office

**FACILITIES:** Rest rooms, water, public phone, and picnic area near park office

**SPECIAL COMMENTS:** Swartswood Lake is a favorite among swimmers, boaters, and fishermen. Call (973) 383-4200 for boat-rental information.

## ▶ IN BRIEF

With so many people drawn to Swartswood Lake and the landscaped lawns that surround it, you should find the more distant trails here delightfully under-populated. That's a net gain, not just for solitude-seekers, but also for enjoying the abundance of birds that flock to the three ponds encountered along the way. A cool, shady hemlock hollow and a hillside hardwood forest, its earthen floor carpeted with a kaleidoscope of wildflowers in spring, add to the charm of this easy jaunt.

## ▶ DESCRIPTION

If you visit Swartswood State Park anytime in summer, you will probably see more boats skimming over the jade-green water of its namesake lake than sail by the South Street Seaport on an average day. With nearly half the acreage here underwater, to most visitors Swartswood Lake is the park; you can swim in it, you can boat on it, and you can cast a fishing line into it. Indeed, Swartswood, which was created by a retreating glacier 15,000 years ago, is considered to be one of New Jersey's best lakes for trout, and the scuttlebutt suggests the walleye population may soon rival that. Landlubbers looking for a different

## ▶ DIRECTIONS

Follow I-95/I-80 west across the George Washington Bridge. Leave I-80 at Exit 25 onto US 206 north and drive about 12 miles. In Newton, turn left on Mill Street (CR 519), and after 0.3 miles, left again onto Swartswood Road (CR 622) west. The park is clearly indicated. Continue 4.4 miles and make a left onto East Shore Drive (CR 619). The park entrance and office are 0.5 miles ahead to the right. The trailhead parking is across the street, several yards south along CR 619.

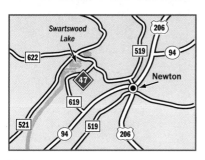

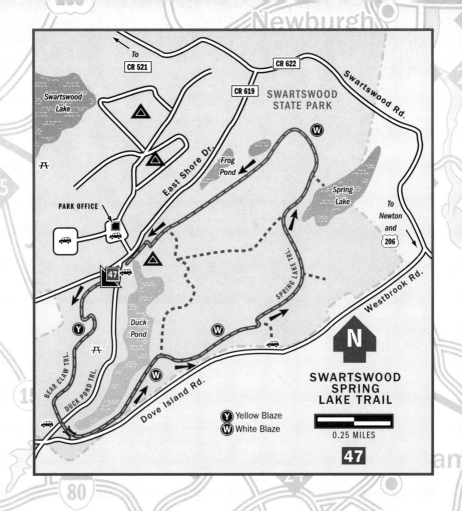

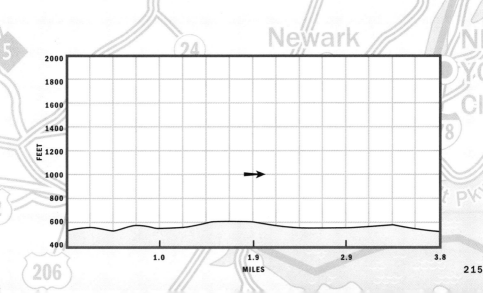

Look but don't taste! This tempting yellow morel makes its appearance in moist weather at Swartswood State Park.

angle on the park, though, don't have to hit the road to scratch their itchy feet. Nope, they just have to cross it, picking up the start of the Bear Claw Trail (BCT, yellow blazes) on the south side of Route 619, catty-corner from the park entrance.

This is not a long hike, and as for ruggedness, let's just say that you are unlikely to develop many blisters. It is in the pulchritude department that Swartswood shines, with the loop drawing you through a hardwood forest, lowland fields, a lakeside community of plants and birds, swamps rife with wildflowers, and a hillside darkened by an antediluvian agglomeration of hemlocks, all in about two hours of walking. The BCT begins to the right a step or two prior to the kiosk. It soars uphill initially, shaded by maples and oaks, with aromatic garlic mustard and white-flowering anemones covering the forest floor. In three minutes, after hopping over a pair of old stone walls, the path peaks and tapers downward toward Duck Pond. It veers to the south and levels off in a couple hundred yards, adhering to the contours of the ridge for a spell, where a handful of hemlocks, ash trees, and dead cedars have filtered in among the usual hardwoods. (If there has been rain at all recently, you may also see rare specimens of cup fungi on the ground.) Resuming the downward trend, the single-file BCT meets another stone wall and parallels it for a few seconds, then shifts left around it and crosses the paved Duck Pond Trail.

This marks the start of the Spring Lake Trail (SLT, white markings). There are a few planks and a short bridge for maneuvering through spillover from Duck Pond, to your left; but for most of the year, the sunlit ground here is dry and firm. In spite of the proximity of Dove Island Road to the right, this is a lovely area, with the path following the shoreline of Duck Pond, where cattail reeds abound. You may notice as well that the heavy overgrowth of the higher Bear Claw area has opened up, with sheep laurel, chokeberry, dogwood, and shagbark hickory providing cover for now, while the soil hosts a plethora of wildflowers like lavender geraniums, yellow asters, and buttercups.

Eventually the serpentine SLT leaves the pond vicinity, heading uphill through chest-high scrub. Turn right at the T, staying with the sunny, grass-sided track as it bends to the left, bumping against sarsaparilla shrubs along the way. After it enters a fern-filled gully (where you may observe jack-in-the-pulpits and—rarely—yellow morels), the SLT arrives at a fork. The route continues to the left (the right spur ends in 250 feet at a small parking area), slipping by an open field and then into the cover of cedar trees. Skip the spur to the right, as the white blazes guide you on to Spring Lake, which seems, oddly, to be somewhat smaller than Duck Pond. The trail swerves left around the foot of the lake, encountering an overgrown trace to the left. From this point on, the views of Spring Lake are minimal; but a right at the next Y, in less than a minute, bolts directly to the rocky shore, where you can dangle your toes in the pristine water and soak up the rays of the morning sun.

Back at the fork, proceed with the SLT as it pulls to the left, passing an open field (which is frequented by bluebirds) and jumping over a collapsed stone wall. Frog Pond, a weed-choked body of water, now looms on your right, ensconced among hemlocks and maples. If you are here during the summer, a croaking chorus of frogs will probably reach your ears, justifying the pond's soubriquet (though turtles are its unsung habitués, too). The trail then gains ground, bounding into a sensational stand of hemlocks. With sunlight filtering through the shady embrace of these conifers, it can be difficult at times to see the blazes, but after a brief climb, the path swings from a southwest direction toward the west, dropping down through a patch of mayapple. In a couple of minutes, Route 619 comes momentarily into view to the right, and a few paces later, the track emerges by the entrance to the group camping area, with Duck Pond straight ahead. Pivot to the right, walk up to the road, and hang a left. The parking lot is 100 yards away, on the left.

### ▶ NEARBY ACTIVITIES

If you'd rather be cool underground than hot with the floating crowd on Swartswood Lake, the Sterling Hill Mining Museum in Ogdensburg offers guided mine tours, and displays of minerals and mining equipment. For information, call (973) 209-7212.

# TALLMAN MOUNTAIN HUDSON RIVER OVERLOOK TRAIL

 **KEY AT-A-GLANCE INFORMATION**

**LENGTH:** 2 miles

**CONFIGURATION:** Elongated balloon

**DIFFICULTY:** Very easy

**SCENERY:** Dense deciduous forest growing on rocky slopes overlooking west bank of the Hudson River and Piermont Marsh grasslands

**EXPOSURE:** Tree cover all the way

**TRAFFIC:** Heavy on summer weekends

**TRAIL SURFACE:** Mix of dirt, rocks, and roots in first half, level cinder on return trail

**HIKING TIME:** 1 hour

**SEASON:** Year-round, 8 a.m.–dusk

**ACCESS:** Third weekend in June–Labor Day, $5 per car, ; pets must be muzzled and leashed

**MAPS:** At gatehouse and office; New York–New Jersey Trail Conference, Hudson Palisades Trails

**FACILITIES:** None along trail, but rest rooms in picnic areas and athletic field are open April–November; vending machines in summer; playground, basketball court, pool, track

**SPECIAL COMMENTS:** The riverside part of this trail overlaps with the Long Path, a 350-mile long (and growing) trail that starts at the George Washington Bridge (New Jersey side) and ends near Albany.

## ▶ IN BRIEF

Stellar views and prime, private picnic spots don't come any easier than this level walk to a high overlook of the Hudson River. Birding and boat-watching are extra attractions, as is the possibility of an extended campaign along a piece of the Long Path, which intersects the trail.

## ▶ DESCRIPTION

We've all heard the argument at one time or another. It starts with a rhetorical question, something on the order of: What's the dividing line between a hike and merely a walk? Some people are guided by distance, others by the degree of effort involved. As far as we're concerned, you might just as well try to determine which came first, the chicken or the egg.

Tallman Mountain falls flatly in the middle of that debate. It came into existence in 1928 when the Palisades Interstate Park Commission appropriated 164 acres along the Palisades cliffs to keep them from being destroyed by industrial developers. Another 540 acres were added 14 years later. So with such a muscular-sounding soubriquet, shouldn't you expect to enjoy something on the order of an 8-mile pinnacles hike, or, at the very least, several hours of rock-scrambling capped by stupendous views? Well, yes, but this is a different sort of state park, one that serves a multitude of interests, devoting much of its land

## ▶ DIRECTIONS

Cross the George Washington Bridge and take the Palisades Interstate Parkway north to Exit 4. At the traffic light, turn left onto US 9W north and proceed for another 2 miles to the park entrance on the right. The parking lot is beyond the park office, to the right.

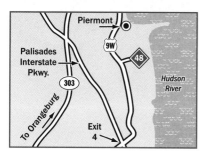

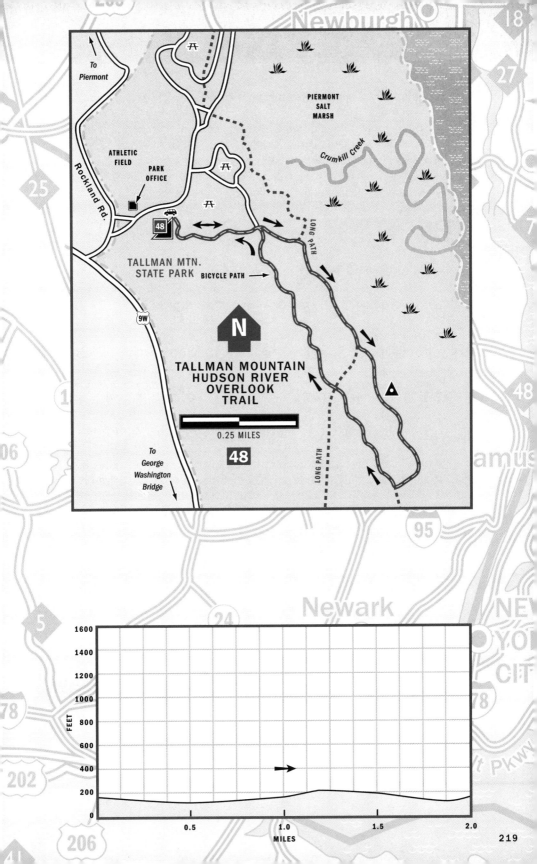

TALLMAN MOUNTAIN
HUDSON RIVER
OVERLOOK
TRAIL

0.25 MILES

**48**

PIERMONT
SALT
MARSH

Crumkill Creek

LONG PATH

ATHLETIC
FIELD

PARK
OFFICE

Rockland Rd.

TALLMAN MTN.
STATE PARK   BICYCLE PATH

9W

To
Piermont

To
George
Washington
Bridge

LONG PATH

to three picnic areas, a sports field and running track, basketball and tennis courts, and even a swimming pool.

Oh, did we forget to mention the hiking in Tallman? A section of the Long Path runs north-south through the entire length of the park and beyond. Overlapping a part of that is a 2-mile jaunt out to the bluffs and back, which some might argue is best described as a *walk*. Split the hairs however you like; this latter Hudson River Overlook Trail, while neither long nor strenuous, has a tremendous payoff in its unsurpassed bird's-eye view of the river and surrounding estuaries.

Look for the trailhead in the large parking area to the right of the park road, just past the office. From the middle of that lot, stroll directly into the lush woodland, dense with sugar maples, black birches, and beech trees. In about 0.25 miles, the somewhat rocky, hard-packed path crosses a paved bicycle lane. One hundred yards beyond that is an intersection with the green-blazed Long Path which, if you follow it to the left, leads first to the swimming pools, then departs Tallman for Rockland Lake State Park and, continuing northward, Bear Mountain State Park.

Unless you are up for a highly ambitious hike or are feeling sweaty and in need of a dip, stay to the right. Though well trafficked, this stretch of trail feels fairly wild, with many stones protruding from the earth and an occasional tulip tree arching over the way. You may detect a bit of brininess to the air if the breeze is blowing from the east, but views of the Hudson are initially obscured, at least in summer, by the over-growth crowding the path.

The vistas improve as the narrow passage descends toward the marshland abut-ting the Hudson, fords a stream (dry in summer), then climbs gradually upward again. In roughly 0.3 miles, after hopping over a few fallen trees, the Long Path veers off to the right. Bear left for a prolongation of the Hudson views. When you have been out from 20 to 30 minutes, you'll reach a granite ledge that protrudes from the bluff several hundred feet above the Piermont salt marsh, providing an excellent vantage point from which to survey the Hudson River and its surroundings, including the Tap-pan Zee Bridge far to the left, and the Piermont Pier. If you brought a pair of binocu-lars along, this is where you'll want to use them. It is also an ideal outpost for enjoying a sandwich.

Walk straight ahead at the next trail junction, in 15 yards, as the way becomes increasingly congested with scrub and tree debris. A few steps farther, and you'll be edging inland and uphill, finally reaching the bike lane you crossed earlier (this seg-ment being composed of cinder). Head right on the wide, easy surface and return to the spur to the parking area, taking a left once the cinder morphs into asphalt.

## ▶ NEARBY ACTIVITIES

Acrophobes disinclined to lunch at the Hudson River overlook should plan to hit the park's shady picnic groves. And if you are looking to cool off, the swimming pool is open from the third weekend in June through Labor Day. For information, call the park at (845) 359-0544.

# TEATOWN LAKE LOOP

### ▶ IN BRIEF

A lake with an island devoted to wildflowers, a couple of streams, and a number of boardwalks and bridges make this a can't-miss for family outings. The wild-at-heart should beat a path to the forested hillsides, too, where granite outcroppings, bogs, and meadows round out this diverse park. Teatown is crosscut by numerous paths, including a stretch of the Briarcliff-Peakskill Trail, so you can create as long or short a hike as fits your time or energy.

### ▶ DESCRIPTION

Some people feel that a hike is not complete without at least one animal sighting. A lone deer grazing on spruce needles, a fuzzy-tailed squirrel gathering acorns, even a swarm of bloodsucking mosquitoes in some intangible way validates the experience of being outdoors for a few hours. No hike comes with a guarantee, of course, that a focus on things feral will come to fruition. But Teatown Lake does the next best thing: it offers up a fail-safe selection of animals within its half-timbered, cream-colored nature center.

Want to know what a corn snake looks like? The nature center has one, along with a black rat

### ▶ DIRECTIONS

*By car:* Follow the New York State Thruway (I-87) north to Exit 9 (Tarrytown) and proceed on US 9 north to Ossining. About 0.4 miles after the junction with SR 133, take a right onto Cedar Lane, which becomes Spring Valley Road, and continue for 3.8 miles past the nature center on the left. Take Blinn Road to the left and drive into the Lakeside parking lot on the left.

*By public transportation:* The Metro North Hudson Line goes to Croton-Harmon Station. A taxi ride from there is roughly 5 miles long.

### ℹ KEY AT-A-GLANCE INFORMATION

**LENGTH:** 4.5 miles; add 1.3 miles for optional Overlook Trail

**CONFIGURATION:** Figure eight

**DIFFICULTY:** Easy/moderate

**SCENERY:** Well-marked, gently rolling trails meander through shady forest of deciduous trees, laurel, and hemlock, around lake and a few swamps

**EXPOSURE:** Dense, protective canopy and only one open meadow

**TRAFFIC:** Light on Hidden Valley Trail across Blinn Road, but Lakeside Trail is quite popular on summer weekends

**TRAIL SURFACE:** Dirt with occasional rocks and roots, and a few patches of boardwalk

**HIKING TIME:** 2.25 hours

**SEASON:** Year-round, dawn–dusk

**ACCESS:** No fee, donations welcome, dogs must be leashed, no bicycles

**MAPS:** At nature center

**FACILITIES:** Water and rest rooms at nature center; picnic area and public phone

**SPECIAL COMMENTS:** For a fee, you may take a guided tour of the Wildflower Island, a 2-acre sanctuary accessible via boardwalk. Open mid-April–September. Be sure to preregister on weekends; call (914) 762-2912.

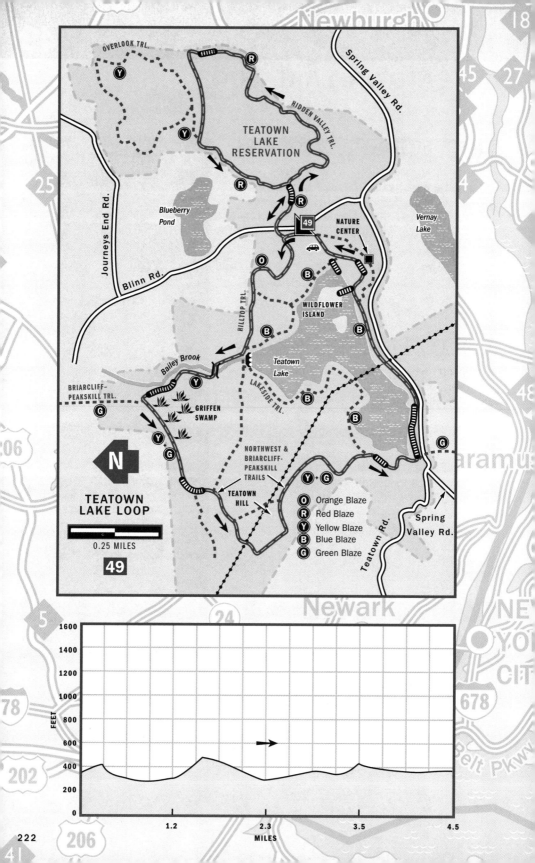

TEATOWN LAKE RESERVATION

Blueberry Pond

NATURE CENTER

Vernay Lake

Overlook Trl.

Hidden Valley Trl.

Spring Valley Rd.

Journeys End Rd.

Blinn Rd.

Hilltop Trl.

WILDFLOWER ISLAND

Bailey Brook

Teatown Lake

Lakeside Trl.

BRIARCLIFF-PEAKSKILL TRL.

GRIFFEN SWAMP

N

TEATOWN LAKE LOOP

0.25 MILES

49

NORTHWEST & BRIARCLIFF-PEAKSKILL TRAILS

TEATOWN HILL

Teatown Rd.

Spring Valley Rd.

Orange Blaze
Red Blaze
Yellow Blaze
Blue Blaze
Green Blaze

FEET

1600
1400
1200
1000
800
600
400
200
0

1.2          2.3          3.5          4.5
MILES

snake, a garter snake, green and gray tree frogs, a bearded dragon, a couple of cuddly ferrets, a bobcat, coyote, barn owl, and moose. Well, okay, the last four are stuffed, but you get the idea: This is very much a family-friendly operation. Managed by a nonprofit corporation, Teatown was established in 1963 with just 190 acres. It has since grown to 759 acres, which consist of a large lake and wildflower island, and several scenic loops showcasing swampland, meadows, hardwood and conifer forests, and a craggy gorge.

Most of these features may be seen over a couple of loops that amount to 4.5 miles of fairly easy walking. Both circuits start near the road on the right side of the parking lot, and yes, there is indeed a good chance of encountering wildlife along the way. The trail forks as you leave the lot, with the orange-blazed Hilltop heading left and the red-slashed Hidden Valley cutting across the road. Keep to the left for now (careful of the poison ivy); you'll return to the Hidden Valley Trail in about an hour and a half. Initially the fairly open dirt track parallels the parking lot, followed in a few minutes by private dwellings to the right, in addition to a number of weather-stained erratics. The path brushes by maples, shagbark hickories, hemlocks, and a handful of withered cedars, then shifts downhill through a shady patch of pines.

It arrives near the base of that slope at the north end of Teatown Lake, with the latter's shimmering green surface lit up by lily pads. Cross the concrete edge of the dam and then, after a short wooden walkway, hang a right onto the Northwest Trail (yellow blazes). This gravel-lined track hugs Bailey Brook (more rocks than water much of the year) for perhaps 200 yards before crossing a bridge and continuing to the right, away from the lake. Diverging slowly from the brook, this northwest route threads precariously through the moist, mucky Griffen Swamp (look for red cardinal flowers among the slippery rocks), with grass and ferns at ankle level, and maple, beech, and tulip trees towering above.

On the far side of a wooden span is a fork; stick with the yellow (now paired with green) blazes to the left. From there, the meandering begins in earnest, and like a magician dazzling his audience with a succession of tricks, there will be fleeting glimpses of a high, rocky ridge rising dramatically to the right, more swampy conditions along a couple of boardwalks, another boulder-filled bluff, maybe a red-tailed hawk soaring low over the birch trees, and then a series of intersections. Stride straight through the first junction (by the boardwalk), and bear right—still on yellow—at the next. Ten minutes of marching uphill should put you among laurels, hemlocks, and a mound of jagged granite.

Savor this setting, for in a few more steps, the scenery takes a definite—though momentary—turn for the worse, as you emerge on an open hillside under a nucleus of power lines. The climb continues in the shadow of those cables and their colossal support stanchions, with blueberry bushes, sassafras, and wild grapes thriving beneath the sun's strong glare. Stay to the left at the ensuing four-way intersection, and keep stomping up the steep, rock-filled slope. Finally at the top, canter left and descend on the other side of the power lines through knee- to waist-high grass and winged sumac. The yellow-green blazes veer off to the right at the base of one stanchion, bending at last away from those eyesores and back into the shade of maples and oaks, among a range of rocky ridgelines.

The trail shifts left by a stone wall, near a boggy patch, yielding in the process a pretty fair view of Teatown Lake. From there, it's downward by an imposing series of boulders, seemingly frozen in place as they were cascading down the hill. Roll right on the 20-foot long boardwalk at the junction with the blue-blazed Lakeside Trail and, as soon as you've hit the west side of the lake, shift left (just prior to the road) onto a pontoon boardwalk that runs directly over a section of the water. This is the segment of the hike in which your decision to bring field specs is rewarded, as the birding is typically excellent, and it is easy to whittle time off the clock counting mallards and Canada geese (and occasionally something more exotic).

In due time, press onward through the shady nook by the shore, over the next span, and into a second maple-shaded recess. Note the spruce grove near the small access pavilion to Wildflower Island; the farmers who tilled the earth here planted it as a windbreak more than a century ago. Moving east by the water, lope left at the wooden stairs to the nature center and pass over the boardwalk. Once by the enormous tulip tree, go straight across the trail junction (left leads down a boardwalk to a view of Wildflower Island through a bird blind), then hop off of blue to the right and return to the parking area.

Once more at the trailhead by the road, follow this time the red blazes of the Hidden Valley Trail across the asphalt for an entirely different look at the park. Proceed through the rock wall and over the boardwalk, into a grassy, fern-speckled meadow, with an apple orchard on one side, black walnut trees on another, and a handful of dogwoods, maples, and sycamores tossed in for good measure. Shuffle right at the four-way junction and remain with the red blazes throughout the entire 1.6-mile loop, seeing along the way thick clusters of pines and hemlocks, and several dramatic escarpments, with rocks spilling down their angular sides. There is even another boardwalk by an extended marsh.

A right option to the Overlook Trail occurs a couple of minutes past an impressively high granite formation. If your soles still have good spring, consider adding this 1.3-mile loop to the tour. Of course, it is easy to get carried away in this part of the park, where the untamed, rough-cut beauty is so highly appealing, and the flush of wildflowers in the spring adds to its allure. In any case, the red blazes show the way back to the meadow, and from there to the parking lot.

## ▶ NEARBY ACTIVITIES

In nearby Ossining, exhibits at the Ossining Heritage Area Park Visitor Center focus on historic town buildings, the Old Croton Aqueduct, and such Sing Sing–related themes as weapons made by prisoners, replicas of cells, and an electric chair. Free admission; for information, call (914) 941-3189.

# THOMPSON PARK
# RED AND BLUE COMBO

In this county park, you will find a healthy balance of what makes central Jersey such a garden spot: a scattering of silver-barked beech trees, a pinch of pine barrens, healthy bogs and wetlands, and a slow-moving river. The fairly secluded hike is seldom challenging, but you may have your hands—and boots—full in spring, when the water level of its streams and swamps is highest.

▶ **DESCRIPTION**

Before heading out to Thompson Park, you had better check your bearings. It is not that this is so deep a pocket of wilderness that you are liable to lose your way, only to be discovered when a flock of buzzards circling overhead points the search party to your position. No, the problem is that there are two Thompson Parks in the vicinity, one each in Monmouth and Middlesex Counties. The former's Thompson has little to interest hikers, and if you end up there by mistake, well, you could always practice your putting.

The highly attractive Thompson Park in Middlesex County, on the other hand, is intersected by a small network of foot-friendly trails

▶ **DIRECTIONS**

*By car:* Follow I-95 across the George Washington Bridge into New Jersey and continue south on the New Jersey Turnpike (I-95). Take Exit 8A and go east (left) on Forsgate Road to a 4-way stop sign. Turn right on Perrineville Road and proceed for 1 mile, then hang a left on Fir Drive into the park. Continue straight for 0.25 miles to the trailhead parking on the right.

*By public transportation:* The closest you can get is Monroe, via the New Jersey Transit bus 138/139 from the New York Port Authority. From Monroe, the park is less than a 3-mile taxi ride away.

**KEY AT-A-GLANCE INFORMATION**

**LENGTH:** 3.1 miles

**CONFIGURATION:** Loop

**DIFFICULTY:** Very easy

**SCENERY:** Wetland valleys intersected by network of streams, lushly forested hills, and even a remnant of pine barrens

**EXPOSURE:** Hardly any

**TRAFFIC:** Can get busy on weekends, light during week

**TRAIL SURFACE:** Dirt and roots, with hidden bog pots in spring and fall

**HIKING TIME:** 1.5 hours

**SEASON:** Year-round, 8 a.m.–dusk

**ACCESS:** No fee, pets must be leashed

**MAPS:** At trailhead; www.monmouthcountyparks.com

**FACILITIES:** Rest rooms and water across Fir Drive, public phone

**SPECIAL COMMENTS:** Be alert at the Conrail train tracks; they are still used, albeit only occasionally.

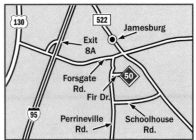

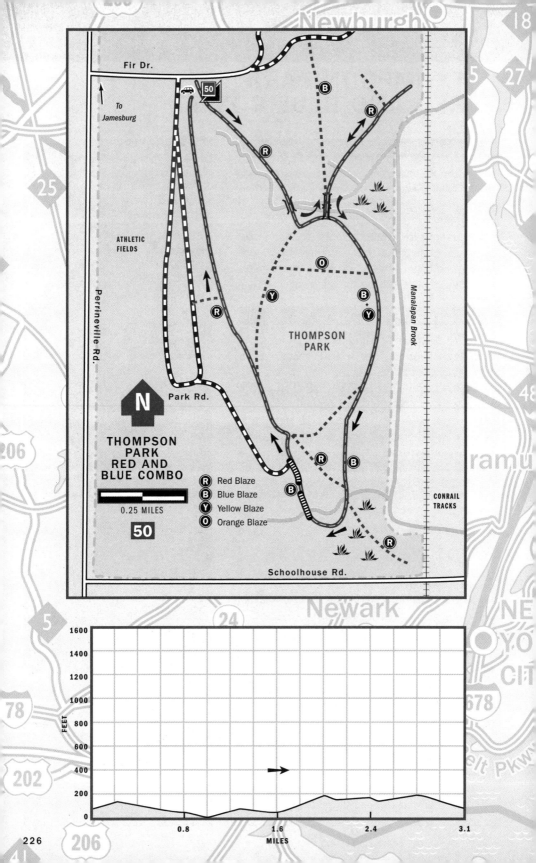

THOMPSON
PARK
RED AND
BLUE COMBO

**R** Red Blaze
**B** Blue Blaze
**Y** Yellow Blaze
**O** Orange Blaze

0.25 MILES

50

N

Fir Dr.

To Jamesburg

50

ATHLETIC
FIELDS

Perrineville Rd.

Park Rd.

THOMPSON
PARK

Manalapan Brook

CONRAIL
TRACKS

Schoolhouse Rd.

that offers a taste of upland woods, low wetlands, pine barrens, and a great variety of bird life. You might also stop by the petting zoo to say hello to the emu, golden pheasants, dwarf goats, and pigs, and perhaps plan to picnic by its large reservoir, where huge flocks of Canada geese reign. This, clearly, is a place where you might spend an entire day and go home with more than trail dirt on your shoes.

Look for the trailhead at the northeast corner of the dirt parking area. Note that colored discs are used as blazes in Thompson, so pay no attention to the many maverick markings that are painted on trees. Follow the red discs directly into the forest and onward through the staggered four-way junction. As the path moves downhill, it zigzags past oaks, birches and many, many silver-barked beech trees, while a low arroyo slices through the root-entangled real estate. A sign points to the right where a bridge fords that stream, then, at a slight rise, bear left at the T. For the moment, the red discs overlap with the yellow trail, a wide inner loop. In perhaps 40 yards, red branches away to the left, leading out to a remnant of the area's pine barrens. Take that turn, which is shared by blue discs, and proceed downward over the boardwalk. Remain with red at the fork as it diverges from blue, jog left at the dry wash, cross the bridge, and keep walking to the right.

This is a singularly attractive bit of woodland, graced in part by sassafras and mature tulip trees, with a picturesque stream flowing by. As a study in contrasts, in a couple of minutes you'll be standing among a lonely concentration of white pines, the last of the area's pine barrens. A couple of spurs here offer bushwhacking possibilities, but the red trail dead-ends in a few more yards by the Conrail tracks. The wide, slowly flowing water you see to the right is Manalapan Brook.

Return to the yellow-blazed loop, and head left as it tapers gracefully uphill for a laughable elevation gain of only 15 feet. Manalapan slithers through a boggy wetland down below on your port side, while the ground opposite rises among cat briar and beech trees to drier conditions. An orange-blazed option to the right is a cutthrough to the other side of the loop, which is useful to know if you've come up lame and need to return to the trailhead. Otherwise, leave the inner loop a few yards later as blue forks to the left. This route provides an elevated panorama of Manalapan Brook, a commanding perch for observing wading waterfowl. In due time, this blue trail tilts steeply toward the brook, only to climb again after reaching its moist bank.

On pushing into a marshy grassland, the path brushes against a different leg of the red trail. That joins blue in dropping left off the slope, as the track continues to shadow the eddying Manalapan. There are many side streams in this locale, and more than a couple of bog pots—so if you value dry feet, watch where you step. Stay with the blue discs when red branches off, as the former's parabola arcs out of the bog and over a couple of boardwalks, toward higher turf. Once atop the ridge, a period of level walking ensues, with a soccer field appearing in a while through the cat briar to the left. Blue's trailhead—and thus its endpoint—lies in that direction.

Change over to red there. At first it appears to overlap yellow on the wide inner loop, which meets blue as the latter expires. As yellow pulls away toward the right in a handful of yards, though, red veers slightly to the left of center in a northwest trajectory. In a couple of minutes, red jogs right at a fork, reaching the parking lot in a few moments more. Near the end of the trail is a board nailed about 12 feet up a tree,

A crimson cardinal is an appropriate sighting on Thompson Park's Red Trail.

an interpretive sign depicting the differences between deer and elk tracks. No question: There is a multitude of deer romping through the forest. As for elk . . . let's just say you are more likely to encounter Ichabod Crane screaming down the trail.

## ▶ NEARBY ACTIVITIES

History buffs should plan to check out Monmouth Battlefield State Park in Freehold. One of the longest battles in the American Revolution took place in this now-peaceful, rural setting. Call (732) 462-9616 for information.

# TURKEY–EGYPT CONNECTION

## ▶ IN BRIEF

It doesn't take a trip on the Orient Express to experience exotic scenery, as this exhilarating hike proves. The myriad trails of this beautiful county park profile a wilder, untamed side of nature while leading to historic cabin ruins, a waterfall, countless swampy streams, mysterious erratics, far-reaching views, a grassy cedar grove, rich birding opportunities, and even the chance of seeing black bears.

## ▶ DESCRIPTION

Our hiking pals out west tend to rattle on with a peacock's pride about their treks through glacier-wracked terrain. Sure, there are still some glaciers on the Left Coast that haven't yet succumbed to global warming. But when it comes to seeing up close the impact a glacier can have on its environment, we in the New York region have no reason to hang our heads—not with so much of our landscape scooped and carved into gorges, gullies, gulches, kettles, and ravines by the last Ice Age. Not when so many mountain lakes and eccentric erratics have been left behind as reminders of those melting blocks of snow.

One block in particular, the Wisconsin Glacier, was responsible for much of the beauty

## ▶ DIRECTIONS

*By car:* Follow I-95/I-80 west across the George Washington Bridge. Leave I-80 at Exit 41 onto I-287 north. Take Exit 44 (Main Street) in Boonton. At the intersection with Boonton Avenue (CR 511), turn right. Proceed for 3.3 miles on CR 511. The parking lot and Visitor Center are on the left.

*By public transportation:* From Penn Station, connect with the New Jersey Transit Montclair–Boonton Line to Boonton Station. From there, it is about 4 miles by taxi to the park.

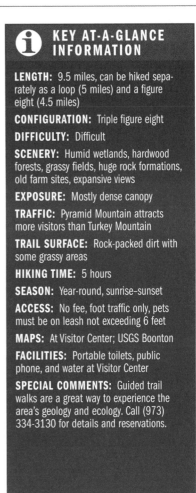

## ① KEY AT-A-GLANCE INFORMATION

**LENGTH:** 9.5 miles, can be hiked separately as a loop (5 miles) and a figure eight (4.5 miles)

**CONFIGURATION:** Triple figure eight

**DIFFICULTY:** Difficult

**SCENERY:** Humid wetlands, hardwood forests, grassy fields, huge rock formations, old farm sites, expansive views

**EXPOSURE:** Mostly dense canopy

**TRAFFIC:** Pyramid Mountain attracts more visitors than Turkey Mountain

**TRAIL SURFACE:** Rock-packed dirt with some grassy areas

**HIKING TIME:** 5 hours

**SEASON:** Year-round, sunrise–sunset

**ACCESS:** No fee, foot traffic only, pets must be on leash not exceeding 6 feet

**MAPS:** At Visitor Center; USGS Boonton

**FACILITIES:** Portable toilets, public phone, and water at Visitor Center

**SPECIAL COMMENTS:** Guided trail walks are a great way to experience the area's geology and ecology. Call (973) 334-3130 for details and reservations.

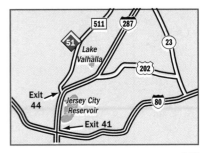

**TURKEY-EGYPT CONNECTION**

N

0.25 MILES

51

Y Yellow Blaze
G Green Blaze
R Red Blaze
B Blue Blaze
O Orange Blaze
W White Blaze
D White Diamond Blaze

Stony Brook Rd.
North Valhalla Brook
Brook Valley Rd.
Botts Pond
LIMESTONE QUARRY CABIN RUINS
TURKEY MTN. 892'
Taylortown Reservoir
STONE RUINS
Boonton Ave.
100 STEPS
EAGLE CLIFF
WHALE HEAD ROCK
BIG CAT SWAMP
Mars Ct.
LITTLE CAT SWAMP
TRIPOD ROCK
51
VISITOR CENTER
BEAR SWAMP
CAT ROCKS
LUCY'S OVERLOOK
PYRAMID MTN. 934'
CR 511
BEAR ROCK
RUINS
Bear House Brook
Stony Brook

Quirk of nature or Paleolithic sundial? Tripod Rock is one of the many dramatic geological attractions of Turkey and Pyramid Mountains.

on display at Pyramid Mountain Natural Historical Area, a Morris County park. When it disappeared about 18,000 years ago, the Wisconsin Glacier deposited a number of extraordinary boulders, including Bear Rock, estimated to be the largest erratic in the Garden State, and Tripod Rock, a unique combination of one enormous stone supported by three diminutive ones. The numerous swamps and streams, as well as a dramatic waterfall, also reflect that climatic heritage. Those, in turn, help nourish the amazing array of wildflowers, in addition to the bears, bobcats, black-capped chickadees, and pileated woodpeckers (to name just a few) that dwell in this densely forested park.

When "developers" threatened to bulldoze Pyramid and Turkey Mountains in the 1990s, conservationists successfully teamed with Morris County officials in the creation of this preserve. More than 1,000 acres of land are now protected—land so unspoiled, so beautiful, we know exactly where to take our Western hiking friends on their next visit. This prolonged trek incorporates both mountains, situated on opposite sides of Boonton Avenue. It may be broken into two shorter loops, though, if you lack the time for the full circuit. We like to start with Turkey Mountain, saving the more dramatic Pyramid Mountain for last. From the park exit, stroll to the other side of Boonton Avenue and step around the pipe gate. Stay with this forest road, blazed yellow, as it passes a spur on the right, a bog on the left, and crosses a four-way intersection. Beech trees are the dominant hardwood in this shady hollow, with ample support from oaks, maples, black birches, and tulip poplars.

Remain with the yellow markings as they swing left at the T, at the bottom of the slope. Walk by the cabin ruins, and in a couple of minutes, rock-hop over the confluence of swamp streams, a picturesque spot made all the prettier by the presence of skunk cabbage and ferns. The track begins to climb after that, leveling off in five minutes by a fork and flowering dogwoods. If you would like to detour to the limestone quarry, strike off to the right. Otherwise, continue straight, skipping also the left option that surfaces in three strides. As the Yellow Trail loses elevation, it arcs to the southeast by knee-high ferns, a handful of cedars, sarsaparilla, and, above to the right, boulders and hemlocks. Shortly after a trace to the left, the yellow blazes break from this wide track, making a hairpin turn to the left. Head that way, bounding over some small seasonal streams while approaching a broad swamp. The birding is great, incidentally, by Botts Pond, down the spur to the right, with warblers, scarlet tanagers, and indigo buntings among the warm-weather visitors.

There are numerous erratics in this vicinity, many impressively large, as you ascend to a power-line break. Look for a yellow blaze on the right leg of the stanchion and bear to the right, as the path returns to the woods a second later. This is a wonderfully wild nook of the bog, with oversize rocks rising off the fern-dappled ground and silver-barked beech saplings gleaming in the sunlight. A few minutes of rolling with the undulating terrain brings you to a four-way intersection. The hike proceeds to the right, but there is a sensational waterfall straight ahead, where you can see the cascade drop 20 feet to a dark pool, then gurgle noisily through a rocky streambed.

If you can pull yourself away from this plashy splasher, cross the bridge and cut up the middle of the three trails that appear immediately after it. This crawls above the falls, paralleling North Valhalla Brook while meandering up and down, through swamp and forest, for the next mile. There is so little foot traffic in this part of the park that you are just as likely to see the paw prints of bears, bobcats, or beavers in the muddy stream banks as anything left behind by the sole of a biped. You may also observe odd red stones larded with specks of white quartzite. These are conglomerates known colloquially as puddingstone (supposedly because it resembles English meat pudding), which are common to Bearfort Mountain, in Wawayanda State Park.

In about 20 minutes, the path comes to a T and shifts right, then squiggles left, avoiding Stony Brook Road, visible through the trees. Several minutes hence, the trail merges with the road, glides left, crosses the bridge, and hops to the left back into the forest, still beside the lovely North Valhalla Brook. The resident naturalist reports that bears inhabit the woods higher up the slope, including some mommas with cubs, so remain vigilant and you may observe much more than the dark cup fungi that often dot the soil. The yellow blazes dart to the left at a fork that follows, gradually gaining elevation among mountain laurels and a fair peppering of glacial debris. Edge right at the ensuing fork, where a green-blazed route branches left. The path crests by a grassy knoll amid cedars and oaks, and ends at a T with a red-blazed track. Turn right on red, as they say at traffic school, and keep your eyes open for white-tailed deer which like to frolic among the cedars. The altitude here, if you scale the gray rock that towers nearby, is 892 feet.

The trail forks in three minutes, with the diverging legs rejoining in approximately 800 feet on the other side of this grass-decked dome. The presence of flowering fruit trees by a stone wall reinforces the notion that this little patch of Eden was once cultivated turf. The path then descends to a marshy bog as cedars yield to chestnut oaks and other hardwoods, before abruptly surging uphill again and ending in the open expanse of the power-line cut. You can pick up the Blue Trail in roughly 25 paces to the right. First, though, jog left to the top of the slope. As you maneuver through the scrub of sumac, sheep laurel, blueberry bushes, and dwarf oaks toward the next stanchion, search for a trace to the left, overgrown with wisteria. That leads to a sizable cabin ruin, with its imposing double-sided chimney largely intact.

Continuing toward the stanchion, there is a second ruin to the right where the unblazed path ends. Tucked among spicebush and covered—in spring—with colorful columbine, this stone foundation was once the summer cabin of an artist who toiled for the Museum of Natural History early in the last century. He reportedly abandoned the place when the power lines were installed. It is easy to understand the attraction of this setting, what with the vista to the east from atop the hill. On a clear day, you may not be able to see forever, but the Manhattan skyline is certainly a possibility.

Reverse course and scoot back down the cut, picking up the blue blazes as you cling to the exposed ground. There is yet another fine vantage point here, this time facing the hills to the west, beyond Pyramid Mountain. Immediately after that are the 100 Steps, a series of stones assembled like a staircase to simplify maintenance access to the utility lines. On different occasions, we've counted 138 and 147 steps—but never 39 (nor 100, for that matter). No matter what the tally, though, this is a surprisingly fun descent, in part because the path threads through a thick overgrowth of maple, chestnut oak, spicebush, cedar, and flowering azalea, effectively concealing the power lines overhead.

You trough at a boggy wetland, surrounded by moss, ferns, and a few white birch trees, and in five minutes recross Boonton Avenue. The Blue Trail proceeds ahead, but if you are ready to call it quits, grab the trace to the left, marked with white diamonds, which returns to the parking lot. Blue merges with another track by a bridge in about 550 feet, then plugs to the right, leaping over several wooden planks. Pivot left in 100 feet, where a yellow-blazed path lunges to the right. As the climb becomes steeper, keep right of the power-line stanchion, staying with the blue markings until the junction with the White Trail (WT, white blazes), which you follow to the left. A dip ensues, with two wooden spans over a seasonal stream; then it is steadily uphill along the break to another stanchion, at which point the WT veers right, into the cover of the forest. The stone foundation by the crook of the brook is all that remains of the Morgan farmstead, once used as a hideout by the Tar Rope Gang, a group notorious for "borrowing" merchandise from local stores.

Skip the red-blazed route that merges from the right in 100 feet by another disintegrating foundation, and in three minutes the path arrives at the humongous Bear Rock, so named, some say, because the Lenape Indians associated the etched lines on the rock with the claw marks of a bear. (Others insist that the 25-foot-high, 45-foot-long erratic earned its soubriquet from its resemblance, seen at certain angles, to a sleeping bear.) When you are finished admiring this impressive monolith, head right over the bridge and boardwalk, and then scamper left at the fork (where the yellow blazes angle to the right). That is Bear Swamp over your left shoulder, where the skunk cabbage is a backdrop to violets, yellow asters, gentians, and cardinal flowers. A steep ascent over a moraine field, requiring your best eggbeater gait, concludes in four minutes—and an elevation gain of 180 feet—at an oak- and laurel-covered ridge. Go left with the WT at the next fork, where the blue markings diverge in the opposite direction.

There are a number of glacial erratics along this knobby ridge, but nothing quite so unique as Tripod Rock, 400 feet from the last junction. Some believe that Paleolithic peoples used it in conjunction with neighboring rocks as a kind of cosmic sundial to predict the summer solstice and best harvest time. To judge by the impromptu fire rings in the vicinity, primitive rites are still being observed here. The WT continues north on this shelf, rubbing up against Big Cat Swamp, where bobcats reportedly roam, and arrives in eight minutes at your left onto the Red Trail (RT, red markings). Before you leave the ridge, though, we suggest you persist with the WT for another five minutes to its junction with the Orange Trail, where a granite-based vista point (800 feet elevation) overlooks the Taylortown Reservoir.

Back with the RT, the stretch moving toward a low rocky bluff known as Eagle Cliff is a colorful, visually appealing area of puddingstone and erratics, with many of the latter so oddly shaped they are easily assigned zoomorphic identities. After encountering an oversize elliptical erratic, known as Whale Head Rock, slip through a fissure in the bedrock and begin to descend. Slice to the left on the trace as you drop off that ledge—the wider track straight ahead peters out among blueberry bushes in a few strides. In three minutes of navigating through a slanted rubble field, you hit the bottom, then cross over two boggy streams via a couple of short spans and some rock-hopping. Swing left at the T, now with blue blazes, and in ten minutes you will be back at Bear Rock, facing its north side. Trot left there, once more crossing over the bridge and boardwalk. This time, though, keep to the right on the Yellow Trail and traipse on up the hill.

The jagged ledges flanking the rocky track are known collectively as Cat Rocks, for the bobcats that reputedly reside here. (The wild turkey tail feathers we once found on this spot may have been evidence of a feline feast.) Heave to the right at the top of the ridge, as blue blazes coalesce with the yellow, and take a right again in 150 feet, as the two colors diverge. With beech, oak, maple, and birch trees occupying much of the arable space, the autumn foliage season is a great time to do this stretch. A number of spurs to the left end at great viewpoints facing east to Turkey Mountain and the surrounding hills, with the blue-blazed path arriving at one momentarily. The peak of this plateau follows, though views in summer from its crown, at 934 feet, are limited by scrub oaks. And then it is down the side of the mountain over bedrock, loose rock, and dirt. The RT merges from the right in a couple of minutes, and the path swerves left at the power-line cut. Hang with this all the way back to the bridge, rolling right on the broad track, which returns you to the parking area.

## ▶ NEARBY ACTIVITIES

Tired of mountains, and craving a lake? The Split Rock Loop Trail will take you along its namesake reservoir and into the Farny Highlands, with some fine views and remnants of an iron mine. For more details, visit www.nynjtc.org.

# TURKEY SWAMP SAMPLER

## ▶ IN BRIEF

The flat ground of New Jersey's Coastal Plain contributes to the ease of walking through this compact county park, making it ideal for families with young hikers-in-training. Vibram veterans will find much to enjoy here, too, including a peaceful pocket of pitch pines, an array of oaks, wildflower-dappled bog land, and a lake where waterfowl frequently cavort.

## ▶ DESCRIPTION

Anyone looking to bag a gobbler by gun or camera at Turkey Swamp will come away with their tail feathers tucked between their legs. This Monmouth County park does not allow hunting, nor is it named for the ungainly bird so many of us like to feast on come late November. No, Turkey Swamp owes its soubriquet to the nearby town of Adelphia.

How is that again? It seems that Adelphia, New Jersey, was once known as Turkey, a name stuffed with many possible interpretations. Over time, the locals may have brooded about being called Turks, Turkians, Turkeyists, and just plain Turkeys. Reluctant to fly the coop, they hatched the idea of renaming their nest, and thus Adelphia was born.

All of which may have left Turkey Swamp high, but certainly not dry. With its water table just below the sandy soil, swampy conditions are a constant throughout much of the 1,180-acre

## ▶ DIRECTIONS

Follow I-95 across the George Washington Bridge into New Jersey, and proceed south on the New Jersey Turnpike (I-95), switching at Exit 11 to the Garden State Parkway south. Take Exit 98 and continue on I-195 west to Exit 28. Head north on US 9 for 1 mile, then turn west on West Farm Road. Continue for 3 miles (West Farm becomes Georgia Road) to the park entrance on the left.

## ⓘ KEY AT-A-GLANCE INFORMATION

**LENGTH:** 2.9 miles

**CONFIGURATION:** Loop

**DIFFICULTY:** Very easy

**SCENERY:** Mostly level terrain features pine barrens, mixed oak woodlands, and open fields surrounding partially secluded lake

**EXPOSURE:** Half protected, half open

**TRAFFIC:** Very lively on summer weekends

**TRAIL SURFACE:** Dirt, some patches of sand, a few rooty stretches

**HIKING TIME:** 1.5 hours

**SEASON:** Year-round, 8 a.m.–dusk

**ACCESS:** No fee, pets must be leashed

**MAPS:** At park office near shelter, www.monmouthcountyparks.com

**FACILITIES:** Rest rooms and water near trailhead; also public phone, vending machines, picnic area, campground and playground

**SPECIAL COMMENTS:** Look out for wet areas around swamps, and bring insect repellent from late spring through summer. In winter, there is ice-skating on the lake.

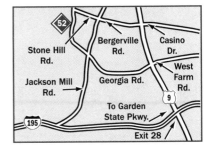

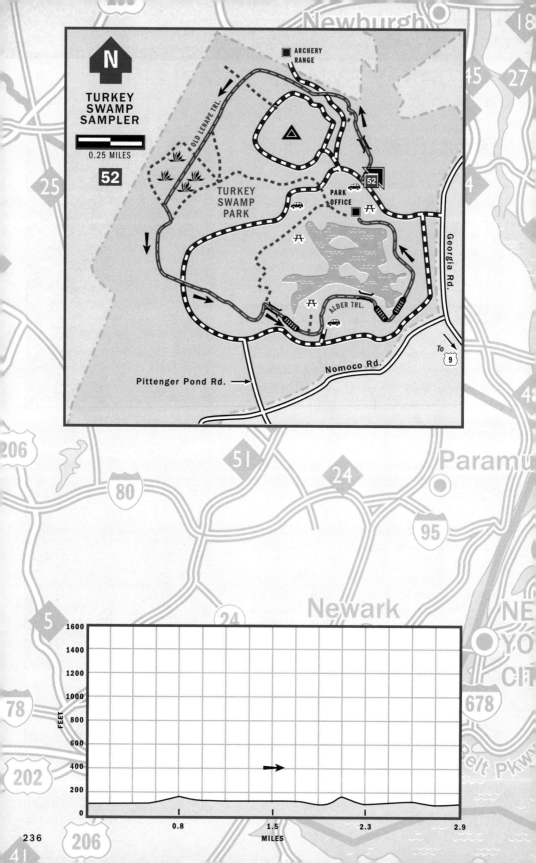

park. Not that hip waders are *de rigueur* for hiking here. Nope, a decent pair of boots or chukkas and a bottle of insect repellant should do the trick. And when you are through with this short hike through pitch pine and oak forests, you might drop a line in the 17-acre lake. Yes, it will take quite a few bass, bluegills and catfish to make a Thanksgiving meal, but the angling is legal, and it is easier on the ears than bagging a bird with a shotgun.

Turkey Swamp has recently redesigned its trails, conforming now to the countywide practice of putting colored blazes on taupe posts. The economical deployment of those posts often finds the hiker at trail junctions without a sure sense of where to go. As an alternative to winging it, we suggest the following route.

Standing in the parking area with your back to the office, walk to the exit of the lot, to the right. Just across the access road is the start of the Old Lenape Trail, marked by a post with a green circle at its top. From the outset, there is a pine barren aura to the path, as it passes among white pines, oaks, black birch trees, and cat briar. Veer left by the power lines, crossing a small footbridge shortly after that. Continue for another 500 yards, as the park road shadows your left side, treading to the right when you come to a fence. In a few steps, the track cuts left by another fence. Several minutes more brings you to a slanted T, where you march right (left returns to the road).

Remain with the trail as it crosses the dirt park road and abruptly launches off to the right. In just a minute or so, it runs into a wider track, joining it to the left. Now venturing into the thick of the preserve's pine barrens, where pitch pines proliferate, you should slow down your pace to enjoy the especially tranquil atmosphere. Once the path has executed a 90-degree bend, stroll straight through a four-way junction. Scoot right at the next intersection, in about ten minutes—longer if you accepted our advice and dallied among the evergreens. Notice how the surroundings have suddenly evolved to swampland habitat, with maples, sweet gum, sassafras, and birch vying for space amid the conifers?

Bypass the succeeding four-way junction, but jog left at the following intersection onto a packed-gravel path. In three minutes, it hits a road by an open meadow. Enter the field and stay along its thorny south side, where a few slender white-barked saplings are struggling to survive. At the end of this expanse, lope left on the Alder Trail, keeping to the east as it edges toward the lake. There, in the corner nearest the water, the route advances, slipping ever-so-slightly downhill and over a boardwalk bridge, meanwhile providing a great vantage point from which to survey the geese and ducks on the lake.

Inevitably the path begins to rise, with a left-hand turn to the picnic pavilion at its crest. An additional 75 yards delivers you to a dirt parking lot. The trail resumes to the left by the handicapped parking slips, where a paved walkway leads by newly refurbished latrines. Unless "nature" calls, persevere as the pavement gives way to earth, and the wide track loops closely around the contours of the lake. On crossing a bridge and then a boardwalk, head left at the T, where another boardwalk awaits. Look for frogs and turtles in this scenically swampy stretch before you shift back toward pines. Didn't see any amphibians? No matter, you'll get another shot, as the left fork at the Y junction hops back to the lake. Keep your eyes on the tiny islands, too, where waterfowl often take refuge.

A patina of ice on the lake at Turkey
Swamp Park marks the advent of winter.

Walk dead ahead when you emerge by the open field, with the lake to the left, opposite the picnic area, and the Visitor Center just beyond the sandy beach. Turkey Swamp, incidentally, operates a family campground, which is open from March 15 through Thanksgiving weekend.

## ▶ NEARBY ACTIVITIES

Give your legs a rest after the hike and rent a canoe (summer only) to paddle to the peaceful center of the lake. Drop a line and you may even hook your dinner. Or practice another way of putting food on the table at the public archery range adjacent to the park. Call (732) 462-7286 for details, or visit www.monmouthcountyparks.com.

# UPLANDS FARM LOOP

From the heart of an old dairy farm, complete with a silo, this double-loop meanders from bird and butterfly meadows through a successional forest, deep into a laurel- and pine-shaded ravine, and back again. An abundance of rabbits along the easy, mostly level trail contributes to a fun, family-friendly hike.

▶ **DESCRIPTION**

True to its name, Uplands Farm Sanctuary retains very much the appearance of a still-functioning dairy farm, with wide-open meadows and a large silo just off the trailhead parking lot. Which is not to imply that you will have to hopscotch over cow pies and similar sorts of organic landmines that are the hallmarks of rustic living. No, stones are the worst obstacles you are apt to encounter in this 97-acre preserve, given that the Nature Conservancy, which manages it, does not permit horses—let alone cattle—on the trails.

According to park literature, the soil here is so gravel-filled and acidic that the cultivation of

▶ **DIRECTIONS**

*By car:* Follow the Long Island Expressway (I-495) east and take Exit 45. At the end of the exit ramp, bear right on Manetto Hill Road. After 0.2 miles, turn right onto Woodbury Road. Continue for 3.4 miles and make a left onto Harbor Road (SR 108). Proceed 1.6 miles and go right on Lawrence Hill Road. Uplands Farm is less than 0.5 miles ahead on the right. Follow the access road and veer left of the farm complex to the parking area.

*By public transportation:* Take the Long Island Railroad (Port Jefferson Branch) to Huntington. From there hop in a cab to the sanctuary, about 4 miles away.

**KEY AT-A-GLANCE INFORMATION**

**LENGTH:** 2.5 miles

**CONFIGURATION:** Figure eight

**DIFFICULTY:** Very easy

**SCENERY:** Former dairy farm surrounded by old grassy fields, hilly deciduous woods, laurel thickets, and a stand of white pine

**EXPOSURE:** Fairly open, with a few secluded woodland sections

**TRAFFIC:** On the light side

**TRAIL SURFACE:** Grass, root-woven dirt, pebbles

**HIKING TIME:** 1.5 hours

**SEASON:** Year-round, sunrise–sunset

**ACCESS:** No fee, foot traffic only, no pets

**MAPS:** At trailhead kiosk

**FACILITIES:** None

**SPECIAL COMMENTS:** The open space and habitat diversity of the sanctuary's 97 acres provide excellent educational opportunities. If you'd like to participate in a nature walk or educational program, call (631) 367-3225.

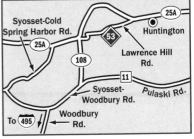

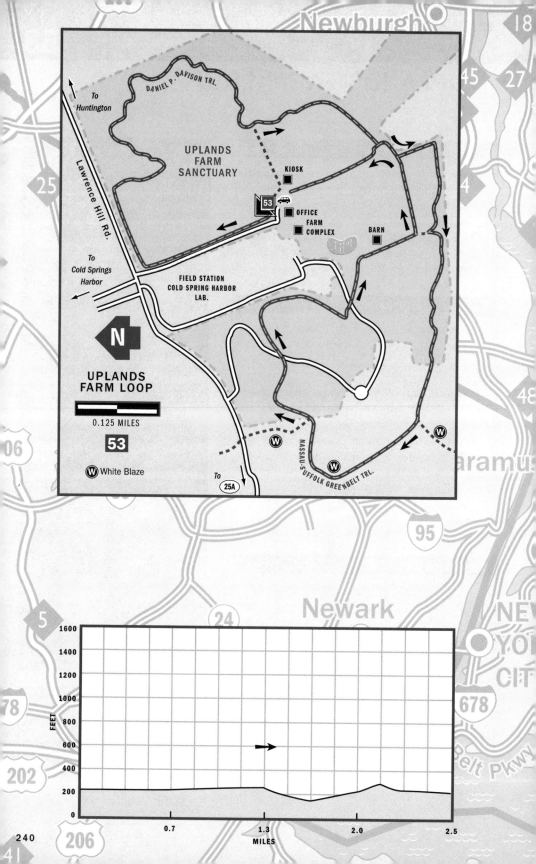

UPLANDS
FARM
SANCTUARY

DANIEL P. DAVISON TRL.

To
Huntington

Lawrence Hill Rd.

To
Cold Springs
Harbor

KIOSK

53

OFFICE
FARM
COMPLEX

BARN

FIELD STATION
COLD SPRING HARBOR
LAB.

**N**

**UPLANDS
FARM LOOP**

0.125 MILES

53

Ⓦ White Blaze

Ⓦ

NASSAU-SUFFOLK GREENBELT TRL.

Ⓦ

Ⓦ

To
25A

FEET

1600

1400

1200

1000

800

600

400

200

0

0.7

1.3

2.0

2.5

MILES

crops was an extremely onerous and unproductive activity. As early as the Colonial era, the grounds were devoted to sheep ranching; for the first half of the twentieth century, the Nichols family bred cattle here while operating a dairy. That activity ceased in 1962, and within 20 years, Jane Nichols, matriarch of the brood, had passed the property on to the Nature Conservancy. Roughly half of this double-loop hike wends through grassy fields, where you are likely to see red-winged blackbirds, bluebirds, Baltimore orioles, and a bevy of butterflies (including tiger and spicebush swallowtails) flutter and frolic. If you are visiting from early spring through midsummer, you may also brush up against ticks, so take the precaution of rolling your slacks into your socks and lathering the latter with insect repellant. Be aware, too, that sun exposure can be intense, particularly in summer.

Pick up a trail map at the Daniel P. Davison Trail kiosk, a few feet from the parking area, then return to the lot and head toward the entrance drive; the hike begins on the field side of the rail fence that parallels that lane. Follow this level, mowed-grass path all the way to where it bends sharply right, back by Lawrence Hill Road. In about 500 feet, the track bolts right again, pulling now in a southern direction. The fields you are ambling around, with oaks and flowering dogwoods growing at their periphery, are cut annually by the Nature Conservancy to preserve both open space and habitat diversity. If untouched, the land would very soon be covered with the sort of successional scrub that the trail guides you to next, as it veers left under a large gnarly tree, into a shady bower of black birch, oak, cedar, and maple, with false lilies and garlic mustard (very flavorful and nutritious as a salad green) part of the undergrowth. In gaining negligible elevation, the path snakes by an occasional holly tree and a large patch of fragrant lilies of the valley before corkscrewing downward by a wild pear tree. Hang a left on emerging from this hollow, back on the border of an open meadow. Stick with the mowed path, while ignoring the spur to the left that feeds into an elongated field, and swing to the right in 500 feet. Go left at the ensuing T, and in ten steps take a second left, strolling now along the side of a narrow, rectangular field, a favorite haunt of cottontail rabbits.

Just as it seems the West Loop is luring you to the front door of an oversize McMansion imperfectly screened from the preserve by maple saplings, it hooks to the right, by an ivy-draped, decaying wooden fence. Having left this field for the next, stride to the left up the rising hill. This, too, is an active rabbit habitat, with so many sets of long ears in evidence on our last visit it looked like a *Watership Down* reunion. In a moment, the track slips by a couple of birches into a forest and starts to descend, first by a few yew trees, then an odd mound of stones. As you approach a wooden platform, the path jogs right, maintaining its downward trend. In a delightful contrast to the meadows you were just plodding through, this ravine offers not only blessed shade, but also a raw, untamed appearance, with a handful of glacial erratics tossed in among an increasing presence of pines.

The spur to the left that drops lower over a set of retaining steps is a southbound stretch of the Nassau-Suffolk Greenbelt Trail (NSG), connecting to Stillwell Woods County Preserve and—ultimately—Massapequa, 21 miles away. Unless you are bounding with energy, bear right, as the West Loop and the northward NSG overlap through a thick cluster of mountain laurels, with an impressive stand of white pines looming uphill. In about 0.5 miles, the NSG diverges to the left, reaching Cold Spring Harbor, down the steep slope, in 1 mile. From here, the main route gradually ascends, popping out from the laurel jungle by a paved driveway.

Directly across the macadam is a blaze at the foot of a snag, with the West Loop edging to the left, back into grassland. Shift to the right of the split-rail fence and shadow it to the far side of the field, where the loop breaks hard to the right, still with the rails. Lunge left at the end of the fence, by a large white pine, and cross the driveway. Stay with the blazes, marching on the mowed-grass path in an east direction. In a couple of minutes, a pond will come into view; roll right on the driveway just after that. Strut past the white barn, the aged oak, and apple trees, turning left by the flowering dogwood, where the pavement ends. In a matter of moments the path is engulfed, shadily flanked by maples, weeds, withered cedars, and vines. Continue straight at the end of that botanical tunnel, scooting left when the trail forks by the entrance to a field you entered earlier, and go left again at the next bifurcation. Now steaming northward under the open sky, the Daniel P. Davison kiosk is dead ahead in about 600 feet.

If you have an extra minute or two after finishing this short trek, take a breather in the diminutive garden by the grain silo. Some of the labeled plants will help put names to the vegetation you may have encountered on the trail, including juneberry, silky dogwood, black chokeberry, and *Pyrrhus arbutifolia* in the rose family.

## ▶ NEARBY ACTIVITIES

You cannot visit the Uplands Farmhouse, but the Huntington Historical Society has two house museums open to the public. The David Conklin Farm House, circa 1750, and the Dr. Daniel W. Kissam House, circa 1795, both contain period furnishings that reflect very different lifestyles. For more details, call (631) 427-7045.

# WALT WHITMAN REVISITED

## ▶ IN BRIEF

The seaside vistas are overgrown from when Walt Whitman roamed this historic woodland, but the densely forested hills still provide a poetic setting for a short hike. A labyrinth of trails snakes by a picturesque pond amid laurels, white pines, and rhododendrons—as well as a full complement of hardwoods—on the way to Jayne's Hill, the highest point on Long Island.

## ▶ DESCRIPTION

"West Hills is a romantic and beautiful spot. It is the most hilly and elevated part of Long Island . . . afford[ing] an extensive and pleasant view," Walt Whitman wrote in 1850 of the hills that rise above his boyhood home. In Whitman's day it was possible to view the Connecticut shore from atop the highest peak, Jayne's Hill, and watch schooners sailing by Fire Island to the south. Those vistas are gone now—overgrown by mountain laurel, beech, and birch trees—but this remains a delightful place, no

## ▶ DIRECTIONS

*By car:* Follow the Long Island Expressway (I-495) east and take Exit 42 to merge onto the Northern State Parkway east. Leave the Parkway at Exit 40S and drive 0.25 miles south on Walt Whitman Road (SR 110). Turn right on Old Country Road and continue 0.3 miles, then go right again on Sweet Hollow Road. Proceed 0.5 miles to the parking lot and picnic area on the right.

*By public transportation:* Take the Long Island Railroad (Port Jefferson Branch) to Hicksville. From there, hop on the Long Island N79 bus to the Walt Whitman Mall and descend at Sweet Hollow Road. Walk about 1.5 miles south on Sweet Hollow to the trailhead at the picnic area on the right.

## ⓘ KEY AT-A-GLANCE INFORMATION

**LENGTH:** 3.8 miles

**CONFIGURATION:** Loop

**DIFFICULTY:** Easy

**SCENERY:** Rolling, mixed deciduous forest hiding a quiet pond, gnarly laurel thickets, and Long Island's highest point

**EXPOSURE:** Lush canopy protection

**TRAFFIC:** Light on weekdays, can get really busy on weekends

**TRAIL SURFACE:** Dirt, roots, and pebbles

**HIKING TIME:** 2 hours

**SEASON:** Year-round, sunrise-sunset

**ACCESS:** $2 for Suffolk County residents, $5 for tourists Memorial Day–Labor Day, free rest of year; no bicycles, pets must be leashed

**MAPS:** At picnic area entrance booth, Long Island Greenbelt Trail Conference

**FACILITIES:** Rest rooms, water, public phone, and playground at picnic area

**SPECIAL COMMENTS:** Riding stables are right behind the picnic area. For information, call (631) 351-9168.

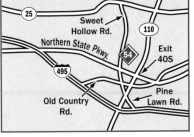

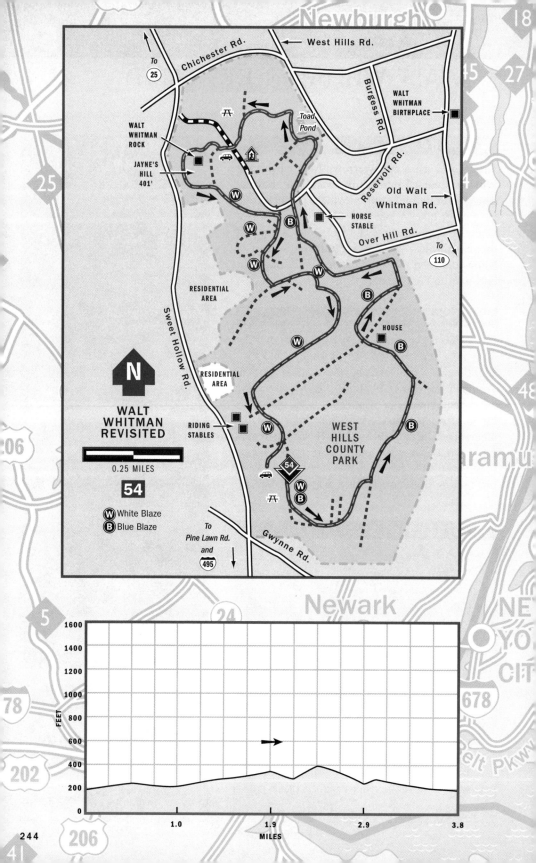

Newburgh

West Hills Rd.

Chichester Rd.

To
25

Burgess Rd.

WALT
WHITMAN
BIRTHPLACE

Toad
Pond

WALT
WHITMAN
ROCK

Reservoir Rd.

JAYNE'S
HILL
401'

Old Walt
Whitman Rd.

W

Over Hill Rd.

W

B

HORSE
STABLE

W

To
110

W

RESIDENTIAL
AREA

W

B

HOUSE

B

N

RESIDENTIAL
AREA

WALT
WHITMAN
REVISITED

0.25 MILES

W

B

54

Sweet Hollow Rd.

RIDING
STABLES

WEST
HILLS
COUNTY
PARK

B

54

W
B

W White Blaze
B Blue Blaze

To
Pine Lawn Rd.
and
495

Gwynne Rd.

Newark

244

1600
1400
1200
1000
800
600
400
200
0

FEET

1.0        1.9        2.9        3.8
MILES

206

less hilly and inspiring today than it once was to one of our country's great poets.

In 1825, when Silas Wood, an early historian of Long Island, had "High Hill" surveyed, its top crested at 354 feet of elevation. While paltry by western standards, that was enough to rank this mount as highest on the island. Its name was later changed to Jayne's Hill, after the family that lived here, and having been resurveyed a number of times since, it now officially tops out at 400.9 feet above sea level. This meandering hike circles through the colorful forests of the West Hills, crossing the top of Jayne's Hill about halfway out. There are many maverick bike and bridle trails intersecting your route, but the main path is well blazed and fairly easy to follow.

The trail begins at the far side of the picnic grounds by the edge of the woods. Keep to the right, walking toward the fenced field, looking for white blazes on a few of the oak trees. Stay with those as the markings glide to the left (or wooded) side of the corral. Once past the corner of the fence, there is a path to the left blazed with blue paint.

These words by Walt Whitman, who was born nearby, mark Long Island's highest point, Jayne's Hill.

Turn there and then left again on the sandy bridle path. Stick with the blue blazes as they veer right at the Y, and right another time in an additional ten steps. Now drifting among birches, oaks, and an occasional dogwood—to say nothing of scads of mountain laurel—the well-indicated, pebbly track shifts left at a T. It then passes a number of spurs as it ascends steadily to higher ground, swinging left in five minutes at the T junction with a bridle trail. For hikers with a good sense of orientation, the many side trails in this forest offer great bushwhacking possibilities.

In due time, the well-blazed trail loops to the left of a gray house. About a minute later, it meets a wide crossing with a bridle path, where it continues straight ahead, Indian file, until it merges with another horse track, where you pivot left. Bear left once more at the next broad fork, steering away from the private dwellings. With laurels now the dominant plant, the blue blazes swerve sharply right off the main route in 150 feet, adhering closely to the line of a ridge. Vault to the right when you hit the slanted T with a bridle path, and a couple of minutes after passing a horse stable to the right just beyond the park boundary, you will come to a set of erosion-control piling steps.

The access lane to Jayne's Hill is at the top of that staircase. Instead of following the road, though, stroll across the pavement, picking up the white blazes on its opposite side near a chain-link fence. With that barrier to the right and white pines towering overhead, you have now started the more enjoyable half of the hike. On reaching a small rise, the path descends sharply away from the majestic conifers, moving swiftly into a beech- and birch-shaded gully. The trail levels off briefly, trots right at a Y, goes straight through an unblazed crossing, then dives downhill again among a green carpet of false lilies of the valley. The white blazes hop left at the succeeding fork, and in a few paces guide you to Toad Pond. Though marred by a metal fence stretched over its right end, this is an attractive (albeit small) body of water, shaped like a crooked, elongated smile.

Ignore the steps that lead away from the pond and proceed along its boggy bank. A few strides later, the white blazes branch to the left, with the path fording a small stream via a log corduroy in another moment or two. With the track running beside a bog, the next several yards can be quite wet in spring, but soon enough the ground grows steadily steeper, plugging upward toward Jayne's Hill. It only takes a minute to get by the most precipitous part of that climb, one breathtaking, heart-pounding minute. From there, the elevation gain is more gradual, almost impercepti-ble. Heave to the left on the bridle path, and in a few dozen strides the trail spits you out at the Jayne's Hill parking lot.

Hug the right side of the lot, circling around a pine tree and hewing hard to the right when a swing set and dilapidated latrine come into view. Stick with this wide, white-blazed track, which is lined with lavender-flowering vinka, dogwoods, and oaks, as it cruises to the right at the subsequent fork and left at the fork after that. The terrain grows more lush with every step you take, as mountain laurels, white pines, and black birches creep back into the forested mix. The top of Jayne's Hill lies just ahead, a site marked by a bench, a rock with a plaque on it, and a pale blue water tower. Second-growth trees now block out the view that Whitman enjoyed from this, the highest ground on Long Island, but you may still derive pleasure from the tran-quility of the spot, as well as the Whitman quote that adorns the plaque.

The trail continues to the right of the rock, down several steps through an over-grown tangle of briar, chokeberry, and poison ivy. It levels off in a minute among ferns and oaks, then rolls with the undulating texture of the hillside. This pleasantly secluded, moss-sided track ends at a split-rail fence, where you scoot right onto a bri-dle path. In 30 yards, the white-blazed foot trail scuttles to the left at a four-way cross-ing, descends through briar, maples, birches, and cedars, and then crosses another four-way intersection. From a leveling off, the path rises negligibly, culminating in a left turn at a T. Pull to the left at the ensuing fork, and with the white blazes clearly visi-ble, hang a right at the next major turn. Fifty feet later, the track diverges to the left and, having descended briefly, darts through a narrow livestock barrier.

You remain on this ridge for awhile, slightly above the trees of the surrounding hills, as rhododendrons make a surprise appearance, blanketing the sides of the slope. A further descent over log steps leads to a second livestock barrier. Once through that, the white blazes shift to the left, crossing the bridle path and slipping through a rail fence. In a few minutes of walking, you should see the roof of the riding stables to the right. A short descent follows, delivering you to yet another set of rails. The horse trails here trot left, right, and straight ahead, with your route running between the right and straight options. A few furlongs more and the path ends, dropping you off by the jun-gle gym, at the far side of the picnic grounds with the parking lot directly beyond.

## ▶ NEARBY ACTIVITIES

What better place to start (or unwind from) this hike than the Walt Whitman Birth-place State Historic Site? Displays in this early nineteenth-century farmhouse include portraits of Whitman, his poetry, letters, a tape recording of his voice, and more. Call (631) 427-5240 for details.

# WARD POUND RIDGE MAIN LOOP

## ▶ IN BRIEF

You could easily while away a couple of days on the trails here and still not see the entire park. Its sublime scenery is a marvelous medley of hardwood forests, glacial ridges, lowland bogs, granite outcroppings and high-rising bluffs, with a couple of ravines, a river, and a far-reaching viewpoint as added attractions. The main trails are wide and very popular with family groups, while many narrower routes provide a more rugged experience.

## ▶ DESCRIPTION

Ward Pound Ridge Reservation—or, simply Pound Ridge—is the largest preserve in the Westchester County Parks system, with 35 miles of trails slicing seamlessly, almost artistically, through its 4,700 acres. It is also the most beautiful of the county's parks, where litter on the ground is as rare as candy in a dentist's office, and the camping shelters (stone lean-tos constructed by the CCC more than 60 years ago) are raked clean by park personnel.

A nucleus of 32 abutting farms was purchased back in 1924 to create the reservation. Extensive tracts have since been added, and with almost every step you take, Pound Ridge's agricultural antecedents are evident in the form of the

## ▶ DIRECTIONS

*By car:* Take the Hutchinson River Parkway north to White Plains, transferring to I-684 north to Katonah. Exit onto SR 35 East and drive 4 miles to Cross River. Turn right (south) at the junction with SR 121. The reservation entrance is immediately to the left. Continue straight for 0.5 miles to the entrance booth. About 0.2 miles beyond, steer right onto Michigan Road and proceed for 0.75 miles to the parking lot.

*By public transportation:* The Metro North railroad stops in Katonah via its Harlem Line. The reservation is less than 5 miles by taxi to the east.

## ⓘ KEY AT-A-GLANCE INFORMATION

**LENGTH:** 5 miles, 5.6 miles with Leatherman's Cave side trip

**CONFIGURATION:** Loop

**DIFFICULTY:** Easy/moderate

**SCENERY:** Swamps, hemlock, laurel, and hardwood forests, impressive rock outcroppings, scenic overlook of Cross River Reservoir, and historic cave

**EXPOSURE:** Shady canopy cover in summer, more open in winter

**TRAFFIC:** Heavy in summer and autumn weekends, but seldom crowded

**TRAIL SURFACE:** Packed dirt, rocks, roots

**HIKING TIME:** 2.75 hours

**SEASON:** Year-round, dawn–dusk

**ACCESS:** $4 with Westchester County Parks Pass, $8 without pass; pets must be leashed, no bicycles

**MAPS:** At entrance booth; posted at trailhead; USGS Peach Lake; www.westchestergov.com

**FACILITIES:** Rest rooms and water at park office and some picnic areas, telephone at park office

**SPECIAL COMMENTS:** Mountain laurel blooms in early June; in autumn this is a lovely place for leaf-peeping; and in winter, sledding and skiing are prime activities.

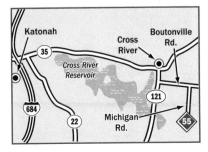

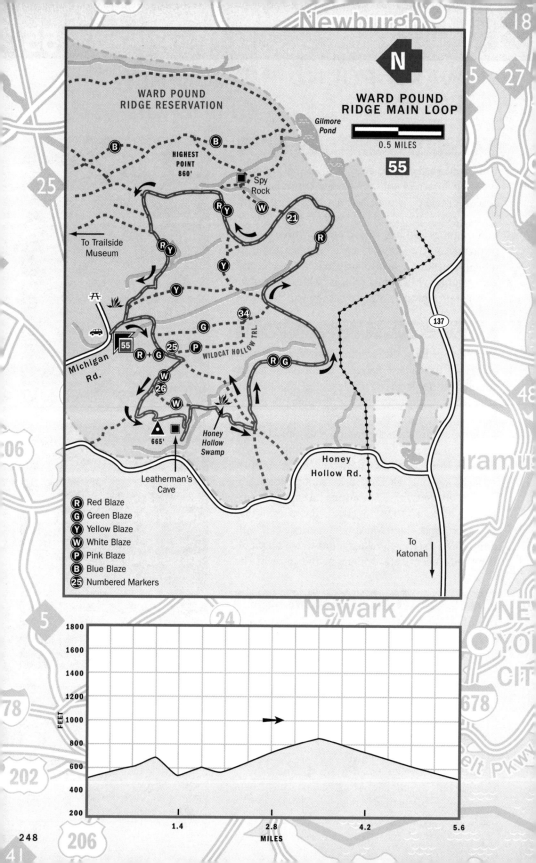

WARD POUND
RIDGE RESERVATION

**N**

WARD POUND
RIDGE MAIN LOOP

0.5 MILES

55

HIGHEST
POINT
860'

Gilmore
Pond

Spy
Rock

To Trailside
Museum

137

Michigan
Rd.

WILDCAT HOLLOW TRL.

Honey
Hollow
Swamp

665'

Leatherman's
Cave

Honey
Hollow Rd.

To
Katonah

R  Red Blaze
G  Green Blaze
Y  Yellow Blaze
W  White Blaze
P  Pink Blaze
B  Blue Blaze
25 Numbered Markers

rock walls running from the upland forests through the lowland swamps. A Trailside Nature Museum recounts some of this history, as well as that of the Indians who earlier occupied the land, and it also has exhibits on indigenous wildlife.

At times white-tailed deer seem the most commonplace, yet it remains a thrill to see them dart through the hemlock and beech groves, bound over granite ridges, or spring past the park's rippling streams. And if the most one can boast of is having witnessed a turkey vulture fly overhead, or heard a chipmunk yelping its squeaky alarm from within the chinks of an ancient wall—well, spending a few hours in such a wild, uncorrupted setting, without a house in view or car horn audible, is reward enough.

It is hard to go wrong with any of Pound Ridge's trails, but for a good overview of the park, we suggest the red-blazed 5-mile circuit. It is a wide, lilting loop, clearly marked and easy to follow, crossed by many other paths that can be used to create a longer or shorter hike. Begin at the Michigan Road trailhead, to the right of the picnic area. Almost immediately, there is a fork in the trail, near a couple of cedar trees; keep to the right. The red-blazed route (RT) runs first through a low swamp, highlighted by stands of hickory and black birch; then, after 0.25 miles, it starts edging up a pebbly slope. Bear left at the next intersection, as the upward slant gives way to a more rolling terrain, with dark boulders scattered through the surrounding woods.

During one of the level stretches that ensue, look for a slight trace branching off to the left, indicated by the number "25" mounted on a tree. That leads through Wildcat Hollow, a more challenging, highly appealing ravine trek of 0.8 miles. This secluded detour is marked with pink blazes, which zigzag from side to side of the creek, exiting the ravine at its southeast end. This pink spur emerges on the Green Trail (GT), a main conduit, and you can return to the parking lot by taking it to the left or resume the longer loop by going right, and then, in five minutes, veering left back onto the RT.

If, on the other hand, you forego the Wildcat Hollow side trip, the well-marked trail to the Leatherman's Cave lies just ahead. This, too, is a wonderful patch of the preserve, not so much for its namesake cave (which is really more of an indentation at the base of a rocky bluff), but for the splendid views from atop that bluff, and the varied topography you pass along the way. Try to adhere to the spur's white blazes, which have been haphazardly applied to trees. The forest (initially dominated by silvery-barked beech, later giving way to maples and oaks) is fairly open as the grass-lined track moseys uphill away from the bog and passes in about six minutes a turnoff to the left by a tree tagged with a "26," before hitting a T at the base of a lichen-spotted granite rise. Steer left (the other way exits the park), and slog on to the top of the next rise. There are many traces worn into the mossy ground here, but you should see, straight ahead beyond a few fallen limbs and rotting logs, a bench that crowns an open viewpoint. This summit, at 665 feet, is nearly 200 feet lower than Pound Ridge's highest point, where a fire tower once stood. Nonetheless, the isolated aerie offers far and away the finest, most far-reaching vista in the park, with the Cross River Reservoir to the west ssuming center stage.

The most direct way to get to the Leatherman's Cave is to shoot south from the bench along the blazed trail, over a slick of bedrock, by the mound of granite to the left. The path then snakes to the right past the rocky uplift and swings back to the left, or south, along an extension of the ridge. Keep to the right on the white-blazed route as it descends from the bluff, passing by and under an angular overhang as it nears the bottom and approaches a stone wall. Just before you reach the kiosk by that wall turn right and march up the deeply eroded rut, the rubble of the bluff now to your right. In about a minute you'll find the recess where the "leatherman," Jules Bourglay, periodically sought shelter. Seen by some to be a tramp, Bourglay was the ur-hiker, reportedly covering 365 miles in 30 days, a cycle he maintained for 30 years in peregrinations throughout western Connecticut and the Hudson Valley. To resume the White Trail, backtrack to the stone wall and jog left onto the wide track.

Skip the red-over-white blazed turnoff to the left that appears in roughly two minutes, remaining instead on the broad path as it bends to the south. For a few hundred yards you'll be treading through swamp country, this particular area going by the handle of Honey Hollow. The next intersection is a critical and rather convoluted junction, a kind of triangle in which the straight option exits the preserve. Head to the left and in 15 strides, when you arrive at a 4-way junction, continue directly ahead, in a resumption of the RT.

In approximately 20 minutes, the GT, which has run concurrently with the RT thus far, diverges to the left. (You may pick up the far end of the previously described Wildcat Hollow Trail by walking five minutes down the GT and turning left on the vague trace by a tree with the number "34" on it.) The RT, meanwhile, forges onward, branching right at a Y in another five minutes.

The hard-packed track alternately gains and loses ground after that turn, while heading first toward the southeast, before swooping around toward the north. Once it begins to tack to the left, now in a northwest direction, you will come to a "21," which marks a descending path to Spy Rock, a picturesque jumble of grass-topped boulders set among an overgrown, laurel-filled wetland. (A continuation of the spur, blazed white, leads to Pound Ridge's highest point.) In another ten minutes, the RT hits a T, where it is joined by a yellow-blazed route, and shifts to the right. The return leg from Spy Rocks appears on the right at the following major fork, while the red and yellow blazes swerve to the left.

Now heading north, 15 minutes of brisk walking brings you to a further series of turns, with the first and third rights leading to the Pell Hill picnic area and the Trailside Nature Museum (1 mile away), respectively. Keep with the clearly marked blazes as they head west, with the RT finally branching off to the right away from the Yellow through an open parcel of grassland. They merge once more in nearly a thousand feet, just before the trailhead. As you amble by the kiosk with the marsh nearby, you may catch sight of the glistening black domes of turtles among the tufts of grass, while being serenaded by peepers and bullfrogs.

## ▶ NEARBY ACTIVITIES

Bring your observations and questions to the naturalists on duty at the quaint Trailside Nature Museum, and take a moment to check out its animal and American Indian exhibits. Or if you care to test your angling acumen, try fishing in the Cross River; parking is available in a small lot to the left of the park entrance. Call the park office for details at (914) 864-7317.

If you didn't spot a single specimen of wildlife, perhaps a visit to the Wolf Conservation Center in South Salem is in order. Visit www.nywolf.org or call (914) 763-2373 for information.

# WATCHUNG SIERRA SAMPLER

## ▶ IN BRIEF

Don't be put off by the overdeveloped nature of this county park. With several miles of trails, there are plenty of opportunities to lose yourself among the hardwoods and conifers that flavor so much of the domain. A couple of ponds, a long narrow lake (where oddly-shaped erratics decorate its shoreline), and the well-preserved remnants of a mill town-cum-resort community contribute to the delights of the hike. Other highlights include the diverse bird populations that thrive around water holes, and herds of deer that chomp through the woods.

## ▶ DIRECTIONS

*By car:* Access I-78 west via the Holland Tunnel. Take Exit 43, and at the traffic light, go right onto McMane Avenue. At the next traffic light, turn left onto Glenside Avenue, and in 1.3 miles hang a right into the reservation, then proceed past Lake Surprise to the traffic circle. The first right, Summit Lane (which becomes New Providence Road), leads to the trailhead on the left, across from the Trailside Nature & Science Center parking lot and the nearby Visitor Center.

*By public transportation:* From the New York Port Authority Terminal, take New Jersey Transit bus 114. Get off in Mountainside at the intersection of New Providence Road and US 22. Cross the pedestrian overpass and walk along New Providence Road until it swings sharply to the right, at which point you should follow the left fork, Deer Path, and march past Tracy Drive to Ackerman Avenue. Veer right there and follow Ackerman to Coles Avenue, making another right onto Coles. Walk to the end of Coles Avenue, to the reappearance of New Providence Road. The trailhead is located along New Providence to the left, with the Trailside Nature & Science Center straight ahead.

## ℹ KEY AT-A-GLANCE INFORMATION

**LENGTH:** 6.5 miles

**CONFIGURATION:** Loop

**DIFFICULTY:** Easy/moderate

**SCENERY:** Gently rolling terrain boasts mixed forests, placid lake, several bogs, abandoned village, and some exceptionally tall tulip trees

**EXPOSURE:** Semi-shady

**TRAFFIC:** Can get really heavy on summer weekends

**TRAIL SURFACE:** Mix of dirt, roots, rocks and grass

**HIKING TIME:** 3 hours

**SEASON:** Year-round, dawn–dusk

**ACCESS:** No fee, pets must be leashed

**MAPS:** At Visitor Center

**FACILITIES:** None along trail, but Visitor Center has rest rooms, water, and public phone; park offers picnic areas, playground, and campground

**SPECIAL COMMENTS:** In springtime, the dogwoods and rhododendrons flower abundantly.

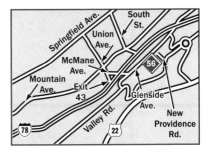

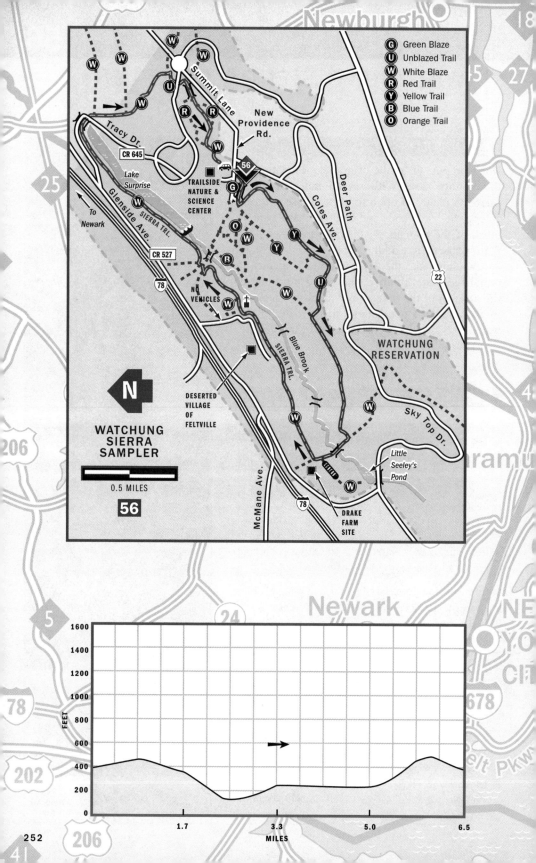

**Green Blaze**
**Unblazed Trail**
**White Blaze**
**Red Trail**
**Yellow Trail**
**Blue Trail**
**Orange Trail**

New Providence Rd.

Summit Lane

Tracy Dr.

CR 645

Lake Surprise

SIERRA TRL.

Glenside Ave.

CR 527

78

To Newark

TRAILSIDE NATURE & SCIENCE CENTER

56

Coles Ave.

Deer Path

22

NO VEHICLES

Blue Brook

SIERRA TRL.

WATCHUNG RESERVATION

Sky Top Dr.

N

WATCHUNG SIERRA SAMPLER

0.5 MILES

56

DESERTED VILLAGE OF FELTVILLE

McMane Ave.

Little Seeley's Pond

DRAKE FARM SITE

78

*Gesundheit!* That, in a word, is the response we hear most often on bringing Watchung into a conversation (it's actually a corruption of "wachunk," a Lenape Indian word for "high hills"). Two soaring ridges of the Watchung Mountains run the length of the park, with a bubbling brook and Lake Surprise nestled in between. Even so, hoofing it through Watchung is hardly a rugged wilderness experience. On the contrary, this is a highly developed park that features a playground, greenhouse, various gardens, a riding stable, ball fields, scout camp, picnic area, trailside museum—even a planetarium. There are also several well-preserved buildings from a nineteenth-century company town and the ruins of its mill.

Considering all that, the hiking in Watchung is pretty darn good. An intricate network of trails covers almost every inch of the reservation's 2,000 acres, with the Sierra Trail (ST, white blazes) circling the perimeter for a total of 10 miles. The following trek overlaps a large segment of the ST and provides a fine introduction to the varied topography of the largest preserve in Union County's park system. Note that not all trails are blazed, and distances on the park map vary in scale.

Start at the southwest corner of the parking lot and stride west over the paved road to the archway entrance of the Nature Trail. The path descends swiftly, passing via a bridge over a rocky arroyo, then cuts upward through a pleasant knoll festooned with benches and birdhouses. Two more seasonal streams follow, as well as some ups and downs. Just as you begin to wend to the right, a yellow-blazed spur appears to the left; take it. Stay left again as yellow gains ground and meanders into an overgrown forest of maples, oaks, and tulip trees, with sassafras sprinkled throughout.

Leave yellow in five minutes, for the unblazed stem to the left. Ignore all the side traces and increase your pace, as this route brushes against a residential neighborhood, picking up such native noises as barking dogs and lawn mowers. Hang a left at the T onto the ST, then slide through the succeeding junction. A series of enjoyable undulations ensues as Sierra descends slightly, snakes upward past beech trees, then drops once more through a couple of gentle switchbacks before yielding to another gradual climb. The grass-sided track finally arches downhill, colliding with a bridle path, where you swerve left.

In less than two minutes, the level, gravel-strewn trail moves to the right, toward Blue Brook. Hop over the bridge and press onward, bypassing the left toward a boardwalk and Little Seeley's Pond. The next right is yours, but before turning on it, stroll a few more steps up-trail to the ruins of the Drake Farm Site, where a large pine now hangs over the stone and concrete foundations. If you enter the ruin in warm weather, remember that rattlesnakes occasionally doze unseen by the feet of such walls.

The ST now travels in an eastward direction, evolving meanwhile into a somewhat wilder stretch of trail. The ground slants steeply to the right and a couple of streams sluice through the path as the surrounding forest, highlighted by white pines, cedars, and locust trees, is slowly swallowed by vines; you may have to scramble over several fallen trees here. Don't be drawn off the ST by the miscellaneous side trails; the Deserted Village of Feltville lies directly ahead.

No, that's not the title of a new Stephen King horror flick. Feltville originated as a company mill town in 1845, though the remaining buildings were modified when the property was later converted to a resort community. Though the resort was eventually abandoned, the site was placed on the National Register of Historic Places in 1980. Off-white with green trim, the houses look invitingly intact and well maintained. Look more closely, though, and aside from three that are still inhabited, most are in various stages of decay and may be dangerous to approach. White-tailed deer like to graze in this area.

Stick with the paved road as it leads from Masker's Barn past three houses and a trail to the right that cuts by the old mill site. Another pair of houses (with a second duo down below them) follows, and then the road starts to bend to the left. There is a turnoff to the right for the cemetery just as the pavement reaches the old church and store, a massive salmon-colored structure trimmed in red. Go with that spur to the pocket graveyard. Contrary to what the five headstones suggest, the small fenced plot is believed to hold something like two dozen bodies. The only original stone is on the far right, and supposedly none of them marks the correct grave. Maybe there's a Stephen King angle to this place after all.

Pick up the white blazes of the ST by the front side of the cemetery as it nudges northeast back into the forest. Go right at the T, joining a wide bridle path; when the trail arcs downhill, lurch left at the second option, about 30 feet beyond the first. In another eight steps, scuttle right onto the narrow conduit between two towering tulip trees. This lush, sward-like setting gives way to Lake Surprise, where ducks often bob on the jade-green surface. In traversing the lakeside, note the large erratics, the first rocks of any significant size up to now.

Continuing along the lake, the Sierra and bridle path join for a kiss, then diverge again, with your route running to the right. Now it gets tricky. On reaching County Road 645, keep to the right shoulder, pass over the bridge, then cross to the left side of the road. Bear left on the cinder driveway, just a few paces beyond the bridge, then turn right at the first intersection. Skip the spur that surfaces in 30 feet, and in a couple of minutes swing away from the road on the wide, smooth track. Those are the Watchung stables roughly 200 yards to the left as you walk by a clutch of tulip trees. The ST reunites with the track from that direction, but sheers off to the left near the road.

Steer to the right on the cinder track, cross the road, then jump left at the first fork and right at the second, as the ST once more joins the path. At the next Y, after fording a bridge, head left, with red blazes briefly joining Sierra. Remain with the ST all the way back to the nature center and the parking lot.

### ▶ NEARBY ACTIVITIES

The Trailside Nature & Science Center on New Providence Road is a great resource with exhibits on taxidermy, animal life, fossils, and energy, as well as a planetarium and various gardens for herbs and wildflowers. Call (908) 789-3670 for information. Fishermen might try their luck in Lake Surprise, while equestrians can join a guided trail ride.

West Orange is less than 20 miles north and well worth a stop for the Edison National Historic Site. It has been closed since 2002, but renovations should be completed in 2005. Call (973) 736-0550 or visit www.nps.gov/edis.

# WAWAYANDA WAY WAY YONDER

## ▶ IN BRIEF

If you feel pangs of pain on finishing this hike, those may owe more to the regret of leaving such a pristine environment than any blisters accumulated during the marathon. From the heights of its puddingstone paradise to the depths of a sprawling rhododendron swamp, there is nothing run-of-the-mill about Wawayanda State Park. Spend a day on the challenging trails of this wa-wa-wonderful property, and you are bound to see wildflowers and wildlife, but relatively few people.

## ▶ DESCRIPTION

There are about 6 miles of the Appalachian Trail coursing through Wawayanda State Park. We once asked a ranger what to expect of that stretch. "Views, I guess, but you might as well be hiking in Kansas," he huffed. His preferred stomping grounds were two of the natural areas, Wawayanda Swamp and Bearfort Mountain, tucked within the 16,679 acres comprising this wild, remote preserve. We offer the following trek as a hearty endorsement of that recommendation. This lengthy jaunt is peppered from start to finish with an awe-inspiring beauty that reaches its pinnacle, both figuratively and literally, at the otherworldly

## ▶ DIRECTIONS

Follow I-95/I-80 west across the George Washington Bridge. Leave I-80 at Exit 53 onto SR 23 north. Drive about 17 miles, then head north on Union Valley Road (CR 513). After approximately 6.5 miles, go through a stop sign and two traffic lights, turning left at the second light. Proceed 1.5 miles, and bear left at the fork. Continue for 0.1 mile, then make a left onto the Warwick Turnpike. The park entrance is 4 miles ahead to the left. Follow Wawayanda Road to the left turnoff for the lake beach and drive to the boat launch and rentals area, to the far left.

## ⓘ KEY AT-A-GLANCE INFORMATION

**LENGTH:** 15.5 miles total, 4.5 miles for Bearfort Mountain Natural Area Loop

**CONFIGURATION:** Double loop

**DIFFICULTY:** Very difficult

**SCENERY:** Lush swamps, cool ravines, scenic mountains, several bodies of water, fascinating geology, and abundant wildlife

**EXPOSURE:** Mainly shady trails, but lakeshore is exposed

**TRAFFIC:** Well trafficked on summer weekends, but Bearfort Mountain Natural Area usually remains pleasantly solitary

**TRAIL SURFACE:** From grass to pine needles, from pebbly to rocky, from packed dirt to puddingstone

**HIKING TIME:** 8 hours

**SEASON:** Year-round, sunrise–sunset

**ACCESS:** Memorial Day–Labor Day, $5 weekdays, $10 weekends; free rest of year; $50 parks pass gives access to all New Jersey state parks for one calendar year

**MAPS:** At park office; USGS Wawayanda; New York–New Jersey Trail Conference, North Jersey Trails

**FACILITIES:** Rest rooms, water, phone at park office; portable toilets at parking lot; playground and picnic area nearby

**SPECIAL COMMENTS:** Pick up a trail-blaze identification sheet at the park office, because park maps do not list trails by blaze color. Waterproof boots recommended for swamp crossings.

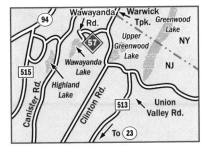

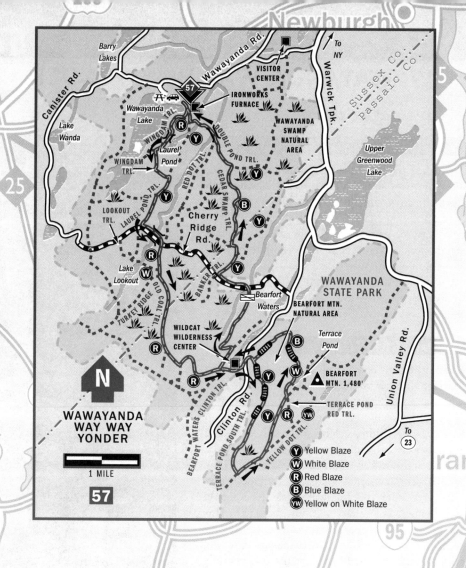

**WAWAYANDA WAY WAY YONDER**

1 MILE

57

- Ⓨ Yellow Blaze
- Ⓦ White Blaze
- Ⓡ Red Blaze
- Ⓑ Blue Blaze
- ⓎⱲ Yellow on White Blaze

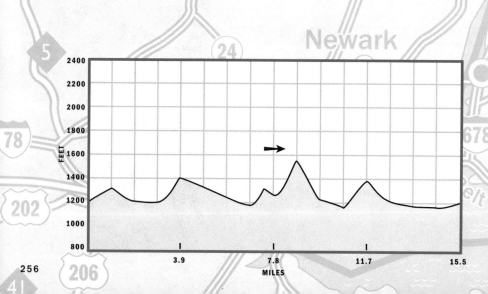

ridgetop setting of Bearfort Mountain. It is the hike for which you've been training—one so enchanting it is likely to draw you back again and again.

Just 300 feet from the north shore of Wawayanda Lake are the disintegrating remnants of Double Pond, a nineteenth-century iron-smelting village. The most striking survivor from that distant era is the charcoal blast furnace, a mortarless stone-block behemoth that measures 30 feet across at its base and a staggering 37 feet high. The furnace was in use from 1846 to 1857, producing pig iron of such high quality that it was formed into train wheels, as well as Union cavalry swords during the Civil War. More recently, during the first half of the 1900s, the New Jersey Zinc Co. logged this region, using the timber for props to strut up its far-flung mines. The vast network of forest roads here dates from that time.

For some people, the name of this park easily takes the form of "way-way-yonder," in part because of its remote position in the Highlands of New Jersey, and partly due to the ambitious hikes engaged in here. In truth, though, Wawayanda is a Lenape Indian word that means "winding, winding water." No question about it: An exhilarating all-day trek through this wilderness wonderland will wind you from one watery spot to another. If you lack the sole for that sort of distance, try splitting the walk into shorter segments, venturing only as far as the Clinton Road, for instance, and looping back from there. Or you might park at the dirt pullout on the Clinton Road, just east of the Project U.S.E. Wildcat Wilderness Center, and concentrate on the Bearfort Mountain Natural Area.

This marathon begins at the parking area by Wawayanda Lake's boat-rental facility. Facing the water, stroll to the far left corner of the lot and proceed along the gravel lane through the picnic area, staying near the lake. Keep to the right, by the railing, and march over the earthen dam. The blue-blazed Wingdam Trail (WT) starts here, by a massive uplift of rounded gray stone that looks like a beached sperm whale. Your return route, the Laurel Pond Trail (LPT, yellow blazes), forks off to the left. For the next mile, the WT rises and falls, mimicking the undulations of this hilly terrain. It drifts between two ridges, well shaded by hemlock, cedar, beech, black birch, and oak trees, and brings you to a lily marsh, fringed with rhododendrons and fed by spill-off from the lake. There is a brief opening in the canopy as you stride over a bridge, and then it is uphill among rhododendrons, with granite boulders on either side of the path and dirt and stones crunching underfoot. In five-minutes, the trail levels off on a grassy plateau, at an altitude of 1,200 feet.

The WT arcs east from there, passing over rocks and descending the hill. Hang a right when it re-encounters the LPT, going now with yellow blazes as the path hugs an impressively rocky ridge, with a great view across a gaping ravine. As is common in these highland woods, the scenery changes from moment to moment, with the beech trees and boulders being replaced by a resurgence of rhododendrons and hemlocks—part of the sprawling Wawayanda Swamp. While the forest road climbs away from this lowland, your route hooks left on an unpaved piece of the Cherry Ridge Road. Carry on for seven or eight minutes until, after walking over a short bridge, you see a red-blazed trace to the right. This is the Old Coal Trail (OCT), with which you will remain for the next 2 miles.

Although fewer boulders wrack the environs here, a number of modest erratics furnish texture for a forest floor that blossoms with lavender geraniums, violets, anemones, and sweet-scented honeysuckle in spring. Scoot left at the fork with the white-blazed Lookout Trail, and left again, in two minutes, at the junction with Turkey Ridge, an unblazed option. The path continues through a small bog, picturesquely bordered by cattails, then rises among white pine, mountain laurel, and sundry hardwoods. When the track reaches the pipeline cut, it tacks directly across the break and starts to gain elevation, cresting in eight minutes at 1,300 feet. Swing left at the fork, go left once more at the Y as you leave the high ground, and forget the odd spurs that occur as the trail drops down to a low bog—a beautiful birding area where the endangered barred owl may be heard hooting over the croaking of frogs. Sticking with the red blazes, continue straight at the large intersection. (Make a mental note of this turnoff; the return loop heads to the left here.) Lope left two minutes later at the base of the hill onto a gravel drive. This level track passes a log cabin and the Project U.S.E. Wildcat Wilderness Center, and then bisects the swampy foot of Bearfort Waters (runoff from Upper Greenwood Lake), ending at a white gate by Clinton Road.

Turn left on the macadam and carefully cross the road. In 250 feet (opposite the dirt parking area) the path jumps back into the forest and forks. Take the Terrace Pond South Trail (TPS, yellow blazes) to the right, a narrow, moss-sided route that meanders up the slanted hill. The trees here are similar to what you saw earlier, but the terrain is far wilder, partly due to its corrugated, rock-and-ridge texture, and in part because fewer of the trails overlap forest roads. Also, several of its swampy sections rise like floodwaters from late winter through mid-spring, requiring a fun rock-hop two-step to ford them. One such boggy stretch occurs within a few minutes, where a boardwalk, log corduroys, and rocks ease the way. After a second set of planks, the serpentine TPS slithers uphill, while showcasing a number of appealing boulders, many split by vertical fissures. The next dip is met with another series of boards, often slick with moss. Then there is a five-minute ascent into a head-high thicket of rhododendrons. Ignore the trace to the right atop the rocky plateau, and lean left in another minute as a forest road merges from the right. Stay with the yellow blazes, bypassing the next pair of traces, both on the left, and then steer left by the brown signboard at a wide intersection.

Next up is an algae-covered pond, though not the Terrace Pond to which this trail's name refers. Nor is the black body of water that follows, which you reach after holding to the left at a Y. From that second dark pool, where glacial erratics, mountain laurels, and white pines flavor the setting, the bayou expands, with huge, stride-stopping puddles often straddling the path. You may have to scuttle over the rocks to the right to get by these obstructions, or resign yourself to hiking in wet boots. The whittled twigs by the water's edge are the work of beavers, and a lodge lies cloaked by foliage to the left as you bolt over a pair of large drainage pipes. When the Yellow Dot Trail (yellow spots on white rectangles) surfaces on the right, vault left, still with the TPS.

Gradually, the track draws away from the watery bog, rising circuitously to the top of the hill, part of an extended ridge of accordion compressions and rocky fins that compose Bearfort Mountain. This is one of the most exhilarating stretches of trail *anywhere,* and not solely because the bedrock, a quartzite-spiked red stone, is of an unusual conglomerate known as puddingstone (think of liver larded with quail eggs).

Nor is the main attraction the yellow and pink penstemon that cover the mount in spring, nor even the surprising appearance of pink lady's slipper orchids at the base of the rocks. No, those are all gravy to the feast of near-continuous scrambling from rocky point to rocky point, with far-reaching views and access to the pristine Terrace Pond tossed in as a sweet dessert. Any wildlife you may stumble upon, like bears, otters—or the barred owl we once startled—simply add to the thrills of this breathtaking area.

Switch left at the junction with the Terrace Pond Red Trail (red markings), navigating further through this puddingstone paradise. Take your time, snack on a sandwich, and enjoy the crow's-nest vistas and the uniqueness of this otherworldly landscape. Canter left at the slanted T and persevere with the white-blazed trail to the edge of Terrace Pond, elevation 1,380 feet, where hooded mergansers frolic and fish. If you have braved this sun-struck area in summer, go ahead and refresh yourself with the cool water of this Castalian fountain—just remember that swimming is not allowed. On finishing with that backwoods baptism, lope left at the north end of the pond onto the blue-blazed track. More craggy crossings ensue, capped in many cases with spicebush, sheep laurel, scrub oak, and pitch pine. Eventually, the path leaves this memorable mountain, diving left on a pipeline cut. Descend via the overlapping traces to a fairly level spot near a cluster of hemlocks and black birches, where the blue blazes veer left into the cover of trees.

In a handful of minutes, and a leisurely bog slog, the trail emerges at Clinton Road. Backtrack to the the Wildcat Wilderness Center; go past the cabin, and uphill to the intersection noted above. Surge right on the unblazed forest road, grab the left fork in about six minutes, and follow it downhill into a fern-filled dell. An additional half mile brings you to the pipe break—for the third time today. Traipse on ahead to the wide dirt logging lane, and stride through the gate. Some of the land in this hemlock hollow is posted as private property, but don't let that throw you. In a moment, after arcing to the left, you will be back on Cherry Ridge Road. Heave to the left on the hard packed lane, and in a hair less than half a mile, just as the road levels off at a turnaround, pivot right onto the Banker Trail (BT, yellow blazes).

Heading directly into the woods, the BT brushes by boulders and laurel, encountering in a couple of minutes an aged, rusting automobile half buried under leaves and mud. The dense patch of rhododendrons that follows, as well as a reed marsh and overall boggy conditions, are reminders that you are back in the Wawayanda Swamp Natural Area. It may not have the high drama of the Bearfort region, but there is a certain serenity to this secluded swale, and a subtle beauty, too. As the conifers recede amid a lustrously luminous bower of beech saplings, a fork materializes to the left—take it. This is the Cedar Swamp Trail (blue blazes), which travels at times through rhododendron alamedas (with a fabulous display of pale pink flowers in mid-July), alternately gaining and losing ground, occasionally relying on moss-covered stones and pontoon roots to get by the swampy overflow.

This a warm-up to the real treat of trucking through the natural area. Shortly after the trail jogs left by yet another rusty old car being swallowed by vegetation, it enters the cedar swamp in earnest. Here commences a quarter mile of continuous planks (they're too narrow to be described as a boardwalk!), a string of lumber that makes it possible to wander this wild, uncorrupted bayou without getting one's feet too wet. (If it is rainy weather, though, these boards can be treacherously slick.) From early spring through mid-summer, the air is filled with the alien calls of peeper frogs and sundry birds hunting for insects. When the path rises from this sweet locale it merges with the Double Pond Trail (yellow blazes), bending to the left. Skip the Red Dot Trail, which appears on the left in a couple of minutes, and cruise past an extension of the swamp and over a wooden bridge. Look for the beaver lodge 300 feet to the right, concealed among the scrub.

Finally back on higher turf, the path slips around a green gate, bringing you to the dirt road of the group campsite. Stay with that as it drifts left briefly, merges with the LPT, and goes straight by the vaulted toilets to a five-way intersection. Dominating this scene is the massive stone blast furnace of the Wawayanda ironworks that once filled the sky with black smoke. To return to the parking lot, seize the second trail from the left, an uphill route. In two minutes, it drops you by the dam at the edge of Wawayanda Lake, where you totter to the right, back on the WT.

## ▶ NEARBY ACTIVITIES

No need, no time—you're supposed to be a vegetable by now. Congratulations! However, why not treat yourself to a restoring experience at the lively Krogh's Restaurant & Brew Pub in Sparta? Menu, directions, and events are posted at www.kroghs.com, or call (973) 729-8428 for details.

# WEIR POND AND SWAMP LOOPS

## ▶ DESCRIPTION

You don't have to be a big fan of American Impressionist paintings to enjoy Weir Farm's easy, 1.8-mile woodland hike. If the names Julian Alden Weir, Childe Hassam, and John Thwachtman are tantamount to Tom, Dick, and Harry, it won't detract a whit from your pleasures by the pond or the serenity of the swamp. Still, Weir Farm, Connecticut's sole national park, offers a unique opportunity to learn about an important period in American art history, to visit an artist's studio,

## ❶ KEY AT-A-GLANCE INFORMATION

**LENGTH:** 1.8 miles (from parking lot)

**CONFIGURATION:** Figure-eight balloon

**DIFFICULTY:** Easy

**SCENERY:** Peaceful woodlands surrounding lily pond, bog, and hidden cascade

**EXPOSURE:** Mostly shady

**TRAFFIC:** Moderate on summer weekends, very light otherwise

**TRAIL SURFACE:** Dirt and exposed roots, some rocky stretches

**HIKING TIME:** 1 hour

**SEASON:** Year-round, dawn–dusk

**ACCESS:** No fee, no dogs, no bicycles

**MAPS:** At Visitor Center; www.nps.gov/wefa

**FACILITIES:** Portable toilets near Visitor Center, no water

**SPECIAL COMMENTS:** The Visitor Center is open Wednesday–Sunday, year-round; closed January 1, Thanksgiving, and December 25.

## ▶ DIRECTIONS

*By car:* Drive north on the Hutchinson River Parkway, continuing as it changes to the Merritt Parkway. Take Exit 39 and go north on Route 7, then west on Route 102 (after the Branchville Station). In 0.3 miles, make a left on Old Branchville Road, followed by another left on Nod Hill Road. Parking is available on the left side of the road, across from the Visitor Center.

*By public transportation:* Take Metro North's New Haven Line to Branchville Station. From there it is 1.8 miles by taxi to Weir Farm. You may also walk west on Branchville Road and turn left on Old Branchville Road. Hang a left again on Nod Hill Road and proceed straight ahead to the Visitor Center on your right.

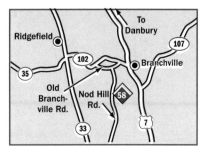

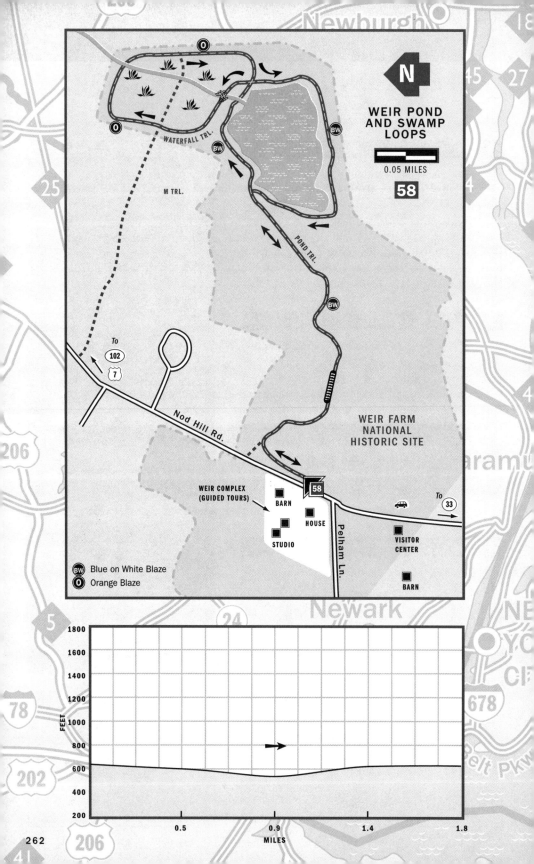

N

## WEIR POND AND SWAMP LOOPS

0.05 MILES

**58**

O

WATERFALL TRL.

M TRL.

BW

BW

POND TRL.

BW

BW

To
102
7

Nod Hill Rd.

WEIR FARM
NATIONAL
HISTORIC SITE

WEIR COMPLEX
(GUIDED TOURS)

BARN

HOUSE

STUDIO

**58**

To 33

VISITOR
CENTER

BARN

Pelham Ln.

BW Blue on White Blaze
O Orange Blaze

| FEET | | | | | |
|---|---|---|---|---|---|
| 1800 | | | | | |
| 1600 | | | | | |
| 1400 | | | | | |
| 1200 | | | | | |
| 1000 | | | | | |
| 800 | | | | | |
| 600 | | | | | |
| 400 | | | | | |
| 200 | | | | | |

0.5    0.9    1.4    1.8
MILES

and to tour a nineteenth-century farm, while also getting in a decent little hike. Talk about having your cake and eating it, too.

J. Alden Weir bought his namesake farm in 1882. He summered there for the next 37 years, until his death, while the bucolic beauty of the locale, reflected in its forests, pond, rock walls, and open fields, became the subject of many of his and his colleagues' paintings. Pressures from suburban development by the late 1970s led to a grassroots drive to protect the property, with the result that the 60-acre Weir Farm was designated a national historic site in 1990.

The Visitor Center, across the road from the parking lot, is only open from Wednesday through Sunday, but the grounds are accessible every day of the week. Views of the pond are best from late fall through early spring, when the water level of its streams and swamp is also greater. That is balanced, of course, against the fact that the many private dwellings besieging the park are more visible then. To reach the pond, turn right on leaving your car and follow the road to the next corner, where Pelham Lane meets Nod Hill, and the Weir house sits catty-corner across the street. Pass through the gap in the wall, directly opposite the red farmhouse, and stick with the mown-lawn path as it tapers along the edge of a small meadow and hits the Pond Trail (blue line over white blazes) by a cedar tree. Roll to the right and enter the woods, highlighted at this stage by oaks, maples, black birches, and shagbark hickory trees.

As is typical in these here parts, a labyrinth of old walls courses through the forest, and you'll see a part of that near a short boardwalk over a fern-flecked patch of bog as you gradually descend toward the water. The trace to the right, which appears within a couple of minutes, leads to a rocky shelf that overlooks the pond (though in summer it is pretty well screened-in by trees). On reaching the bottom of this slight slope, swing to the left side of the pond by the large beech tree, and step over the runoff. The plank that fords this stream was missing on our last visit, but it's an easy jump across.

A sign at the northeast corner of the pond points the way to the Waterfall Trail (orange blazes), to the left. The "waterfall" is really more of a trickle cascading over a series of stones, but this secondary loop is an excellent, bite-size dip into a cooler, wilder habitat, largely one of marshland and glacial ridges. The path is less maintained, with initially a good—or bad—number of rocks underfoot. Before you know it, in perhaps 80 yards, you'll be past the dribbling flow that passes for a waterfall and heading toward a towering mound of granite that comes to a dull point, like an eroded pyramid, 25 feet off the ground. Now moss-covered, the track moves to the left of that, drifting among many ferns and poplars en route to a junction. The circuit continues straight ahead on the Rock Walk.

As the trail moseys downhill, you'll notice a series of three-foot-high white poles spaced in a staggered line through the forest. Keep your eyes peeled for a right fork in this area; it's not well marked. Following that, the descent becomes rockier, delivering you finally to the bottom of an appealing shelf of angular granite. For the next few minutes, you'll walk a fine line between this buttress on the left and a fetid, fecund swamp to the right. Then—presto!—the path veers east, leaving the granite-graced ground behind. There are two seasonal streams to rock-hop over—you may see (or hear) frogs here—after which it is back in a southerly direction toward the pond.

Oaks and laurels shade this high ground route—but not enough, alas, to shield the steady series of private homes from view to the left, just beyond the boundary of the park. These hallmarks of "civilization" remind us, of course, to be grateful for such conservation efforts as those that helped preserve Weir Farm. Still, you may want to direct your gaze toward the right across unsullied expanse of forest and bog. In due time, a turnoff to the right surfaces, which leads back to the Waterfall Trail and Nod Hill. Skip that, and in a few minutes, the trail ends by the pond. Turn left to resume the previous loop, and having circled the pond, retrace your earlier steps up the hill to the parking area. If you would like to see more of this rustic region, the trail to the Nature Conservancy's Weir Preserve, an adjacent domain, begins by the Burlingham Barn, just past the Visitor Center.

### ▶ NEARBY ACTIVITIES

Do make time for a guided tour of Weir Farm to learn about American Impressionist art. Check the events calendar for exhibits and concerts, or call (203) 834-1896.

You can extend your hiking by well more than a mile at the Weir-Leary-White Preserve, a Nature Conservancy property abutting Weir Farm. Trails cut through a successional forest, open fields, and laurel covered hills. For more information, call (860) 344-0716.

# WESTCHESTER WILDERNESS WALK

## ▶ IN BRIEF

Some trails naturally overlap animal paths or ancient forest roads, while others are created from scratch to showcase the wilds with a minimum impact. This hike takes a third approach—playfully, artistically, and circuitously winding around old walls and glacial erratics, through an attractive blend of hardwood highlands (complete with craggy bluffs) and soggy lowlands—where stepping-stone staircases draw visitors into the middles of streams and cascades.

## ▶ DESCRIPTION

*Pssst*—can you keep a secret? Like most hikers, we have our favorite stomping grounds, little-known secluded spots where one is more likely to see wildlife than an ambling ambassador of civilization. The Westchester Wilderness Walk (WWW) is one such oasis. It's a relatively new preserve of a little more than 150 acres tucked into the heart of suburban Pound Ridge, just over the Connecticut state line. On paper, the acreage of WWW is unimpressive, and by most standards

## ▶ DIRECTIONS

*By car:* Drive north on the Hutchinson River Parkway, continuing as it changes to the Merritt Parkway. Take Exit 34 onto Long Ridge Road (SR 104) north, and drive approximately 5 miles to Upper Shad Road. Turn right on Upper Shad and continue for 0.3 miles to a tiny parking lot on the left, opposite a small pond.

*By public transportation:* Take a Metro North New Haven Line train to Stamford Station, then hop on Connecticut Transit bus 32 (Long Ridge Road). Get off at the intersection with Rock Rimmon Road. Walk north on Long Ridge for about 1.5 miles, then turn right onto Upper Shad Road. The trailhead is 0.3 miles ahead on the left.

## ⓘ KEY AT-A-GLANCE INFORMATION

**LENGTH:** 6.5 miles total; Southern Loop is a 3-mile self-guided nature hike

**CONFIGURATION:** Quadruple loop

**DIFFICULTY:** Easy/moderate

**SCENERY:** Mixed hardwood forest containing upland rocky ridges, lowland swamps, and lots of stepping-stones

**EXPOSURE:** Only in winter, when dense canopy is absent

**TRAFFIC:** Pleasantly light for rather populated area

**TRAIL SURFACE:** Mostly dirt and rocks, with occasional streambed rock-hopping

**HIKING TIME:** 2.5 hours

**SEASON:** Year-round

**ACCESS:** No fee, pets must be leashed

**MAPS:** At trailhead kiosk

**FACILITIES:** None

**SPECIAL COMMENTS:** This preserve is very attractive in spring, after snowmelt has filled the creeks and rock-hopping over streambeds is a fun challenge. The Southern Loop is an interpretive trail that showcases some the park's more colorful features.

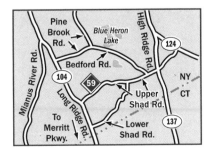

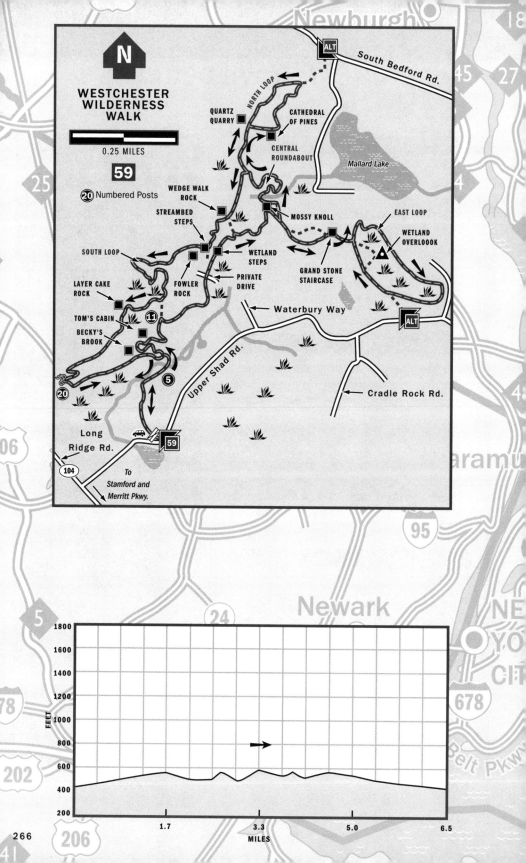

# WESTCHESTER WILDERNESS WALK

**N**

0.25 MILES

**59**

**20** Numbered Posts

North Loop

Quartz Quarry

Cathedral of Pines

Central Roundabout

Mallard Lake

Wedge Walk Rock

Streambed Steps

Mossy Knoll

East Loop

Wetland Overloook

South Loop

Wetland Steps

Private Drive

Grand Stone Staircase

Layer Cake Rock

Fowler Rock

Tom's Cabin

Becky's Brook

Waterbury Way

Cradle Rock Rd.

Upper Shad Rd.

Long Ridge Rd.

To Stamford and Merritt Pkwy.

South Bedford Rd.

calling it a wilderness is a bit of a stretch. Creative trail construction, though, has resulted in four interconnected loops, amounting to 6.5 miles of densely forested pathways that wind circuitously through skunk cabbage–filled bogs, over seasonal streams, and by high-rising granite bluffs.

From the trailhead parking area (four- to five-vehicle capacity), slip through the rail fence and pick up a map at the wooden kiosk. (There are also Self-Guided Nature Hike pamphlets keyed to numbered posts along the first loop.) Proceed north on the forest road, noting the green plastic blazes that mark the way. In a few minutes, the carriageway narrows to single-file and brushes up against a swamp—minor rock-hopping required—before hitting a low stone wall by post 5. Jump up on the wall and head left, keeping the murky, meandering creek to your right. The trail resumes at the end of this span, shifting to the left before meeting a fork. Bear right, gaining a bit of elevation as you leave the lush wetland habitat behind—for now—and enter into a hardwood forest. Gneiss and schist, metamorphic rock outcroppings deposited by the Wisconsin glacier when it withdrew from the area 12,000 to 15,000 years ago, lend an air of drama to the understory here.

In a moment or three, the path plunges through a gap in a wall and arrives at Becky's Brook, a small cascade tumbling over an array of rocks. A trace just prior to that leads to the right and a low embankment, but it's more fun to simply walk up the stream itself. That's correct, *up* the stream. In a whimsical bit of trail construction that recurs later in the hike, a crude stone stairway has been set directly into the flow, providing an over-the-top view of the water as it rolls and spills downhill. The main route, near the top of the cascade, presses onward above the top of a granite fin.

From this colorful spot, the green-blazed track doglegs right, then left, shuffling through the ruins of an old cabin. Although it is known locally as Tom's Cabin, no one really knows who lived here. The site, much overgrown by hemlocks and beech trees, was left to squirrels and raccoons decades ago—and not much remains beyond its fireplace and foundation stones. The trail loops by a jumble of gray boulders, then swings left and ascends that mound via an improvised stair of stones. Stroll by post 11, which commemorates the decline of the American chestnut (due to a fungus accidentally introduced from overseas a century ago), and vault right at the fork in 25 yards.

The trail holds largely to the well-treed high ground for the next 0.1 mile, zigzagging between oaks, maples, and miscellaneous chunks of granite. On descending by a network of old mortarless walls toward a swamp on the right, it crosses a private drive, and continues into an extension of the wetland. A staggered line of oversize stone steps, fringed appealingly with large-leaf skunk cabbage, aids in fording a particularly wet portion of this bayou before the path once again starts to ascend. A couple of minutes' steady striding brings you to an intersection, with the hike proceeding to the right on a loop dubbed the Central Roundabout (CR).

As the leaf-strewn track rises gently, a stone bench appears in a little more than 0.1 mile, providing a splendid overlook of a serpentine stream coursing through the bog below. This is listed as Mossy Knoll on the map, with the turnoff to the right, a few paces away, the new East Loop (EL). Its layout was still a work in progress on our last foray here, and it may have been altered by the time you hit the park. Basically, though, the 1.5-mile EL surges through an open half acre of grassy meadow (a favorite hunting ground of red-shouldered hawks) before reaching a craggy bluff. A series of steps, officially dubbed the Grand Stone Staircase, have been crafted into the far edge of that gray precipice—quite an impressive display of amateur masonry—to deliver hikers to the lower terrain. Hang with the path as it tapers downhill in an east direction. In one minute, the trail diverges; take the hard left toward the north (you will return on the right spur). The ensuing area has a wild aura, with a boulder-littered bluff extending to your left, and an expansive swamp simmering to the right. Within five minutes, the trace bends to the right, away from the rocky high ground, only to emerge at a newly paved road. Heave to the right there and remain on the shoulder for roughly 75 paces, slicing right again when the blazes reenter the forest. Hew to the right at the subsequent juncture (the EL trailhead lies to the left) and persevere with the undulating loop as it reconnects, in five more minutes, with your earlier turnoff. Scoot left and proceed to the foot of the bluff, using the stone stairs to reach its top. Backtrack from there to the CR, where you cruise right.

The CR earns its title of Roundabout during the succeeding quarter mile, as it hugs the undulating terrain, darting to the right or left of various trees, loping around glacial debris, and cutting through ubiquitous bogs. Stay straight when you come to a left fork across a small stream by a hefty erratic, but remember that spur—you'll need to grab it on your return. This is the start of the North Loop, which rises initially before dipping toward a slightly lower elevation. In five minutes, as the Cathedral of Pines grove of conifers comes into view toward the east, the green blazes diverge, with your tour branching to the right.

Over the next ten minutes, the trail approaches that large patch of pines, then lurches over some oblong stepping-stones, slips through gaps in a couple of stone walls, and drops down toward a watery, fern-flecked swamp. You may require the steely vision of a French trapper here to spot the return spur to the left, as the natural flow of the trail appears to be straight onward, a rock-skipping route through the marsh. Don't worry if you miss the intersection, because the South Bedford Road trailhead (no parking) is only a couple of minutes away, and you can easily double-back from there.

The return from this shady, appealing swamp can be concluded in a fairly expeditious five minutes, after a brief climb and more stepping-stone marsh crossings. The miniloop's end occurs just beyond the Quartz Quarry, where you transfer to the right and retrace your steps back to the earlier junction by the stream, beside the large, dark erratic. Before you hasten on, though, dawdle a moment to inspect this small quarry site. Digging here ceased in the first half of the nineteenth century, and from then on the cavity was used as a garbage pit, with some of the trash, which consists largely of odd bottles and an occasional earthenware jug, reportedly dating back to the Civil War.

Having spun right at the fork by the stream, you are now traveling once more on the CR. The path gains a touch of elevation initially and then—predictably—loses it, meandering meanwhile around several sizable globs of granite and gliding over a handful of stone steps, with rock-hopping through a slow-moving creek preceding the CR's terminus. Tack right at the intersection and slip between the fractured rocks, listed on the map as Wedge Walk Rock, as the track gradually edges uphill. The minimal effort involved in this climb yields, in a moment or two, a fine overview of the surrounding swamp. Then it is downward again, drifting beneath the bluff. On reaching a stream, the track veers left, only to cut suddenly to the right, where it ascends, as at Becky's Brook, over the very center of a trickling cascade. Well-positioned stones make this enjoyable stretch child's play, but as always when striding on wet rocks, be careful of your footing.

This improvised walkway arcs to the left away from the water in a couple of seconds, grinding up to a pair of erratics and a four-way intersection. Dead ahead is Fowler Outlook, a viewpoint from atop a large rock, with the hike continuing to the right on the faintly discernible trace. (Left is a cutoff that returns to the private road you crossed earlier.) A few spindly hemlocks leaven the hardwood mix of trees as you sputter upward by some fair-size boulders, and after an additional pair of lookout ledges, the

Water trickles and rushes and bubbles all over the Streambed Steps on the Westchester Wilderness Walk.

green blazes guide you by a seasonal stream and alongside a broad bog. When you hit the T, bolt right.

This final portion of the hike is a resumption of the interpretive loop, with the numbered posts interspaced with such playfully named natural phenomenon as Pooh's Stump, Layer Cake Rock, World's Largest Poison Ivy Vine, and so forth. The latter, by the way, is at post 20, by a small, attractive cascade, where Dutchmans britches flower in early spring. The trail hooks left there, descending over stone steps to the fairly level ground of a bog. Remain straight on meeting the fork to the left—where you turned off at the hike's beginning—and, now retracing the first leg of the trek, scamper to the right atop the low wall. Stay with the path all the way back to the parking area, a walk of about five minutes.

## ▶ NEARBY ACTIVITIES

The Bartlett Arboretum in North Stamford is of a more manicured nature. Swamps and ponds thrive next to woodlands and meadows, and the unique collection of champion trees makes this a special place. Visit bartlett.arboretum.uconn.edu or call (203) 322- 6971 for information.

# WESTMORELAND GRAND TOUR

## KEY AT-A-GLANCE INFORMATION

**LENGTH:** 5.6 miles

**CONFIGURATION:** Loop

**DIFFICULTY:** Easy/moderate

**SCENERY:** Mixed forest houses rock cliffs and stone walls, lush swamps, cascading streams, and kettle-hole pond

**EXPOSURE:** Mostly shady except for a couple of meadow crossings

**TRAFFIC:** Heavy on some weekends or when student programs take place, but usually light on Coles Kettle Trail

**TRAIL SURFACE:** Packed dirt, rocks, and roots

**HIKING TIME:** 2.75 hours

**SEASON:** Year-round, dawn–dusk

**ACCESS:** No fee, no pets, no bicycles

**MAPS:** At entrance kiosk; USGS Mount Kisco; www.westmorelandsanctuary.org

**FACILITIES:** Rest rooms and water inside Museum & Nature Center

**SPECIAL COMMENTS:** The organization that operates this sanctuary offers a great range of public programs, such as an annual fall festival, maple sugaring, bird-watching, slide shows, etc. Call (914) 666-8448 to inquire about special activities.

## IN BRIEF

With paths ranging from wide and smooth to narrow and rocky, family groups and hardened hikers alike can find the circuit that suits their interests—the common denominator is sensational scenery. Over the course of a handful of miles through rolling forestland, you will see impressive rock outcroppings, seasonal streams, and a few ponds where birds often flock. Deer sightings are virtually guaranteed early and late in the day.

## DESCRIPTION

A bearded dragon is housed among the animals on exhibit in Westmoreland's nature center, but don't let that deter you from heading into the woods of this attractive sanctuary. This abandoned pet is native to Australia—not Westchester County—and was adopted by the resident naturalist. The most threatening animals you are likely to encounter along the 7 miles of trails that rope through Westmoreland's 625 acres are the snapping turtles that inhabit its three ponds.

Which is not to suggest that this is a buttoned-down suburban park with all the beauty of a backyard tomato garden. On the contrary, Westmoreland offers an opportunity for a good up-and-down workout along some of the area's more exciting granite bluffs, in addition to a striking kettle-hole pond dating to the last Ice Age.

## DIRECTIONS

*By car:* Take the Hutchinson River Parkway north to White Plains, then I-684 north to Exit 4. Drive west on SR 172 for 0.3 miles. Turn left onto Chestnut Ridge Road and proceed for 1.3 miles. The entrance and parking lot are on the left.

*By public transportation:* Metro North's Harlem Line stops at Mount Kisco Station. It is less than 3 miles by taxi from there.

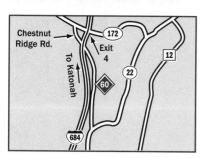

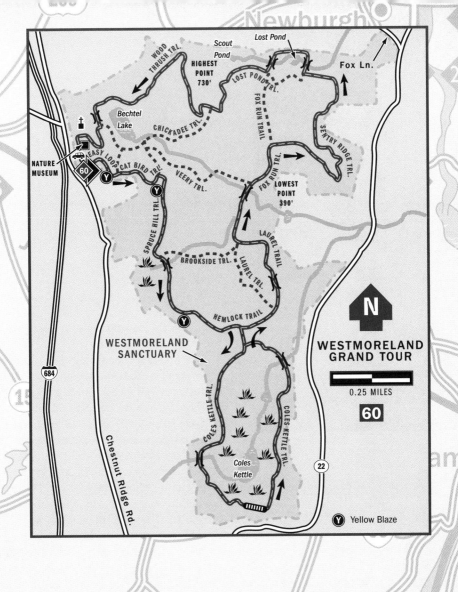

WESTMORELAND
SANCTUARY

**WESTMORELAND
GRAND TOUR**

0.25 MILES

**60**

Y Yellow Blaze

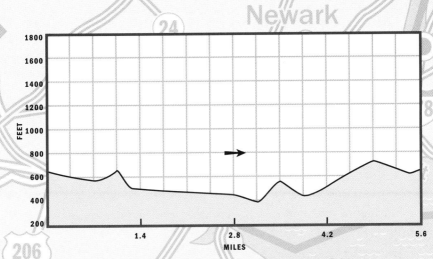

Swallowtail butterflies descend on Westmoreland Sanctuary during the summer, attracted by milkweed and other aromatic flora.

Deer herds teem through groves of oaks, beeches, and black birch trees, and the abundance of water, including numerous streams and minor seasonal cascades, draws a wide range of songbirds, as well as downy, pileated, and red-bellied woodpeckers, turkey vultures, and red-tailed hawks.

This circumference of the park starts on the Easy Loop, by a wooden arch (where maps are usually available) to the right of the nature center. Stay with the yellow blazes as they trend downhill past a few maples and spruce trees, and bear right in 0.1 mile through a break in the stonewall onto the Catbird Trail. More stone walls and a couple of open fields ensue as you persist downward, and in two or three minutes, swing right at the junction with Spruce Hill Trail (SHT).

With pines hanging low over short stretches of the ascending path, this section of the sanctuary feels appealingly wild. After a 40-yard stretch, the SHT crests by an uplifted mound of glacial moraine, one of many dark, lichen-mottled ridges that run through Westmoreland. Spruce Hill then descends into a concentration of beech trees, where it meets Brookside and Hemlock trails. Step right onto Hemlock and cross the rickety bridge fording a marshy stream. Wild lilac grows nearby, and in July and August its sweet perfume fills the air, attracting swallowtail butterflies in search of nectar.

The trail, still blazed yellow, moves uphill, past desiccated hemlocks and a few shagbark hickories. On leveling off in 150 to 200 yards, it enters a bog that can be very, very moist in winter and early spring. As you begin to descend once more, take a glance behind at a hitherto hidden granite outcropping that rises an impressive 30 feet off the forest floor.

The right-hand turnoff to Coles Kettle Trail, a 1.5-mile miniloop, is signposted, but that indicator faces the opposite direction. In any case, you are unlikely to miss so clear an intersection. The kettle-hole, or pond, measuring about 100 yards wide by 170 yards long, is at the far end of the loop. Because it is ringed by green briar and a variety of hardwood trees, it is most visible in winter and early spring. That is also the time, alas, when the trail is likely to be soggy with snowmelt and a surfeit of water. No matter; this less-trafficked circuit, part of which runs along a boardwalk, is well worth the detour. Remain wide-eyed, not just for wild turkeys, of which we spied a dozen here recently, but also for the path, as many blazes are either faded or missing.

On your return from the Coles Kettle, roll right on the eastern stretch of the Hemlock Trail. It presses forward another 0.14 miles, descending past a cluster of maple trees in advance of an intersection with the Laurel Trail. March right and pass over a couple of small bridges, with some hefty boulders and a massive moraine field on either side of the laurel-fringed path. The rugged rock outcroppings extend for

A snowy carpet adds fresh dimension to the shady byways of the Westmoreland Sanctuary, where deer tracks outnumber boot prints.

0.25 miles, at which point the track emerges at a slightly sloping, grassy meadow. Head directly across this birdhouse-festooned sward, keeping to its southern side, until you hit the intersection with the Brookside Trail, where you veer right along the stone wall.

This trail is bordered by a wide stream (dry in summer) while tapering downward among beech, birch, maple, and (later on) hemlock trees. Ultimately, Brookside bottoms out at 390 feet of elevation, which is the lowest point in the sanctuary, before—you guessed it!—beginning a gradual ascent. Cross over a sizable wooden bridge, step through a rock wall, and hew to the right on Fox Run at the trail junction.

Here starts one of the steeper stretches in Westmoreland, though it only lasts for something like 150 yards. A dramatic bluff looms to the left, extending outward as the trail levels off, culminating in a protrusion of boulders 50 feet above the ground. A hitching post, roughly 0.25 miles up the path, marks your turn onto Sentry Ridge. Prior to hanging a right there, check out the solidly built stone wall that runs directly up the opposite hill, finishing in a nearly vertical position. This sturdy relic is circumstantial evidence of why so many farming families emigrated westward in search of flat, arable land.

As its name implies, Sentry Ridge offers pretty fair views, although a good portion of those are of Route 22, well below and to the east. This stretch features a series of uphill-downhill bursts past rocky knobs, through a congregation of maples, and around a ledge and granite ridge, before finally meeting the right-hand turnoff to Lost Pond. There is a bench at the northeast side of this a man-made pond, providing a fine spot to idle and look for frogs among the lilies. Your Walden-like reverie concluded, follow the trail away from the water as it threads through a bog, across a small bridge, and uphill to the next intersection, where you point your paws to the right.

For the upcoming 0.25 miles, the trail shifts steadily higher into a rocky landscape, skipping by Scout Pond—really more of a marshy flat—and its adjacent bird blind along the way. The ascent continues for a short spell on the Wood Thrush Trail to the right, reaching, at 730 feet, the highest elevation in Westmoreland. The path then wends slightly to the left into a shady grove of beech trees, passes a striking ridge of granite and encounters, as it courses downhill, a rock slide of scattered glacial boulders.

Several massive tulip poplars, their lower trunks measuring four feet or more in diameter, appear a few minutes later in the vicinity of a couple of foot bridges. Bechtel Lake, one of the more popular family destinations in the sanctuary, is just beyond. Poison ivy thrives in this locale, but you should also be vigilant for the turnoff to the right on the latter segment of the Easy Loop Trail. This final 0.21 miles leads by a large stand of white pines, a couple of old-fashioned outhouses, and the Neighborhood Burying Ground (from 1824 to 1915), ultimately terminating by the nature center.

Plan to make time for a peak inside that facility. Sure, other than the bearded dragon, most exhibits are rather folksy. But look more closely at the taupe-colored, clapboard-sided building itself. This 200 year-old colonial structure was once the Presbyterian Church in nearby Bedford Village. When the people there outgrew it, the private, not-for-profit corporation that operates Westmoreland stepped in and had it taken apart and reassembled at its current location.

## ▶ NEARBY ACTIVITIES

When we are feeling energetic, we like to combine this hike with a shorter spin through the Arthur W. Butler Memorial Sanctuary, less than half a mile away. See listing on page 40.

History buffs should enjoy the John Jay Homestead State Historic Site, the farmhouse—maintained with period furnishings—where the first U.S. chief justice retired; it's on SR 22 in Katonah. Call (914) 232-5651 for details.

# 60 Hikes
## *within* 60 MILES

### NEW YORK CITY
#### INCLUDING NORTHERN NEW JERSEY, WESTERN LONG ISLAND, AND SOUTHWESTERN CONNECTICUT

## APPENDIXES
## & INDEX

# APPENDIX A:
# OUTDOOR SHOPS

**Blue Ridge Mountain Sports**
www.brmsstore.com

Princeton Shopping Center
North Harrison Street
Princeton, NJ 08540
(609) 921-6078

23 Main Street
Madison, NJ 07940
(973) 377-3301

**Campmor**
www.campmor.com
810 Route 17 North
Paramus, NJ 07653
(201) 445-5000

**Eastern Mountain Sports**
www.ems.com

952 High Ridge Road
Stamford, CT 06905
(203) 461-9865

277 Woodbridge Center Drive
Woodbridge, NJ 07095
(732) 634-8787

820 Route 17 North
Paramus, NJ 07652
(201) 670-4646

591 Broadway (at Mercer)
New York, NY 10012
(212) 966-8730

20 West 61st Street
New York, NY 10023
(212) 397-4860

**Hiking and Backpacking**
www.hikingandbackpacking.com

**Hudson Valley Outfitters**
www.hudsonvalleyoutfitters.com
63 Main Street
Cold Spring, NY 10516
(845) 265-0221, (866) TO-KAYAK

**Jagger's Camp & Trail Outfitters**
www.jaggerscamptrail.com
351 Adams Street
Bedford Hills, NY 10507
(914) 241-4448

**L. L. Bean**
www.llbean.com
1 Church Street, Suite 93
Flemington, NJ 08822
(800) 441-5713, (908) 806-3473

**Paragon Sports**
www.paragonsports.com
867 Broadway (at 18th Street)
New York, NY 10003
(800) 961-3030, (212) 255-8036 x237

**Ramsey Outdoor**
www.ramseyoutdoor.com

835 Route 17 South
Ramsey, NJ 07446
(201) 327-8141

240 Route 17 North
Paramus Towne Square
Paramus, NJ 07652
(800) 699-5874, (201) 261-5000

1039 Route 46
Ledgewood, NJ 07852
(973) 584-7799

**Tent and Trails**
www.tenttrails.com
21 Park Place
New York, NY 10007
(800) 237-1760, (212) 227-1760

# APPENDIX B:
# WHERE TO BUY MAPS

**Altrec**
www.altrec.com
(800) 369-3949

**The Backpacker**
www.thebackpacker.com

**Campmor**
www.campmor.com
810 Route 17 North
Paramus, NJ 07653
(201) 445-5000

**Delorme**
www.delorme.com
(800) 642-0970, (800) 561-5105

**Eastern Mountain Sports**
www.ems.com

952 High Ridge Road
Stamford, CT 06905
(203) 461-9865

277 Woodbridge Center Drive
Woodbridge, NJ 07095
(732) 634-8787

820 Route 17 North
Paramus, NJ 07652
(201) 670-4646

591 Broadway (at Mercer)
New York, NY 10012
(212) 966-8730

20 West 61st Street
New York, NY 10023
(212) 397-4860

**Jagger's Camp & Trail Outfitters**
www.jaggerscamptrail.com
351 Adams Street
Bedford Hills, NY 10507
(914) 241-4448

**Maps a la Carte**
www.topozone.com
73 Princeton Street, Suite 305
North Chelmsford, MA 01863
(978)-251-4242

**New York–New Jersey Trail Conference**
www.nynjtc.org
156 Ramapo Valley Road (SR 202)
Mahwah, NJ 07430
(201) 512-9348

**Ramsey Outdoor**
www.ramseyoutdoor.com

835 Route 17 South
Ramsey, NJ 07446
(201) 327-8141

240 Route 17 North
Paramus Towne Square
Paramus, NJ 07652
(800) 699-5874, (201) 261-5000

1039 Route 46
Ledgewood, NJ 07852
(973) 584-7799

**REI**
www.rei.com
(800) 426-4840

**Tamassee**
www.tamassee.com
(888) 770-5463

**Wildernet**
www.wildernet.com
(877) 587-9004

# APPENDIX C:
# HIKING CLUBS

**Adirondack Mountain Club**
(Long Island/Ramapo/North Jersey/
New York/Albany/Mid-Hudson/Mohican/
Knickerbocker Chapter)
www.adk.org, www.adk-nyc.org
814 Goggins Road
Lake George, NY 12845
(800) 395-8080, (518) 668-4447

**Adventures for Women**
www.adventuresforwomen.org
15 Victoria Lane
Morris Township, NJ 07960
(973) 644-3594

**Appalachian Mountain Club New York–**
 **North Jersey Chapter**
www.amc-ny.org, www.amc-ny.org/
 amcnynj.shtml
5 Tudor City Place
New York, NY 10017
(212) 986-1430, (212) 986-1432

**Appalachian Trail Conference**
www.atconf.org
799 Washington Street, P.O. Box 807
Harpers Ferry, WV 25425-0807
(304) 535-6331

**Audubon New York**
www.ny.audubon.org
200 Trillium Lane
Albany, NY 12203
(518) 869-9731

**Audubon New Jersey/Weis Ecology**
 **Center/Weis Wyanokie Wanderers**
www.njaudubon.org
150 Snake Den Road
Ringwood, NJ 07456
(973) 835-2160

**Chinese Mountain Club of New York**
www.cmcny.org
837-B Donaldson Street
Highland Park, NJ 08904
(732) 985-2685

**German–American Hiking Club**
www.nynjtc.org/clubpages/gah.html
1577 Third Avenue
New York, NY 10128

**Interstate Hiking Club**
28 Bergen Avenue
Haskell, NJ 07420
(973) 839-0292

**Long Island Greenbelt Trail Conference**
www.hike-li.com/ligtc
P.O. Box 5636
Hauppauge, NY 11788
(631) 360-0753

**New York Hiking Club**
www.nynjtc.org/clubpages/nyh.html
1408 East 49th Street
Brooklyn, NY 11234
(718) 258-7276

**New York–New Jersey Trail Conference**
www.nynjtc.org
156 Ramapo Valley Road (SR 202)
Mahwah, NJ 07430
(201) 512-9348

**New York Ramblers**
www.nyramblers.org
(212) 260-4879

**Monmouth County Park System**
www.monmouthcountyparks.com
805 Newman Springs Road
Lincroft NJ 07738
(732) 842-4000 x4236

**Morris County Park Commission**
www.morristrails.org
P.O. Box 834
Lake Hopatcong, NJ 07849
(973) 663-0200

**Morris Trails Conservancy**
Morris County Trails
c/o MCPC, Box 1295
Morristown, NJ 07962-1295

# APPENDIX C: HIKING CLUBS
## (continued)

**Mosaic Outdoor Mountain Club of Greater New York**
www.mosaic-gny.org
P.O. Box 647
Copaigue, NY 11726
(212) 502-0820

**Nassau Hiking and Outdoor Club**
www.nhoc.org
(516) 483-8606

**Sierra Club**
New York City Field Office
www.sierraclub.org/ny
116 John Street, Suite 3100
New York, NY 10038
(212) 791-9291

Atlantic Chapter
www.newyork.sierraclub.org
P.O. Box 886
Syosset, NY 11791-0886

**Urban Trail Club**
www.nynjtc.org/clubpages/utc.html
P.O. Box 264 Bowling Green
New York, NY 10274
(718) 274-0407

**Westchester Trails Association**
www.nynjtc.org/clubpages/wta.html

**Woodland Trail Walkers**
www.nynjtc.org/clubpages/wtw.html
17 Bent Tree Lane
Kinnelon, NJ 07405
(973) 492-4855

# APPENDIX D: AGENCIES

**Mercer County Parks**
www.mercercounty.org/parks

**Middlesex County Parks**
www.co.middlesex.nj.us/parksrecreation

**Monmouth County Parks**
www.monmouthcountyparks.com

**Morris County Parks**
www.morrisparks.net
(973) 326-7600

**Nassau County Parks**
www.co.nassau.ny.us/parks.html
(516) 572-0200

**National Parks Service, Northeast Region**
www.nps.gov
U.S. Custom House
200 Chestnut Street, Fifth Floor
Philadelphia, PA 19106
(215) 597-7013

**National Wildlife Refuges**
refuges.fws.gov

**Great Swamp National Wildlife Refuge**
www.greatswamp.fws.gov
152 Pleasant Plains Road
Basking Ridge, NJ 07920-9615
(973) 425-1222

**The Nature Conservancy**
www.nature.org

Eastern New York Chapter
19 North Moger Avenue
Mt. Kisco, NY 10549
(914) 244-3271 x21

New Jersey Field Office
200 Pottersville Road
Chester, NJ 07930
(908) 879-7262

Long Island Chapter
250 Lawrence Hill Road
Cold Spring Harbor, NY 11724
(631) 367-3225

Connecticut Field Office
55 High Street
Middletown, CT 06457
(860) 344-0716

**New Jersey Department of Environmental Protection**
P. O. Box 402
Trenton, NJ 08625-0402
(800) 843-6420, (609) 984-0370

New Jersey Division of Parks and Forestry
www.state.nj.us/dep/parksandforests

Green Acres (NJDEP)
www.state.nj.us/dep/greenacres
501 East State Street
Station Plaza Building 5, Ground Floor
Trenton, NJ 08625
(609) 984-0500

**New York State Department of Environmental Conservation (DEC)**
www.dec.state.ny.us
625 Broadway
Albany, NY 12233
(609) 984-0500

**New York State Parks**
www.nysparks.state.ny.us
Albany, NY 12238
(518) 474-0456, (518) 486-1899 (TDD)

**Open Space Institute**
www.osiny.org
1350 Broadway, Suite 201
New York, NY 10018-7799
(212) 629-3981

**Palisades Interstate Park Commission**
Administration Building
Bear Mountain State Park
Bear Mountain, NY 10911-0427
(845) 786-2701

**Sierra Club**
www.sierraclub.org/ny
New York City Field Office
116 John Street, Suite 3100
New York, NY 10038
(212) 791-9291

**Somerset County Parks**
www.park.co.somerset.nj.us
P.O. Box 5327
North Branch, NJ 08876
(908) 722-1200

# APPENDIX D: AGENCIES
## (continued)

**Suffolk County Parks**
www.co.suffolk.ny.us
P.O. Box 144, Montauk Highway
West Sayville, NY 11796
(631) 854-4949

**Union County Parks**
www.unioncountynj.org

**Westchester County Parks**
Westchester County Department of Parks,
    Recreation, and Conservation
25 Moore Avenue
Mt. Kisco, NY 10549

County of Westchester
www.westchestergov.com
148 Martine Avenue
White Plains, NY 10601
(914) 995-TELE

**Westchester Land Trust**
www.westchesterlandtrust.org
11 Babbitt Road
Bedford Hills, NY 10507
(914) 241-6346

# INDEX

# INDEX

# INDEX

# INDEX

# INDEX

# INDEX

# INDEX

# NOTES

# NOTES

# NOTES